RETRIEVING THE *American Past*

A CUSTOMIZED U.S. HISTORY READER

EDITED BY

DAVID MCDANIEL

INTRODUCTION TO AMERICAN HISTORY

Director of Database Publishing: Michael Payne
Sponsoring Editor: Natalie Danner
Development Editor: Katherine R. Gehan
Editorial Assistant: Laura Krier
Marketing Manager: Kerry Chapman
Operations Manager: Eric M. Kenney
Production Project Manager: Jennifer M. Berry
Rights Editor: Francesca Marcantonio
Cover Designer: Renée Sartell

Cover Art: Courtesy of Christie's Images, Granger Collection, Corbis, and Getty Images.

Printed in the United States of America

Please visit our website at *www.pearsoncustom.com*
Attention bookstores: For permission to return any unsold stock, contact Pearson Custom Publishing at 1-800-777-6872.

ISBN: 0536146411

PEARSON CUSTOM PUBLISHING
75 Arlington St., Suite 300
Boston, MA 02116

CONTRIBUTORS

Senior Editor
Saul Cornell

Managing Editor
David Staley

Copy Editor
Ann Heiss

Assistant Managing Editor
Denice Fett

Contributing Editors

Tyler Anbinder
Kenneth J. Andrien
Jean Harvey Baker
Michael Les Benedict
Mansel Blackford
Paul C. Bowers
Rowland Brucken
John D. Buenker
John C. Burnham
Joan E. Cashin
William R. Childs
Albert J. Churella
Steven Conn
Saul Cornell
Nick Cullather
Jeanette Davis
Merton L. Dillon
Daniel Feller
Charles Coleman Finlay
Emily Greenwald
Mark Grimsley
Bernard N. Grindel
Peter L. Hahn
James Hansen
Susan M. Hartmann
Mary Ann Heiss
Earl J. Hess
Michael J. Hogan
R. Douglas Hurt
Bruce Karhoff
Michael Kazin
Terence Kehoe
K. Austin Kerr
Frank Lambert
Valerie Mendoza
James McCaffrey
Allan R. Millett
Pamela J. Mills
Daniel Nelson
Margaret E. Newell
Josef Ostyn
Carla Gardina Pestana
Patrick D. Reagan
Randolph A. Roth
Hal K. Rothman
John A. M. Rothney
Leila J. Rupp
Richard D. Shiels
David Sicilia
C. Edward Skeen
Amy L. S. Staples
David L. Stebenne
David Steigerwald
Marshall F. Stevenson, Jr.
Warren R. Van Tine
Christopher Waldrep
J. Samuel Walker

Your *Retrieving the American Past* purchase includes access to online resources designed to complement your readings. This Companion Website is located at the following URL:

http://www.pearsoncustom.com/dbrtap/rtap/student

When prompted, enter the User Name: **rtapstudent** and Password: **rtaplearn**

(*Note:* The User Name and Password are case-sensitive, so be sure to use upper and lower case characters exactly as shown above.)

Once logged in, you will have access to the following resources:

- ***Link Library.*** A collection of vetted web links, organized by key terms and historical figures, which offer you background and context for many of the selections you'll be reading.
- ***Documents.*** Access (via links) to the full text of historical documents, which can furnish a backdrop to events that might have preceded, or followed, their drafting.
- ***The Writing Process.*** Advice that can aid you during the writing process. Included are guidelines and suggestions for each phase of writing, from start to finish.
- ***Plagiarism.*** Suggestions to help you maintain academic honesty, with illustrative examples.
- ***Style Guide.*** A brief guide to help you follow either MLA or Chicago Manual styles in citing your sources. The Modern Language Association style is widely used for papers in English composition, literature, and foreign languages. History, the fine arts, and some fields in the humanities (but not literature) use traditional footnotes or endnotes, which should conform to standards set by *The Chicago Manual of Style.*

We invite you to explore!

Contents

The Historical Legacies of Christopher Columbus

Kenneth J. Andrien

Introduction

Few historical figures have generated as much controversy over the last five hundred years as Christopher Columbus. For some he remains a heroic figure, advancing the frontiers of western civilization. For others his voyages are responsible for the ultimate deaths of millions of indigenous peoples and the destruction of the landscape that prevailed in the Americas before 1492. Despite the controversies surrounding his historical place in American and world history, Christopher Columbus remains an enigmatic figure. He left few documents for historians to analyze; even his journal of the first voyage was lost in the sixteenth century. From the scanty historical record, however, it seems clear that Columbus never really comprehended the consequences of his historic voyages, maintaining stubbornly to his death that he had reached Asia, not "discovered" a New World. From his return to Europe in 1493, his contemporaries also expressed widely divergent views about the man and his importance. These divisions have endured over time, so that modern historians most often speak of the multiple historical legacies of Christopher Columbus. Regardless of whether he is viewed as a hero or a villain, it is clear that his voyages began the process of global interdependency that characterizes our own modern world.

Columbus's Legacy in the Documentary Record

The principal documentary source about the first voyage of Christopher Columbus is his journal or logbook, intended to inform the monarchs of Castile about his journey. In this work, Columbus often focused on what might have pleased the crown, rather than simply recording events. In addition, it is clear that Columbus did not always understand the ecological, human, and geographical landscape that he encountered. An even more serious problem with interpreting the journal, however, is that all of the original copies were lost sometime in the sixteenth century. The only remaining copy is a transcription of the original made in the 1550s by the Dominican friar, Bartolomé de las Casas, who used it as a source in writing his Historia de las Indias. *Las Casas, a vigorous champion of the Amerindians, introduced his own biases, made numerous copying errors, often summarized or omitted points, and even interjected his own comments. The result is a primary source that must be used very carefully by any student of the period.*

The only original documentary record of the first voyage is the 1493 letter of Columbus, but this document too has its limitations. It reads like an advertising brochure designed to encourage future investments in a second voyage of Columbus to the New World.

The remaining documents in this collection deal with the wide impact of the Columbian voyages on the course of world history. Nevertheless, they too contain exaggerations, reflecting the biases of their authors and the limited abilities of contemporaries to understand the magnitude of the changes affecting their lives.

The Journal of Christopher Columbus

The document that follows serves as the introduction to the journal of Columbus. It recounts how the monarchs of "the Spains" agreed to support Columbus after their formal conquest of the Muslim city of Granada in 1492, followed by the expulsion of the Jews from the country shortly afterward.[1] *Columbus links his own voyage to the monarch's "triumphs" by promising to spread the Christian faith after his arrival in Asia. He also reminds them of the many titles granted to his family and promises to record his voyage faithfully in the ensuing journal. This selection is taken from* The Journal of Christopher Columbus, *trans. Cecil Jane (London, 1968), 3–4, 6.*

Journal Introduction

Most Christian and most exalted and most excellent and most mighty princes, King and Queen of the Spains and of the islands of the sea, our Sovereigns: Forasmuch as, in this present year of 1492, after that Your Highnesses had made an end of the war with the Moors who reigned in Europe, and had brought that war to a conclusion in the very great city of Granada, . . . and afterwards in that same month, on the ground of information which I had given to Your Highnesses concerning the lands of India, and concerning a prince who is called 'Grand Khan,' which is to say in our Romance tongue 'King of Kings,' how many times he and his ancestors had sent to Rome to beg for men learned in our holy faith, in order that they might instruct him therein, and how the Holy Father had never made provision in this matter, and how so many nations had been lost, falling into idolatries and taking to themselves doctrines of perdition, and Your Highnesses, as Catholic Christians and as princes devoted to the holy Christian

[1] Spain was not a nation-state in 1492; it was united when Ferdinand of Aragon and Isabel of Castile married in 1469 and ascended their respective thrones ten years later. Thus, it was merely a dynastic union, and the institutions of both kingdoms remained separate. Columbus recognizes this tenuous unity by referring to Ferdinand and Isabel as monarchs of the "Spains."

faith and propagators thereof, and enemies of the sect of Mahomet and of all idolatries and heresies, took thought to send me, Christopher Columbus, to the said parts of India, to see those princes and peoples and lands and the character of them and of all else, and the manner which should be used to bring about their conversion to our holy faith, and ordained that I should not go by land to the eastward, by which way it was the custom to go, but by way of the west, by which down to this day we do not know certainly that any one has passed; therefore, after having driven out all the Jews from your realms and lordships, in the same month of January, Your Highnesses commanded me that, with a sufficient fleet, I should go to the said parts of India and for this accorded to me great rewards and ennobled me so that from that time henceforward I might style myself 'don' and be high admiral of the Ocean Sea and viceroy and perpetual governor of the islands and continent which I should discover and gain and which from now henceforward might be discovered and gained in the Ocean Sea, and that my eldest son should succeed to the same position, and so on from generation to generation. And I departed from the city of Granada on the twelfth day of the month of May in the same year of 1492, on a Saturday, and came to the town of Palos, which is a port of the sea, where I made ready three ships, very suited for such an undertaking, and I set out from that port, well furnished with very many supplies and with many seamen, on the third day of the month of August of the same year, on a Friday, half an hour before the rising of the sun, and I steered my course for the Canary Islands of Your Highnesses, which are in the Ocean Sea, thence to set out on my way and to sail until I should arrive in the Indies, and deliver the embassy of Your Highnesses to those princes and perform all that you had commanded me to do. To this end, I thought to write all this journey very carefully, from day to day, all that I might do and see and experience, as will be hereafter seen.

The next journal entry records the first landfall of the voyage and the initial encounter with the indigenous peoples of the Caribbean. Columbus dutifully claimed the lands for his sovereigns and noted the good relations that developed between his crew members and the inhabitants of the islands. He obviously viewed the Amerindians as human beings but as technologically inferior. Columbus also alluded to the apparent animosity that existed between these people and their neighbors, who sought to enslave them. Notice how Las Casas interposes himself into the narrative at various places. This excerpt is taken from The Journal of Christopher Columbus, *22–24.*

Thursday, October 11th/[12th]

He navigated to the west-south-west; . . . Two hours after midnight land appeared, at a distance of about two leagues from them. They took in all sail, remaining with the mainsail, which is the great sail without bonnets, and kept jogging, waiting for day, a Friday, on which they reached a small island of the Lucayos, which is called in the language of the Indians "Guanahaní." Immediately they saw naked people, and the admiral went ashore in the armed boat, and Martin Alonso Pinzón and Vicente Yañez, his brother, who was captain of the *Niña*. The admiral brought out the royal standard, and . . . [w]hen they had landed, they saw very green trees and much water and fruit of various kinds. The admiral called the two captains and the others who had landed, and Rodrigo de Escobedo, secretary of the whole fleet, and Rodrigo Sanchez de Segovia, and said that they should bear witness and testimony how he, before them all, took possession of the island, as in fact he did, for the King and Queen, his Sovereigns, making

A seventeenth-century engraving, showing newly discovered America as a paradise.

the declarations which are required, as is contained more at length in the testimonies which were there made in writing. Soon many people of the island gathered there. What follows are the actual words of the admiral, in his book of his first voyage and discovery of these Indies.

"I," he says, "in order that they might feel great amity towards us, because I knew that they were a people to be delivered and converted to our holy faith rather by love than by force, gave to some among them some red caps and some glass beads, which they hung round their necks, and many other things of little value. At this they were greatly pleased and became so entirely our friends that it was a wonder to see. Afterwards they came swimming to the ships' boats, where we were, and brought us parrots and cotton thread in balls, and spears and many other things, and we exchanged for them other things, such as small glass beads and hawks' bells, which we gave to them. In fact, they took all and gave all, such as they had, with good will, but it seemed to me that they were a people very deficient in everything. They all go naked as their mothers bore them, and the women also, although I saw only one very young girl. And all those whom I did see were youths, so that I did not see one who was over thirty years of age; they were very well built, with very handsome bodies and very good faces. Their hair is coarse almost like the hairs of a horse's tail and short; they wear their hair down over their eyebrows, except for a few strands behind, which they wear long and never cut. Some of them are painted black, and they are the colour of the people of the Canaries, neither black nor white, and some of them are painted white and some red and some in any colour that they find. Some of them paint their faces, some their whole bodies, some only the eyes, and some only the nose. They do not bear arms or know them, for I showed to them swords and they took them by the blade and cut themselves through ignorance. They have no iron. Their spears are certain reeds, without iron, and some of these have a fish tooth at the end, while others are pointed in various ways. They are all generally fairly tall, good looking and well proportioned. I saw some who bore marks of wounds on their bodies, and I made signs to them to ask how this came about, and they indicated to me that people came from other islands, which are near, and wished to capture them, and they defended themselves. And I believed and still believe that they come here from the mainland to take them for slaves. They should be good servants and of quick intelligence, since I see that they very soon say all that is said to them, and I believe that they would easily be made Christians, for it appeared to me that they had no creed. Our Lord willing, at the time of my departure I will bring back six of them to Your Highnesses, that they may learn to talk. I saw no beast of any kind in this island, except parrots." All these are the words of the admiral.

The journal returns to the theme of warfare among the indigenous peoples by introducing the Caribs, who are pictured as cannibals. These entries are very controversial among historians because the supporting evidence for cannibalism or even the existence of a separate Carib people is very scanty. Some scholars believe that Columbus introduced these passages to justify the violent skirmishes that broke out between his men and indigenous groups. Others even speculate that these references to cannibalism, which Europeans considered a particularly inhumane or "barbaric" practice, were merely excuses for the subjugation of these indigenous peoples. The passage is taken from The Journal of Christopher Columbus, *146–48.*

Sunday, January 13th

He sent the boat to land at a beautiful beach, in order that they might take *ajes* [edible tropical plants] to eat, and they found some men with bows and arrows, with whom they paused to talk, and they bought two bows and many arrows, and asked one of them to go to speak with the admiral in the caravel, and he came. The admiral says that he was more ugly in appearance than any whom he had seen. He had his face all stained with charcoal, although in all other parts they are accustomed to paint themselves with various colours; he wore all his hair very long and drawn back and tied behind, and then gathered in meshes of parrots' feathers, and he was as naked as the others. The admiral judged that he must be one of the Caribs who eat men and that the gulf, which he had seen yesterday, divided the land and that it must be an island by itself. He questioned him concerning the Caribs, and the Indian indicated to him that they were near there to the east, and the admiral says that he sighted this land yesterday before he entered that bay. The Indian told him that in that land there was much gold, and pointing to the poop of the caravel, which was very large, said that there were pieces of that size. He called gold "tuob," and did not understand it by "caona," as they call it in the first part of the island, or by "nozay," as they name it in San Salvador and in the other islands. . . . The admiral says further that in the islands which he had passed they were in great terror of Carib: in some islands they call it "Caniba," but in Española "Carib"; and they must be a daring people, since they go through all the islands and eat the people they can take. He says that he understood some words, and from them he says that he gathered other things, and the Indians whom he carried with him understood more, although they found a difference of languages, owing to the great distance between the lands. He ordered food to be given to the Indian, and gave him pieces of green and red cloth, and glass beads, to which they are very much attached, and sent him back to shore. And he told him to bring him gold, if there was any, which he believed to be the case from certain small ornaments which he was wearing. When the boat reached the shore, there were behind the trees quite fifty-five men, naked, with very long hair, as women wear their hair in Castile. At the back of the head, they wore tufts of parrot feathers and feathers of other birds, and each one carried his bow. The Indian landed and caused the others to lay aside their bows and arrows and a short stick, . . . which they carry in place of a sword. Afterwards they came to the boat and the people from the boat landed, and they began to buy from them their bows and arrows and other weapons, because the admiral had ordered this to be done. When two bows had been sold, they would not give more, but prepared rather to assault the Christians and capture them. They went running to collect their bows and arrows, where they had laid them aside, and came back with ropes in their hands, in order, as he says, to bind the Christians. Seeing them come running towards them, the Christians, being on guard, as the admiral always advised them to be, fell upon them, and they gave an Indian a great slash on the buttocks and they wounded another in the breast with an arrow. When they saw that they could gain little, although the Christians were not more than seven and they were fifty and more, they turned in flight, so that not one remained, one leaving his arrows here and another his bow there. The Christians, as he says, would have killed many of them, if the pilot who went with them as their captain had not prevented it.

The Letter of Columbus to Ferdinand and Isabel

The following excerpt from the letter of Christopher Columbus to King Ferdinand and Queen Isabel was undoubtedly intended to publicize the successes of the first voyage. The size and potential richness of the islands are apparently exaggerated to impress the monarchs (and any other potential investors) and generate support for any future voyages by Columbus. Although he scarcely refers to the Caribs, Columbus does emphasize the exotic qualities of the newly discovered lands, particularly the nudity of the inhabitants. Apart from illustrating the "primitive" social system of the native peoples, these references were probably also meant to evoke (in the reading audience) an image of the biblical Garden of Eden. This copy of the letter may be found in The Journal of Christopher Columbus, *191, 194, 196–98, 200–201.*

SIR: Since I know that you will be pleased at the great victory with which Our Lord has crowned my voyage, I write this to you, from which you will learn how in thirty-three days I passed from the Canary Islands to the Indies, with the fleet which the most illustrious King and Queen, our Sovereigns, gave to me. There I found very many islands, filled with innumerable people, and I have taken possession of them all for their Highnesses, done by proclamation and with the royal standard unfurled, and no opposition was offered to me.

To the first island which I found I gave the name "San Salvador," in remembrance of the Divine Majesty, Who had marvellously bestowed all this; the Indians call it "Guanahani." To the second, I gave the name the island of "Santa Maria de Concepcion," to the third, "Fernandina," to the fourth, "Isabella," to the fifth island, "Juana," and so each received from me a new name. . . .

Española is a marvel. The sierras and the mountains, the plains, the champaigns, are so lovely and so rich for planting and sowing, for breeding cattle of every kind, for building towns and villages. The harbours of the sea here are such as cannot be believed to exist unless they have been seen, and so with the rivers, many and great, and of good water, the majority of which contain gold. In the trees, fruits and plants, there is a great difference from those of Juana. In this island, there are many spices and great mines of gold and of other metals.

The people of this island and of all the other islands which I have found and of which I have information, all go naked, men and women, as their mothers bore them, although some of the women cover a single place with the leaf of a plant or with a net of cotton which they make for the purpose. They have no iron or steel or weapons, nor are they fitted to use them. This is not because they are not well built and of handsome stature, but because they are very marvellously timorous. They have no other arms than spears made of canes, cut in seeding time, to the ends of which they fix a small sharpened stick. Of these they do not dare to make use, for many times it has happened that I have sent ashore two or three men to some town to have speech with them, and countless people have come out to them, and as soon as they have seen my men approaching, they have fled, a father not even waiting for his son. This is not because ill has been done to any one of them; on the contrary, at every place where I have been and have been able to have speech with them, I have given to them of that which I had, such as cloth and many other things, receiving

Native Americans congregate as ships arrive from the New World in this German woodcut.

nothing in exchange. But so they are, incurably timid. It is true that, after they have been reassured and have lost this fear, they are so guileless and so generous with all that they possess, that no one would believe it who has not seen it. They refuse nothing that they possess, if it be asked of them; on the contrary, they invite any one to share it and display as much love as if they would give their hearts. They are content with whatever trifle of whatever kind that may be given to them, whether it be of value or valueless. I forbade that they should be given things so worthless as fragments of broken crockery, scraps of broken glass and lace tips, although when they were able to get them, they fancied that they possessed the best jewel in the world. So it was found that for a thong a sailor received gold to the weight of two and a half castellanos, and others received much more for other things which were worth less. As for new blancas, for them they would give everything which they had, although it might be two or three castellanos' [gold coins] weight of gold or an arroba or two of spun cotton. They took even the pieces of the broken hoops of the wine barrels and, like savages, gave what they had, so that it seemed to me to be wrong and I forbade it. I gave them a thousand handsome good things, which I had brought, in order that they might conceive affection for us and, more than that, might become Christians and be inclined to the love and service of Your Highnesses and of the whole Castilian nation, and strive to collect and give us of the things which they have in abundance and which are necessary to us.

They do not hold any creed nor are they idolaters; but they all believe that power and good are in the heavens and were very firmly convinced that I, with these ships and men, came from the heavens, and in this belief they everywhere received me after they had mastered their fear. This belief is not the result of ignorance, for they are, on the contrary, of a very acute intelligence and they are men who navigate all those seas, so that it is amazing how good an account they give of everything. It is because they have never seen people clothed or ships of such a kind.

As soon as I arrived in the Indies, in the first island which I found, I took some of the natives by force, in order that they might learn and might give me information of whatever there is in these parts. And so it was that they soon understood us, and we them, either by speech or signs, and they have been very serviceable. At present, those I bring with me are still of the opinion that I come from Heaven, for all the intercourse which they have had with me. They were the first to announce this wherever I went, and the others went running from house to house, and to the neighbouring towns, with loud cries of, "Come! Come! See the men from Heaven!" So all came, men and women alike, when their minds were set at rest concerning us, not one, small or great, remaining behind, and they all brought something to eat and drink, which they gave with extraordinary affection. . . .

In all these islands, I saw no great diversity in the appearance of the people or in their manners and language. On the contrary, they all understand one another, which is a very curious thing, on account of which I hope that their Highnesses will determine upon their conversion to our holy faith, towards which they are very inclined.

I have already said how I went one hundred and seven leagues in a straight line from west to east along the seashore of the island of Juana, and as a result of this voyage I can say that this island is larger than England and Scotland together, for, beyond these one hundred and seven leagues, there remain to the westward two provinces to which I have not gone. One of these provinces they call "Avan," and there people are born with tails. These provinces cannot have a length of less than fifty or sixty leagues, as I could understand from those Indians whom I have and who know all the islands.

The other island, Española, has a circumference greater than all Spain from Collioure by the seacoast to Fuenterabia in Vizcaya, for I voyaged along one side for one hundred and eighty-eight great leagues in a straight line from west to east. It is a land to be desired and, when seen, never to be left. I have taken possession of all for their Highnesses, and all are more richly endowed than I know how or am able to say, and I hold all for their Highnesses, so that they may dispose of them as they do of the kingdoms of Castile and as absolutely. But especially, in this Española, in the situation most convenient and in the best position for the mines of gold and for all trade as well with the mainland here as with that there, belonging to the Grand Khan, where will be great trade and profit, I have taken possession of a large town, to which I gave the name "Villa de Navidad," and in it I have made fortifications and a fort, which will now by this time be entirely completed. In it I have left enough men for such a purpose with arms and artillery and provisions for more than a year, and a fusta, and one, a master of all seacraft, to build others, and I have established great friendship with the king of that land, so much so, that he was proud to call me "brother" and to treat me as such. . . .

In conclusion, to speak only of what has been accomplished on this voyage, which was so hasty, their Highnesses can see that I will give them as much gold as they may need, if their Highnesses will render me very slight assistance; presently, I will give them spices and cotton, as much as their Highnesses shall command; and mastic, as much as they shall order to be shipped and which, up to now, has been found only in Greece, in the island of Chios, and the Seignory sells it for what it pleases; and aloe, as much as they shall order to be shipped; and slaves, as many as they shall order, and who will be from the idolaters. I believe also that I have found rhubarb and cinnamon, and I shall find a thousand other things of value, which the people whom I have left there will have discovered, for I have not delayed at any point, so far as the wind allowed me to sail, except in the town of Navidad, in order to leave it secured and well established, and in truth I should have done much more if the ships had served me as reason demanded. . . .

This is an account of the facts, thus abridged.

Done in the caravel, off the Canary Islands, on the fifteenth day of February, in the year one thousand four hundred and ninety-three.

The Amerindians and the "Garden of Eden"

The attempt to picture the Amerindians as an innocent and childlike race, so apparent in the Columbus letter, was a common theme in the sixteenth century. Members of the clergy often used this image to prove that the indigenous peoples were "real" human beings (rather than some form of savage animals), to protect them from exploitation from the settlers, and also to gain control over their conversion to Christianity from rival clerical or lay organizations. The following passage is filled with language meant to evoke an image of the Garden of Eden, not the realities of Amerindian life in the Americas. The passage is taken from Bartolomé de las Casas, Very Brief Account of the Destruction of the Indies, *trans. Francis Augustus MacNutt in* Bartholomew De Las

Casas: His Life, His Apostolate, and His Writings *(New York, 1909), 314–15.*

God has created all these numberless people to be quite the simplest, without malice or duplicity, most obedient, most faithful to their natural Lords, and to the Christians, whom they serve; the most humble, most patient, most peaceful, and calm, without strife nor tumults; not wrangling, nor querulous, as free from uproar, hate and desire of revenge, as any in the world.

They are likewise the most delicate people, weak and of feeble constitution, and less than any other can they bear fatigue, and they very easily die of whatsoever infirmity; so much so, that not even the sons of our Princes and of nobles, brought up in royal and gentle life, are more delicate than they; although there are among them such as are of the peasant class. They are also a very poor people, who of worldly goods possess little, nor wish to possess: and they are therefore neither proud, nor ambitious, nor avaricious. . . .

They are likewise of a clean, unspoiled, and vivacious intellect, very capable, and receptive to every good doctrine; most prompt to accept our Holy Catholic Faith, to be endowed with virtuous customs; and they have as little difficulty with such things as any people created by God in the world.

Once they have begun to learn of matters pertaining to faith, they are so importunate to know them, and in frequenting the sacraments and divine service of the Church, that to tell the truth, the clergy have need to be endowed of God with the gift of preeminent patience to bear with them: and finally, I have heard many lay Spaniards frequently say many years ago, (unable to deny the goodness of those they saw) certainly these people were the most blessed of the earth, had they only knowledge of God.

The "Sins" of the Spanish Invasion

Militant friars like Las Casas and many of his fellow Dominicans also tried to picture the Spanish conquistadors and settlers as vicious and cruel exploiters. These tales had some basis in reality, but they were also

Bartolome de Las Casas, (1474–1566), missionary leader.

aimed at convincing a European audience that the excesses of the conquest had to be curbed and the powers of the crown and the clergy expanded in the New World. Along with the images of the indigenous peoples as innocents reminiscent of the Garden of Eden, they created a powerful picture of European excesses. According to many friars, these abuses undermined the chances for salvation of all Christians who tolerated such "sins" against humanity. The selection below is taken from Bartolomé de las Casas, Very Brief Account of the Destruction of the Indies, *trans. Francis Augustus MacNutt in* Bartholomew De Las Casas, *319–20.*

The Christians, with their horses and swords and lances, began to slaughter and practise strange cruelty among them. They penetrated into the country and spared neither children nor the aged, nor pregnant women, nor those in child labour, all of whom they ran through the body and lacerated, as though they were assaulting so many lambs herded in their sheepfold.

They made bets as to who would slit a man in two, or cut off his head at one blow: or they opened up his bowels. They tore the babes from their mothers' breast by the feet, and dashed their heads against the rocks. Others they seized by the shoulders and threw into the rivers, laughing and joking, and when they fell into the water they exclaimed: "boil body of so and so!" They spitted the bodies of other babes, together with their mothers and all who were before them, on their swords.

They made a gallows just high enough for the feet to nearly touch the ground, and by thirteens, in honour and reverence of our Redeemer and the twelve Apostles, they put wood underneath and, with fire, they burned the Indians alive. . . .

And because all the people who could flee, hid among the mountains and climbed the crags to escape from men so deprived of humanity, so wicked, such wild beasts, exterminators and capital enemies of all the human race, the Spaniards taught and trained the fiercest boar-hounds to tear an Indian to pieces as soon as they saw him, so that they more willingly attacked and ate one, than if he had been a boar. These hounds made great havoc and slaughter.

The Onset of the Epidemics

The introduction of European diseases brought unprecedented devastation upon the Amerindian peoples. In Mexico, for example, some historical demographers estimate the precontact Amerindian population at 20-25 million; within one hundred years that number had fallen to 1.5 million, largely as a result of epidemic diseases. Often the epidemics arrived even before the Spanish forces, spread by indigenous peoples who had contact with the Europeans. The following passage, taken from an indigenous (Aztec) source recounts the devastation of a smallpox epidemic in the valley of Mexico, which preceded the arrival of the Spaniards, weakened the indigenous peoples, and paved the way for the conquistadores' ultimate victories. This excerpt is taken from Fray Bernardino de Sahagún, Florentine Codex: General History of the Things of New Spain, *trans. Arthur J. O. Anderson and Charles E. Dibble (Santa Fe, 1955), 12:81.*

And [even] before the Spaniards had risen against us, a pestilence first came to be prevalent: the smallpox. It was [the month of] Tepeilhuitl when it began, and it spread over the people as great destruction. Some it quite covered [with pustules] on all

From the *Florentine Codex: General History of the Things of New Spain* by Fray Bernardino de Sahagún. Arthur J. O. Anderson and Charles E. Dibble, Translators. Published by The School of American Research and The University of Utah, 1955.

parts—their faces, their heads, their breasts, etc. There was great havoc. Very many died of it. They could not walk; they only lay in their resting places and beds. They could not move; they could not stir; they could not change position, nor lie on one side, nor face down, nor on their backs. And if they stirred, much did they cry out. Great was its destruction. Covered, mantled with pustules, very many people died of them. And very many starved; there was death from hunger, [for] none could take care of [the sick]; nothing could be done for them.

And on some the pustules were widely separated; they suffered not greatly, neither did many [of them] die. Yet many people were marred by them on their faces; one's face or nose was pitted. Some lost their eyes; they were blinded.

At this time, this pestilence prevailed sixty days, sixty day signs. When it left, when it abated, when there was recovery and the return of life, the plague had already moved toward Chalco, whereby many were disabled—not, however, completely crippled. When it came to be prevalent, [it was the month of] Teotl eco. And when it went, weakened, it was Panquetzaliztli. Then the Mexicans, the chieftains, could revive.

And after this, then the Spaniards came.

Amerindians View the Spanish Invasion

For the highly advanced Amerindian civilizations, the arrival of the Europeans signaled a massive change in their religious, social, and economic way of life. Many Amerindians resisted these changes, clinging to their traditional ways and changing them as little as possible. The following passage from the Mayan peoples of Mesoamerica has a nostalgic quality, harkening back to better days before the Europeans arrived. It is taken from The Book of Chilam Balam of Chumayel, *trans. Ralph L. Roys (Norman, Oklahoma, 1967), 83.*

They did not wish to join with the foreigners; they did not desire Christianity. They did not wish to pay tribute, did those whose emblems were the bird, the precious stone, the flat precious stone and the jaguar, those with the three magic <emblems>. Four-hundreds of years and fifteen score years was the end of their lives; then came the end of their lives, because they knew the measure of their days. Complete was the month; complete, the year; complete, the day; complete, the night; complete, the breath of life as it passed also; complete, the blood, when they arrived at their beds, their mats, their thrones. In due measure did they recite the good prayers; in due measure they sought the lucky days, until they saw the good stars enter into their reign; then they kept watch while the reign of the good stars began. Then everything was good.

Then they adhered to <the dictates of> their reason. There was no sin; in the holy faith their lives <were passed>. There was then no sickness; they had then no aching bones; they had then no high fever; they had then no smallpox; they had then no burning chest; they had then no abdominal pains; they had then no consumption; they had then no headache. At that time the course of humanity was orderly. The foreigners made it otherwise when they arrived here. They brought shameful things/when they came. They lost their innocence in carnal sin.

The Columbian Exchange

The first European explorers and settlers were often astounded by the rich and diverse plant and animal life, much of it unknown to them. Indeed, the concept of the Americas as a "New World" stemmed in part from the very different natural environment. As the passage below catalogs, the Americas had rich supplies of plant and animal life, which enriched the food supply of many parts of the world after 1492. Before the Columbian voyages, for example, Ireland had no potatoes, and commodities like corn or chocolate were unknown outside of the Western Hemisphere. Even the coca leaf was a traditional Andean crop. This passage is taken from José de Acosta, Historia natural y moral de las Indias *(Mexico City, 1940), in* Latin American Civilization: History and Society, 1492 to the Present, *ed. Benjamin Keen, 4th ed. (Boulder, 1986), 76–79.*

The Indians have their own words to signify bread, which in Peru is called *tanta* and in other parts is given other names. But the quality and substance of the bread the Indians use is very different from ours, for they have no kind of wheat, barley, millet, panic grass, or any grain such as is used in Europe to make bread. Instead they have other kinds of grains and roots, among which maize, called Indian wheat in Castile and Turkey grain in Italy, holds the first place. . . .

Maize is the Indian bread, and they commonly eat it boiled in the grain, hot, when it is called *mote* . . . ; sometimes they eat it toasted. There is a large and round maize, like that of the Lucanas, which the Spaniards eat as a delicacy; it has better flavor than toasted chickpeas. There is another and more pleasing way of preparing it, which consists in grinding the maize and making the flour into pancakes, which are put on the fire and later placed on the table and eaten piping hot; in some places they call them *arepas*. . . .

Maize is used by the Indians to make not only their bread but also their wine; from it they make beverages which produce drunkenness more quickly than wine made of grapes. They make this maize wine in various ways, calling it *azua* in Peru and more generally throughout the Indies *chicha*. The strongest sort is made like beer, steeping the grains of maize until they begin to break, after which they boil the juice in a certain way, which makes it so strong that a few drinks will produce intoxication. . . .

The cacao tree is most esteemed in Mexico and coca is favored in Peru; both trees are surrounded with considerable superstition. Cacao is a bean smaller and fattier than the almond, and when roasted has not a bad flavor. It is so much esteemed by the Indians, and even by the Spaniards, that it is the object of one of the richest and largest lines of trade of New Spain; since it is a dry fruit, and one that keeps a long time without spoiling, they send whole ships loaded with it from the province of Guatemala. Last year an English corsair burned in the port of Guatulco, in New Spain, more than one hundred thousand *cargas* of cacao. They also use it as money, for five cacao beans will buy one thing, thirty

---

Selections by José de Acosta, reprinted from *Latin American Civilization: History and Society, 1492 to the Present*, Fourth Edition, Benjamin Keen, editor, translator.

another, and one hundred still another, and no objections are made to its use. They also use it as alms to give to the poor.

The chief use of this cacao is to make a drink that they call chocolate, which they greatly cherish in that country. But those who have not formed a taste for it dislike it, for it has a froth at the top and an effervescence like that formed in wine by dregs, so that one must really have great faith in it to tolerate it. In fine, it is the favorite drink of Indians and Spaniards alike, and they regale visitors to their country with it; the Spanish women of that land are particularly fond of the dark chocolate. They prepare it in various ways: hot, cold, and lukewarm. They usually put spices and much chili in it; they also make a paste of it, and they say that it is good for the chest and the stomach, and also for colds. Be that as it may, those who have not formed a taste for it do not like it. . . .

The cacao does not grow in Peru; instead they have the coca, which is surrounded with even greater superstition and really seems fabulous. In Potosí alone the commerce in coca amounts to more than 5,000,000 pesos, with a consumption of from 90 to 100,000 hampers, and in the year 1583 it was 100,000. . . . This coca that they so greatly cherish is a little green leaf which grows upon shrubs about one *estado* high. . . . It is commonly brought from the Andes, from valleys of insufferable heat, where it rains the greater part of the year, and it costs the Indians much labor and takes many lives, for they must leave their highlands and cold climates in order to cultivate it and carry it away. . . .

The Indians prize it beyond measure, and in the time of the Inca kings plebeians were forbidden to use coca without the permission of the Inca or his governor. Their custom is to hold it in their mouths, chewing and sucking it; they do not swallow it; they say that it gives them great strength and is a great comfort to them. Many serious men say that this is pure superstition and imagination. To tell the truth, I do not think so; I believe that it really does lend strength and endurance to the Indians, for one sees effects that cannot be attributed to imagination, such as their ability to journey two whole days on a handful of coca, eating nothing else, and similar feats.

Ecological Change

The Americas also underwent massive ecological changes brought about, in large part, by the introduction of European plant and animal life. The passage below provides some indication of the magnitude of these changes that followed the first Columbian voyages in 1492. The following document is also taken from José de Acosta, Historia natural y moral de las Indias *(Mexico City, 1940), in* Latin American Civilization: History and Society, 1492 to the Present, *ed. Benjamin Keen, 4th ed. (Boulder, 1986), 80–82.*

The Indies have been better repaid in the matter of plants than in any other kind of merchandise; for those few that have been carried from the Indies into Spain do badly there, whereas the many that have come over from Spain prosper in their new homes. I do not know whether to attribute this to the excellence of the plants that go from here or to the bounty of the soil over there. Nearly every good thing grown in Spain is found there; in some regions they do better than in others. They include wheat, barley, garden produce and greens and vegetables of all kinds, such as lettuce, cabbage, radishes, onions, garlic, parsley, turnips, carrots, eggplants, endive, salt-wort, spinach, chickpeas, beans, and lentils—in short, whatever grows well here, for those who have gone to the Indies have been careful to take with them seeds of every description. . . .

The trees that have fared best there are the orange, lemon, citron, and others of that sort. In some parts there are already whole forests and groves of orange trees. Marvelling at this, I asked on a certain island who had planted so many orange trees in the fields. To which they replied that it might have happened that some oranges fell to the ground and rotted, whereupon the seeds germinated, and, some being borne by the waters to different parts, gave rise to these dense groves. This seemed a likely reason. I said before that orange trees have generally done well in the Indies, for nowhere have I found a place where oranges were not to be found. . . .

Peaches and apricots also have done well, although the latter have fared better in New Spain. . . . Apples and pears are grown, but in moderate yields; plums give sparingly; figs are abundant, chiefly in Peru. Quinces are found everywhere, and in New Spain they are so plentiful that we received fifty choice ones for half a *real*. Pomegranates are found in abundance, but they are all sweet, for the people do not like the sharp variety. The melons are very good in some regions, as in Tierra Firme and Peru. Cherries, both wild and cultivated, have not so far prospered in the Indies. . . . In conclusion, I find that hardly any of the finer fruits is lacking in those parts. . . .

By profitable plants I mean those plants which not only yield fruit but bring money to their owners. The most important of these is the vine, which gives wine, vinegar, grapes, raisins, verjuice, and syrup—but the wine is the chief concern. Wine and grapes are not products of the islands or of Tierra Firme; in New Spain there are vines which bear grapes but do not yield wine. The reason must be that the grapes do not ripen completely because of the rains which come in July and August and hinder their ripening; they are good only for eating. Wine is shipped from Spain and the Canary Islands to all parts of the Indies, except Peru and Chile, where they have vineyards and make very good wine. This industry is expanding continually, not only because of the goodness of the soil, but because they have a better knowledge of winemaking. . . .

The silk which is made in New Spain goes to other provinces—to Peru, for example. There was no silk industry before the Spaniards came; the mulberry trees were brought from Spain, and they grow well, especially in the province called Misteca, where they raise silkworms and make good taffetas; they do not yet make damasks, satins, or velvets, however.

The sugar industry is even wider in scope, for the sugar not only is consumed in the Indies but is shipped in quantity to Spain. Sugar cane grows remarkably well in various parts of the Indies. In the islands, in Mexico, in Peru, and elsewhere they have built sugar mills that do a large business. I was told that the Nasca [Peru] sugar mill earned more than thirty thousand pesos a year. The mill at Chicama, near Trujillo [Peru], was also a big enterprise, and those of New Spain are no smaller, for the consumption of sugar and preserves in the Indies is simply fantastic. From the island of Santo Domingo, in the fleet in which I came, they brought eight hundred and ninety-eight chests and boxes of sugar. I happened to see the sugar loaded at the port of Puerto Rico, and it seemed to me that each box must contain eight *arrobas*.

The sugar industry is the principal business of those islands—such a taste have men developed for sweets!

Olives and olive trees are also found in the Indies, in Mexico, and in Peru, but up to now they have not set up any mills to make olive oil. Actually, it is not made at all, for they prefer to eat the olives, seasoning them well. They find it unprofitable to make olive oil, and so all their oil comes from Spain.

Questions

1. *How does Columbus portray the indigenous peoples? Does he present contradictory images of them? How does he gather his information about the customs, beliefs, and culture of the Amerindians when he does not speak their language? What role do you think Columbus envisioned for the indigenous peoples after the Europeans established their control?*
2. *Why did Las Casas and other clergymen present such an idealized picture of the Amerindians? Why did they picture the Spanish settlers as such barbarians? Do you think these portrayals are accurate or mere propaganda? Why?*
3. *What role did disease have in the European victories over the Amerindian empires of Mesoamerica and South America? Do the two indigenous accounts indicate that the Amerindians submitted passively to Spanish rule after the initial victories of the conquistadores? What factors do you think gave rise to the success of the Europeans?*
4. *Why did the people, plants, and animals of Europe fare so well in the New World? To what extent was the expansion of Europe made possible by this success? To what extent was the so-called Columbian exchange of plants, animals, and biota beneficial for the world?*

FURTHER READING

The literature on Christopher Columbus and his historical legacies is immense, but the standard treatment in English is by William D. Phillips, Jr. and Carla Rahn Phillips, The Worlds of Christopher Columbus *(New York, 1992). An older but still stimulating treatment of the impact of European expansion in the Caribbean is Carl Ortwin Sauer,* The Early Spanish Main *(Berkeley, 1966). An updated and expanded book on the ecological impact of global interdependency is by Alfred W. Crosby, Jr.,* Ecological Imperialism: The Biological Expansion of Europe, 900–1900 *(New York, 1986). A positive scholarly treatment of the life and times of Christopher Columbus is P. E. Taviani,* Christopher Columbus: The Grand Design *(London, 1985). A challenging literary treatment of the "encounters" in the New World is by Peter Hulme,* Colonial Encounters: Europe and the Native Caribbean, 1492–1797 *(New York, 1986).*

What Did it Mean to Be a Puritan?

Carla Gardina Pestana

Introduction

Puritans suffer from a bad reputation. Since the early twentieth century when American social critic H. L. Mencken ridiculed the first English settlers in New England, the word "puritan" conjures up images of sexual prudery, censoriousness, and hypocrisy. Although American school children are told that the Puritans came to America to establish religious freedom, as adults we learn that they in fact repressed dissent. Not only that, they limited political participation to (adult male) church members, even though admission to the church was by no means automatic. Many college students learning anew about early New England history wonder: Why would anyone be a Puritan?

The English men and women who migrated to New England between 1630 and 1642 to settle the Massachusetts Bay Colony would probably not be surprised that they have an unflattering image. By the time they left England they were accustomed to being ridiculed. In part they departed because they were committed to a religious movement that was increasingly coming under attack. In their view, the Church of England (established by Henry VIII in 1534) ought to participate more fully in the Protestant Reformation that had converted many on the European continent. Their criticisms of religious practices and social mores had ceased to be tolerated in the years leading up to their exodus, and Archbishop William Laud was intent on suppressing their movement. Financial hardships and religious woes combined to persuade over thirteen thousand people to leave the island of their birth to travel to northern North America in the dozen years after 1629.

They carried on—in spite of the travails they experienced—because they believed that God required it of them. To understand the Puritans, we must think about that conviction and the meaning that it gave to their lives. Many women and men braved first the displeasure of the English authorities and then the dangers of colonization because of their belief that they were fulfilling God's will. Early New England residents embraced the faith that we call "Puritan" out of the sense of personal commitment to reformed Protestantism. Theologically, they generally followed the teachings of John Calvin, a leading Protestant reformer of the previous century. The Puritans' church organization has been described as "non-separating congregationalism." Congregationalists rejected the ecclesiastical hierarchy of the Church of England (with its bishops, like their old nemesis Archbishop Laud, and its system of courts); they believed that the individual congregation should be autonomous, with the power to call a minister and to admit and discipline members. They earned the appellation "non-separating" because—unlike the separatists ("Pilgrims") who settled Plymouth—they refused to renounce their affiliation with the Anglican church, claiming that they wished to work for its reformation from within. Although we may find it difficult to comprehend their beliefs and the depth of their convictions, we must understand the Puritans as people dedicated to a cause. This cause guided them to New England in the first place and led them to create a unique society once they arrived. Their commitment to their cause was their reason for being Puritans.

PURITAN FAITH: THE PERSONAL AND THE POLITICAL

Since the popular negative image of Puritanism is a fairly recent development, the Puritans themselves did not respond systematically to the various charges that have been levelled against them. Thus, the written records they left—a sampling of which is reprinted below—do not necessarily address our issues. For the Puritans, the compelling question—Am I saved or damned?—was unanswerable in this life. Unable to know their fates, each wondered how can I handle not knowing my fate, and how does God require me to live my life? As they struggled with these issues, they produced a wide variety of documents that can suggest to us why they made the choice to join the Puritan movement and what that decision meant for the society that they created in New England.

God's Judgment as a Lesson

Increase Mather (1639–1723), an influential Boston minister, wrote a best-selling book that recounted examples of "God's Providence"—that is, God's direct intercession in people's lives. Mather collected stories from all over New England to illustrate that God did take an active role in daily life. In the preface to his book, he related the following incident from an earlier English manuscript that made his point quite well; Mather criticizes then-prevailing religious practices (such as church discipline) even as he approvingly relates the tale of poor Mr. Juxon. From the unpaginated preface to An Essay for the Recording of Illustrious Providences . . . *(Boston, 1684).*

This M. *SS.* [manuscript] doth also mention some most *Remarkable Judgments* of God upon Sinners, as worthy to be Recorded for Posterity to take notice of. It is there said, that when Mr. *Richard Juxon* was a Fellow of *Kings Colledge* in *Cambridge*, he led a most vicious life: and whereas such of the Students as were serious in matters of Religion, did endeavour by solemn Fasting and Prayer to prepare themselves for the Communion which was then (this was about the year 1636) on *Easter-Day*. This *Juxon* spent all the time of preparation in Drunken wild Meetings, and was up late and Drunk on . . . Saturday night. Nevertheless, on the Lords day, he came with others to the Communion, and sat next to the Relator [storyteller], who knowing his Disorder the night before, was much troubled: but had no remedy; Church-Discipline not being then so practiced as ought to have been. The Communion being ended, such of the Scholars as had the fear of God in their hearts, repaired to their Closets [or small rooms]. But this *Juxon* went immediately to a Drunken-meeting, and there to a Cock-fight, where he fell to his accustomed madness, and pouring out a volley of Oaths and Curses; while these were between his Lips, God smote him dead in the twinkle of an eye. And though *Juxon* were but young, and of a comely person, his Carcase was immediately so corrupted as that the stench of it was insufferable, insomuch that no house would receive it; and his Friends were forced to hire some base Fellows to watch the Carcase till night; and then with Pitch and such like Gums covered him in a Coffin, and so made a shift to endure his Interment. There stood by a Scholar, whose name was *George Hall*, and who acted his part with *Juxon* in his prophaneness: but he was so astonished with this amazing Providence of God, as that he fell down upon his knees, begging pardoning mercy from Heaven, and vowing a Reformation; which vow the Lord enabled him to keep, so as that afterwards he became an able and famous Minister of the Gospel.

Preface to "An Essay for the Recording of Illustrious Providences," by Increase Mather, published by Samuel Green for Joseph Browning, Boston, 1684.

John Dane Grapples with His Sinfulness

Every Puritan thought about his (or her) spiritual state, confronting the sinful inclinations inherent in human nature and praying for God's help in overcoming temptation. Shortly before his death in 1683, John Dane (born in 1612) composed an autobiography intended to edify his children and grandchildren, from which the following excerpt is extracted. His narrative gives some insight into the attitudes of lay people. Taken from "A Declaration of Remarkabell Prouedenses in the Corse of My Lyfe," in New England Historical Genealogical Register, *(Boston 1854) 8:149–51) [In the following selection, the Latin "u" is often substituted for the English "v".]*

Consarning my self; when I was but a lettell boy, being edicated under godly parents, my Conshans [conscience] was ueary apt to tell me of euells that I should not doe. Being now about aight yers ould, I was giuen mutch to play and to run out without my fathers Consent and againe his comand. One a time, I haueing gone out most parte of the day, when my father saw me cum home, he toke me and basted [beat] me. I then cept [kept] home, and folowed my busenes two or thre dase. My father and mother Comended me, and tould me that god would bles me if I obeyed my parents, and what the contrary would ishew [issue] in. I then thout in my harte, o that my fatther would beat me more when I did amis. I fard [feared], if he did not, I should not be good. . . .

I did think myself in a good condishon. I was conuinsed that I should pray and durst doe no other, and Red and here sarmons and durst doe no other; yet I was giuen to pastime and to dansing, and that I thout lawfull. Now uppone a time, when I was groune 18 yers of age or thare abouts, I went to a dansing scoll to larne to dans. My father hering of it, when I cam home tould me, if I went agayne, he would bast me. I tould him, if he did he should neuer bast me againe. With that, my father toke a stick and basted me. I toke it patiently, and said nothing for a day or [two], but on morning betimes I Res and toke 2 shurts on my back and the best sute I had, and a bybell in my pocet, and set the dores open and went to my fathers chamber dore and said, god by father, god by mother. Why, whether are you going? To seke my fortin, I answared. Then said my mother, *goe whare you will, god he will find you out.* This word, the point of it, stuck in my breast, and afterwards god struck it home to its head.

Allthough I thout my fatther was two Strict, I thout Soloman said, be not holy ouer mutch, and daued [David] was a man after gods oun harte, and he was a danser [dancer]: but yet I went my Journey, and was from him half a yere before he hard whare I was. I first settled in barcumsted, and thare Rought on a shobord that had bene improud that waie. On a nyte [night], when most folke was a bead, a mayd cam into the shopbord and sat with me, and we Jested togetther; but at the last she cared it so, and put huself in sutch a poster, as that I made as If I had sum speshall ocashon abrod and went out; for I fared, If I had not, I should haue cumitted foley with hur. But I ofen thout that it was the prayers of my parents that preuaild with god to kepe me. I then gaue my self mutch to dansing and staying out and heatting myself and lying in haymowes, the pepell being a bed whare I abod that I lost my culler and neuer Recuferd it a gaine. . . .

I now being at harford, M'[ister] Goodin preacht thare, and he preacht consarning prayer. But on saboth day, not being in that trim that i would haue bene in [i.e., not being able to dress as he would like], . . . I would not goe to metting but walkt in the filds close by a meadow sid. Thare was, whetther fly, wasp or hornet, I cannot tell, but it struck my finger, and watter and blod cam out of it and paind me mutch. I went up to a hous and shoud it, but thay knew not what a sting I had at my harte. Now I thout of my mothers words, that god would find me out. I hastend home to the Chamber I lay in, at my masters house; and when i cam thare I toke my bybell and lokt ouer sum instructions my father had Ret, and I weapt sorly. The payne and swelling increast & sweld up to my shoulder. I prayd ernistly to god that he would pardon my sinn and heall my arme. I went to a surgin and askt him what it was. He said it was *the take*. I askt him what he meant. He said it was taken by the prouedens [providence] of god. This knoct home on my hart what my mother said, *god will find you out*. Now I made great promises that if god would here me this time I would Reforme.

An Artist Contemplates the Struggle to Overcome Sin

The Puritan poet Anne Bradstreet (1612?–1672) approaches the struggle over sin that engaged John Dane and indeed all Puritans from a more philosophical perspective in the poem reprinted below. In "The Flesh and The Spirit" the natural (or sinful) side of the Christian believer debates with the spiritual side. Note that the spirit derides worldly pleasures, contrasting these with spiritual pleasures to come. Reprinted from The Complete Works of Anne Bradstreet, *ed. Joseph R. McElrath, Jr., and Allan P. Robb (Boston, 1981), 175–77.*

The Flesh and the Spirit.

In secret place where once I stood
Close by the Banks of *Lacrim* flood
I heard two sisters reason on
Things that are past, and things to come;
One flesh was call'd, who had her eye
On worldly wealth and vanity;
The other Spirit, who did rear
Her thoughts unto a higher sphere:
Sister, quoth Flesh, what liv'st thou on
Nothing but Meditation?
Doth Contemplation feed thee so
Regardlesly to let earth goe?
Can Speculation satisfy
Notion without Reality?
Dost dream of things beyond the Moon
And dost thou hope to dwell there soon?
Hast treasures there laid up in store
That all in th' world thou count'st but poor?
Art fancy sick, or turn'd a Sot
To catch at shadowes which are not?
Come, come, Ile shew unto thy sence,

"The Flesh and the Spirit," by Anne Bradstreet, reprinted from *The Complete Works of Anne Bradstreet,* Joseph R. McElrath, Jr. and Allan P. Robb, editors. Published by Twayne Publishers, 1981.

Industry hath its recompence.
What canst desire, but thou maist see
True substance in variety?
Dost honour like? acquire the same,
As some to their immortal fame:
And trophyes to thy name erect
Which wearing time shall ne're deject.
For riches dost thou long full sore?
Behold enough of precious store.
Earth hath more silver, pearls and gold,
Then eyes can see, or hands can hold.
Affect's thou pleasure? take thy fill,
Earth hath enough of what you will.
Then let not goe, what thou maist find,
For things unknown, only in mind.
Spir. Be still thou unregenerate part,
Disturb no more my setled heart,
For I have vow'd (and so will doe)
Thee as a foe, still to pursue.
And combate with thee will and must,
Untill I see thee laid in th' dust.
Sisters we are, yea twins we be,
Yet deadly feud 'twixt thee and me;
For from one father are we not,
Thou by old Adam wast begot,
But my arise is from above,
Whence my dear father I do love.
Thou speak'st me fair, but hat'st me sore,
Thy flatt'ring shews Ile trust no more.
How oft thy slave, hast thou me made,
When I believ'd, what thou hast said,
And never had more cause of woe
Then when I did what thou bad'st doe.
Ile stop mine ears at these thy charms,
And count them for my deadly harms.
Thy sinfull pleasures I doe hate,
Thy riches are to me no bait,
Thine honours doe, nor will I love;
For my ambition lyes above.
My greatest honour it shall be
When I am victor over thee,

And triumph shall, with laurel head,
When thou my Captive shalt be led,
How I do live, thou need'st not scoff,
For I have meat thou know'st not off;
The hidden Manna I doe eat,
The word of life it is my meat.
My thoughts do yield me more content
Then can thy hours in pleasure spent.
Nor are they shadows which I catch,
Nor fancies vain at which I snatch,
But reach at things that are so high,
Beyond thy dull Capacity;
Eternal substance I do see,
With which inriched I would be:
Mine Eye doth pierce the heavens, and see
What is Invisible to thee.
My garments are not silk nor gold,
Nor such like trash which Earth doth hold,
But Royal Robes I shall have on,
More glorious then the glistring Sun;
My Crown not Diamonds, Pearls, and gold,
But such as Angels heads infold.
The City where I hope to dwell,
There's none on Earth can parallel;
The stately Walls both high and strong,
Are made of pretious *Jasper* stone;
The Gates of Pearl, both rich and clear,
And Angels are for Porters there;
The Streets thereof transparent gold,
Such as no Eye did e're behold,
A Chrystal River there doth run,
Which doth proceed from the Lambs Throne:
Of Life, there are the waters sure,
Which shall remain for ever pure,
Nor Sun, nor Moon, they have no need,
For glory doth from God proceed:
No Candle there, nor yet Torch light,
For there shall be no darksome night.
From sickness and infirmity,
For evermore they shall be free,
Nor withering age shall e're come there,

But beauty shall be bright and clear;
This City pure is not for thee,
For things unclean there shall not be:
If I of Heaven may have my fill,
Take thou the world, and all that will.

Drawing Upon Faith in the Face of Affliction

Although Puritans—like religious peoples in many other faith traditions—feared divine judgment, they also found solace in their religious faith. When dealing with the death of a loved one, Puritans often sought comfort in their religious beliefs. Anne Bradstreet wrote the following poem while struggling to come to terms with the death of her granddaughter. From The Complete Works of Anne Bradstreet, *ed. Joseph R. McElrath, Jr., and Allan P. Robb (Boston, 1981), 187.*

In memory of my dear grand-child . . .
Who deceased June 20. 1669. *being three years and*
seven Moneths old.
With troubled heart & trembling hand I write,
The Heavens have chang'd to sorrow my delight.
How oft with disappointment have I met,
When I on fading things my hopes have set?
Experience might 'fore this have made me wise,
To value things according to their price:
Was ever stable joy yet found below?
Or perfect bliss without mixture of woe.
I knew she was but as a withering flour,
That's here to day, perhaps gone in an hour;
Like as a bubble, or the brittle glass,
Or like a shadow turning as it was.
More fool then I to look on that was lent,

As if mine own, when thus impermanent.
Farewel dear child, thou ne're shall come to me,
But yet a while, and I shall go to thee;
Mean time my throbbing heart's chear'd up with this
Thou with thy Saviour art in endless bliss.

"To Walke Together": The Role of the Puritan Congregation

The preceding selections from Mather, Dane, and Bradstreet dealt with religion on a personal level, but Puritans believed that their spirituality ought to have a public component as well. One way in which they expressed their commitment publicly was by joining a church. In seventeenth-century Massachusetts and Connecticut, only those who seemed to their peers to be saved—that is, to have undergone a legitimate conversion experience—could become church members. Once accepted into a congregation, new members entered into a church covenant. In many churches, such as the one founded in Salem, Massachusetts in 1629, a written covenant was publicly endorsed by all members. The text of the Salem covenant explains why the Puritans thought it necessary to organize churches. Taken from The Records of the First Church in Salem Massachusetts, *1629–1736, ed. Richard D. Pierce (Salem, Massachusetts, 1974), 3–5.*

Wee whose names are here under written, members of the present Church of Christ in Salem, haveing found by sad experience how dangerous it is to sitt loose to the Covenant wee make with our God: and how apt wee are to wander into by pathes, even to the looseing of our first aimes in entring into Church fellowship: Doe therefore, solemnly in the presence of the Eternall God both for our owne comforts and those which shall or maye be joyned unto us renewe that Church covenant we find this Church bound unto at theire first begining. vizt: That we Covenant with the Lord and one with an other, and doe bynd our selves in the presence of God, to walke together in all his waies, according as he is pleased to reveale him selfe unto us in his Blessed word of truth. And doe more explicitely in the name and feare of God, profess and protest to walke as followeth through the power and grace of our Lord Jesus.

1. first wee avowe the Lord to be our God, and our selves his people in the truth and simplicitie of our Spirits

2. Wee give our selves to the Lord Jesus Christ, and the word of his grace, fore the teaching, ruleing and sanctifyeing of us in matters of worship, and conversation resolveing to cleave to him alone for life and glorie; and oppose all contrarie wayes, cannons and constitutions of men in his worship.

3. Wee promise to walk with our brethren and sisters in the Congregation with all watchfullness, and tendernis avoyding all jelousies, suspitions, backbyteings, conjurings, provoakings, secrete riseings of spirit against them, but in all offences to follow the rule of the Lord Jesus, and to beare and forbeare, give and forgive as he hath taught us.

4. In publick or private, we will willingly doe nothing to the ofence of the Church but will be willing to take advise for ourselves and ours as ocasion shall be presented.

5. Wee will not in the Congregation be forward eyther to show our owne gifts or parts in speaking or scrupuling [2] or there discover the fayling of our brethren or sisters butt attend an orderly cale there unto; knowing how much the Lord may be dishonoured, and his Gospell in the profession of it, sleighted by our distempers, and weaknesses in publyck.

6. Wee bynd ourselves to studdy the advancment of the Gospell in all truth and peace, both in regard of those that are within, or without, noe waye sleighting our sister Churches, but useing theire Counsell as need shalbe; nor laying a stumbling block, before any, noe not the Indians, whose good we desire to promote, and soe to converse, as wee may avoyd the verrye appearance of evill,

7. Wee hereby promise to carrye ourselves in all lawfull obedience, to those that are over us in Church or Common weale, knowing how well pleasing it wilbe to the Lord, that they should have incouragement in theire places, by our not greiveing theyre spirites through our iregulareties.

8. Wee resolve to prove our selves to the Lord in our particular calings, shunning ydlenes as the bane of any state, nor will wee

deale hardly, or opressingly with Any, wherein wee are the Lords stewards: alsoe

9. promyseing to our best abilitie to teach our children and servants, the knowledge of God and his will, that they may serve him alsoe and all this, not by any strength of our owne, but by the Lord Christ, whose bloud we desire may sprinckle this our Covenant made in his name.

A Puritan Justifies Intolerance

The New England Puritans were criticized for more than leaving England at a time of intense struggle; they were also attacked as religious bigots. In the following selection, Puritan legal scholar Nathaniel Ward (1570–1653) attempts to justify intolerance. Although he and his co-religionists were criticized for these attitudes in their own day, we must bear in mind that principled opposition to religious diversity was fairly common among their contemporaries. This passage is taken from The Simple Cobler of Aggawam in America, *5th ed. (Boston, 1713), 5–6. Aggawam was an early name for the town of Ipswich, Massachusetts.*

My heart hath natura'ly detested four things: The standing of the Apocrypha in the Bible; Forainers dwelling in my Country, to crowd out Native Subjects into the corners of the Earth; Alchymized Coines; Tolerations of divers Religions, or of one Religion in segregant shapes: He that willingly assents to the last, if he examines his heart by day-light, his Conscience will tell him, he is either an Atheist, or an Heretick, or an Hypocrite, or at best a captive to some Lust: Poly-piety is the greatest impiety in the World. True Religion is *Ignis probation is* which doth *congregare homogenea & segregare heterogenea [True Religion is a Testing Fire which doth Bring Together the alike and drive away the different or heterodox].*

Excerpted from *The Simple Cobler of Aggawam in America,* Fifth Edition, by Nathaniel Ward a.k.a. Theodore de la Guard, printed by J.D. & R.I. Reprinted for Daniel Henchman at his shop in King Street, Boston, Massachusetts, 1713.

Not to tolerate things meerly indifferent to weak Consciences, argues a Conscience too strong: pressed uniformity in these, causes much disunity: To tolerate more than indifferents, is not to deal indifferently with God: He that doth it, takes his Scepter out of his hand, and bids him stand by. Who hath to do to institute Religion but God. The power of all Religion and Ordinances, lies in their Purity: their Purity in their Simplicity: then are mixtures pernicious. I lived in a City, where a Papist Preached in one Church, a Lutheran in another, a Calvinist in a third; a Lutheran one part of the day, a Calvinist the other, in the same Pulpit: the Religion of that Place was but motly and meagre, their affections Leopard-like.

If the whole Creature should conspire to do the Creator a mischief, or offer him an insolency, it would be in nothing more, than in erecting untruths against his Truth, or by sophisticating his Truths with humane medleyes: the removing of some one iota in Scripture, may draw out all the life, and traverse all the Truth of the whole Bible: but to authorize an untruth, by a Toleration of State, is to build a Sconce against the walls of Heaven, to batter God out of his Chair: To tell a practical lye, is a great Sin, but yet transient; but to set up a Theorical untruth, is to warrant every lye that lyes from its root to the top of every branch it hath, which are not a few.

Edward Johnson Exhorts All People to Follow Christ

In this final excerpt, lay author Edward Johnson interrupts his history of early New England to call all nations to Christ. Because he sees New England as the fulfillment of God's plan for humanity, this call seems to him not an interruption, but an integral part of the history he is relating. The language he uses in this passage is inspired by the Bible. Taken from Edward Johnson, A History of New-England *[better known as* Wonder-working Providence*] (London, 1654), 32–33.*

An Exhortation to all People, Nations and Languages, to indeavour the advancing of the Kingdome of Christ in the purity of his Ordinances, seeing he hath done such admirable Acts for these poore shrubs.

AND now all you whose affections are taken with wonderfull matters (Attend) and you that thinke Christ hath forgotten his poore despised people (Behold) and all you that hopefully long for Christs appearing to confound *Antichrist* (Consider) and rejoyce all yee his Churches the World throughout, for the Lambe is preparing his Bride, and oh! yee the antient Beloved of Christ, whom he of old led by the hand from *Egypt* to *Canaan,* through that great and terrible Wildernesse, looke here, behold him whom you have peirced, preparing to peirce your hearts with his *Wonder-working Providence,* and to provoke you by this little handfull of his people to looke on him, and mourne. Yet let no man think these few weake Wormes would restraine the wonderfull Workes of Christ, as onely to themselves, but the quite contrary, these but the Porch of his glorious building in hand, and if hee have shewed such admirable acts of his providence toward these, what will he doe when the whole Nation of *English* shall set upon like Reformation according to the direct Rule of his Word? Assured confidence there is also for all Nations, from the undoubted promise of Christ himselfe.

The Winter is past, the Raine is changed and gone, come out of the holes of the secret places, feare not because your number is but small, gather into Churches, and let Christ be your King, yee *Presbytery,* Lord it not over them or any Churches, but feed every one, that one flock over which Christ hath made you overseers, and yee people of Christ give your *Presbytery* double honours, that they with you may keepe the watch of the Lord over his Churches. Yee *Dutch* come out of your hods-podge, the great mingle mangle of Religion among you hath caused the Churches of Christ to increase so little with you, standing at a stay like Corne among Weeds, Oh, yee *French*! feare not the great swarmes of *Locusts,* nor the croking *Frogs* in your Land, Christ is reaching out the hand to you, look what hee hath done for these *English,* and sure hee is no Respecter of Persons, &c. yee *Germanes* that have had such a bloudy bickering, Christ is now comming to your aide, then cast off your loose, and carelesse kinde of Reformation, gather into Churches, and keepe them pure, that Christ may delight to dwell among you: oh *Italy!* The Seat and Center of the Beast, Christ will

Excerpted from *A History of New England,* better known as *Wonder-working Providence,* printed for Nath. Brooke at the *Angel* in Corn Hill, 1654.

now pick out a People from among you for himselfe, see here what wonders hee workes in little time. Oh! yee *Spaniards* and *Portugalls*, Christ will shew you the abominations of that beastly Whore, who hath made your Nations drunke with the Wine of her Fornication. Dread not that cruell murtherous Inquisition, for Christ is now making Inquisition for them, and behold, here how hee hath rewarded them, who dealt cruelly with these his people.

Finally, oh all yee Nations of the World, behold great is the worke the glorious King of Heaven and Earth hath in hand; beware of neglecting the call of Christ: and you the Seed of *Israel* both lesse and more, the ratling of your dead bones together is at hand, Sinewes, Flesh and Life.

Questions

1. *Some of the passages above suggested that these religious beliefs caused people to feel fearful, other passages suggested that these religious beliefs that they served as a source of comfort. Which aspect of the experience seems comprehensible to you? Can the fear and comfort be integrated somehow? How did the Puritans integrate them?*
2. *What obligations did the Puritans' faith place upon them, in terms of their personal behavior, their churches, and their society?*
3. *What impact do you think Puritanism as a social or religious force had on the history of New England?*
4. *Why would a seventeenth-century English man or woman have found the Puritan message and movement appealing? Why would some people have been outraged by the very existence of such a movement?*

FURTHER READING

Edmund Morgan's biography of John Winthrop, The Puritan Dilemma: The Story of John Winthrop *(Boston, 1958), offers a good starting place on the early history of Puritanism in Massachusetts.* Worlds of Wonder, Days of Judgment: Popular Religious Belief in Early New England *(New York, 1989) by David D. Hall treats popular religion in New England. A fairly basic general account of the experiences of the first migrants to Puritan New England can be found in Virginia DeJohn Anderson,* New England's Generation: The Great Migration and the Formation of Society and Culture in the Seventeenth Century *(New York, 1991). John Demos's* A Little Commonwealth: Family Life in Plymouth Colony *(New York, 1970), addresses the social history of an early New England settlement.*

The Causes of Bacon's Rebellion

Carla Gardina Pestana
and Charles Coleman Finlay

INTRODUCTION

By 1675, the royal colony of Virginia concentrated its agricultural efforts on growing tobacco for export. Tobacco cultivation demanded a large labor force, and the planters relied mainly on English, Irish, and Scottish indentured servants, some of them poor young men and women, others convicts sentenced to a period of labor in the New World. When their terms of servitude expired, they wanted land for themselves, which put them in competition with plantation owners (their former masters) who wanted to expand their holdings to replace land that had been depleted by the overcultivation of tobacco. New land was becoming scarce, because the colony was reaching the limits of its boundaries. Beyond those boundaries lived various groups of Native Americans who opposed continued English expansion onto their lands. The royally appointed governor, Sir William Berkeley, sought to avoid further conflicts with the Indians by reaching boundary agreements with them. These agreements primarily hurt the ex-indentured servants and the newly arrived planters, since these people would benefit most if additional lands were made available for settlement. Some of these people went to live on (or beyond) the borders of the colony, where their presence sparked the hostilities that Berkeley sought to avoid.

In 1675 and early 1676, a series of confrontations occurred along the Potomac River in the Chesapeake region, pitting Doeg and Susquehannock Indians against these English planters. Nathaniel Bacon, a well-born Englishman who had recently migrated to Virginia, sought official sanction for a general attack against the natives. After Governor Berkeley refused to authorize

Bacon's request, Bacon led a group of volunteers to massacre one of the friendly tribes. When Berkeley declared Bacon a rebel and moved to arrest him, the young man launched an attack on the governor, and the entire colony collapsed into civil war. The rebels burned Jamestown, the capital, to the ground, and a period of plunder ensued in which partisans on both sides looted the homes and property of their enemies.

For most of 1676 Virginia was engulfed by civil war. The uprising against Berkeley, led by Bacon and named after him, was the largest armed revolt against English authority in the American colonies until the Revolution a century later. It was only put down after King Charles II dispatched an expeditionary force to quell the rebellion. After they had helped Berkeley restore order to the colony, the king's commissioners replaced Berkeley and sent him back to England to justify himself to the king. After an extended career (1642–52, 1660–77) as governor in the first royal colony in America, Berkeley died in disgrace in England shortly after his return there.

Although Berkeley's handling of the crisis (along with some of the policies that led up to it) resulted in his fall from power, the rebels were judged yet more harshly at the time. Many of them lost their lives after the rebellion was put down. During the revolutionary era, however, it became popular to present Bacon as the heroic forerunner of later Virginian revolutionaries like George Washington and Patrick Henry. More recently, scholars have been less inclined to side wholeheartedly with Bacon. They now tend to study the rebellion for what it reveals about serious divisions within late-seventeenth-century Chesapeake society. Bacon's Rebellion was the only colonial revolt to involve Native Americans, Europeans, and Africans. As such, it offers a glimpse of the social and political development of early Virginia.

Contemporary Views of the Rebellion

Only a few of the participants left records about their roles in the rebellion, and those were mostly the wealthy men who served as leaders of either faction. While we know that several different groups of Native Americans were involved, that women participated actively in both the Bacon and Berkeley camps, and that the last rebels out in the field were mostly European indentured servants and African or African-American slaves, we have few, if any, records from these people to explain their actions. The motives of all parties can only be interpreted through the limited existing records. (Throughout these documents, archaic abbreviations have been silently edited for greater clarity.)

Tensions on the Frontier

In the aftermath of the rebellion, commissioners sent from England by the king interviewed people and collected information about the rebellion to discover why it happened. The following selection describes the conflicts with local Native Americans that sparked a desire for revenge in Bacon and other frontier dwellers. Taken from the commissioners' report entitled "A True Narrative of the Rise, Progresse, and Cessation of the Late Rebellion in Virginia . . ." in Narratives of the Insurrections, 1675–1690, *ed. Charles M. Andrews (New York, 1952), 105–7.*

Few or none had bin the Damages sustained by the English from the Indians, other than occasionally had happen'd sometimes upon private quarells and provocations, untill in July, 1675, certain Doegs and Susquahanok Indians on Maryland side, stealing some Hoggs from the English at Potomake on the Virginia shore (as the River divides the same), were pursued by the English in a Boate, beaten or kill'd and the hoggs retaken from them; whereupon the Indians repairing to their owne Towne, report it to their Superiors, and how that one [Thomas] Mathewes (whose hoggs they had taken) had before abused and cheated them, in not paying them for such Indian trucke [goods] as he had formerly bought of them, and that they took his hogs for Satisfaction [of the debt]. Upon this (to be Reveng'd on Mathews) a warr Captain with some Indians came over to Potomake and killed two of Mathewes his servants, and came also a second time and kill'd his sonne.

It happen'd hereupon that Major George Brent and Col. George Mason pursued some of the same Indians into Maryland, and marching directly up to the Indian Towne with a Party of 30 Virginians came to a certaine House and there killed an Indian King and 10 of his men upon the place; the rest of the Indians fled for their lives. . . .

The Indians persisting to Revenge themselves Inforted [fortified their position] in Maryland and now began to be bold and formidable to the English who Besieged them; their Boldness and daring behavior of late tymes and their promptnesse to Fire arms, being (indeed) wonderfull, over what they seem'd formerly indued with, which doubtlesse was of some advantage extraordinary to them considering their Small Body, [and the fact that] the Virginians and Marylanders that Besieged them being said to make neer a thousand men. The siege held 7 weekes, during which tyme the English lost 50 men, besides some Horses which the Indians tooke, and serv'd themselves to subsist on. But Provisions growing very scarce with them during this siege the Indians sent out 5 greate men to Treate of Peace, who were not Permitted to return to the Fort, but being kept Prisoners Some tyme were at last murdered by the English.

At length (whether through negligence or cowardize) the Indians made theire escape through the English, with all their wives, children and goods of value, wounding and killing some at their sally and going off. After which the English returning (as Report Saith), the Marylanders composed a Peace with the Salvages, and soe diverted the warr from themselves. . . .

But about the beginning of January, 1675–6, a Party of those abused Susquahanocks in Revenge of the Maryland businesse came suddainly down upon the weak Plantations at the head of Rappahanock and Potomaque and killed at one time 36 persons and then immediately (as their Custome is) ran off into the woods.

Berkeley Declares Bacon a Rebel

When Governor William Berkeley refused to authorize attacks against the Susquehannocks, Nathaniel Bacon, a wealthy planter, took matters into his own hands, leading a group of volunteers in a massacre of friendly Indians. In the selection below, Berkeley defends his own actions and declares Bacon a rebel. Originally printed in the Collections of the Massachusetts Historical Society, *4th Series, (Boston, 1871) 9:178–81.*

Since that time that I returned into the Country [as Governor of Virginia: about 1660], I call the great God, Judge of all things in heaven and earth to wittness, that I doe not know of any thing relateive to this Country, wherein I have acted unjustly, corruptly, or negligently, in distributeing equall Justice to all men, & takeing all possible care to preserue [preserve] their proprietys, & defend them from their barbarous enimies. . . .

And now I will state the Question betwixt me as a Governor and Mr Bacon, and say that if any enimies should invade England, any Councellor Justice of peace, or other inferiour officer, might raise what forces they could to protect his Majesty's subiects [subjects], But I say againe, if after the Kings knowledge of this inuasion, any the greatest peere [or nobleman] of England, should raise forces against the kings p'hibition this would be now, & ever was in all ages & Nations accompted [accounted as] treason. Nay I will goe further, that though this peere was truly zealous for the preservation of his King, & subiects, and had better & greater abillitys than all the rest of his fellow subiects, to doe his King and Country seruice, yett if the King (though by false information) should suspect the contrary, itt were treason in this Noble peere to p'ceed after the King's prohibition, and for the truth of this I appeale to all the laws of England, and the Laws and constitutions of all other Nations in the world. . . .

Now my friends I have lived 34 yeares amongst you, as vncorrupt and dilligent as ever [a] Governor was, Bacon is a man of two yeares amongst you, his p'son and qualities vnknowne to most of you, & to all men else, by any vertuous action that ever I heard of, And that very action which he boasts of [the massacre of the Occaneechee Indians], was sickly & fooleishly, & as I am informed treacherously carried to the dishonnor of the English Nation, yett in itt, he lost more men then I did in three yeares Warr [against an Indian uprising several decades earlier], and by the grace of God will putt myselfe to the same daingers & troubles againe when I have brought Bacon to acknowledge the Laws are above him, and I doubt not but by God's assistance to have better success then Bacon hath had, the reason of my hopes are, that I will take Councell of wiser men then my selfe, but Mr Bacon hath none about him, but the lowest of the people.

Yett I must further enlarge, that I cannot without your helpe, doe any thinge in this but dye in defence of my King, his laws, & subiects, which I will cheerefully doe, though alone I doe itt, and considering my poore fortunes, I can not leave my poore Wife and friends a better legacy then by dyeing for my King & you: for his sacred Majesty will easeily distinguish betweene Mr Bacons actions & myne, and Kinges have long Armes, either to reward or punish. . . .

Lastly my most assured ffriends I would have preserued those Indians that I knew were howerly att our mercy, to have beene our spyes and intelligence, to finde out our bloody enimies, but as soone as I had the least intelligence that they alsoe were trecherous enimies, I gave out Comissions to distroy them all as the Comissions themselues will speake itt.

To conclude, I have don what was possible both to friend and enimy, have granted Mr Bacon three pardons, which he hath scornefully reiected, suppoaseing himselfe stronger to subuert [the laws] than I and you [are] to maineteyne the Laws, by which onely and Gods assisting grace and mercy, all men must hope for peace and safety. I will add noe more though much more is still remaineing to Justifie me & condemne Mr Bacon, but to desier that this declaration may be read in every County Court in the Country.

The Queen of Pamunkey Negotiates for Her People

Once Bacon began attacking the frontier Indians, Virginia's leaders sought assistance from the Pamunkeys, the most powerful of the tributary, or "friendly," Indians. In the following passage, Thomas Mathew, an eyewitness, relates how and why the Queen of Pamunkey tried to keep her people from becoming involved. Taken from Thomas Mathew, "The Beginning, Progress, and Conclusion of Bacon's Rebellion . . .," reprinted in, Tracts and Other Papers, Relating Principally to the Origin, Settlement, and Progress of the Colonies in North America *. . . , ed. Peter Force, (Washington, D.C., 1836) 1:14–15.*

Our comittee being sat, the Queen of Pamunky (descended from Oppechankenough a former Emperor of Virginia) was introduced, who entred the chamber with a comportment gracefull to admiration, bringing on her right hand an Englishman interpreter, and on the left her son a stripling twenty years of age, she having round her head a plat of black and white wampum peague three inches broad in imitation of a crown, and was cloathed in a mantle of dress't deer skins with the hair outwards and the edge cut round 6 inches deep which made strings resembling twisted frenge from the shoulders to the feet; thus with grave courtlike gestures and a majestick air in her face, she walk'd up our long room to the lower end of the table, where after a few intreaties she sat down; th' interpreter and her son standing by her on either side as they had walked up, our chairman asked her what men she woud [would] lend us for guides in the wilderness and to assist us against our enemy Indians, she spake to th' interpreter to inform her what the chairman said, (tho' we believed she understood him) he told us she bid him ask her son to whom the English tongue was familiar, and who was reputed the son of an English colonel, yet neither woud he speak to or seem to understand the chairman but th' interpreter told us, he referred all to his mother, who being againe urged she after a little musing with an earnest passionate countenance as if tears were ready to gush out and a fervent sort of expression made a harangue about a quarter of an hour often, interlacing (with a high shrill voice and vehement passion) these words "Tatapatamoi Chepiack, i.e. Tatapatamoi dead["] Coll. Hill being next me, shook his head, I ask'd him what was the matter, he told me all she said was too true to our shame, and that his father was generall in that battle, where diverse years before Tatapatamoi her husband had led a hundred of his Indians in help to th' English against our former enemy Indians, and was there slaine with most of his men; for which no compensation (at all) had been to that day rendered to her wherewith she now upbraided us.

Her discourse ending and our morose chairman not advancing one cold word towards asswaging the anger and grief her speech . . . nor taking any notice of all she had said, . . . he rudely push'd againe the same question "what Indians will you now contribute, &c.?["] of this disregard she signified her resentment by a disdainfull aspect, and turning her head half aside, sate mute till that same question being press'd, a third time, she not returning her face to the board, answered with a low slighting voice in her own language "six,["] but being further importun'd she sitting a little while sullen, without uttering a word between said "twelve,["] tho' she then had a hundred and fifty Indian men, in her town, and so rose up and gravely walked away, as [if] not pleased with her treatment.

Bacon Justifies Rebellion on Behalf of "the People"

Within months, the colony divided into factions that supported either Berkeley or Bacon, and both sides took up arms. On 30 July 1676, Bacon issued "The Declaration of the People," in which he defended his actions and attacked the policies of Berkeley's government. Reprinted from the Collections of the Massachusetts Historical Society, *4th Series, (Boston, 1871), 9:184–85.*

1st. For haveing . . . raised greate unjust taxes vpon the Comonality for the aduancement of private favorites & other sinister ends, but [without having] . . . in any measure aduanced this hopefull Colony either by fortifications Townes or Trade.

2d. For haveing abused & rendred contemptable the Magistrates of Justice, by aduanceing to places of Judicature, scandalous and Ignorant favorites.

3. For haveing wronged his Majestys prerogative & interest, by assumeing Monopolony of the Beaver trade, & for haveing in that unjust gaine betrayed & sold his Majestys Country & the lives of his loyall subiects to the barbarous heathen.

4. For haveing, protected, favoured, & Imboldned the Indians against his Majestys loyall subiects, never contriveing, requireing, or appointing any due or proper meanes of satisfaction for theire many Inuasions, robbories, & murthers comitted vpon vs.

5. For haveing when the Army of English was just vpon the track of those Indians, who now in all places burne, spoyle, murther & when we might with ease have distroyed them who then were in open hostillity, for then haveing expressly countermanded, & sent back our Army, by passing his word for the peaceable demeanour of the said Indians, who imediately p'secuted theire evill intentions, comitting horred murthers & robberies in all places, being p'tected by the said ingagement & word past of him the said Sir Wm Berkeley, haveing ruined & laid desolate a greate part of his Majestys Country, & have now drawne themselves into such obscure & remote places, & are by theire success soe imboldned & confirmed, by theire confederacy soe strengthned that the cryes of blood are in all places, & the terror, & constirnation of the people soe greate, are now become, not onely a difficult, but a very formidable enimy, who might att first with ease haue beene distroyed.

6th. And lately when vpon the loud outcryes of blood the Assembly had with all care raised & framed an Army for the preventing of further mischiefe & safeguard of this his Majestys Colony.

7th. For haveing with onely the privacy of some few favorites, without acquainting the people, onely by the alteration of a figure, forged a Comission, by we know not what hand, not onely without, but even against the consent of the people, for the raiseing & effecting civill warr & destruction, which being happily & without blood shed prevented, for haveing the second time attempted the same, thereby calling downe our forces from the defence of the fronteeres & most weekely expoased places.

8. For the prevention of civill mischeife & ruin amongst ourselues, whilst the barbarous enimy in all places did invade, murther & spoyle vs, his majestys most faithfull subiects.

Edward Hill Explains His Opposition to Nathaniel Bacon

Colonel Edward Hill, a Berkeley loyalist, vigorously suppressed the rebellion in Charles City County where he lived. When other planters in the area criticized his brutality, he countered with a description of the treatment he and his family received from the rebels, which he clearly believed justified his own actions. The following excerpt is taken from the Virginia Magazine of History and Biography, *3 (1895–1896): 250.*

I must with trouble and sorrow say that I am grieved to see the spirit of rebellion soe strong and fresh in the hearts of these people that would make it a grievance of the County for to obey those just comands which I received from his honor [the governor], and I should think theire true grievance should be that they were soe active and mischievous as they were from the beginning of the rebellion to the end thereof, and were the first that against the King's Governor's comands went out upon the Occaneechees, were the very men to help Bacon to force his comission, and marched a hundred miles out of theire own country [county] as low as Lower Norfolk to fight the king's loyall subjects, and over into Gloucester, and indeed all over the country, and in fine were the first in armes, and the laste that opposed and faced the King's Governor's power, yet these noe grievances, And I bless God, and truely rejoice in the great goodness and mercey of our most gracious king that they are pardoned; but me thinks with modesty they mought [might] have given me leave to have had my grievances that my house was plundered of all I had, my sheep all destroyed, my hoggs and cattle killed, all my grain taken and destroyed, wheat, barley, oates, & Indian graine, to the quantity of seven, or eight hundred bushels, and to compleat theire jollity draw my brandy, Butts of wyne and syder [cider, a mildly alcoholic beverage] by payles full, and [toasting] to every health instead of burning theire powder [shooting off their guns], burnt my writings, bills, bonds, acc'ts to the true vallue of forty thousand pounds of tobacco and to finish theire barbarism, take my wife bigg with child [pregnant] prisoner, beat her with my Cane, tare [tore] her childbed linen out of her hands, and with her ledd away my children where they must live on corne and water and lye on the ground.

Indentured Servants and Slaves Resist Surrender

Along with poor freemen, indentured servants and slaves who had deserted their masters formed a large part of Bacon's army. As the rebellion collapsed, they still held the fort at West Point. As the passage below indicates, Berkeley and his supporters were not above lying to trick such people into putting down their arms. Thomas Grantham was a ship captain who helped Berkeley suppress the uprising. From "A Narrative of the Indian and Civil Wars in Virginia . . .," in Tracts and Other Papers *. . ., ed. Peter Force, 1:44–45.*

What number of soulders was, at this time, in Garrisson at West Point, I am not certaine: It is saide about 250, sumed up in freemen, sarvants and slaves; these three ingredience being the compossition of Bacons Army, ever since that the Governour left Towne. These was informed (to prepare the way) two or three days before that Grantham came to them, that there was a treaty on foote betwene there Generall, and the Governour; and that Grantham did manely promote the same, as he was a parson [person] that favoured the cause, that they were contending for.

When that Grantham arived, amongst these fine fellowes, he was receved with more then an ordnary respect; which he haveing repade, with a suteable deportment, he acquaints them with his commission, which was to tell them, that there was a peace concluded betwene the Governour and their Generall; an since himself had (in some measure) used his indeviours, to bring the same to pass, hee begged of the Governour, that he might have the honor to com and acquaint them with the terms; which he saide was such, that they had all cause to rejoyce at, than any ways to thinke hardly of the same; there being a compleate satisfaction to be given (by the Articles of agreement) according to every ones particuler intress; which he sumed up under these heads. And first, those that were now in Arms (and free men) under the Generall, were still to be retained in Arms, if they so pleased, against the Indians. Secondly, and for those who had a desire for to return hom, to their owne abodes, care was taken for to have them satisfide, for the time they had bin out, according to the alowance made the last Assembley. And lastly, those that were sarvants in Arms, and behaved themselves well, in their imployment, should emediately receve discharges from their Indentures, signed by the Governour or Sequetary of State; and their Masters to receve, from the publick, a valluable satisfaction, for every sarvant, so set free (marke the words) proportionably to the time that they have to sarve.

Upon these terms, the soulders forsake West Point, and goe with Grantham to kiss the Governours hands (still at Tindells point) and to receve the benefitt of the Articles, mentioned by Grantham; where when they came (which was by water, themselves in one vessill, and their arms in another; and so contrived by Grantham, as he tould me himselfe, upon good reason) the sarvants and slaves was sent hom to their Masters, there to stay till the Governour had leasure to signe their discharges; or to say better, till they were free according to the custom of the countrey [which meant finishing their indentures, plus serving extra time for being runaways], the rest was made prissoners, or entertained by the Governour, as hee found them inclined.

Mrs. Cheisman's Attempt to Save Her Husband

Mrs. Cheisman's husband was an officer in Bacon's army who was captured at the end of the rebellion. The selection below describes her effort to protect her husband from a death sentence by claiming responsibility for his rebellious actions. Assuming she honestly stated her views in this interview, she stands as one of the female supporters of the rebellion whom we can identify. If this account had not been recorded by an anonymous participant, we would not know today that Mrs. Cheisman existed (and we shall probably never know her first name). Her husband was never tried for his crime, dying in prison of "feare, griefe, or bad useage," as the author of this narrative put it. Excerpted from "A Narrative of the Indian and Civil Wars in Virginia . . .," in Tracts and Other Papers *. . ., ed. Peter Force, 1:34*

There is one remarkable passage reported of this Major Cheismans Lady [or wife], which because it sounds to the honor of her sex, and consequently of all loveing Wives, I will not deny it a roome in this Narrative.

When that the Major was brought into the Governours presence, and by him demanded, what made him to ingage in Bacons designes? Before that the Major could frame an answer to the Governours demand; his Wife steps in and tould his honour that it was her provocations that made her Husband joyne in the cause that Bacon contended for; ading, that if he had not bin influenced by her instigations, he had never don that which he had done. Therefore (upon her bended knees) she desired of his honour, that since what her husband had done, was by her meanes, and so, by consequence, she most guilty, that she might be hanged, and he pardoned. Though the Governour did know, that what she had saide, was neare to the truth, yet he said litle to her request.

Thomas Hansford's Execution

Thomas Hansford, who was a colonel in Bacon's army, was captured by Berkeley supporters as the rebellion collapsed. The excerpt below, describes his capture and death. Taken from the same anonymous "A Narrative of the Indian and Civil Wars in Virginia . . .," printed in Tracts and Other Papers *. . ., ed. Peter Force, vol. 1:33.*

[P]resently after that he [Thomas Hansford, a soldier] came to Accomack, he had the ill luck to be the first Verginian borne that dyed [meaning the first person of English descent born in Virginia to die] upon a paire of Gallows. When that he came to the place of

Execution (which was about a mile removed from his prison) he seemed very well resolved to undergo the utmost mallize [malaise] of his not over kinde Destinies, onely complaineing of the maner of his death. Being observed neather at the time of his tryall (which was by a Court Martiall) nor afterwards, to supplicate any other faviour, than that he might be shot like a soulder, and not to be hanged like a Dog. But it was tould him, that what he so passionately petitioned for could not be granted, in that he was not condemned as he was merely a soldier, but as a Rebell, taken in Arms, against the king, whose laws had ordained him that death. During the short time he had to live after his sentence he approved to his best advantage for the wellfare of his soul, by repentance and contrition for all his sins, in generall, excepting his Rebellion, which he would not acknowledge; desireing the people at the place of execution, to take notis that he dyed a loyal subject, and a lover of his countrey; and that he had never taken up arms, but for the destruction of the Indians, who had murthered so many Christians.

Questions

1. *Why did Berkeley believe it significant that only "the lowest of the people" supported Bacon?*
2. *Do you think that Bacon was really speaking on behalf of the "people" when he issued the "Declaration"?*
3. *What motivated the various individuals whose actions are described or whose words are quoted in these documents?*
4. *Do you think there was one rebellion or several rebellions, according to the accounts you have read?*
5. *How did the rebellion appear from the perspective of various Native American groups who fought against or refused to fight against Bacon?*

FURTHER READING

Thomas Wertenbaker's Torchbearer of the Revolution: The Story of Bacon's Rebellion in Virginia *(Princeton, 1940) and Wilcomb Washburn's* The Governor and The Rebel: A History of Bacon's Rebellion in Virginia *(Chapel Hill, 1957) are still the two most important full-length books on Bacon's Rebellion.* 1676: The End of American Independence *(New York, 1984), written by Stephen Saunders Webb, connects Bacon's Rebellion with other developments in English-Indian relations on the North American continent that occurred simultaneously. Warren M. Billings has re-explored the long-term economic and political conditions that led to the conflict in "The Causes of Bacon's Rebellion: Some Suggestions," an article in the October 1970 issue of the* Virginia Magazine of History and Biography. *Martha W. McCartney examines in detail the Queen of Pamunkey and her role in Virginia politics before, during, and after Bacon's Rebellion in "Cockacoeske, Queen of Pamunkey: Diplomat and Suzerain," an essay in* Powhatan's Mantle: Indians in the Colonial Southeast, *ed. Peter H. Wood, Gregory A. Waselko, and M. Thomas Hatley (Lincoln, Nebraska, 1989).*

The Salem Witchcraft Scare

Carla Gardina Pestana

INTRODUCTION

English colonists brought with them beliefs about witches and, once in America, occasionally suspected some residents of practicing witchcraft. According to contemporary wisdom, witches entered into a pact with Satan and thereby acquired supernatural powers. They used these powers to harm their neighbors, in acts of witchcraft known as maleficum. Individuals were suspected of witchcraft in many English colonies in the seventeenth century, including Connecticut, Maryland, Massachusetts, the Somers Island (or Bermuda), and Virginia. Nowhere in Anglo-America, however, were more witches accused than in Massachusetts, the most populous and powerful of the "Puritan" colonies of New England. The bulk of the accusations and trials there occurred in 1692 in the northeastern part of the colony, in a witchcraft scare that has come to be associated with the town of Salem, where the outbreak began.

In 1692, some residents of the coastal town of Salem became convinced that many of their neighbors had become witches. The scare began with a group of adolescent girls and young women who were dabbling in occult practices in an effort to learn about the future. When a number of them fell into strange fits, a physician diagnosed these as the work of a witch. The afflicted then made a series of accusations, adult community members supported their charges and fingered others, and the "witch hunt" was on.

At the time of the outbreak the colony had only a provisional government, while it awaited a new royal charter and the arrival of a governor. (This state of uncertainty had developed since the revocation of the charter in 1686. At that time, the colony had been subsumed under a new "Dominion of New England," but it later rose in revolt hoping to get support from King William and Queen Mary for a return to its old charter. This support had not materialized, so the colony rather nervously awaited a new charter and a new governor in 1692.) With no legitimate claim to govern, the colony's leaders were loath to try capital crimes such as witchcraft. So, as the number of accused witches soared to over a hundred, the authorities simply jailed the suspects while awaiting word from England. By the time the new governor, Sir William Phipps, arrived, the jails were overflowing. Many colonists were certain that witches were conspiring to take over the colony. The governor appointed an emergency court with broad powers to try the cases and it ordered nineteen people hanged in the months that followed.

The crisis came to a close that autumn for a number of reasons. Popular support for the trials waned as more individuals with good reputations (some of them drawn from the ranks of the elites) were accused. The populace may also have felt revulsion at the violence of the many executions. When a group of ministers led by the influential Increase Mather publicly questioned some of the evidence the judges were accepting, the authority of the court was seriously undermined. In October the governor replaced the first court with a new one that had more limited powers; his instructions to the second court indicated a need for greater restraint. He reprieved the few witches that it did convict and then granted a general pardon, emptying the jails of the remaining suspects.

Participants in the trials and scholars subsequently have struggled to make sense of one of the most dramatic and disturbing episodes in colonial history. After 1692, colonists gave up the practice of witch hunting, and no major outbreak followed the one that has made Salem infamous. But colonists were slower to give up their belief that the devil played an active role in their lives. Indeed, the first attempts to explain what had gone wrong at Salem attributed the debacle to a "delusion of Satan" that caused the community to see a witch conspiracy where none existed. Since that time, many interpretations have been offered to explain the witchcraft crisis. Modern Americans, inclined to believe that the religious bigotry of the Puritans can explain anything distressing in their history, find it surprising that the ministers helped to halt the trials. Other aspects of the witch scare may surprise you as well.

Contemporary Ideas About Witches and the Events at Salem

The documents that follow examine Salem witchcraft from a number of different perspectives. The case against Bridget Bishop includes depositions taken largely from lay people who came forward to accuse this woman of witchcraft. The statement by a group of ministers lays out the somewhat belated clerical opposition to the trials, which played a key role in ending them. The documents authored by Increase and Cotton Mather present some of their views, penned either while the trials were still going on or ten years after they had ended. Together, these documents provide a glimpse of attitudes toward the supernatural in late-seventeenth-century New England.

The Case Against Bridget Bishop

One of nineteen people executed as a witch in 1692, Bridget Bishop had some of the classic attributes her New England neighbors were inclined to associate with a witch. For one thing, she was alienated from the religious faith of the community, having never attended worship services. In addition, she ran a tavern, where excessive drinking and game playing were common. She seems to have been seen as embodying relaxed sexual attitudes; deponents elsewhere mention her red bodice and a number of men may have had illicit thoughts about her, as they recount nocturnal visits to their beds by her specter (or ethereal image).

The excerpts below from the depositions taken against her offer typical examples of behavior attributed to alleged witches: she caused illness or death to people and animals, her image could appear as a specter, and she could change herself into other shapes. On one count, however, Bridget Bishop was unique. Only she was accused of keeping puppets (or "popites") to use in tormenting her victims. This evidence, contained in a deposition given below, caused one modern student of Salem witchcraft to conclude that Bishop was a witch, intent on using magical powers to harm her neighbors. Bishop was the wife of Edward Bishop at the time of her trial and execution, but she had previously been married to a man named Oliver, and the trial records refer to her by both names. These documents are taken from The Salem Witchcraft Papers: Verbatim Transcripts of the Legal Documents of the Salem Witchcraft Outbreak of 1692, *ed. Paul Boyer and Stephen Nissenbaum, (New York, 1977), 1:94–101, 103. Punctuation has been added and abbreviations expanded to clarify meaning.*

Deposition 1: Samuel Gray, May 30, 1692

Samuell Gray of Salem Aged aboute 42 yeares Testifieth and sayth that about fourteen years agoe he goeing to bed well one Lords Day at night, and after he had beene asleep some time, he awakened & looking up, saw the house light as if a candle or candles were lighted in it and the dore locked & that little fire there, was Raked up. He did then see a woman standing between the Cradle in the Roome and the Bed side and seemed to look upon him. Soe he did Rise up in his bed and it vanished or disappeared. Then he went to the dore and found it locked. And unlocking and Opening the dore, he went to the Entry dore and looked out, and then againe did see the same Woman he had a little before seene in the Rome [room], and in the same garbe she was in before. Then he said to her "in the name of God what doe you come for?" Then she vanished away. Soe he Locked the dore againe & went to bed. And between sleepeing & wakeing he felt some thing Come to his mouth or lipes cold, & thereupon started & looked up & againe did see the same woman with some thing betweene both her hands holding before [it] his mouth. Upon which she moved. And the Child in the Cradle gave a great screech out as if it was greatly

"Depositions," excerpted from *The Salem Witchcraft Papers: Verbatim Transcripts of the Legal Documents of the Salem Witchcraft Outbreak of 1692*, Paul Boyer and Stephen Nissenbaum, editors, Harvard University Press, 1977.

hurt. And she [the specter] disappeared. And [he] takeing the child up could not quiett it in some howres. From which tyme, the child that before was a very likely thriveing Child did pine away and was never well, althow it Lived some moneths after, yet in a sad Condition and soe dyed. . . .

Deposition 2: The Reverend John Hale, May 20, 1692

The said Bishop did entertaine people in her house at unseasonable houres in the night, to keep drinking and playing at shovel-board, whereby discord did arise in other families & young people were in danger to bee corrupted &. . . . The said [Christian, wife of John Trask, a neighbor] Trask knew these things & had once gon into the house; & fynding some at shovel-board had taken the peices thay played with & thrown them into the fyre & had reprooved the said Bishop for promoting such disorders, But received no satisfaction from her about it. . . .

But as to Christian Trask, the next news I heard of her was that she was distracted; & asking her husband [John] Trask when she was so taken [he told] mee shee was taken distracted that night after shee [came from] my house when shee complained against Goody Bishop.

She continueing some time Distracted, wee sought the Lord by fasting & prayer & the Lord was pleased to restore the said [Trask] to the use of her reason agen [again]. I was with her often in [her] distraction (& took it then to bee only distraction, yet fearing sometimes somewhat worse). But since I have seen the fitts of those bewitched at Salem Village I call to mind some of hers to be much like some of theirs. . . .

Her distraction (or bewitching) continued about a month and in those intervalls wherein shee was better shee earnestly desired prayers. & the Sabboth befere she dyed I received a note for prayers on her behalf which her husband said was written by her selfe; & I judge was her owne hand writing, beeing well acquainted with her hand.

As to the wounds she dyed of, I observed 3 deadly ones; apeice of her wind pipe cutt out. & another wound above that threww the windpipe & Gullet & the veine they call jugular. So that I then judge & still doe apprehend it impossible for her with so short a pair of cissars [scissors] to mangle her selfe so, without some extraordinary work of the devill or witchcraft.

Deposition 3: Samuel Shattock, June 2, 1692

Sundry other tymes she came in a Smooth flattering maner in very Slighty Errants [errands]; we have thought Since [that she did this] on purpos to work mischief. At or very near this tyme our Eldest Child, who promised as much health & understanding both by Countenance and actions as any other Children of his years, was taken in a very drooping Condition. And as She Came oftener to the hous he grew wors & wors. As he would be standing at the door, [he] would fall out & bruis his face upon a great Step Stone, as if he had been thrust out bye an invisible hand, often tymes falling & hitting his face in a very miserable maner. . . .

. . . [H]e grew wors in his fits; and [when he was] out of them, would be allmost allways crying, [so] that for many months he would be crying till nature's strenght was spent & then would fall a sleep and then awake & fall to crying & moaning: that his very Countenance did bespeak Compassion. And at length wee perceived his understanding decayed, Soe that wee feared (as it has Since proved) that he would be quite bereaft of his witts; for Ever Since he has bin Stupified and voide of reason, his fitts still following of him. . . .

Deposition 4: John Louder, June 2, 1692

John Louder of Salem Aged aboute thurtey two Yeares Testifieth and sayth that aboute seaven or Eight years since [ago], I then Liveing with Mr John Gedney in Salem and haveing had some Controversy with Bridgett Bushop the wife of Edward Bushop of Salem, Sawyer [wood finisher], aboate her fowles that used to Come into our orchard or garden. Some little tyme after which, I goeing well to bed, aboute the dead of the night [I] felt a great weight upon my Breast. And awakening [I] looked and, it being bright moonlight, did clearly see said Bridget Bushop or her likeness sitting upon my stomake. . . . [I put] my Armes of[f] of the bed to free myselfe from that great oppression, [but] she presently layd hold of my throat and allmost Choked mee. And I had noe strenth or power in my hands to resist or help my selfe. And in this Condition she held mee to [until] almost day. Some tyme after this, my Mistress Susannah Gedney was in our orchard and I was then with her. And said Bridget Bushop, being then in her Orchard which was next adjoyneing to ours, my Mistress told said Bridget that I said or afirmed that she came one night & satt upon my brest as aforesaid, which she denyed and I afirmed to her face to be true and that I did plainely see her. Upon which discourse with her, she Threatened mee. And some tyme after that I being not very well stayed at home on a Lords day. And on the afternoon of said day, the dores being shutt, I did see a black pig in the Roome Coming towards mee; soe I went towards itt to kick it and it vanished away.

Immediately after I satt down in an Narrow Bar and [I] did see a black thing Jump into the window; and [it] came & stood Just before my face, upon the bar. The body of itt looked like a Munky only the feete ware like a Cocks feete with Claws and the face somewhat more like a mans than a Munkiey. And I being greatly affrighted, not being able to speake or help my selfe by Reason of fear, I suppose; soe the thing spake to mee and said 'I am a Messenger sent to you, for I understand you are trobled in mind, and if you will be Ruled by mee, you shall want for Nothing in this world.' Upon which I endeavered to clap my hands upon itt, and sayd 'You devill I will Kill you.' But I could feale noe substance. . . .

I Againe did see that or the like creture that I before did see within dores, in such a posture as it seemed to be agoeing to fly at mee. Upon which I cryed out: 'the whole armor of god be between mee and you.' Soe itt sprang back and flew over the apple tree, flinging the dust with its feet against my stomake. Upon which I was struck dumb, and soe Continued for aboute three days tyme. And also shook many of the apples of[f] from the tree which it flu over.

Deposition 5: John Bly, Sr., and William Bly, June 2, 1692

Jno Blye Senior aged about 57 years & William Blye aged about 15 years both of Salem Testifieth and sayth that, being Imployed by Bridgitt Bushup Alies Oliver of Salem to help take downe the Cellar wall of The owld house she formerly Lived in, wee the said Deponants, in holes of the said owld wall Belonging to the said sellar, found Severall popitts made up of Raggs And hoggs Brusells with headles pins in Them, with the points out ward & this was about Seaven years Last past.

Deposition 6: John Bly, Sr., and Rebecca Bly, no date

Jno Bly Bought a Sow of Edward Bushop of Salem . . . and Bridgett, the wife of Said Edward Bushop, because she could not have the mony or vallue agreed for, payd unto her, she [came] to the house of the deponents in Salem and Quarrelled with them aboute it. Soon after which the sow haveing piged, she was taken with strange fitts, Jumping up and knocking hir head against the fence and seemed blind and deafe and would not Eat neither Lett her pigs suck, but foamed at the mouth . . . wee did then Apprehend or Judge & doe still that said Bishop had bewitched said sow.

Bringing the Witch Trials to an End

Increase Mather, the leading minister in the colony in 1692, returned from London, where he had been negotiating a new charter for the Massachusetts government, and confronted the witch scare. After observing the proceedings for a time, he joined with other ministers to produce the statement reprinted below. The effect of their declaration was to bring the trials to a halt, since in it the ministers questioned the judges' use of evidence. Whereas the judges were willing to believe that the appearance of one's specter proved that one was a witch, the ministers suggested that the devil might cause an innocent person's likeness to appear as a way to bring charges down on the godly. Because ministers were experts on the theological questions raised by witchcraft prosecutions, their opinions mattered to the governor and his council, to whom this statement was addressed. This document was printed in Increase Mather's Cases of Conscience *(Boston, 1693), unpaginated appendix.*

The Return of several Ministers consulted by his Excellency, and the Honourable Council, upon the present Witchcrafts in *Salem* Village.

Boston, June 15. 1692

I. The afflicted State of our poor Neighbours, that are now suffering by Molestations from the Invisible World, we apprehend so deplorable, that we think their Condition calls for the utmost help of all Persons in their several Capacities.

II. We cannot but with all Thankfulness acknowledge, the Success which the merciful God has given unto the sedulous and assiduous Endeavors of our honourable Rulers, to detect the abominable Witchcrafts which have been committed in the Country; humbly *praying that the discovery of these mysterious and mischievous Wickednesses, may be perfected.*

III. We judge that in the prosecution of these, and all such Witchcrafts, there is need of a very critical and exquisite Caution, left by too much Credulity for things received only upon the Devil's Authority, there be a Door opened for a long Train of miserable Consequences, and Satan get an Advantage over us, for we should not be ignorant of his Devices.

IV. . . .'tis necessary that all Proceedings thereabout be managed with an exceeding tenderness toward those that may be complained of; especially if they have been Persons formerly of an unblemished Reputation.

V. When the first Enquiry is made into the Circumstances of such as may lie under any just Suspicion of Witchcrafts, we could wish that there may be admitted as little as is possible, of such Noise, Company, and Openness, as may too hastily expose them that are examined; and that there may nothing be used as a Test, for the Trial of the suspected, the Lawfulness whereof may be doubted among the People of God; but that the Directions given by such Judicious Writers as Perkins and Bernard, be consulted in such a Case.

At the close of his pamphlet opposing the witch trials, Increase Mather added a postscript protesting that he did not want to be misunderstood. In particular, Mather feared that readers might think he did not believe in witches or that he intended to criticize the trial judges. These excerpts from his postscript reveal how uncomfortable New England elites felt about publishing their differences; in addition they suggest that Mather did not want to be seen as contributing to irreligion by denying again the existence of the supernatural.

The Design of the preceding *Dissertation,* is not to plead for Witchcrafts, or to appear as an Advocate for Witches: I have therefore written another Discourse proving that there are such horrid Creatures as Witches in the World; and that they are to be extripated and cut off from amongst the People of God, which I have Thoughts and Inclinations in due time to publish; and I am abundantly satisfied that there have been, and are still most cursed Witches in the Land. More then one or two of those now in

Prison, have freely and credibly acknowledged their Communion and Familiarity with the Spirits of Darkness; and have also declared unto me the Time and Occasion, with the particular Circumstances of their Hellish Obligations and Abominations.

Nor is there designed any Reflection on those worthy Persons who have been concerned in the late Proceedings at *Salam:* They are wise and good Men, and have acted with all Fidelity according to their Light, and have out of tenderness declined the doing of some things, which in our own Judgments they were satisfied about: Having therefore so arduous a Case before them, Pitty and Prayers rather than Censures are their due; on which account I am glad that there is published to the World (by my Son) a *Breviate of the Tryals* of some who were lately executed, whereby I hope the thinking part of Mankind will be satisfied, that there was more than that which is called *Spectre Evidence* for the Conviction of the Persons condemned.

Cotton Mather Assesses the Witch Trials

In the following passage, Cotton Mather—also a Boston minister like his father, Increase Mather—addresses three questions. First, what had been the principle evidence in the witch trials; second, what led him to conclude that the trials went too far; and, third, what were the most serious mistakes made at Salem? Note that Mather, like his father, continued to believe that Satan works evil in the world through witches, even as he suggests that witches may not have been the source of the problem in this particular case. The following is taken from Mather's monumental history of early New England, Magnalia Christi Americana *(1702); this excerpt was taken from the 1820 edition, 2:413–14.*

By these things you may see how this matter was carry'd on, *viz.* chiefly by the complaints and accusations of the afflicted (bewitch'd ones, as it was suppos'd) and then by the confessions of the *accus'd* condemning themselves and others. Yet experience shew'd, that the more there were apprehended, the more were still afflicted by satan; and the number of confessors increasing, did but increase the number of the *accused;* and the executing of

Cotton Mather (1663–1728) was a clergyman in one of the Boston churches in 1692. Because he had previously assisted with the case of a girl who was apparently bewitched, he was considered something of an expert on the supernatural. In this, he followed in the footsteps of his powerful and important father, Increase Mather who—along with Cotton and other ministers—helped to bring the trials to an end (Courtesy of the New York Public Library.)

some, made way for the apprehending of others: For still the afflicted complain'd of being tormented by new objects, as the former were remov'd. So that those that were concern'd, grew amaz'd at the number and quality of the persons accus'd, and feared that satan by his wiles had enwrapped innocent persons under the imputation of that crime. And at last, it was evidently seen, that there must be a stop put, or the generation of the children of God, would fall under that condemnation. Henceforth therefore the juries generally acquitted such as were tried, fearing they had gone too far before. And Sir *William Phips* the Governour, repriev'd all that were condemn'd, even the confessors as well as others. And the confessors generally fell off from their confession, some saying, *They remembred nothing of what they had said;* others said, *They had belied themselves and others.* Some broke prison and ran away, and were not strictly searched after. Some acquitted, some dismissed, and one way or other, all that had been accused, were set or left at liberty. . . .

It may be queried, How doth it appear that there was a going too far in this *affair?*

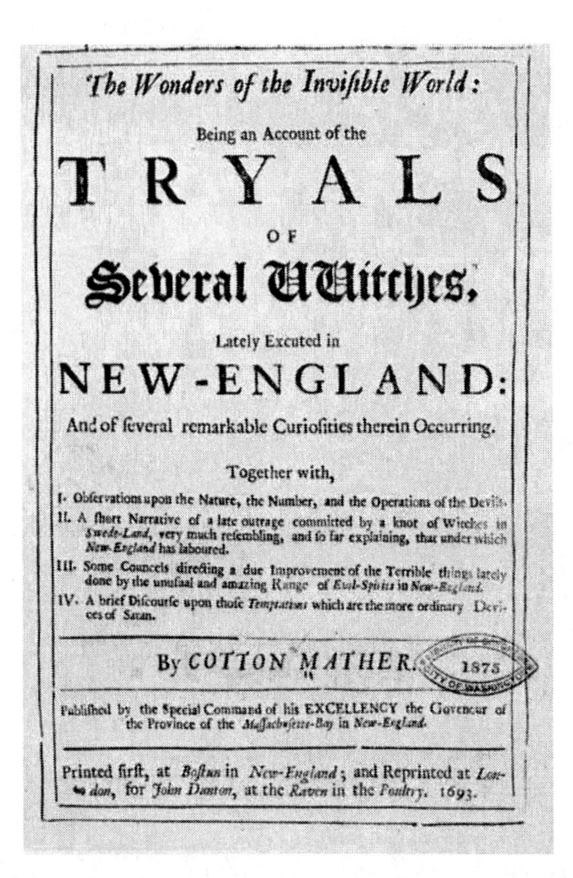

The Wonders of the Inviſible World:

Being an Account of the

TRYALS

OF

Several Witches,

Lately Excuted in

NEW-ENGLAND:

And of ſeveral remarkable Curioſities therein Occurring.

Together with,

I. Obſervations upon the Nature, the Number, and the Operations of the Devils.

II. A ſhort Narrative of a late outrage committed by a knot of Witches in *Swede-Land*, very much reſembling, and ſo far explaining, that under which *New-England* has laboured.

III. Some Councels directing a due Improvement of the Terrible things lately done by the unuſual and amazing Range of *Evil-Spirits* in *New-England*.

IV. A brief Diſcourſe upon thoſe *Temptations* which are the more ordinary Devices of Satan.

By *COTTON MATHER*.

Publiſhed by the Special Command of his EXCELLENCY the Govenour of the Province of the *Maſſachuſetts-Bay* in *New-England*.

Printed firſt, at *Boſtun* in *New-England*; and Reprinted at *London*, for *John Dunton*, at the *Raven* in the *Poultry*. 1693.

Title page to Cotton Mather, The Wonders of the Invisible World *(London, 1693). Mather, who had grave reservations about the work of the court that tried the witchcraft cases in 1692, nonetheless felt compelled to defend it against critics. His account, contained in this pamphlet, reveals his conflicted attitudes. The title of his pamphlet refers back to an early work by his father, Increase Mather, that argued in favor of "an invisible world" against skeptics. (Courtesy of the Library of Congress.)*

By the numbers of the persons accus'd, which at length increas'd to about an hundred; and it cannot be imagin'd that in a place of so much knowledge, so many in so small a compass of land, should so abominably leap into the devil's lap all at once.

The quality of several of the accus'd was such, as did bespeak *better things, and things that accompany salvation;* Persons, whose blameless and holy lives before did testifie for them; Persons that had taken great pains to bring up their children in the nurture and admonition of the Lord; such as we had charity for, as for our own souls: And charity is a christian duty commended to us.

The number of the afflicted daily increased until about fifty persons were thus vex'd by the devil. This gave just ground to suspect some mistake, which gave advantage to the *accuser of the brethren* to make a breach upon us.

It was considerable, that *nineteen* were executed, and all denied the crime to the death, and some of them were knowing persons, and had before this been accounted blameless *livers*. . . .

When this prosecution ceas'd, the Lord so *chain'd up satan,* that the afflicted grew presently well: The accused are generally quiet; and for five years since, we have no such molestation by them.

It sways much with me, which I have since heard and read, of the like mistakes in other places. As in Suffolk in England, about the year 1645 was such a prosecution, until they saw, that unless they put a stop, it would bring all into blood and confusion. The like hath been in France, until nine hundred were put to death. And in some other places the like So that New-England is not the only place circumvented by the *wiles of the wicked and wily serpent in this kind*. . . .

As to our case at *Salem,* I conceive it proceeded from some mistaken principles: As, that satan cannot assume the shape of an innocent person, and in that shape do mischief to the bodies and estates of mankind: and that the devil, when he doth harm to persons in their body or estate, it is (at least, most commonly, generally and frequently) by the help of our neighbour, some witch in covenant with the devil; and that when the party suspected looks on the parties suppos'd to be bewitch'd, and they are thereupon struck down into a fit, as if struck with a cudgel, it is a proof of such a covenant.

Questions

1. *If they continued to believe in the existence of witchcraft, how did various leading colonists come to oppose the trials?*
2. *What do the depositions reveal about popular attitudes regarding witches?*
3. *Can you see any differences between lay and clerical thinking when you compare the depositions and the ministers' statements?*

FURTHER READING

The most popular book on Salem witchcraft among undergraduates remains Salem Possessed: The Social Origins of Witchcraft, *by Paul Boyer and Stephen Nissenbaum (Cambridge, Massachusetts, 1974). John Putnam Demos's* Entertaining Satan: Witchcraft and the Culture of Early New England *(New York, 1982) and Carol Karlsen's* The Devil in the Shape of a Woman: Witchcraft in Colonial New England *(New York, 1987) examine the Salem accusations in the context of the long history of witch fears in colonial New England.* The Devil's Dominion: Magic and Religion in Early New England *(New York, 1992), by Richard Godbeer, includes two chapters on Salem. Trial transcripts are available in* The Salem Witchcraft Papers: Verbatim Transcripts of the Legal Documents of the Salem Witchcraft Outbreak of 1692, *ed. Paul Boyer and Stephen Nissenbaum, 3 vols. (New York, 1977); other original documents can be found in* Witch-hunting in Seventeenth-Century New England: A Documentary History, 1638–1692, *ed. David D. Hall (Boston, 1991).*

Colonial American Political Culture: Deference or Democracy?

Margaret E. Newell

Introduction

A number of tensions shaped colonial political culture in the century before the Revolution. On the one hand, economic, cultural, and political ties with England grew stronger in the 1700s. Many Americans gloried in the privileges and "rights of Englishmen" that they enjoyed as members of the British empire. They also praised the British Constitution as the best form of government. Rather than a single document or frame of government, the British Constitution referred to the three estates of English society—the king, the aristocracy, and the people. English men and women regarded a proper tension and balance between these groups as essential to the stability of their nation. They believed that the king and the English Parliament—which included the House of Lords and the House of Commons—gave each group proper representation in government and prevented any one group from dominating the rest. Americans believed that they replicated this perfect system in their colonial assemblies, where the royal governor took the place of the king, an upper house or council took the place of the Lords, and the lower house or assembly represented all the people. Yet despite their approving rhetoric, the colonists' actions challenged English notions of balance and power. During the eighteenth century, the lower houses of the colonial assemblies regularly challenged the royal governors' authority; most colonies also lacked a hereditary aristocracy capable of turning colonial councils into another House of Lords. This meant that the elective colonial assemblies exerted far more influence than was proper under the British Constitution, which worried many imperial authorities.

The distribution of political power within the colonies themselves generated another set of tensions. Both religious teachings and social custom instructed people to obey political authorities. England, including its colonies, was a monarchy, and the king occupied the top position in a hierarchical social structure. Few Americans questioned the justice of this inequality in the colonial period; indeed, most believed that inequality and the deference of inferiors to superiors were crucial to the maintenance of political and social order. Members of the colonial elite—merchants in northern port cities, slaveholding planters in the South—dominated political office in the colonies. Women, blacks, and those white men without property were prevented from voting. Yet because of the availability of land and economic opportunity, many colonists (as many as 50 to 90 percent of white males over twenty-one in some areas) were able to meet the property requirements for voting. Far more Americans could participate in political life and influence elections than in contemporary England, where, by the mid-eighteenth century, a man needed the equivalent of $80,000 to vote. But did the right to participate translate into democracy? Or did customs of deference and hierarchy continue to influence voters? Did the growing power of the assemblies translate into a fairer, more democratic government for all?

State and Society: Theory and Practice

The following documents either offer insight into the political theories of the seventeenth and eighteenth centuries or explore the relationship between economic and political equality in colonial America. In sermons, diaries, public speeches, and pamphlets, civil and religious leaders discussed the duty of citizens to obey and of rulers to guard the people's well-being; they defined patriotism and public service in exalted terms as an unselfish desire to advance the common good. These first five selections represent an ideal, not necessarily a reality; nonetheless, they reveal important concepts that shaped the colonists' political understanding.

The Rulers and the Ruled: John Winthrop's Definition of Liberty

One of the original planners of the Massachusetts Bay Colony, John Winthrop (1588–1649) served as governor or deputy governor almost every year from 1630 until his death. He delivered the following speech after his acquittal in a trial in which he was accused of exceeding his authority. Excerpted from The History of New England from 1630 to 1649, *ed. James Savage (Boston, 1826), 2:228–30.*

The great questions that have troubled the country, are about the authority of the magistrates [officeholders] and the liberty of the people. It is yourselves who have called us to this office, and being called by you, we have our authority from God, in way of an ordinance, such as hath the image of God eminently stamped

John Winthrop was one of the original planners of the Massachusetts Bay Colony and also one of its chief political figures for two decades. (Courtesy of the American Antiquarian Society.)

upon it, the contempt and violation whereof hath been vindicated with examples of divine vengeance. I entreat you to consider, that when you choose magistrates, you take them from among yourselves, men subject to like passions as you are. Therefore when you see infirmities in us, you should reflect upon your own, and that would make you bear the more with us, and not be severe censurers of the failings of your magistrates. . . .

For the other point concerning liberty, I observe a great mistake in the country about that. There is a twofold liberty, natural (I mean as our nature is now corrupt) and civil or federal. The first is common to man with beasts and other creatures. By this, man, as he stands in relation to man simply, hath liberty to do what he lists [likes]; it is a liberty to evil as well as to good. This liberty is incompatible and inconsistent with authority, and cannot endure the least restraint of the most just authority. The exercise and maintaining of this liberty makes men grow more evil, and in time to be worse than brute beasts. . . . This is that great enemy of truth and peace, that wild beast, which all the ordinances of God are bent against, to restrain and subdue it. The other kind of liberty I call civil or federal, it may also be termed moral, in reference to the covenant between God and man, in the moral law, and the politic covenants and constitutions, amongst men themselves. This liberty is the proper end and object of authority, and cannot subsist without it; and it is a liberty to that only which is good, just and honest. This liberty you are to stand for, with the hazard (not only of your goods, but) of your lives, if need be. Whatsoever crosseth this, is not authority, but a distemper thereof. This liberty is maintained and exercised in a way of subjection to authority; it is of the same kind of liberty wherewith Christ hath made us free. The woman's own choice makes such a man her husband; yet being so chosen, he is her lord, and she is to be subject to him, yet in a way of liberty, not of bondage; and a true wife accounts her subjection her honour and freedom, and would not think her condition safe and free, but in her subjection to her husband's authority. Such is the liberty of the church under the authority of Christ, her king and husband; his yoke is so easy and sweet to her as a bride's ornaments; and if through frowardness or wantonness &c. she shake it off, at any time, she is at no rest in her spirit, until she take it up again; and whether her lord smiles upon her, and embraceth her in his arms, or whether he frowns, or rebukes, or smites her, she apprehends the sweetness of his love in all, and is refreshed, supported and instructed by every such dispensation of his authority over her. On the other side, ye know who they are that complain of this yoke and say, let us break their bands &c. we will not have this man to rule over us. Even so, brethren, it will be between you and your magistrates. If you stand for your natural corrupt liberties, and will do what is good in your own eyes, you will not endure the least weight of authority, but will murmur, and oppose, and be always striving to shake off that yoke; but if you will be satisfied to enjoy such civil and lawful liberties, such as Christ allows you, then will you quietly and cheerfully submit unto that authority which is set over you, in all the administrations of it, for your good. Wherein, if we fail at any time, we hope we shall be willing (by God's assistance) to hearken to good advice from any of you, or in any other way of God; so shall your liberties be preserved, in upholding the honour and power of authority amongst you.

Jonathan Mayhew on the Limits of Obedience

Jonathan Mayhew, Congregationalist minister of Boston's West Church, offered another perspective on the relationship between magistrates and the populace in this 1750 sermon. Starting from a New Testament text, St. Paul's Letter to the Romans, Mayhew rebuts the notion that the Bible called for unlimited obedience and outlines the conditions under which the people might remove a leader who violated the public trust. Taken from Jonathan Mayhew, A Discourse Concerning Unlimited Submission and Non-Resistance to the Higher Powers . . . *(Boston, 1750),* 12, 28–30.

There is one very important and interesting point which remains to be inquired into; namely, the *extent* of that subjection *to the higher powers,* which is here enjoined as a duty upon all christians. . . .

. . . [St. Paul's] arguments to enforce submission, are of such a nature, as to conclude only in favour of submission *to such rulers as he himself describes;* i.e. such as rule for the good of society, which is the only end of their institution. Common tyrants, and public oppressors, are not intitled to obedience from their subjects, by virtue of any thing here laid down by the inspired apostle.

I now add, farther, that the apostle's argument is so far from proving it to be the duty of people to obey, and submit to, such rulers as act in contradiction to the public good, and so to the design of their office, that it proves *the direct contrary.* For, please to observe, that if the end of all civil government, be the good of society; . . . it follows, that when no such good end can be answered by submission, there remains no argument or motive to enforce it; if instead of this good end's being brought about by submission, a *contrary end* is brought about, and the ruin and misery of society effected by it, here is a plain and positive reason against submission in all such cases, should they ever happen. And therefore, in such cases, a regard to the public welfare, ought to make us with-hold from our rulers, that obedience and subjection which it would, otherwise, be our duty to render to them. If it be our duty, for example, to obey our king, merely for this reason, that he rules for the public welfare, (which is the only argument the apostle makes use of) it follows, by a parity of reason, that when he turns tyrant, and makes his subjects his prey to devour and to destroy, instead of his charge to defend and cherish, we are bound to throw off our allegiance to him, and to resist. . . . Let me make use of this easy and familiar *similitude* to illustrate the point in hand—Suppose God requires a family of children, to obey their father and not to resist him; . . . Suppose this parent at length runs distracted, and attempts, in his mad fit, to cut all his children's throats: Now, in this case, is not the reason before assigned, why there children should obey their parent while he continued of a sound mind, namely, *their common good,* a reason equally conclusive for disobeying and resisting him, since he is become delirious, and attempts their ruin?

William Livingston on Patriotism and the Duty of Public Service

New York lawyer and politician William Livingston (1723–1790) published a series of essays on politics in a periodical called The Independent Reflector. *In this essay, Livingston defined patriotism as a willingness to suppress selfish interest in favor of the common good. Because of his stress on unity, Livingston viewed political parties as illegitimate, since they represented special interest groups and created political conflict. Taken from William Livingston, "Of Patriotism,"* The Independent Reflector, *3 May 1753, 93–94.*

He is a Patriot who prefers the Happiness of the Whole, to his own private Advantage; who, when properly called upon, is ready to rise up in its Defence, and with a manly Fortitude, shield it from Danger. He is a Patriot, the ruling Object of whose Ambition, is the public Welfare: Whose Zeal, chastised by Reflection, is calm, steady and undaunted: He whom lucrative Views cannot warp from his Duty: Whom no partial Ties can prevail on to act traitorously to the Community, and sacrifice the Interest of the *Whole* to that of a *Part*: He whom Flattery cannot seduce, nor Frowns dismay, from supporting the public Interest when it is in his Power: Who mourns for their Vices, and exerts his Abilities to work a Reformation: Who compassionates their Ignorance, and endeavours to improve their Understandings: He who aims to cultivate Urbanity and social Harmony. To conclude, he is a true Patriot whose Love for the Public is not extinguished, either by their Insensibility or Ingratitude; but goes on with unwearied Benevolence in every public-spirited Attempt. . . .

The noisy intemperate Froth of a political Enthusiast, is as far removed from a steady Principle of Patriotism, as the Dignity of solid Understanding from the Fumes of poetical Madness.—

Party-Faction and personal Resentment, have often imposed themselves upon Mankind for the divine Operations of public Spirit. We shall find Hypocrites of this sort, more frequently inveighing against Men, than reasoning upon Facts: Ridicule is their favourite Engine—to mislead the Judgment by warming the Imagination, is their peculiar Art.

The superstitious Zealot, and the religious Bigot, have not so much as an Idea of a Public: When they presume to act the Part of Patriots, there is something so unnatural and absurd in their Manner, that they can scarcely deceive any but their own Herd.

When these Characters lay Claim to Patriotism, we may be sure they are Imposters, and we should treat them as Hypocrites.

Landon Carter Defines Representation

Representation in the eighteenth century Anglo-American world meant something very different from representation today. Rather than representing the particular interest of local constituents, English Members of Parliament believed that they represented all the people, and therefore

Reprinted from *The Diary of Colonel Landon Carter of Sabine Hall, 1752–1778*, Vol. I, edited by Jack P. Greene, published by The University Press of Virginia, 1965.

were free to make their own decisions regarding which measures were in the common interest. In the following selection, Virginia planter-politician Landon Carter (1710–1778) describes a debate in the Virginia House of Burgesses between defenders of this English conception of representation and others who were moving towards a more "popular" constituent-responsive definition of representation. Abridged from The Diary of Colonel Landon Carter of Sabine Hall, *1752–1778, ed. Jack P. Greene (Charlottesville, Virginia, 1965), 1:116–17.*

[T]he question was Whether a Representative was obliged to follow the directions of his Constituents against his own Reason and Conscience or to be Governed by his Conscience. The Arguments for implicit obedience [to his constituents' wishes] were that the first institution of a Representative was for the avoiding the Confusion of a Multitude in assembly. He, therefore, was to Collect the sentiments of his Constituents and whatever that Majority willed ought to be the rule of his Vote. Thus argued the favourers of Popularity, who were all headed by the Speaker, for these were nearly his own words. The Admirers of Reason and Liberty of Conscience distinguished upon it and said, where the matter related particularly to the interest of the Constituents alone, there implicit obedience ought to Govern, but, where it was to affect the whole Community, Reason and Good Conscience should direct, for it must be absurd to Suppose one part of the Community could be apprized of the good of the whole without Consulting the whole. For that Part, therefore, to order an implicit vote must be absurd and the Representative acting accordingly could only augment the Absurdity because he must suppose his people so perverse as not to be moved by Reasons ever so good that might be advanced by other parts of the Community. Many other Arguments do so naturally arise to support this last and best Opinion that I need not insert them.

The Practice of Politics: How to Get Elected—An Eighteenth-Century Guide

In 1770, Robert Munford, a colonel in the Virginia militia and office-holder at many levels of local government, wrote a play about electioneering in his home colony. Although satirical and comic, The Candidates *contains some realistic accounts of political practices in pre-revolutionary Virginia. The main character, Mr. Wou'dbe (i.e. "would be"), wishes to run for the House of Burgesses. As a gentleman, Wou'dbe scorns campaigning and expresses mixed feelings about serving in public office. He believes that voters should recognize the quality of gentlemen candidates and automatically elect them to office. But in order to defeat his opponents—Sir John Toddy, Mr. Strutabout, and Mr. Smallhopes—Wou'dbe adopts a number of not-so-idealistic strategies. Munford describes the practice of "treating" voters with rum, barbecues, and breakfasts before elections and recounts conversations in which candidates make various promises to the freeholder constituents. Taken from "Robert Munford's* The Candidates,*" ed. Jay B. Hubbell and Douglass Adair* The William and Mary Quarterly *5 (April 1948): 231, 237–44.*

Act I. Scene I. *Mr. Wou'dbe's house. Enter Wou'dbe with a newspaper in his hand.*

. . . Well, our little world will soon be up, and very busy towards our next election. Must I again be subject to the humours of a fickle croud? Must I again resign my reason, and be nought but what each voter pleases? Must I cajole, fawn, and wheedle, for a place that brings so little profit? . . .

[In the next scene, Wou'dbe discusses the proper qualifications for serving in the House of Burgesses with a freeholder (voter), Guzzle.]

Wou'dbe. I'm sorry Mr. Guzzle, you are so ignorant of the necessary qualifications of a member of the house of burgesses. . . . I'll make it a point of duty to dispatch the business, and my study to promote the good of my county.

Guzzle. Yes, damn it, you all promise mighty fair, but the devil a bit do you perform; there's Strutabout, now, he'll promise to move mountains. He'll make the rivers navigable, and bring the tide over the tops of the hills, for a vote.

Strutabout. You may depend, Mr. Guzzle, I'll perform whatever I promise.

Guzzle. I don't believe it, damn me if I like you. . . .

Wou'dbe. Don't be angry, John, let our actions hereafter be the test of our inclinations to serve you. . . . who are you for?

Guzzle. For the first man that fills my bottle: so Mr. Wou'dbe, your servant.

Wou'dbe. Ralpho, go after him, and fill his bottle. . . .

Wou'dbe. (pulling out his watch.) 'Tis now the time a friend of mine has appointed for me to meet the freeholders at a barbecue; well, I find, in order to secure a seat in our august senate, 'tis necessary a man should either be a slave or a fool; a slave to the people, for the privilege of serving them, and a fool himself, for thus begging a troublesome and expensive employment.

To sigh, while toddy-toping sots rejoice,
To see you paying for their empty voice,
From morn to night your humble head decline,
To gain an honour that is justly thine,
Intreat a fool, who's your's at this day's treat,
And next another's, if another's meat,
Is all the bliss a candidate acquires,
In all his wishes, or his vain desires. . . .

[The next scene takes place at a barbecue Wou'dbe has sponsored in order to woo the voters. Freeholders Twist, Stern, Prize, and their wives discuss the candidates. Sir John Toddy arrives with his aide, Guzzle, and proceeds to "glad-hand" the voters. Note that Guzzle has to whisper their names to Sir John, who pretends that he knows his constituents. Finally, Twist presses Mr. Wou'dbe about what he specifically would do for the voters once in office.]

Stern. Pray, gentlemen, what plausible objection have you against Mr. Wou'dbe? he's a clever civil gentleman as any, and as far as my poor weak capacity can go, he's a man of as good learning, and knows the punctilios of behaving himself, with the best of them. . . .

Lucy. If the wives were to vote, I believe they would make a better choice than their husbands.

Twist. You'd be for the funnyest—wou'dn't you?

Lucy. Yes, faith; and the wittiest, and prettiest, and the wisest, and the best too; you are all for ugly except when you choose me.

Catharine. Well done, Lucy, you are right, girl. If we were all to speak to our old men as freely as you do, there would be better doings.

Stern. Perhaps not, Kate. . . .

Catharine. Husband, you know Mr. Wou'dbe is a clever gentleman; he has been a good friend to us.

Stern. I agree to it, and can vote for him without your clash.

Sarah. I'll be bound when it comes to the pinch, they'll all vote for him. . . .

Enter Sir John Toddy.

Sir John. Gentlemen and ladies, your servant, hah! my old friend Prize, how goes it? how does your wife and children do?

Sarah. At your service, sir. *(making a low courtsey.)*

Prize. How the devil come he to know me so well, and never spoke to me before in his life? *(aside.)*

Guzzle. (whispering [to] Sir John) Dick Stern.

Sir John. Hah! Mr. Stern, I'm proud to see you; I hope your family are well; how many children? does the good woman keep to the old stroke?

Catharine. Yes, an't please your honour, I hope my lady's well, with your honour.

Sir John. At your service, madam.

Guzzle. (whispering [to] Sir John) Roger Twist.

Sir John. Hah! Mr. Roger Twist! your servant, sir. I hope your wife and children are well.

Twist. There's my wife. I have no children, at your service. . . .

Twist. [to Mr. Wou'dbe] . . . I've heard a 'sponsible man say, he could prove you were the cause of these new taxes.

Wou'dbe. Do you believe that too? or can you believe that it's in the power of any individual member to make a law himself? If a law is enacted that is displeasing to the people, it has the concurrence of the whole legislative body, and my vote for, or against it, is of little consequence.

Guzzle. And what the devil good do you do then?

Wou'dbe. As much as I have abilities to do.

Guzzle. Suppose, Mr. Wou'dbe, we were to want you to get the price of rum lower'd—wou'd you do it?

Wou'dbe. I cou'd not.

Guzzle. Huzza for Sir John! he has promised to do it, huzza for Sir John!

Twist. Suppose, Mr. Wou'dbe, we should want this tax taken off—cou'dyou do it?

Wou'dbe. I could not.

Twist. Huzza for Mr. Strutabout! he's damn'd, if he don't. Huzza for Mr. Strutabout!

Stern. Suppose, Mr. Wou'dbe, we that live over the river, should want to come to church on this side, is it not very hard we should pay ferryage; when we pay as much to the church as you do?

Wou'dbe. Very hard.

Stern. Suppose we were to petition the assembly could you get us clear of that expence?

Wou'dbe. I believe it to be just; and make no doubt but it would pass into a law.

Stern. Will you do it?

Wou'dbe. I will endeavour to do it.

Stern. Huzza for Mr. Wou'dbe! Wou'dbe forever!

Prize. Why don't you burgesses, do something with the damn'd pickers *[tobacco inspectors]*? If we have a hogshead of tobacco refused, away it goes to them; and after they have twisted up the best of it for their own use, and taken as much as will pay them for their trouble, the poor planter has little for his share.

Wou'dbe. There are great complaints against them; and I believe the assembly will take them under consideration.

Prize. Will you vote against them?

Wou'dbe. I will, if they deserve it.

Prize. Huzza for Mr. Wou'dbe! you shall go, old fellow; don't be afraid; I'll warrant it.

Equality and Opportunity in Eighteenth-Century America

Since the colonies required a minimum property holding of those white males who wished to qualify for suffrage, the extent to which Americans had access to land and economic opportunity affected political participation. In this selection, J. Hector St. John (1735–1813), a French immigrant who settled in New York in 1765, compares American and European society, stressing the relatively egalitarian nature of the colonies. Crèvecoeur's essay, first published in 1782, focuses on the political and economic consequences of the lack of social hierarchy. Excerpted from J. Hector St. John, Letters From An American Farmer . . . *(Philadelphia, 1793), 42–46.*

I wish I could be acquainted with the feelings and thoughts which must agitate the heart and present themselves to the mind of an enlightened Englishman, when he first lands on this continent. . . . He is arrived on a new continent; a modern society offers itself to his contemplation, different from what he had hitherto seen. It is not composed, as in Europe, of great lords who possess every thing, and of a herd of people who have nothing. Here are no aristocratical families, no courts, no kings, no bishops, no ecclesiastical dominion, no invisible power giving to a few a very visible one; no great manufacturers employing thousands, no great refinements of luxury. The rich and the poor are not so far removed from each other as they are in Europe.

Some few towns excepted, we are all tillers of the earth, from Nova Scotia to West Florida. We are a people of cultivators, scattered over an immense territory, communicating with each other by means of good roads and navigable rivers, united by the silken bands of mild government, all respecting the laws without dreading their power, because they are equitable. We are all animated with the spirit of industry, which is unfettered and unrestrained, because each person works for himself. If he travels through our rural districts, he views not the hostile castle, and the haughty mansion, contrasted with the clay-built hut and miserable cabbin, where cattle and men help to keep each other warm, and dwell in meanness, smoke, and indigence. A pleasing uniformity of decent competence appears throughout our habitations. The meanest of our log-houses is a dry and comfortable habitation. Lawyer or merchant are the fairest titles our towns afford; that of a farmer is the only appellation of the rural inhabitants of our country. It must take some time ere he can reconcile himself to our dictionary, which is but short in words of dignity, and names of honour. There, on a Sunday, he sees a congregation of respectable farmers and their wives, all clad in neat homespun, well mounted, or riding in their own humble waggons. There is not among them an esquire, saving the unlettered magistrate. There he sees a parson as simple as his flock, a farmer who does not riot on the labour of others. We have no princes, for whom we toil, starve, and bleed: we are the most perfect society now existing in the world. Here man is free as he ought to be; nor is this pleasing equality so transitory as many others are. . . .

. . . Every thing has tended to regenerate them; new laws, a new mode of living, a new social system; here they are become men: in Europe they were as so many useless plants, wanting vegetative mould, and refreshing showers; they withered, and were mowed down by want, hunger, and war: but now, by the power of transplantation, like all other plants they have taken root and flourished! Formerly they were not numbered in any civil list of their country, except in those of the poor; here they rank as citizens. By what invisible power has this surprizing metamorphosis been performed? By that of the laws and that of their industry. The laws, the indulgent laws, protect them as they arrive, stamping on them the symbol of adoption; they receive ample rewards for their labours; these accumulated rewards procure them lands; those lands confer on them the title of freemen; and to that title every benefit is affixed which men can possibly require. This is the great operation daily performed by our laws. From whence proceed these laws? From our government. Whence that government? It is derived from the original genius and strong desire of the people, ratified and confirmed by government. This is the great chain which links us all.

A Vertical Society: Hierarchy in Colonial Virginia

In this fragment from his 1806 autobiography, Devereux Jarratt (1732–1801), an Episcopalian minister from Virginia, remembers—and expresses nostalgia for—the yawning social and material gulf that separated freeholders from elites in early America. Note that when Jarratt began to ascend the social ladder in taking a position as schoolmaster, he did so only with the help of a wealthy patron and that he sought out a wig, the sign of a gentleman, symbolic of his new station in life. Abridged from Devereux Jarratt, The Life of the Reverend Devereux Jarratt . . . *(Baltimore, 1806), 12–16, 25–26.*

I was born in *New Kent*, a county in Virginia, about 25 miles below Richmond, on January 6th, 1732–3, O. S. [Old Style dating].

I was the youngest child of *Robert Jarratt* and *Sarah* his wife. My grand-father was an Englishman, born, I believe, in the city of *London*. . . . My grand-mother, as I was told, was a native of *Ireland*. Both she and my grand-father died before I was born, and I have had no account of them, except that they were poor people, but industrious, and rather rough in their manners. They acquired a pretty good tract of land, of near 1200 acres, but they had no slaves—probably they were prejudiced against that kind of property. . . .

My father was brought up to the trade of a carpenter, at which he wrought till the very day before he died. He was a mild, inoffensive man, and much respected among his neighbors. My mother was the daughter of Joseph Bradley, of *Charles City*, a county bordering on *New Kent*. None of my ancestors, on either side, were either rich or great, but had the character of honesty and industry, by which they lived in credit among their neighbors, free from real want, and above the frowns of the world. This was also the habit, in which my parents were. They always had plenty of plain food and raiment, wholesome and good, suitable to their humble station, and the times in which they lived. Our food was altogether the produce of the farm, or plantation, except a little sugar, which was rarely used; and our raiment was altogether my mother's manufacture, except our hats and *shoes*, the *latter* of which we never put on, but in the winter season. We made no use of *tea* or *coffee* for breakfast, or at any other time; nor did I know a single family that made any use of them. Meat, bread and milk was the ordinary food of all my acquaintance. I suppose the *richer sort* might make use of *those* and other luxuries, but to such people I had no access. We were accustomed to look upon, what were called *gentle folks*, as beings of a superior order. For my part, I was quite shy of *them*, and kept off at a humble distance. A *periwig*, in those days, was a distinguishing badge of *gentle folk*—and when I saw a man riding the road, near our house, with a wig on, it would so alarm my fears, and give me such a disagreeable feeling, that, I dare say, I would run off, as for my life. Such ideas of the difference between *gentle* and *simple*, were, I believe, universal among all of my rank and age. But I have lived to see, a vast alteration, in this respect, and the contrary extreme prevail. In our high *republican times*, there is more *levelling* than ought to be, consistent with good government. I have as little notion of oppression and tyranny as any man, but a due subordination is essentially requisite in every government. . . .

My parents neither sought nor expected any titles, honors, or great things, either for themselves or children. Their highest ambition was to teach their children to read, write, and understand the fundamental rules of arithmetic. I remember also, they taught us short prayers, and made us very perfect in repeating the *Church Catechism*. They wished us all to be brought up in some honest calling, that we might earn our bread, by the sweat of our brow, as they did. . . .

One of the most remote means, as I consider it, which led me to the station, which I now fill, was my being called from the *ax* to the *quill*. . . . One *Jacob Moon*, living in Albemarle county, . . . sent me word, that he should be glad to employ me as a schoolmaster . . . I readily embraced the proposal, and soon packed up my *all*, which consisted in such things, as made no great baggage, for I think I carried the whole on my back, except one shirt. . . . My whole dress and apparel consisted in a pair of coarse breeches, one or two oznaburgs shirts, a pair of shoes and stockings, an old felt hat, a bear skin *coat*, which, by the by, was the first coat I ever had made for me, since my childhood. And that I might appear something more than common, in a strange place, and be counted somebody, I got me an old wig, which, perhaps being cast off by the master, had became [become] the property of his slave, and from the slave it was conveyed to me.

Who Could Vote and for Whom Did They Vote? The Statistics from Massachusetts

The following tables provide information regarding the distribution of wealth, eligibility for suffrage and patterns of voting in Massachusetts. Table 1 offers estimates of the percentage of adult males who could vote in several Massachusetts towns. In Table 2, Gary Nash notes change over time in the proportion of "polls"—people with enough property to be taxed who formed the pool from which voters were selected—in the overall population of Boston. In Table 3, Robert Gross examines the socio-economic background of the men who served as selectman—a town government office—in Concord, Massachusetts; in Table 4 Gross calculates who controlled the wealth and resources in Concord. Table 1 is taken from Robert E. Brown, Middle-Class Democracy and the

Table 1
Estimated Percentage of Voters in the Adult Male Population

Town	County	No. of reps.	Least no. of voters	No. of polls	Est. polls 16 to 21	Est. No. adult males	Est. % of adult male voters
Roxbury	Suff.	3	220	356	89	267	82.4
Watertown	Mid.	2	120	185	46	139	86.3
Northampton	Hamp.	4	320	451	113	338	94.6 (1777)
Worcester	Worc.	4	320	438	109	329	97.2
Charlton	Worc.	3	220	308	77	231	95.2
Boston	Suff.	12	1120	2664	666	1998	56.0
Salem	Essex	7	620	1193	298	895	69.2
Ipswich	Essex	5	420	1016	254	762	55.1
Marblehead	Essex	5	420	1047	262	785	53.5
Gloucester	Essex	5	420	939	235	704	59.6
Newbury	Essex	5	420	704	176	528	79.5
Medford	Mid.	2	120	190	47	143	83.9
Monson	Hamp.	2	120	197	49	148	81.0 (1777)
Bridgewater	Ply.	6	520	1130	282	848	61.3
Leicester	Worc.	2	120	212	53	159	75.4 (1777)
New Braintree	Worc.	2	120	185	46	139	86.3 (1777)
Sheffield	Berk.	3	220	338	84	254	86.6 (1777)

Reprinted from *Middle-Class Democracy and the Revolution in Massachusetts, 1691–1780* by Robert E. Brown, published by Russell & Russell, 1968.

Revolution in Massachusetts, 1691–1780 *(New York, 1955), 50. Table 2 is from Gary Nash, "Urban Wealth and Poverty in Pre-Revolutionary America,"* The Journal of Interdisciplinary History 6 *(Spring 1976): 465. Tables 3 and 4 are from Robert A. Gross,* The Minutemen and Their World *(New York, 1976), 196, 212.*

Table 2
Rateable Polls in Boston, 1728–1771

Year	Population	Polls
1728	12,650	c3,000
1733	15,100	c3,500
1735	16,000	3,637
1738	16,700	3,395
1740	16,800	3,043
1741	16,750	2,972
1745	16,250	2,660
1750	15,800	c2,400
1752	15,700	2,789
1756	15,650	c2,500
1771	15,500	2,588

Table 3
Percentage Distribution of the Selectmen in Quintiles Over Time

	Top 20%	UM20%	Mid 20%	Bottom 20%	N
1745–54	81	12	6	0	16
175[5]–64	71	8	12	0	17
1765–74	69	31	0	0	13

[Key: Top 20%=wealthiest 20% of white males eligible for office; UM 20%=next wealthiest 20%; Mid 20%=next wealthiest 20%; N=size of sample, i.e. number of selectmen that Gross studied in each period.]

Table 4
Percentage of Wealth Held in Each Category

Year	Top 10%	Top 20%	Mid 40%	Bottom 40%	N
1746	22.8	38.4	41.6	20.1	346
1757	23.2	38.8	40.9	20.2	289
1770	26.7	42.7	39.2	18.0	292

[Key: Gross is estimating who owned the wealth in Concord. For example, "Top 10%"=amount of wealth and resources owned by wealthiest 10%. N=size of sample, or number of individuals included in the survey.]

Questions

1. *What was the relationship between ideals and practice in colonial politics? Did Munford's candidates live up to the standards of patriotism, integrity, and unselfishness that William Livingston and Landon Carter outlined?*
2. *What changed between John Winthrop's discussion of the relationship between authority and liberty in 1645 and Jonathan Mayhew's sermon on the same subject in 1750? Both used the metaphor of a father's authority within the family to describe the relationship between the rulers and the ruled; how did they apply the metaphor differently?*
3. *How democratic was colonial American society? Who voted? Who served in office? Did this change over time? Did the freeholders in The Candidates influence policy in Virginia?*
4. *Does the right to vote translate automatically to democracy? What would Devereux Jarratt think?*
5. *Do the statistics on wealth and officeholding confirm or contradict Crèvecoeur's view of America?*

FURTHER READING

Bernard Bailyn's The Origins of American Politics *(New York, 1968) describes the relationship between royal officials and the colonial assemblies and discusses the extent and limits of elite political power. Gordon S. Wood's* The Creation of the American Republic, 1776–1787 *(Chapel Hill, 1969) offers an excellent analysis of the meaning of the British Constitution and describes the "whig science of politics"—Anglo-American theories of the relationship between power and liberty, balance and stability. For popular and urban politics see Gary Nash's study of Philadelphia, New York, and Boston in the eighteenth century,* The Urban Crucible: Social Change, Political Consciousness, and the Origins of the American Revolution *(Cambridge, Massachusetts, 1979). Patricia Bonomi's* A Factious People: Politics and Society in Colonial New York *(New York, 1971) explores the distinct political culture of New York.*

The Radicalism of the American Revolution

Saul Cornell

Introduction

Americans have debated the meaning of the Revolution for more than two hundred years. Was the Revolution "a war for home rule, or a war for who should rule at home?" For those scholars who believe that the break with Britain was merely a colonial war for independence, the Revolution has been portrayed as hardly revolutionary. In the case of those scholars who believe that the challenge to British authority was part of a broader social and political transformation, the Revolution appears as a distinctly revolutionary event.

Historians have explored many different aspects of the Revolution. The political and constitutional ideas of the Revolution have been analyzed in great detail. The Revolution has also produced a large body of scholarship devoted to exploring "history from the bottom up." In contrast to traditional political and constitutional history, history from the bottom up focuses on the experience of non-elite groups, including artisans, farmers, women, and slaves. The Revolution did not mean the same thing to all Americans. Nor did the Revolution have the same impact on all groups in American society. Given the complexity of the revolutionary experience, it is easy to understand why scholars would be divided when asked to assess the radicalism of the Revolution.

Revolutionary Rhetoric and Reality

One way of measuring the revolutionary character of the events of 1776 is to consider the nature of the social change brought about by Americans. Studies of the American Revolution have used other social upheavals like the English Revolution, the French Revolution, or the Russian Revolution as a yardstick against which the events of 1776 should be judged. In all of these European revolutions there was an ideological challenge to the ideals of aristocracy and monarchy. In each of these historical episodes a revolutionary ideology emerged that championed some form of political and social equality. In all of these revolutions the effort to implement these ideals also resulted in profound and rapid social change.

Another way of exploring the meaning of the Revolution is to consider the relationship between the ideals of the Revolution and the political and economic changes that accompanied the break with Britain. In the Declaration of Independence, Jefferson asserted that:

> *[A]ll men are created equal, that they are endowed by their Creator with certain unalienable Rights, that among these are Life, Liberty, and the pursuit of Happiness—That, to secure these rights, Governments are instituted among Men, deriving their just powers from the consent of the governed,—That whenever any Form of Government becomes destructive of these ends, it is the Right of the People to alter or to abolish it, and to institute new Government. . . .*

To evaluate the degree to which revolutionary rhetoric translated into reality one might begin by asking how radical were Jefferson's claims in the Declaration. The next question that needs to be considered is to what extent did the Revolution fulfill the promise of Jefferson's words. The selections that follow provide several different perspectives on these important questions.

Property and the Right to Vote

Patriot leader John Adams was among the most influential political theorists of the revolutionary generation. His pamphlet, Thoughts on Government, *helped define the principles of republican government for Americans. Adams was an avid and prolific correspondent. Like so many of his generation, he used his personal correspondence to explore important political issues of the day. In his letter to John Sullivan, Adams makes clear the republican idea that ownership of property ought to be a prerequisite for the exercise of the right to vote. Abridged from* Papers of John Adams, *ed. Robert J. Taylor (Cambridge, Massachusetts, 1979), 4:208, 210–12.*

Philadelphia May. 26. 1776

Dear Sir

. . . It is certain in Theory, that the only moral Foundation of Government is the Consent of the People. But to what an Extent Shall We carry this Principle? Shall We Say, that every Individual of the Community, old and young, male and female, as well as rich and poor, must consent, expressly to every Act of Legislation? No, you will Say. This is impossible. How then does the Right arise in the Majority to govern the Minority, against their Will? Whence arises the Right of the Men to govern Women, without their Consent? Whence the Right of the old to bind the Young, without theirs.

But let us first Suppose, that the whole Community of every Age, Rank, Sex, and Condition, has a Right to vote. This Community, is assembled—a Motion is made and carried by a Majority of one Voice. The Minority will not agree to this. Whence arises the Right of the Majority to govern, and the Obligation of the Minority to obey? from Necessity, you will Say, because there can be no other Rule. But why exclude Women? You will Say, because their Delicacy renders them unfit for Practice and Experience, in the great Business of Life, and the hardy Enterprizes of War, as well as the arduous Cares of State. Besides, their attention is So much engaged with the necessary Nurture of their Children, that Nature has made them fittest for domestic Cares. And Children have not Judgment or Will of their own. True. But will not these Reasons apply to others? Is it not equally true, that Men in general in every Society, who are wholly destitute of Property, are also too little acquainted with public Affairs to form a Right Judgment, and too dependent upon other Men to have a Will of their own? If this is a Fact, if you give to every Man, who has no Property, a Vote, will you not make a fine encouraging Provision for Corruption by your fundamental Law? Such is the Frailty of the human Heart, that very few Men, who have no Property, have any Judgment of their own. They talk and vote as they are directed by Some Man of Property, who has attached their Minds to his Interest. . . .

Harrington has Shewn that Power always follows Property. This I believe to be as infallible a Maxim, in Politicks, as, that Action and Re-action are equal, is in Mechanicks. Nay I believe We may advance one Step farther and affirm that the Ballance of Power in a Society, accompanies the Ballance of Property in Land. The only possible Way then of preserving the Ballance of Power on the side of equal Liberty and public Virtue, is to make the Acquisition of Land easy to every Member of Society: to make a Division of the Land into Small Quantities, So that the Multitude may be possessed of landed Estates. If the Multitude is possessed of the Ballance of real Estate, the Multitude will have the Ballance of Power, and in that Case the Multitude will take Care of the Liberty, Virtue, and Interest of the Multitude in all Acts of Government. . . .

The Same Reasoning, which will induce you to admit all Men, who have no Property, to vote, . . . will prove that you ought to admit Women and Children: for generally Speaking, Women and Children, have as good Judgment, and as independent Minds as those Men who are wholly destitute of Property: these last being to all Intents and Purposes as much dependent upon others, who will please to feed, cloath, and employ them, as Women are upon their Husbands, or Children on their Parents. . . .

Depend upon it, sir, it is dangerous to open So fruitfull a Source of Controversy and Altercation, as would be opened by attempting to alter the Qualifications of Voters. There will be no End of it. New Claims will arise. Women will demand a Vote. Lads from 12 to 21 will think their Rights not enough attended to, and every Man, who has not a Farthing, will demand an equal Voice with any other in all Acts of State. It tends to confound and destroy all Distinctions, and prostrate all Ranks, to one common Levell.

The Problem of Women's Suffrage

The logic of Adams's argument excluded women who were not property owners from the vote. But what of widows, the group of women who did own property? In this letter, patriot Richard Henry Lee discusses the possibility of allowing suffrage for widows. In the case of widows the connection between the right to vote and the ownership of property need not have presented a barrier to their participation. This contradiction did not go unnoticed by women at the time, as this letter to Mrs. Hannah Corbin suggests. While female suffrage was hardly common in this period, the state constitution New Jersey adopted enfranchised "all free inhabitants." Women voted in New Jersey until an explicit prohibition on female voting was enacted in 1807. Excerpted from The Letters of Richard Henry Lee, *ed. James Curtis Ballagh (New York, 1911), 1:392–93.*

[March 17, 1778]

You complain that widows are not represented. . . . The doctrine of representation is a large subject, and it is certain that it ought to be extended as far as wisdom and policy can allow; nor do I see that either of these forbid widows having property from voting, notwithstanding it has never been the practice either here or in England. Perhaps 'twas thought rather out of character for women to press into those tumultuous assemblages of men where the business of choosing representatives is conducted. And it might also have been considered as not so necessary, seeing that the representatives themselves, as their immediate constituents, must suffer the tax imposed in exact proportion as does all other property taxed, and that, therefore, it could not be supposed that taxes would be laid where the public good did not demand it. This, then, is the widow's security as well as that of the never married women, who have lands in their own right, for both of whom I have the highest respect, and would at any time give my consent to establish their right of voting. . . . When we complained of British taxation we did so with much reason, and there is great difference between our case and that of the unrepresented in this country. The English Parliament nor their representatives would pay a farthing of the tax they imposed on us but quite otherwise. . . . Oppressions, therefore, without end and taxes without reason or public necessity would have been our fate had we submitted to British usurpation.

The Problem of Slavery

During the bicentennial of the U.S. Constitution, Justice Thurgood Marshall, the first African American to serve on the Supreme Court, shocked many when he attacked the Founding Fathers' support for the institution of slavery. Marshall was hardly the first person to notice the inconsistency between the ideals of the Revolution and the existence of chattel slavery. The English literary figure Samuel Johnson mocked the sincerity of the patriot cause when he wrote, "How is it that we hear the loudest yelps for liberty among the drivers of Negroes?" In Massachusetts a number of slaves were inspired by the rhetoric of the revolutionary ferment to petition for their freedom. This document provides a glimpse into how the rhetoric of the Revolution was interpreted by those enslaved, not by the arbitrary acts of Parliament, but by the acts of American citizens. In New England and parts of the middle-Atlantic states the institution of slavery was gradually eliminated after the Revolution. Slavery was abolished in the Vermont Constitution of 1777. In 1780 the Supreme Court of Massachusetts ruled that slavery was incompatible with the state constitution's claim that "all men are born free and equal." Pennsylvania (1780), Connecticut (1784), and Rhode Island (1784) all enacted laws that freed children born to slave parents. In the South, the institution of slavery continued to remain an integral part of the social and political order. Taken from "To his Excellency Thomas Gage . . .," May 25, 1774, Collections of the Massachusetts Historical Society, *5th Series, (Boston, 1877), 3:432–33.*

The Petition of a Grate Number of Blackes . . .

Humbly Shewing

That your Petitioners apprehind we have in common with all other men a naturel right to our freedoms without Being depriv'd of them by our fellow men as we are a freeborn Pepel and have never forfeited this Blessing by aney compact or agreement whatever. But we were unjustly dragged by the cruel hand of power from our dearest frinds and sum of us stolen from the bosoms of our tender Parents and from a Populous Pleasant and plentiful country and Brought hither to be made slaves for Life in a Christian land. Thus are we deprived of every thing that hath a tendency to make life even tolerable, the endearing ties of husband and wife we are strangers to for we are no longer man and wife then our masters or mestreses thinkes proper. . . . Our children are also taken from us by force and sent maney miles from us. . . . Thus our lives are imbittered to us on these accounts. . . . We therfor Bage [beg] your Excellency and Honours will give this its deu weight and consideration and that you will accordingly cause an act of the legislative to be pessed that we may obtain our Natural right our freedoms.

A Radical Defense of Democracy

The anonymous author of the following pamphlet articulated one of the most egalitarian defenses of democracy written during the Revolution. The pamphlet attacked the argument that property and the suffrage ought to be linked. Excerpted from Anon., The People the Best Governors: or A Plan of Government Founded on the Just Principles of Natural Freedom *(1776), 9–10.*

The question now . . . arises what it is that ought to be the qualification of a representative? In answer we observe, that fear is the principle of a despotic, honour of a kingly, and virtue is the principle of a republican government.—Social virtue and knowledge, I say then, is the best, and only necessary qualification of the person before us. But it will be said, that an estate of two hundred, four hundred pounds, or some other sum is essential. . . . [W]hat will then be come of the genuine principle of freedom? This notion of an estate has the directed tendency to set up the avaricious over the heads of the poor, though the latter are ever so virtuous. Let it not be said in future generations, that money was made by the founders of the American states, an essential qualification in the rulers of a free people.

Virginians Assert Their Rights

The 1776 Virginia "Declaration of Rights," drafted in large part by George Mason, served as a model of the bills of rights that were prefaced to a number of state constitutions. The "Declaration of Rights" not only affirms the ideals of liberty but also states in clear terms the essential principles of republicanism upon which American constitutional government would be based. Excerpted from The Papers of George Mason, 1725–1792, *ed. Robert A. Rutland (Chapel Hill, 1970), 1:287–89.*

A DECLARATION OF RIGHTS made by the Representatives of the good people of VIRGINIA, assembled in full and free Convention; which rights do pertain to (them and their) posterity, as the basis and foundation of Government.

1. That all men are (by nature) equally free and independent, and have certain inherent rights, of which, (when they enter into a state of society,) they cannot, by any compact, deprive or divest their posterity; (namely,) the enjoyment of life and liberty, with the means of acquiring and possessing property, and pursuing and obtaining happiness and safety.
2. That all power is vested in, and consequently derived from, the People; that magistrates are their trustees and servants, and at all times amenable to them.
3. That Government is, or ought to be, instituted for the common benefit, protection, and security of the people, nation, or community;—Of all the various modes and forms of Government that is best which is capable of producing the greatest degree of happiness and safety, and is most effectually secured against the danger of mal-administration;—And that, whenever any Government shall be found inadequate or contrary to these purposes, a majority of the community hath an indubitable, unalienable, and indefeasible right, to reform, alter, or abolish it, in such manner as shall be judged most conducive to the publick weal.
4. That no man, or set of men, are entitled to exclusive or separate emoluments and privileges from the community, but in consideration of publick services; which,

not being descendible, (neither ought the offices) of Magistrate, Legislator, or Judge, (to be hereditary).

5. That the Legislative and Executive powers of the State should be separate and distinct from the judicative; and, that the members of the two first may be restrained from oppression, by feeling and participating the burdens of the people, they should, at fixed periods, be reduced to a private station, return into that body from which they were originally taken, and the vacancies be supplied by frequent, certain, and regular elections, (in which all, or any part of the former members, to be again eligible, or ineligible, as the laws shall direct).
6. That elections of members to serve as Representatives of the people, in Assembly, ought to be free; and that all men, having sufficient evidence of permanent common interest with, and attachment to, the community, have the right of suffrage, (and cannot be taxed or deprived of their property for) publick uses without their own consent or that of their Representative (so elected,) nor bound by any law to which they have not, in like manner assented, for the publick good.
7. That all power of suspending laws, or the execution of laws, by any authority, without consent of the Representatives of the people, is injurious to their rights, and ought not to be exercised.
8. That in all capital or criminal prosecutions a man hath a right to demand the cause and nature of his accusation, to be confronted with the accusers and witnesses, to call for evidence in his favour, and to a speedy trial by an impartial jury of his vicinage, without whose unanimous consent he cannot be found guilty, nor can he be compelled to give evidence against himself; that no man be deprived of his liberty except by the law of the land, or the judgment of his peers.
9. That excessive bail ought not to be required, nor excessive fines imposed, nor cruel and unusual punishments inflicted.
10. That (general) warrants, whereby any officer or messenger may be commanded to search suspected places (without evidence of a fact committed,) or to seize any person or persons (not named or whose offence is) not

particularly described (and supported by evidence,) are grievous and oppressive, and ought not to be granted.

11. That in controversies respecting property, and in suits between man and man, the ancient trial by Jury is preferable to any other, and ought to be held sacred.
12. That the freedom of the Press is one of the greatest bulwarks of liberty, and can never be restrained but by despotick Governments.
13. That a well-regulated Militia, composed of the body of the people, trained to arms, is the proper, natural, and safe defence of a free State; that Standing Armies, in time of peace, should be avoided as dangerous to liberty; and that, in all cases, the military should be under strict subordination to, and governed by, the civil power.
14. That the people have a right to uniform Government; and, therefore, that no Government separate from, or independent of, the Government of *Virginia,* ought to be erected or established within the limits thereof.
15. That no free Government, or the blessing of liberty, can be preserved to any people but by a firm adherence to justice, moderation, temperance, frugality, and virtue, and by frequent recurrence to fundamental principles.
16. That Religion, or the duty which we owe to our *Creator,* and the manner of discharging it, can be directed only by reason and conviction, not by force or violence; and, therefore, all men (are equally entitled to the free) exercise of religion, according to the dictates of conscience; and that it is the mutual duty of all to practise Christian forbearance, love, and charity, towards each other.

Changes in Suffrage and Voting Behavior

The information presented in the first set of tables shows the change in property requirements enacted by four states during the revolutionary era. The data in the second table provides information about the economic status of individuals elected to the lower houses of the various states both before and after the Revolution.

Property Requirements for Voting and Officeholding

Virginia

	1762 election law, reaffirmed in 1769	1776 constitution
HOUSE		
electors	fr. of 25 acres with 12' x 12' house; or fr. of 50 acres unsettled; or town lot with 12' x 12' house *Housekeepers in Williamsburg and Norfolk could also vote if they had served to any trade for 5 years.*	"the right of suffrage . . . shall remain as exercised at present"
candidates		freeholder, or otherwise "duly qualified according to law"

Pennsylvania

	1706 election law	1776 constitution
HOUSE		
electors	fr. of 50 acres, 12 acres thereof "seated and cleared," or pers. est. worth £50 clear of debts	taxpayer, or son of freeholder
candidates	same as electors	

New York

	1699 election law	1777 constitution
HOUSE		
electors	fr. worth £40 free of debts, or being a freeman of the corporation of Albany or the city of New York	fr. worth £20, or rented real est. worth 40s. per year
candidates	fr. worth £40 free of debts	

Massachusetts

	1691 charter	1780 constitution
HOUSE		
electors	fr. worth 40s. per year, or pers. est. worth £40	est. worth £60 or fr. worth £3 per year
candidates		est. worth £200, or fr. worth £100

Economic Status of Representatives to the Lower House Before and After the Revolution

	N.H., N.Y., and N.J.		Md., Va., and S.C.	
	Prewar (percentages)	Postwar (percentages)	Prewar (percentages)	Postwar (percentages)
Wealthy	36	12	52	28
Well-to-do	47	26	36	42
Moderate	17	62	12	30

Adapted from "Government by the People: The American Revolution and the Democratization of the Legislatures," by Jackson Turner Main. Reprinted from The William and Mary Quarterly, 3d. ser., Vol. 23, July 1966, pp. 405.

Questions

1. *Why would men like Adams believe that republican government could not survive if the right to vote was not tied to the ownership of property?*
2. *What do the struggles of women and African Americans tell us about the meaning of the Revolution?*
3. *What, if anything, is radical about the argument of the author of The People the Best Governors?*
4. *Does the information about the changes in suffrage and voting behavior support or refute the claim that the Revolution accomplished a radical change in American government and society?*

Further Reading

Gordon S. Wood's analysis of revolutionary ideas in The Creation of the American Republic, 1776–1787 *(Chapel Hill, 1969), focuses on changing ideas about republican government in the period between the Revolution and the adoption of the Constitution. Linda K. Kerber explores the impact of republicanism on women's roles in* Women of the Republic: Intellect and Ideology in Revolutionary America *(Chapel Hill, 1980). Ira Berlin and Ronald Hoffman's edited volume* Slavery and Freedom in the Age of the American Revolution *(Charlottesville, 1983), traces the impact of the Revolution on the lives of African Americans, including the experiences of slaves and free men and women. Edward Countryman's synthetic account of the Revolution charts the diverse experiences of Americans, and is especially sensitive to how issues of race, class, and gender influenced people's experiences during this period of American history;* The American Revolution *(New York, 1985). See also Gordon S. Wood,* The Radicalism of the American Revolution *(New York, 1992).*

The Struggle over the Constitution: Federalists vs. Anti-Federalists

Saul Cornell

Introduction

The publication of the Constitution prompted Americans from all walks of life to participate in a lively public debate over the meaning of republican government and the nature of constitutionalism. The meaning of the Constitution has been debated since it was first proposed more than two hundred years ago. While most Americans today venerate the Constitution, there was substantial opposition to the Constitution when it was first proposed.

Three issues dominated the debate over ratification: the absence of a bill of rights, the meaning of federalism, and the role of democracy in the new government. The Philadelphia Convention that proposed the Constitution did not include a basic declaration of rights. The Bill of Rights was only added during the First Congress and might never have been added had not Anti-Federalists demanded substantial amendments. Apart from the controversy over the absence of a bill of rights, Federalists and Anti-Federalists argued over the scope of power ceded to the new government. This debate raised questions about the distribution of authority between the states and the new federal government. Another controversial issue was the Anti-Federalist claim that the constitution created an aristocratic government. Federalists disputed this charge and defended the republican character of the new government.

No essay produced during this controversy has exerted a more profound impact on subsequent generations than The Federalist. *Judges and lawyers routinely consult* The Federalist *for insights into the original meaning of the Constitution. While Federalists may have won the battle over ratification, Anti-Feder-*

alist concerns have shaped the language of dissent within the American constitutional tradition. Jeffersonian and Jacksonian thought each owed a significant debt to Anti-Federalist ideas. In contemporary America, their ideas have been rediscovered by the political right and left, who have been drawn to different aspects of Anti-Federalist thought.

Debating and Ratifying the Constitution

Interpreting a document as complex as the Constitution has proven to be an exceedingly difficult task for historians, political scientists, and judges. The debate over ratification involved hundreds of delegates to state conventions and thousands of voters, as well as countless essays and letters, some of which were published in the press and others of which circulated in private. The documents below illustrate some of the sources that historians have used either to prove or refute the claim that the Constitution represented a rejection of the Revolution's principles.

Hamilton Introduces the Federalist Argument

The Federalist Papers were published pseudonymously under the pen name of Publius. By choosing to sign the essays with a name drawn from classical antiquity, the true authors of the essays, Alexander Hamilton, John Jay, and James Madison, hoped to impress readers with their commitment to the ideals of republicanism. The following is the first installment of The Federalist. *Taken from Alexander Hamilton, "The Federalist No. 1" in* The Federalist: A Commentary on the Constitution of the United States, *ed. Paul Leicester Ford (New York, 1898), 1-7.*

October 27, 1787

To the People of the State of New York:

After an unequivocal experience of the inefficiency of the subsisting federal government, you are called upon to deliberate

THE

FEDERALIST:

ADDRESSED TO THE

PEOPLE OF THE STATE OF NEW-YORK.

NUMBER I.

Introduction.

AFTER an unequivocal experience of the ineffi-cacy of the ſubſiſting federal government, you are called upon to deliberate on a new conſtitution for the United States of America. The ſubject ſpeaks its own importance; comprehending in its conſequences, nothing leſs than the exiſtence of the UNION, the ſafety and welfare of the parts of which it is compoſed, the fate of an empire, in many reſpects, the moſt intereſting in the world. It has been frequently remarked, that it ſeems to have been reſerved to the people of this country, by their conduct and example, to decide the important queſtion, whether ſocieties of men are really capable or not, of eſtabliſhing good government from reflection and choice, or whether they are forever deſtined to depend, for their political conſtitutions, on accident and force. If there be any truth in the remark. the criſis, at which we are arrived, may with propriety be regarded as the æra in which

A that

A page of The Federalist *encouraging ratification of the new United States Constitution. (Courtesy of the Library of Congress.)*

on a new Constitution for the United States of America. The subject speaks its own importance; comprehending in its consequences nothing less than the existence of the UNION, the safety and welfare of the parts of which it is composed, the fate of an empire in many respects the most interesting in the world. It has been frequently remarked that it seems to have been reserved to the people of this country, by their conduct and example, to decide the important question, whether societies of men are really capable or not of establishing good government from reflection and choice, or whether they are forever destined to depend for their political constitutions on accident and force. If there be any truth in the remark, the crisis at which we are arrived may with propriety be regarded as the era in which that decision is to be made; and a wrong election of the part we shall act may, in this view, deserve to be considered as the general misfortune of mankind.

This idea will add the inducements of philanthropy to those of patriotism, to heighten the solicitude which all considerate and good men must feel for the event. Happy will it be if our choice should be directed by a judicious estimate of our true interests, unperplexed and unbiased by considerations not connected with the public good. But this is a thing more ardently to be wished than seriously to be expected. The plan offered to our deliberations affects too many particular interests, innovates upon too many local institutions, not to involve in its discussion a variety of objects foreign to its merits, and of views, passions, and prejudices little favorable to the discovery of truth.

Among the most formidable of the obstacles which the new Constitution will have to encounter may readily be distinguished the obvious interest of a certain class of men in every State to resist all changes which may hazard a diminution of the power, emolument, and consequence of the offices they hold under the State establishments; and the perverted ambition of another class of men, who will either hope to aggrandize themselves by the confusions of their country, or will flatter themselves with fairer prospects of elevation from the subdivision of the empire into several partial confederacies than from its union under one government.

It is not, however, my design to dwell upon observations of this nature. I am well aware that it would be disingenuous to resolve indiscriminately the opposition of any set of men (merely because their situations might subject them to suspicion) into interested or ambitious views. Candor will oblige us to admit that even such men may be actuated by upright intentions; and it cannot be doubted that much of the opposition which has made its appearance, or may hereafter make its appearance, will spring from sources, blameless, at least, if not respectable—the honest errors of minds led astray by preconceived jealousies and fears. So numerous indeed and so powerful are the causes which serve to give a false bias to the judgment, that we, upon many occasions, see wise and good men on the wrong as well as on the right side of questions of the first magnitude to society. This circumstance, if duly attended to, would furnish a lesson of moderation to those who are ever so much persuaded of their being in the right in any controversy. And a further reason for caution, in this respect, might be drawn from the reflection that we are not always sure that those who advocate the truth are influenced by purer principles than their antagonists. Ambition, avarice, personal animosity, party opposition, and many other motives not more laudable than these, are apt to operate as well upon those who support as those who oppose the right side of a question. Were there not even these inducements to moderation, nothing could be more ill-judged than that intolerant spirit which has, at all times, characterized political parties. For in politics, as in religion, it is equally absurd to aim at making proselytes by fire and sword. Heresies in either can rarely be cured by persecution.

And yet, however just these sentiments will be allowed to be, we have already sufficient indications that it will happen in this as in all former cases of great national discussion. A torrent of angry and malignant passions will be let loose. To judge from the conduct of the opposite parties, we shall be led to conclude that they will mutually hope to evince the justness of their opinions, and to increase the number of their converts by the loudness of their declamations and by the bitterness of their invectives. An enlightened zeal for the energy and efficiency of government will be stigmatized as the offspring of a temper fond of despotic power and hostile to the principles of liberty. An overscrupulous jealousy of danger to the rights of the people, which is more commonly the fault of the head than of the heart, will be represented as mere pretense and artifice, the stale bait for popularity at the expense of the public good. It will be forgotten, on the one hand, that jealousy is the usual concomitant of love, and that the noble enthusiasm of liberty is apt to be infected with a spirit of narrow and illiberal distrust. On the other hand, it will be equally forgotten that the vigor of government is essential to the security of liberty; that, in the contemplation of a sound and well-informed judgment, their interest can never be separated; and that a dangerous ambition more often lurks behind the specious mask of zeal for the rights of the people than under the forbidding appearance of zeal for the firmness and efficiency of government. History will teach us that the former has been found a much more certain road to the introduction of despotism than the latter, and that of those men who have overturned the liberties of republics, the greatest number have begun their career by paying an obsequious court to the people; commencing demagogues, and ending tyrants.

In the course of the preceding observations, I have had an eye, my fellow-citizens, to putting you upon your guard against all attempts, from whatever quarter, to influence your decision in a matter of the utmost moment to your welfare, by any impressions other than those which may result from the evidence of truth. You will, no doubt, at the same time have collected from the general scope of them, that they proceed from a source not unfriendly to the new Constitution. Yes, my countrymen, I own to you that, after having given it an attentive consideration, I am clearly of opinion it is your interest to adopt it. I am convinced that this is the safest course for your liberty, your dignity, and your happiness. I affect not reserves which I do not feel. I will not amuse you with an appearance of deliberation when I have decided. I frankly acknowledge to you my convictions, and I will freely lay before you the reasons on which they are founded. The consciousness of good intentions disdains ambiguity. I shall not, however, multiply professions on his head. My motives must remain in the depository of my own breast. My arguments will be open to all, and may be judged of by all. They shall at least be offered in a spirit which will not disgrace the cause of truth.

I propose, in a series of papers, to discuss the following interesting particulars:—*The utility of the UNION to your political prosperity—The insufficiency of the present Confederation to preserve that Union—The necessity of a government at least equally energetic with the one proposed, to the attainment of this object—The conformity of the proposed Constitution to the true principles of republican government—Its analogy to your own State constitution*—and lastly, *The additional security which its adoption will afford to the preservation of that species of government, to liberty, and to property.*

In the progress of this discussion I shall endeavor to give a satisfactory answer to all the objections which shall have made their appearance, that may seem to have any claim to your attention. . . .

PUBLIUS.

The Virginia Ratification Debates

The contest for ratification of the Constitution was closely fought. The selection below is from the debates in the constitutional convention of Virginia, which ratified the Constitution in June 1788 by a vote of 89 to 79. The Anti-Federalist position is aired first. Excerpted from The Debates, Resolutions, and Other Proceedings, in Convention, on the adoption of the Federal Constitution . . . *(Washington, 1828), 2:46–47, 56–58.*

Mr. HENRY.—Mr. Chairman, the public mind, as well as my own, is extremely uneasy at the proposed change of government. . . . I consider myself as the servant of the people of this commonwealth, as a centinel over their rights, liberty, and happiness. I represent their feelings, when I say, that they are exceedingly uneasy, being brought from that state of full security, which they enjoyed, to the present delusive appearance of things. A year ago, the mind of our citizens were at perfect repose. Before the meeting of the late federal convention at Philadelphia, a general peace, and an universal tranquillity prevailed in this country; but, since that period, they are exceedingly uneasy and disquieted. When I wished for an appointment to this convention, my mind was extremely agitated for the situation of public affairs. I conceive the republic to be in extreme danger. If our situation be thus uneasy, whence has arisen this fearful jeopardy? It arises from this fatal system—it arises from a proposal to change our government—a proposal that goes to the utter annihilation of the most solemn engagements of the states; a proposal of establishing nine states into a confederacy, to the eventual exclusion of four states. . . . Was our civil polity, or public justice, endangered or sapped: Was the real existence of the country threatened—or was this preceded by a mournful progression of events? This proposal of altering our federal government is of a most alarming nature: make the best of this new government—say it is composed by any thing but inspiration—you ought to be extremely cautious, watchful, jealous of your liberty; for instead of securing your rights, you may lose them forever. If a wrong step be now made, the republic may be lost forever. If this new government will not come up to the expectation of the people, and they should be disappointed—their liberty will be lost, and tyranny must and will arise. I repeat it again, and I beg gentlemen to consider, that a wrong step made now will plunge us into misery, and our republic will be lost. . . . I have the highest veneration for those gentlemen; but, sir, give me leave to demand, what right had they to say, *We, the People?* My political curiosity, exclusive of my anxious solicitude for the public welfare, leads me to ask, who authorized them to speak the language of, *We, the People,* instead of *We, the States?* States are the characteristics, and the soul of a confederation. If the states be not the agents of this compact, it must be one great consolidated national government, of the people of all the states. I have the highest respect for those gentlemen who formed the convention, and were some of them not here, I would express some testimonial of esteem for them. America had on a former occasion put the utmost confidence in them; a confidence which was well placed: and I am sure, sir, I would give up any thing to them; I would cheerfully confide in them as my representatives. But, sir, on this great occasion, I would demand the cause of their conduct. . . . The people gave them no power to use their name. That they exceeded their power is perfectly clear. . . .

[Next the Federalist view was articulated.]

Mr. PENDLETON.—Mr. Chairman, my worthy friend (Mr. HENRY) has expressed great uneasiness in his mind, and informed us, that a great many of our citizens are also extremely uneasy, at the proposal of changing our government: but that a year ago, before this fatal system was thought of, the public mind was at perfect repose. It is necessary to inquire, whether the public mind was at ease on the subject, and if it be since disturbed, what was the cause? What was the situation of this country, before the meeting of the federal convention? Our general government was totally inadequate to the purpose of its institution; our commerce decayed; our finances deranged; public and private credit destroyed: these and many other national evils, rendered necessary the meeting of that convention. If the public mind was then at ease, it did not result from a conviction of being in a happy and easy situation: it must have been an inactive unaccountable stupor. The federal convention devised the paper on your table, as a remedy to remove our political diseases. What has created the public uneasiness since? Not public reports, which are not to be depended upon; but mistaken apprehensions of danger, drawn from observations on governments which do not apply to us. When we come to inquire into the origin of most governments of the world, we shall find, that they are generally dictated by a conqueror at the point of the sword, or are the offspring of confusion, when a great popular leader taking advantage of circumstances, if not producing them, restores order at the expence of liberty, and becomes the tyrant over the people. It may well be supposed, that in forming a government of this sort, it will not be favourable to liberty: the conqueror will take care of his own emoluments, and have little concern for the interest of the people. In either case, the interest and ambition of a despot, and not the good of the people, have given the tone to the government. A government thus formed, must necessarily create a continual war between the governors and governed. Writers consider the two parties (the people and tyrants) as in a state of perpetual warfare, and sounded the alarm to the people. But what is our case? We are perfectly free from sedition and war: we are not yet in confusion: we are left to consider our real happiness and security: we want to secure these objects: we know they cannot be attained without government. Is there a single man in this committee of a contrary opinion?. . . There is no quarrel between government and liberty; the former is the shield and protector of the latter. The war is between government and licentiousness, faction, turbulence, and other violations of the rules of society, to preserve liberty. Where is the cause of alarm? We, the people, possessing all power, form a government, such as we think will secure happiness: and suppose in adopting this plan we should be mistaken in the end; where is the cause of alarm on that quarter? In the same plan we point out an easy and quiet method of reforming what may be found amiss. . . .

But an objection is made to the form: the expression, We, the people, is thought improper. Permit me to ask the gentleman, who made this objection, who but the people can delegate powers? Who but the people have a right to form government? The expression is a common one, and a favorite one with me: the representatives of the people, by their authority, is a mode wholly inessential. If the objection be, that the union ought to be not of the people, but of the state governments, then I think the choice of the former, very happy and proper.—What have the state governments to do with it? . . . It has been said that it has carried us through a dangerous war to a happy issue. Not that confederation, but common danger and the spirit of America, were the bonds of our union: union and unanimity, and not that insignificant paper, carried us through that dangerous war. "United, we stand—divided, we fall!" echoed and re-echoed through America, from congress to the drunken carpenter; was effectual, and procured the end of our wishes, though now forgot by gentlemen, if such there be, who incline to let go this strong hold, to catch at feathers; for such all substituted projects may prove.

This spirit had nearly reached the end of its power when relieved by peace. It was the spirit of America, and not the confederation, that carried us through the war: thus I prove it. The moment of peace showed the imbecility of the federal government: . . . The inefficacy of the general government warranted an idea that we had no government at all. Improvements were proposed and agreed to by twelve states, but were interrupted, because the little state of Rhode Island refused to accede to them; this was a further proof of the imbecility of that government; need I multiply instances to shew that it is wholly ineffectual for the purposes of its institution? Its whole progress since the peace proves it.

The Federalist Defense of the Constitution

James Madison provided one of the most intellectually sophisticated defenses of the Constitution. Madison's argument has since become a classic statement of American constitutional principles. The following is excerpted from James Madison, "Federalist No. 10," in The Federalist: A Commentary on the Constitution of the United States, *ed. Paul Leicester Ford (New York, 1898), 54–60, 62–63.*

November 22, 1787

To the People of the State of New York

Among the numerous advantages promised by a well-constructed Union, none deserves to be more accurately developed than its tendency to break and control the violence of faction.... Complaints are everywhere heard from our most considerate and virtuous citizens, equally the friends of public and private faith and of public and personal liberty, that our governments are too unstable, that the public good is disregarded in the conflicts of rival parties, and that measures are too often decided, not according to the rules of justice and the rights of the minor party, but by the superior force of an interested and overbearing majority....

By a faction I understand a number of citizens, whether amounting to a majority or minority of the whole, who are united and actuated by some common impulse of passion, or of interest, adverse to the rights of other citizens, or to the permanent and aggregate interests of the community....

There are again two methods of removing the causes of faction: the one, by destroying the liberty which is essential to its existence; the other, by giving to every citizen the same opinions, the same passions, and the same interests....

The latent causes of faction are thus sown in the nature of man; and we see them everywhere brought into different degrees of activity, according to the different circumstances of civil society. A zeal for different opinions concerning religion, concerning government, and many other points, as well of speculation as of practice; an attachment to different leaders ambitiously contending for pre-eminence and power; or to persons of other descriptions whose fortunes have been interesting to the human passions, have, in turn, divided mankind into parties, inflamed them with mutual animosity, and rendered them much more disposed to vex and oppress each other than to co-operate for their common good. . . . But the most common and durable source of factions has been the various and unequal distribution of property. Those who hold and those who are without property have ever formed distinct interests in society. Those who are creditors, and those who are debtors, fall under a like discrimination. A landed interest, a manufacturing interest, a mercantile interest, a moneyed interest, with many lesser interests, grow up of necessity in civilized nations, and divide them into different classes actuated by different sentiments and views. The regulation of these various and interfering interests forms the principal task of modern legislation and involves the spirit of party and faction in the necessary and ordinary operations of the government. . . .

It is in vain to say that enlightened statesmen will be able to adjust these clashing interests and render them all subservient to the public good. Enlightened statesmen will not always be at the helm. . . .

The inference to which we are brought is that the *causes* of faction cannot be removed and that relief is only to be sought in the means of controlling its *effects*. . . .

By what means is this object attainable? Evidently by one of two only: Either the existence of the same passion or interest in a majority at the same time must be prevented, or the majority, having such coexistent passion or interest, must be rendered, by their number and local situation, unable to concert and carry into effect schemes of oppression. . . .

From this view of the subject it may be concluded that a pure democracy, by which I mean a society consisting of a small number of citizens, who assemble and administer the government in person, can admit of no cure for the mischiefs of faction. . . . Hence it is that such democracies have ever been spectacles of turbulence and contention; have ever been found incompatible with personal security or the rights of property; and have in general been as short in their lives as they have been violent in their deaths. . . .

A republic, by which I mean a government in which the scheme of representation takes place, opens a different prospect and promises the cure for which we are seeking. Let us examine the points in which it varies from pure democracy, and we shall comprehend both the nature of the cure and the efficacy which it must derive from the Union.

The two great points of difference between a democracy and a republic are: first, the delegation of the government in the latter, to a small number of citizens elected by the rest; secondly, the greater number of citizens and greater sphere of country over which the latter may be extended.

The effect of the first difference is, on the one hand, to refine and enlarge the public views by passing them through the medium of a chosen body of citizens, whose wisdom may best discern the true interest of their country and whose patriotism and love of justice will be least likely to sacrifice it to temporary or partial considerations. . . .

The other point of difference is the greater number of citizens and extent of territory which may be brought within the compass of republican than of democratic government; and it is this circumstance principally which renders factious combinations less to be dreaded in the former than in the latter. The smaller the society, the fewer probably will be the distinct parties and interests composing it; the fewer the distinct parties and interests, the more frequently will a majority be found of the same party; and the smaller the number of individuals composing a majority, and the smaller the compass within which they are placed, the more easily will they concert and execute their plans of oppression. Extend the sphere and you take in a greater variety of parties and interests; you make it less probable that a majority of the whole will have a common motive to invade the rights of other citizens; or if such a common motive exists, it will be more difficult for all who feel it to discover their own strength and to act in unison with each other. . . .

The influence of factious leaders may kindle a flame within their particular States but will be unable to spread a general conflagration through the other States. A religious sect may degenerate into a political faction in a part of the Confederacy; but the variety of sects dispersed over the entire face of it must secure the national councils against any danger from that source. A rage for paper money, for an abolition of debts, for an equal division of property, or for any other improper or wicked project, will be less apt to pervade the whole body of the Union than a particular member of it, in the same proportion as such a malady is more likely to taint a particular county or district than an entire State.

In the extent and proper structure of the Union, therefore, we behold a republican remedy for the diseases most incident to republican government. . . .

PUBLIUS.

The Anti-Federalist Critique of the Constitution

The Centinel essays were among the most widely reprinted Anti-Federalist attacks on the Constitution. Authored by Pennsylvania's Samuel Bryan, the essays rejected the calm disinterested tone favored by many Anti-Federalists in favor of a more polemical style. The following document is excerpted from The Documentary History of the Ratification of the Constitution, *vol. 13,* Commentaries on the Constitution: Public and Private, *ed. John P. Kaminski and Gaspare J. Saladino, (Madison, 1981), 1:332, 334–35.*

I shall now proceed to the examination of the (proposed plan of government, and I trust, shall make it appear to the meanest capacity, that it has none of the essential requisites of a free government; . . . that it is a most daring attempt to establish a despotic aristocracy among freemen, that the world has ever witnessed.) . . .

. . . [I]f the United States are to be melted down into one empire, it becomes you to consider, whether such a government, however constructed, would be eligible in so extended a territory; and whether it would be practicable, consistent with freedom? It is the opinion of the greatest writers, that a very extensive country cannot be governed on democratical principles, on any other plan, than a confederation of a number of small republics, possessing all the powers of internal government, but united in the management of their foreign and general concerns.

It would not be difficult to prove, that any thing short of despotism, could not bind so great a country under one government; and that whatever plan you might, at the first setting out, establish, it would issue in a despotism.

If one general government could be instituted and maintained on principles of freedom, it would not be so competent to attend to the various local concerns and wants, of every particular district; as well as the peculiar governments, who are nearer the scene, and possessed of superior means of information, besides, if the business of the *whole* union is to be managed by one government, there would not be time. Do we not already see, that the inhabitants in a number of larger states, who are remote from the seat of government, are loudly complaining of the inconveniencies and disadvantages they are subjected to on this account, and that, to enjoy the comforts of local government, they are separating into smaller divisions. . . .

Thus, we see, the house of representatives, are on the part of the people to balance the senate, who I suppose will be composed of the *better sort*, the *well born*, &c. The number of the representatives . . . appears to be too few, either to communicate the requisite information, of the wants, local circumstances and sentiments of so extensive an empire, or to prevent corruption and undue influence, in the exercise of such great powers.

Ratification Of The Federal Constitution 1787 - 1788

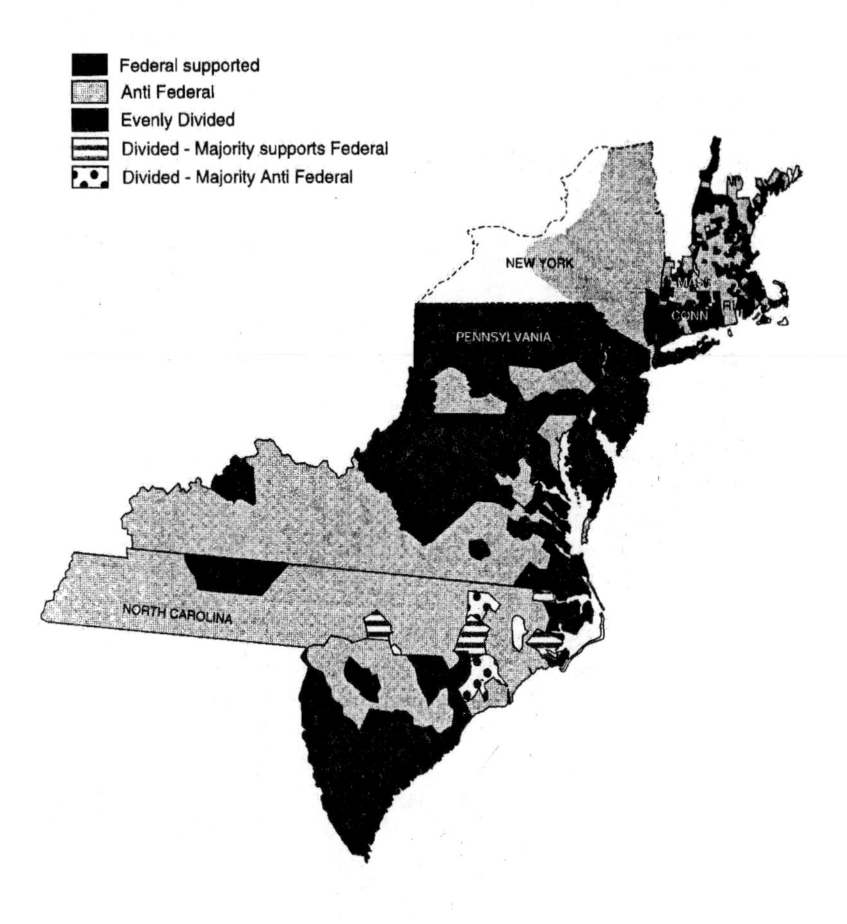

Reprinted from *The Other Founders: Antifederalism and the American Constitutional Tradition* by Saul Cornell (Chapel Hill: University of North Carolina Press, forthcoming).

Questions

1. *What are the essential points of conflict between the Anti-Federalists and the Federalists?*
2. *Does it make sense to view the Anti-Federalists as the spokesmen for democracy?*
3. *When historians interpret texts, they usually ask two questions: Who is the author? Who is the intended audience? With these questions in mind, what rhetorical strategies does Publius use in* Federalist 1 *to persuade his readers?*
4. *How does the approach of Publius compare to that of Centinel?*

FURTHER READING

Gordon S. Wood's The Creation of the American Republic, 1776–1787 *(Chapel Hill, 1969) is a study of the transformation of American political ideas in the period between the Revolution and the Constitution that puts the conflict between Federalists and Anti-Federalists in the larger context of evolving ideas about republicanism. Forrest McDonald's work explores the intellectual influences shaping the participants in the struggle over the Constitution; see* Novus Ordo Seclorum: the Intellectual Origins of the Constitution *(Lawrence, Kansas, 1985). Richard B. Morris describes the immediate political and social context of the debate over the Constitution in* The Forging of the Union, 1781–1789 *(New York, 1987). Finally, the essays in Richard Beeman's volume cover a variety of topics including: Madison's political thought, slavery, Shays's Rebellion, and the legacy of Anti-Federalism; see Richard Beeman et al.,* Beyond Confederation: Origins of the Constitution and American National Identity *(Chapel Hill, 1987).*

Andrew Jackson and Cherokee Removal

Paul C. Bowers

Introduction

In the 1830s, the federal government of the United States forced most of the Native Americans living east of the Mississippi off their homelands. Ostensibly intended to relocate these Indians on sparsely populated and less desirable lands to the west; this massive "removal" resulted in the deaths of many. Because the justification for removal was often framed in terms of savage Indians and civilized whites, the forced migration of the Cherokee people earned the most attention at the time and since. Of the Native American people who were finally forced to leave their lands and migrate across the Mississippi River—Choctaw, Cherokee, Creeks, and others—the Cherokee made the most sustained and successful effort to accommodate to the white man's ways. They aided Andrew Jackson in his victory over the Creeks at the pivotal Battle of Horseshoe Bend, 27 March 1814. They made rapid advancement in agriculture, education, and adoption of the Christian religion. In 1827, the Cherokee adopted a written constitution patterned after the Constitution of the United States and claimed to be a sovereign, independent nation with complete jurisdiction over their territory. Neither the federal nor state governments recognized that claim. Ultimately, their efforts to retain their land and freedom were to no avail.

Soon after the Cherokee adopted their constitution, the states in which they resided, especially Georgia, stepped up efforts to gain control of their land. When Andrew Jackson became president of the United States in 1829, he initiated the first major federal effort to relocate Native American populations. His policy, consonant with that of Georgia and other southern states and reflecting the opinions and desires of most white Americans, was to clear the lands east of the Mississippi River for settlement and exploitation by whites.

Jackson's policy was a success. By the Treaty of New Echota, 29 December 1835, a small group of Cherokee leaders ceded the nation's land east of the Mississippi River to the United States for the sum of $5 million and a promise of sufficient land for their resettlement in the west. The treaty bitterly divided the Cherokee into pro- and anti-removal parties and led to the murder, or execution, of John Ridge, Elias Boudinot, and Major Ridge, who favored the treaty, by members of their own nation.

In 1830, Congress passed the Indian Removal Act, which enabled President Jackson to exchange land west of the Mississippi River for tribal territory in the southeastern states. Almost sixteen thousand Cherokee were forced to emigrate, and, according to one estimate, about one-fourth of them died in concentration camps or along the "Trail of Tears," the Cherokee name for the terrible trek west.

How shall we understand what happened to the Cherokee, and indeed to all Native Americans, following the advent and expansion of Europeans in their land? Andrew Jackson has been accused of genocide, as have, of late, Christopher Columbus and all Europeans who invaded, settled, and conquered the Americas.

What is *genocide?* Webster's New World Dictionary *defines it as: "first applied to the attempted killing or extermination of a whole people or nation." You see the key words: "killing," "extermination," "whole people or nation." Was that Andrew Jackson's intent? Or, if not his intent, was it in any case the result of his policy, abetted by the majority of white Americans? If not, why did what happened happen? Jackson himself believed that what happened was tragic but inevitable. So did many of his contemporaries, and so do many today. Jackson believed the removal and deaths of so many Cherokee was the result of the often-repeated clash between civilization and savagery; between a dynamic, superior culture and a backward, inferior one.*

Was there no other, better, way? You decide.

The Contemporary Debate

Although a number of historians have used the word "inevitable" to describe the final victory of Jackson's removal policy, it is important to realize that Indian removal was vigorously debated at the time. For over a decade, the white citizens of the United States, the spokespeople for the federal and state governments, and Native Americans bitterly contested every aspect of state and national action regarding removal and every encroachment of whites into territory claimed by Native Americans. The issues involved in this extended debate—among them the status of Native American nations in the polity of the United States; the constitutional division of power between states and the federal government; the binding nature of treaties between the colonies, states, federal government and Native American peoples; and the moral and ethical nature of removal—remain a focus for often emotional, even violent, disagreement. We who live in the United States of America have not escaped or outlived the consequences of what happened to the Cherokee and their kin. The following selections provide an introduction to the range of opinions, the depth of emotion, and the breadth of significance for this country occasioned by Indian removal in the nineteenth century.

A Benevolent Policy

In his second annual message to Congress, on 6 December 1830, Andrew Jackson explained and defended his policy of Indian removal. Excerpted from A Compilation of the Messages and Papers of the Presidents, 1789–1897, *ed. James D. Richardson (Washington, 1896), 2:519–23.*

It gives me pleasure to announce to Congress that the benevolent policy of the Government, steadily pursued for nearly thirty years, in relation to the removal of the Indians beyond the white settlements is approaching to a happy consummation. Two important tribes have accepted the provision made for their removal at the last session of Congress, and it is believed that their example will induce the remaining tribes also to seek the same obvious advantages.

The consequences of a speedy removal will be important to the United States, to individual States, and to the Indians themselves. The pecuniary advantages which it promises to the Government are the least of its recommendations. It puts an end to all possible danger of collision between the authorities of the General and State Governments on account of the Indians. It will place a dense and civilized population in large tracts of country now occupied by a few savage hunters. By opening the whole territory between Tennessee on the north and Louisiana on the south to the settlement of the whites it will incalculably strengthen the southwestern frontier and render the adjacent States strong enough to repel future invasions without remote aid. It will relieve the whole State of Mississippi and the western part of Alabama of Indian occupancy, and enable those States to advance rapidly in population, wealth, and power. It will separate the Indians from immediate contact with settlements of whites; free them from the power of the States; enable them to pursue happiness in their own way and under their own rude institutions; will retard the progress of decay, which is lessening their numbers, and perhaps cause them gradually, under the protection of the Government and through the influence of good counsels, to cast off their savage habits and become an interesting, civilized, and Christian community. These consequences, some of them so certain and the rest so probable, make the complete execution of the plan sanctioned by Congress at their last session an object of much solicitude.

Toward the aborigines of the country no one can indulge a more friendly feeling than myself, or would go further in attempting to reclaim them from their wandering habits and make them a happy, prosperous people. I have endeavored to impress upon them my own solemn convictions of the duties and powers of the General Government in relation to the State authorities. For the justice of the laws passed by the States within the scope of their reserved powers they are not responsible to this Government. As individuals we may entertain and express our opinions of their acts, but as a Government we have as little right to control them as we have to prescribe laws for other nations.

With a full understanding of the subject, the Choctaw and the Chickasaw tribes have with great unanimity determined to avail themselves of the liberal offers presented by the act of Congress, and have agreed to remove beyond the Mississippi River. Treaties have been made with them, which in due season will be submitted for consideration. In negotiating these treaties they were made to understand their true condition, and they have preferred maintaining their independence in the Western forests to submitting to the laws of the States in which they now reside. These treaties, being probably the last which will ever be made with them, are characterized by great liberality on the part of the Government. They give the Indians a liberal sum in consideration of their removal, and comfortable subsistence on their arrival at their new homes. If it be their real interest to maintain a separate existence, they will there be at liberty to do so without the inconveniences and vexations to which they would unavoidably have been subject in Alabama and Mississippi.

Humanity has often wept over the fate of the aborigines of this country, and Philanthropy has been long busily employed in devising means to avert it, but its progress has never for a moment been arrested, and one by one have many powerful tribes disappeared from the earth. To follow to the tomb the last of his race and to tread on the graves of extinct nations excite melancholy reflections. But true philanthropy reconciles the mind to these vicissitudes as it does to the extinction of one generation to make room for another. In the monuments and fortresses of an unknown people, spread over the extensive regions of the West, we behold the memorials of a once powerful race, which was exterminated or has disappeared to make room for the existing savage tribes. Nor is there anything in this which, upon a comprehensive view of the general interests of the human race, is to be regretted. Philanthropy could not wish to see this continent restored to the condition in which it was found by our forefathers. What good man would prefer a country covered with forests and ranged by a few thousand savages to our extensive Republic, studded with cities, towns, and prosperous farms, embellished with all the improvements which art can devise or industry execute, occupied by more than 12,000,000 happy people, and filled with all the blessings of liberty, civilization, and religion?

The present policy of the Government is but a continuation of the same progressive change by a milder process. The tribes which occupied the countries now constituting the Eastern States were annihilated or have melted away to make room for the whites. The waves of population and civilization are rolling to the westward, and we now propose to acquire the countries occupied by the red men of the South and West by a fair exchange, and, at the expense of the United States, to send them to a land where their existence may be prolonged and perhaps made perpetual. Doubtless it will be painful to leave the graves of their fathers; but what do they more than our ancestors did or than our children are now doing? To better their condition in an unknown land our forefathers left all that was dear in earthly objects. Our children by thousands yearly leave the land of their birth to seek new homes in distant regions. Does Humanity weep at these painful separations from everything, animate and inanimate, with which the young heart has become entwined? Far from it. It is rather a source of joy that our country affords scope where our young population may range unconstrained in body or in mind, developing the power and faculties of man in their highest perfection. These remove hundreds and almost thousands of miles at their own expense, purchase the lands they occupy, and support themselves at their new homes from the moment of their arrival. Can it be cruel in this Government when, by events which it can not control, the Indian is made discontented in his ancient home to purchase his lands, to give him a new and extensive territory, to pay the expense of his removal, and support him a year in his new abode? How many thousands of our own people would gladly embrace the opportunity of removing to the West on such conditions! If the offers made to the Indians were extended to them, they would be hailed with gratitude and joy.

And is it supposed that the wandering savage has a stronger attachment to his home than the settled, civilized Christian? Is it more afflicting to him to leave the graves of his fathers than it is to our brothers and children? Rightly considered, the policy of the General Government toward the red man is not only liberal, but generous. He is unwilling to submit to the laws of the States and mingle with their population. To save him from this alternative, or perhaps utter annihilation, the General Government kindly offers him a new home, and proposes to pay the whole expense of his removal and settlement. . . .

It is, therefore, a duty which this Government owes to the new States to extinguish as soon as possible the Indian title to all lands which Congress themselves have included within their limits. When this is done the duties of the General Government in relation to the States and the Indians within their limits are at an end. The Indians may leave the State or not, as they choose. The purchase of their lands does not alter in the least their personal relations with the State government. No act of the General Government has ever been deemed necessary to give the States jurisdiction over the persons of the Indians. That they possess by virtue of their sovereign power within their own limits in as full a manner before as after the purchase of the Indian lands; nor can this Government add to or diminish it.

May we not hope, therefore, that all good citizens, and none more zealously than those who think the Indians oppressed by subjection to the laws of the States, will unite in attempting to open the eyes of those children of the forest to their true condition, and by a speedy removal to relieve them from all the evils, real or imaginary, present or prospective, with which they may be supposed to be threatened.

A Divisive Policy

The Congress of the United States provided a national forum for debate over the Indian Removal Bill of 1830. Here follows an excerpt from written records of debate in the House of Representatives, presenting the views of Wilson Lumpkin, a Democratic Representative from Georgia and an advocate of removal. The following material is taken from The American Indian and the United States: A Documentary History, *ed. Wilcomb E. Washburn (New York, 1973), 2:1071, 1080–81.*

I differ with my friend from Tennessee [Mr. Bell] in regard to Indian civilization. I entertain no doubt that a remnant of these people may be entirely reclaimed from their native savage habits, and be brought to enter into the full enjoyment of all the blessings of civilized society. It appears to me, we have too many instances of individual improvement amongst the various native tribes of America, to hesitate any longer in determining whether the Indians are susceptible of civilization. Use the proper means, and success will crown your efforts. The means hitherto resorted to by the Government, as well as by individuals, to improve the condition of the Indians, must, from the present state of things, very soon be withheld from these unfortunate people, if they remain in their present abodes; for they will every day be brought into closer contact and conflict with the white population, and this circumstance will diminish the spirit of benevolence and philanthropy towards them which now exists. . . .

But, sir, upon this subject, this Government has been wanting in good faith to Georgia. It has, by its own acts and policy, forced the Indians to remain in Georgia, by the purchase of their lands in the adjoining States, and by holding out to the Indians strong inducements to remain where they are; by the expenditure of vast sums of money, spent in changing the habit of the savage for those of civilized life. All this was in itself right and proper; it has my hearty approbation; but it should not have been done at the expense of Georgia. The Government, long after it was bound to extinguish the title of the Indians to all the lands in Georgia, has actually forced the Cherokees from their lands in other States, settled them upon Georgia lands, and aided in furnishing the means to create the Cherokee aristocracy.

Sir, I blame not the Indians; I commiserate their case. I have considerable acquaintance with the Cherokees, and amongst them I have seen much to admire. To me, they are in many respects an interesting people. If the wicked influence of designing men, veiled in the garb of philanthropy and christian benevolence, should excite the Cherokees to a course that will end in their speedy destruction, I now call upon this Congress, and the whole American people, not to charge the Georgians with this sin; but let it be remembered that it is the fruit of cant and fanaticism, emanating from the land of steady habits, from the boasted progeny of the pilgrims and puritans.

Sir, my State stands charged before this House, before the nation, and before the whole world, with cruelty and oppression towards the Indians. I deny the charge, and demand proof from those who make it.

Excerpt from a speech made in Congress regarding the Indian Removal Bill of 1830, by Wilson Lumpkin, as it appeared in *The American Indian and the United States: A Documentary History*, Volume II, Wilcomb E. Washburn, editor, 1973.

A Breakdown of National Law?

Worcester v. Georgia (1832)
In the Worcester v. *Georgia (1832) landmark decision the Supreme Court of the United States and Chief Justice John Marshall found that the state of Georgia had acted unconstitutionally in its assertion of control over Cherokee land. Georgia ignored the court's decision; Andrew Jackson ignored it as well. Taken from* Reports of Decisions in the Supreme Court of the United States, *ed. B. R. Curtis (Boston, 1855), 10: 214, 240, 242–44.*

A return to a writ of error from this court to a state court, certified by the clerk of the court which pronounced the judgment, and to which the writ is addressed, and authenticated by the seal of the court, is in conformity to law, and brings the record regularly before this court.

The law of Georgia, which subjected to punishment all white persons residing within the limits of the Cherokee nation, and authorized their arrest within those limits, and their forcible removal therefrom, and their trial in a court of the State, was repugnant to the constitution, treaties, and laws of the United States, and so void; and a judgment against the plaintiff in error, under color of that law, was reversed by this court, under the 25th section of the Judiciary Act, (1 Stats. at Large, 85.)

The relations between the Indian tribes and the United States examined. . . .

From the commencement of our government, congress has passed acts to regulate trade and intercourse with the Indians; which treat them as nations, respect their rights, and manifest a firm purpose to afford that protection which treaties stipulate. All these acts, and especially that of 1802, which is still in force, manifestly consider the several Indian nations as distinct political communities, having territorial boundaries, within which their

---

"Worcester v. The State of Georgia," (1832) excerpted from *Reports of Decisions in the Supreme Court of the United States,* Vol. 10, published by Little Brown & Company, 1855.

authority is exclusive, and having a right to all the lands within those boundaries, which is not only acknowledged, but guaranteed by the United States.

In 1819, congress passed an act for promoting those humane designs of civilizing the neighboring Indians, which had long been cherished by the executive. It enacts, "that, for the purpose of providing against the further decline and final extinction of the Indian tribes adjoining to the frontier settlements of the United States, and for introducing among them the habits and arts of civilization, the President of the United States shall be, and he is hereby authorized, in every case where he shall judge improvement in the habits and condition of such Indians practicable, and that the means of instruction can be introduced with their own consent, to employ capable persons, of good moral character, to instruct them in the mode of agriculture suited to their situation; and for teaching their children in reading, writing, and arithmetic; and for performing such other duties as may be enjoined, according to such instructions and rules as the President may give and prescribe for the regulation of their conduct in the discharge of their duties."

This act avowedly contemplates the preservation of the Indian nations as an object sought by the United States, and proposes to effect this object by civilizing and converting them from hunters into agriculturists. Though the Cherokees had already made considerable progress in this improvement, it cannot be doubted that the general words of the act comprehend them. Their advance in the "habits and arts of civilization," rather encouraged perseverance in the laudable exertions still further to meliorate their condition. This act furnishes strong additional evidence of a settled purpose to fix the Indians in their country by giving them security at home. . . .

The Indian nations had always been considered as distinct, independent political communities, retaining their original natural rights, as the undisputed possessors of the soil, from time immemorial, with the single exception of that imposed by irresistible power, which excluded them from intercourse with any other European potentate than the first discoverer of the coast of the particular region claimed; and this was a restriction which those European potentates imposed on themselves, as well as on the Indians. The very term "nation," so generally applied to them, means "a people distinct from others." The constitution, by declaring treaties already made, as well as those to be made, to be the supreme law of the land, has adopted and sanctioned the previous treaties with the Indian nations, and consequently admits their rank among those powers who are capable of making treaties. The words "treaty" and "nation" are words of our own language, selected in our diplomatic and legislative proceedings, by ourselves, having each a definite and well understood meaning. We have applied them to Indians, as we have applied them to the other nations of the earth. They are applied to all in the same sense. . . .

The Cherokee nation, then, is a distinct community, occupying its own territory, with boundaries accurately described, in which the laws of Georgia can have no force, and which the citizens of Georgia have no right to enter, but with the assent of the Cherokees themselves, or in conformity with treaties and with the acts of congress. The whole intercourse between the United States and this nation is, by our constitution and laws, vested in the government of the United States. . . .

. . . If the review which has been taken be correct, and we think it is, the acts of Georgia are repugnant to the constitution, laws, and treaties of the United States.

They interfere forcibly with the relations established between the United States and the Cherokee nation, the regulation of which, according to the settled principles of our constitution, are committed exclusively to the government of the Union.

They are in direct hostility with treaties, repeated in a succession of years, which mark out the boundary that separates the Cherokee country from Georgia, guarantee to them all the land within their boundary, solemnly pledge the faith of the United States to restrain their citizens from trespassing on it, and recognize the preëxisting power of the nation to govern itself.

They are in equal hostility with the acts of congress for regulating this intercourse, and giving effect to the treaties.

Tragic Decision

Elias Boudinot was a "civilized" Cherokee who, in terms of education, religion, and aspirations, had come far along the white man's path; or so he believed. He agonized over removal, but finally supported it as a last, desperate means of maintaining the existence of his people. His stand cost him his life. The following selection is from editorials written by Boudinot as editor of the Cherokee Phoenix, *reprinted in* Cherokee Editor: The Writings of Elias Boudinot, *ed. Theda Perdue (Knoxville, 1983), 108–9, 142–43.*

[17 June 1829]

From the documents which we this day lay before our readers, there is not a doubt of the kind of policy, which the present administration of the General Government intends to pursue relative to the Indians. President Jackson has, as a neighboring editor remarks, "recognized the doctrine contended for by Georgia in its full extent." It is to be regretted that we were not undeceived long ago, while we were hunters and in our savage state. It appears now from the communication of the Secretary of War to the Cherokee Delegation, that the illustrious Washington, Jefferson, Madison and Monroe were only tantalizing us, when they encouraged us in the pursuit of agriculture and Government, and when they afforded us the protection of the United States, by which we have been preserved to this present time as a nation. Why were we not told long ago, that we could not be permitted to establish a government within the limits of any state? Then we could have borne disappointment much easier than now. The pretext for Georgia to extend her jurisdiction over the Cherokees has always existed. The Cherokees have always had a government of their own. Nothing, however, was said when we were governed by savage laws, when the abominable law of retaliation carried death in our midst, when it was a lawful act to shed the blood of a person charged with witchcraft, when a brother could kill a brother with impunity, or an innocent man suffer for an offending relative. At that time it might have been a matter of charity to have extended over us the mantle of Christian laws & regulations. But how happens it now, after being fostered by the U. States, and advised

Cherokee Indians depicted along the "Trail of Tears" after expulsion from their native lands. (Painting by Robert Lindneux. Original in Wollaroc Museum, Bartesville, Oklahoma. Courtesy of Corbis-Bettmann.)

by great and good men to establish a government of regular law; when the aid and protection of the General Government have been pledged to us; when we, as dutiful "children" of the President, have followed his instructions and advice, and have established for ourselves a government of regular law; when everything looks so promising around us, that a storm is raised by the extension of tyrannical and unchristian laws, which threatens to blast all our rising hopes and expectations?

There is, as would naturally be supposed, a great rejoicing in Georgia. It is a time of "important news"—"gratifying intelligence"—"The Cherokee lands are to be obtained speedily." It is even reported that the Cherokees have come to the conclusion to sell, and move off to the west of the Mississippi—not so fast. We are yet at our homes, at our peaceful firesides, (except those contiguous to Sandtown, Carroll, &c.) attending to our farms and useful occupations. . . .

[12 November 1831]

. . . But alas! no sooner was it made manifest that the Cherokees were becoming strongly attached to the ways and usages of civilized life, than was aroused the opposition of those from whom better things ought to have been expected. No sooner was it known that they had learned the proper use of the earth, and that they were now less likely to dispose of their lands for a mess of pottage, than they came in conflict with the cupidity and self-interest of those who ought to have been their benefactors—Then commenced a series of obstacles hard to overcome, and difficulties intended as a stumbling block, and unthought of before. The "Great Father" of the "red man" has lent his influence to encourage those difficulties. The *guardian* has deprived his *wards* of their rights—The sacred obligations of treaties and laws have been disregarded—The promises of Washington and Jefferson have not been fulfilled. The policy of the United States on Indian affairs has taken a different direction, for no other reason than that the Cherokees have so far become civilized as to appreciate a regular form of Government. They are now deprived of rights they once enjoyed—A neighboring power is now permitted to extend its withering hand over them—Their own laws, intended to regulate their society, to encourage virtue and to suppress vice, must now be abolished, and civilized acts, passed for the purpose of expelling them, must be substituted.—Their intelligent citizens who have been instructed through the means employed by former administrations, and through the efforts of benevolent societies, must be abused and insulted, represented as avaricious, feeding upon the poverty of the common Indians—the hostility of all those who want the Indian lands must be directed against them. That the Cherokees may be kept in ignorance, teachers who had settled among them by the approbation of the Government, for the best of all purposes, have been compelled to leave them by reason of laws unbecoming any civilized nation—Ministers of the Gospel, who might have, at this day of trial, administered to them the consolations of Religion, have been arrested, chained, dragged away before their eyes, tried as felons, and finally immured in prison with thieves and robbers.

Vain Protest

A delegation of Cherokee leaders who opposed the Treaty of New Echota protested to Congress, but in vain. The following excerpt from the "Memorial and Protest of the Cherokee Nation" of 22 June 1836 appears in House Documents, 24th Cong., 1st sess., *vol. 7, Doc. no. 286, CIS US Serial no. 292, microprint, 2–5.*

If it be said that the Cherokees have lost their national character and political existence, as a nation or tribe, by State legislation, then the President and Senate can make no treaty with them; but if they have not, then no treaty can be made for them, binding, without and against their will. Such is the fact, in reference to the instrument intered into at New Echota, in December last. If treaties are to be thus made and enforced, deceptive to the Indians and to the world, purporting to be a contract, when, in truth, wanting the assent of one of the pretended parties, what security would there be for any nation or tribe to retain confidence in the United States? If interest or policy require that the Cherokees be removed, without their consent, from their lands, surely the President and Senate have no constitutional power to accomplish that object. They cannot do it under the power to make treaties, which are contracts, not rules prescribed by a superior, and therefore binding only by the assent of the parties. In the present instance, the assent of the Cherokee nation has not been given, but expressly denied. The President and Senate cannot do it under the power to regulate commerce with the Indian tribes, or intercourse with them, because that belongs to Congress, and so declared by the President, in his message to the Senate of February 22, 1831, relative to the execution of the act to regulate trade and intercourse with the Indian tribes, &c. passed 30th of March, 1802. They cannot do it under any subsisting treaty stipulation with the Cherokee nation. Nor does the peculiar situation of the Cherokees, in reference to the States their necessities and distresses, confer any power upon the President and Senate to alienate their legal rights, or to prescribe the manner and time of their removal.

Without a decision of what ought to be done, under existing circumstances, the question recurs, is the instrument under consideration a contract between the United States and the Cherokee nation? It so purports upon its face, and that falsely. Is that statement so sacred and conclusive that the Cherokee people cannot be heard to deny the fact? They have denied it under their own

---

Excerpt from the "Memorial and Protest of the Cherokee Nation: Memorial of the Cherokee Representatives," reprinted from House Reports, *24th Cong., 1st sess.,* June 22, 1836, Vol. 7, No. 286.

signatures, as the documents herein before referred to will show, and protested against the acts of the unauthorized few, who have arrogated to themselves the right to speak for the nation. The Cherokees have said they will not be bound thereby. The documents submitted to the Senate show, that when the vote was taken upon considering the propositions of the commissioner, there were but seventy-nine for so doing. Then it comes to this: could this small number of persons attending the New Echota meeting, acting in their individual capacity, dispose of the rights and interests of the Cherokee nation, or by any instrument they might sign, confer such power upon the President and Senate?

If the United States are to act as the guardian of the Cherokees, and to treat them as incapable of managing their own affairs, and blind to their true interests, yet this would not furnish power or authority to the President and Senate, as the treaty making power to prescribe the rule for managing their affairs. It may afford a pretence for the legislation of Congress, but none for the ratification of an instrument as a treaty made by a small faction against the protest of the Cherokee people.

That the Cherokees are a distinct people, sovereign to some extent, have a separate political existence as a society, or body politic, and a capability of being contracted with in a national capacity, stands admitted by the uniform practice of the United States from 1785, down to the present day. With them have treaties been made through their chiefs, and distinguished men in primary assemblies, as also with their constituted agents or representatives. That they have not the right to manage their own internal affairs, and to regulate, by treaty, their intercourse with other nations, is a doctrine of modern date. In 1793, Mr. Jefferson said, "I consider our right of pre-emption of the Indian lands, not as amounting to any dominion, or jurisdiction, or paramountship whatever, but merely in the nature of a remainder, after the extinguishment of a present right, which gives us no present right whatever, but of preventing other nations from taking possession, and so defeating our expectancy. That the Indians *have the full, undivided, and independent sovereignty as long as they choose to keep it, and that this may be forever.*" This opinion was recognised and practised upon, by the Government of the United States, through several successive administrations, also recognised by the Supreme Court of the United States, and the several States, when the question has arisen. It has not been the opinion only of jurists, but of politicians, as may be seen from various reports of Secretaries of War—beginning with Gen. Knox, also the correspondence between the British and American ministers at Ghent in the year 1814. If the Cherokees have power to judge of their own interests, and to make treaties, which, it is presumed, will be denied by none, then to make a contract valid, the assent of a majority must be had, expressed by themselves or through their representatives, and the President and Senate have no power to say what their will shall be, for from the laws of nations we learn that "though a nation be obliged to promote, as far as lies in its power, the perfection of others, it is not entitled forcibly to obtrude these good offices on them." Such an attempt would be to violate their natural liberty. Those ambitious Europeans who attacked the American nations, and subjected them to their insatiable avidity of dominion, an order, as they pretended, for civilizing them, and causing them to be instructed in the true religion, (as in the present instance to preserve the Cherokees as a distinct people,) these usurpers grounded themselves on a pretence equally unjust and ridiculous." It is the expressed wish of the Government of the United States to remove the Cherokees to a place west of the Mississippi. That wish is said to be founded in humanity to the Indians. To make their situation more comfortable, and to preserve them as a distinct people. Let facts show how this *benevolent* design has been prosecuted, and how faithful to the spirit and letter has the promise of the President of the United States to the Cherokees been fulfilled—that *"those who remain may be assured of our patronage, our aid, and good neighborhood."* The delegation are not deceived by empty professions, and fear their race is to be destroyed by the mercenary policy of the present day, and their lands wrested from them by physical force; as proof, they will refer to the preamble of an act of the General Assembly of Georgia, in reference to the Cherokees, passed the 2d of December, 1835, where it is said, "from a knowledge of the Indian character, and from the present feelings of these Indians, it is confidently believed, that the right of occupancy of the lands in their possession should be withdrawn, *that it would be a strong inducement to them to treat with the General Government, and consent to a removal to the west;* and whereas, the present Legislature openly avow that their primary object in the measures intended to be pursued *are founded on real humanity to these Indians,* and with a view, in a distant region, to perpetuate them with their old identity of character, *under the paternal care of the Government of the United States;* at the same time frankly disavowing *any selfish or sinister motives towards them in their present legislation."* This is the profession. Let us turn to the practice of *humanity*, to the Cherokees, by the State of Georgia. In violation of the treaties between the United States and the Cherokee nation, that State passed a law requiring all white men, residing in that part of the Cherokee country, in her limits, to take an oath of allegiance to the State of Georgia. For a violation of this law, some of the ministers of Christ, missionaries among the Cherokees, were tried, convicted, and sentenced to hard labor in the penitentiary. Their case may be seen by reference to the records of the Supreme Court of the United States.

Valuable gold mines were discovered upon Cherokee lands, within the chartered limits of Georgia, and the Cherokees commenced working them, and the Legislature of that State interfered by passing an act, making it penal for an Indian to dig for gold within Georgia, no doubt *"frankly disavowing any selfish or sinister motives towards them."* Under this law many Cherokees were arrested, tried, imprisoned, and otherwise abused. Some were even shot in attempting to avoid an arrest; yet the Cherokee people used no violence, but humbly petitioned the Government of the United States for a fulfilment of treaty engagements, to protect them, which was not done, and the answer given that the United States could not interfere. Georgia discovered she was not to be obstructed in carrying out her measures, *"founded on real humanity to these Indians,"* she passed an act directing the Indian country to be surveyed into districts. This excited some alarm, but the Cherokees were quieted with the assurance it would do no harm to survey the country. Another act was shortly after passed, to lay off the country into lots. As yet there was no authority to take possession, but it was not long before a law was made, authorizing a lottery for the lands laid off into lots. In this act the Indians were secured in possession of all the lots touched by their improvements, and the balance of the country allowed to be occupied by white men. This was a direct violation of the 5th article of the treaty of the 27th of February, 1819. The Cherokees made no resistance, still petitioned the United States for protection, and received the same answer that the President could not interpose.

Questions

1. *What, according to his second annual message to Congress, is Jackson's Indian policy? If you were a Cherokee—or Creek, Choctaw, Seminole—why should you trust, or mistrust, Jackson's message?*
2. *What were the important issues involved in the Supreme Court decision in Worcester v. Georgia and in the congressional debates over the Indian Removal Act of 1830?*
3. *If you were a Cherokee, would you have supported the anti- or pro-removal position among the Cherokee people? Why?*

FURTHER READING

The Great Father: The United States Government and the American Indians, *vol. 1 (Lincoln, Nebraska, 1984), by Francis Paul Prucha, contains the latest full treatment of Jackson's Indian policy by this prolific and generally pro-Jackson scholar. Useful for its detailed coverage is Ronald N. Satz,* American Indian Policy in the Jacksonian Era *(Lincoln, Nebraska, 1975). An excellent bibliography covering the removal period is in Thurman Wilkins,* Cherokee Tragedy: The Story of the Ridge Family and the Decimation of a People. *(New York, 1970). For the many books that are highly critical of Jackson's removal policy see the bibliography in Wilkins. William G. McLoughlin, in* Champions of the Cherokees: Evan and John B. Jones *(Princeton, 1990), considers the Cherokee as heroic in their resistance to a terrible injustice.* Cherokee Removal: Before and After, *edited by William L. Anderson (Athens, Georgia, 1991), has several useful articles on various facets of removal and may be used to supplement the bibliographical information in Wilkins. Jackson's role in removal is treated at length by Robert V. Remini in his laudatory biography,* Andrew Jackson and the Course of American Freedom, 1822–1832, *vol. 2 (New York, 1977). An excellent collection of documents on removal is in* The New American State Papers: Indian Affairs, *vol. 9,* Southeast *(Wilmington, Delaware, 1972).*

Transcendentalism

Steven Conn

INTRODUCTION

Transcendentalism has been a subject of study and discussion among scholars from the middle of the nineteenth century. As long ago as 1876, O. B. Frothingham wrote Transcendentalism in New England. *Yet despite all the books written and studies conducted, transcendentalism remains a slippery and elusive phenomenon.*

This much we can agree on: the phenomenon (movement is probably too strong a word) arose in and around Boston in the 1830s under the inspiration of Unitarian minister Ralph Waldo Emerson. Around Emerson gathered a remarkable constellation of writers, thinkers, critics, and philosophers, some in close orbit, others only tangentially so. Even here, historians have debated who should actually be considered a transcendentalist. In addition to Emerson, those usually associated with transcendentalism include Henry David Thoreau, Orestes Brownson, Margaret Fuller, Theodore Parker, and George Ripley. For some, the poet Walt Whitman is part of the transcendentalist phenomenon as well.

Intellectually and spiritually, transcendentalism grew out of the religious controversies taking place in New England. In the late eighteenth century Unitarianism had arisen to replace an eclipsed Puritanism. By the 1830s many who had grown up in a Unitarian tradition, including Emerson, an ordained minister, had grown weary of Unitarianism's stress on the intellectual as opposed to intuitive spirituality, and bored with its emphasis on texts rather than on life experience as the source of education. Expressing his emotional dissatisfaction with Unitarian thought, Emerson famously called it "corpse cold."

Added to this was an exposure to European romanticism, particularly through the English poet Samuel Taylor Coleridge, and German philosophy. The transcendentalists took their name from the writings of philosopher Immanuel Kant.

Transcendentalism grew out of this intellectual soil. Though each of its participants developed his or her own particular vision and ideas, all shared some basic concerns. Transcendentalists were especially interested in exploring how nature showed the way to spiritual insight, and they believed in the boundless possibilities of the individual mind and spirit, what Emerson called "the infinitude of private man." For Emerson, perhaps more so than any of the others, the natural world, the individual soul, and God were all the same, seamless and inseparable, if only people would open their eyes and their hearts.

TRANSCENDENTALIST VOICES

The people associated with Transcendentalism left a tremendous body of writing, and picking a few "representative" samples is virtually impossible. What follows are three of the most well known essays, by three figures most closely associated with Transcendentalism. Taken together they also give a sense not only of different personal styles but of the different kinds of issues with which Transcendentalists wrestled: nature and the soul, the duty to one's conscience, and the political situation of women.

Ralph Waldo Emerson

Historians agree that the loose phenomenon known as "Transcendentalism" began in 1832 when Ralph Waldo Emerson (1803-1882) resigned his Unitarian ministry to pursue a vocation as independent critic, scholar, writer, and thinker.

On a trip to Europe after his resignation, Emerson met some of the leading intellectual figures of the day, including Thomas Car Lyle, William Wordsworth, and Samuel Taylor Coleridge. By 1835 he had settled in Concord, Massachusetts, where he presided over an extraordinary group of writers, reformers, and thinkers.

The following year Emerson published the essay "Nature," excerpted below, which became something of a manifesto for those associated with the group. From its opening lines, "Nature" constitutes a bold plea for a new American cultural identity. Car Lyle called the essay "a true apocalypse," and it stands as America's declaration of cultural independence.

"Nature," like all of Emerson's writings, is a deliberately challenging essay. Emerson wanted his readers to struggle with his ideas. Read it in the spirit of the writer James Russell Lowell, who said, "Emerson's oration began nowhere and ended everywhere and yet, as always with that divine man, it left you feeling that something beautiful had passed that way—something more beautiful than anything else, like the rising and setting of stars." The body of Emerson's writing stands as a remarkable exploration of the relationship between the intellect and the spirit, between humans and God, between society and nature.

Excerpted from Ralph Waldo Emerson, Nature *(Boston, 1836), 5-14, 89-95.*

Our age is retrospective. It builds the sepulchres of the fathers. It writes biographies, histories, and criticism. The foregoing generations beheld God and nature face to face; we, through their eyes. Why should not we also enjoy an original relation to the universe? Why should not we have a poetry and philosophy of insight and not of tradition, and a religion by revelation to us, and not the history of theirs? Embosomed for a season in nature, whose floods of life stream around and through us, and invite us by the powers they supply, to action proportioned to nature, why should we grope among the dry bones of the past, or put the living generation into masquerade out of its faded wardrobe? The sun shines to-day also. There is more wool and flax in the fields. There are new lands, new men, new thoughts. Let us demand our own works and laws and worship.

Ralph Waldo Emerson (1803–1882), critic, poet; he was the focal point around which many who whould be called "Transcendentalists" gathered. (Courtesy of The Library of Congress.)

Undoubtedly we have no questions to ask which are unanswerable. We must trust the perfection of the creation so far, as to believe that whatever curiosity the order of things has awakened in our minds, the order of things can satisfy. Every man's condition is a solution in hieroglyphic to those inquiries he would put. He acts it as life, before he apprehends it as truth. In like manner, nature is already, in its forms and tendencies, describing its own design. Let us interrogate the great apparition, that shines so peacefully around us. Let us inquire, to what end is nature?

All science has one aim, namely, to find a theory of nature. We have theories of races and of functions, but scarcely yet a remote approximation to an idea of creation. We are now so far from the road to truth, that religious teachers dispute and hate each other, and speculative men are esteemed unsound and frivolous. But to a sound judgment, the most abstract truth is the most practical. Whenever a true theory appears, it will be its own evidence. Its test is, that it will explain all phenomena. Now many are thought not only unexplained but inexplicable; as language, sleep, dreams, beasts, sex.

Philosophically considered, the universe is composed of Nature and the Soul. Strictly speaking, therefore, all that is separate from us, all which Philosophy distinguishes as the NOT ME, that is, both nature and art, all other men and my own body, must be ranked under this name, NATURE. In enumerating the values of nature and casting up their sum, I shall use the word in both senses;—in its common and in its philosophical import. In inquiries so general as our present one, the inaccuracy is not material; no confusion of thought will occur. *Nature*, in the common sense, refers to essences unchanged by man; space, the air, the river, the leaf. *Art* is applied to the mixture of his will with the same things, as in a house, a canal, a statue, a picture. But his operations taken together are so insignificant, a little chipping, baking, patching, and washing, that in an impression so grand as that of the world on the human mind, they do not vary the result.

To go into solitude, a man needs to retire as much from his chamber as from society. I am not solitary whilst I read and write, though nobody is with me. But if a man would be alone, let him look at the stars. The rays that come from those heavenly worlds, will separate between him and vulgar things. One might think the atmosphere was made transparent with this design, to give man, in the heavenly bodies, the perpetual presence of the sublime.

Seen in the streets of cities, how great they are! If the stars should appear one night in a thousand years how would men believe and adore; and preserve for many generations the remembrance of the city of God which had been shown! But every night come out these preachers of beauty, and light the universe with their admonishing smile.

The stars awaken a certain reverence, because though always present, they are always inaccessible; but all natural objects make a kindred impression, when the mind is open to their influence. Nature never wears a mean appearance. Neither does the wisest man extort all her secret[s], and lose his curiosity by finding out all her perfection. Nature never became a toy to a wise spirit. The flowers, the animals, the mountains, reflected all the wisdom of his best hour, as much as they had delighted the simplicity of his childhood.

When we speak of nature in this manner, we have a distinct but most poetical sense in the mind. We mean the integrity of impression made by manifold natural objects. It is this which distinguishes the stick of timber of the wood-cutter, from the tree of the poet. The charming landscape which I saw this morning, is indubitably made up of some twenty or thirty farms. Miller owns this field, Locke that, and Manning the woodland beyond. But none of them owns the landscape. There is a property in the horizon which no man has but he whose eye can integrate all the parts, that is, the poet. This is the best part of these men's farms, yet to this their land-deeds give them no title.

To speak truly, few adult persons can see nature. Most persons do not see the sun. At least they have a very superficial seeing. The sun illuminates only the eye of the man, but shines into the eye and the heart of the child. The lover of nature is he whose inward and outward senses are still truly adjusted to each other; who has retained the spirit of infancy even into the era of manhood. His intercourse with heaven and earth, becomes part of his daily food. In the presence of nature, a wild delight runs through the man, in spite of real sorrows. Nature says, — he is my creature, and maugre [in spite of] all his impertinent griefs, he shall be glad with me. Not the sun or the summer alone, but every hour and season yields its tribute of delight; for every hour and change corresponds to and authorizes a different state of the mind, from breathless noon to grimmest midnight. Nature is a setting that fits equally well a comic or a mourning piece. In good health, the air is a cordial of incredible virtue. Crossing a bare common, in snow puddles, at twilight, under a clouded sky, without having in my thoughts any occurrence of special good fortune, I have enjoyed a perfect exhilaration. Almost I fear to think how glad I am. In the woods too, a man casts off his years, as the snake his slough, and at what period soever of life, is always a child. In the woods, is perpetual youth. Within these plantations of God, a decorum and sanctity reign, a perennial festival is dressed, and the guest sees not how he should tire of them in a thousand years. In the woods, we return to reason and faith. There I feel that nothing can befal[l] me in life,—no disgrace, no calamity, (leaving me my eyes,) which nature cannot repair. Standing on the bare ground,—my head bathed by the blithe air, and uplifted into infinite space,—all mean egotism vanishes. I become a transparent eye-ball. I am nothing. I see all. The currents of the Universal Being circulate through me; I am part or particle of God. The name of the nearest friend sounds then foreign and accidental. To be brothers, to be acquaintances,—master or servant, is then a trifle and a disturbance. I am the lover of uncontained and immortal beauty. In the wilderness, I find something more dear and connate than in streets or villages. In the tranquil landscape, and especially in the distant line of the horizon, man beholds somewhat as beautiful as his own nature.

The greatest delight which the fields and woods minister, is the suggestion of an occult relation between man and the vegetable. I am not alone and unacknowledged. They nod to me and I to them. The waving of the boughs in the storm, is new to me and old. It takes me by surprise, and yet is not unknown. Its effect is like that of a higher thought or a better emotion coming over me, when I deemed I was thinking justly or doing right.

Yet it is certain that the power to produce this delight, does not reside in nature, but in man, or in a harmony of both. It is necessary to use these pleasures with great temperance. For, nature is not always tricked in holiday attire, but the same scene which yesterday breathed perfume and glittered as for the frolic of the nymphs, is overspread with melancholy today. Nature always wears the colors of the spirit. . . .

At present, man applies to nature but half his force. He works on the world with his understanding alone. He lives in it, and masters it by a penny-wisdom; and he that works most in it, is but a half-man and whilst his arms are strong and his digestion good, his mind is imbruted and he is a selfish savage. His relation to nature, his power over it, is through the understanding; as by manure; the economic use of fire, wind, water, and the mariner's needle; steam, coal, chemical agriculture; the repairs of the human body by the dentist and the surgeon. This is such a resumption of power, as if a banished king should buy his territories inch by inch, instead of vaulting at once into his throne. Meantime, in the thick darkness, there are not wanting gleams of a better light,—occasional examples of the action of man upon nature with his entire force,—with reason as well as understanding. Such examples are; the traditions of miracles in the earliest antiquity of all nations; the history of Jesus Christ; the achievements of a principle, as in religious and political revolutions, and in the abolition of the Slave-trade; . . . miracles of enthusiasm, . . . many obscure and yet contested facts, now arranged under the name of Animal Magnetism; prayer; eloquence; self-healing; and the wisdom of children. These are examples of Reason's momentary grasp of the sceptre; the exertions of a power which exists not in time or space, but an instantaneous in-streaming causing power. The difference between the actual and the ideal force of man is happily figured by the schoolmen, in saying, that the knowledge of man is an evening knowledge, *vespertina cognitio*, but that of God is a morning knowledge, *matutina cognitio*.

The problem of restoring to the world original and eternal beauty, is solved by the redemption of the soul. The ruin or the blank, that we see when we look at nature, is in our own eye. The axis of vision is not coincident with the axis of things, and so they appear not transparent but opake [opaque]. The reason why the world lacks unity, and lies broken and in heaps, is, because man is disunited with himself. He cannot be a naturalist, until he satisfies all the demands of the spirit. Love is as much its demand, as perception. Indeed, neither can be perfect without the other. In the uttermost meaning of the words, thought is devout, and devotion is thought. Deep calls unto deep. But in actual life, the marriage is not celebrated. There are innocent men who worship God after the tradition of their fathers, but their sense of duty has not yet extended to the use of all their faculties. And there are patient naturalists, but they freeze their subject under the wintry light of the understanding. Is not prayer also a study of truth,—a sally of the soul into the unfound infinite? No man ever prayed heartily, without learning something. But when a faithful thinker, resolute to detach every object from personal relations, and see it in the light of thought, shall, at the same time, kindle science with the fire of the holiest affections, then will God go forth anew into the creation.

It will not need, when the mind is prepared for study, to search for objects. The invariable mark of wisdom is to see the miraculous in the common. What is a day? What is a year? What is summer? What is woman? What is a child? What is sleep? To our blindness, these things seem unaffecting. We make fables to hide the baldness of the fact and conform it, as we say, to the higher law of the mind. But when the fact is seen under the light of an idea, the gaudy fable fades and shrivels. We behold the real higher law. To the wise, therefore, a fact is true poetry, and the most beautiful of fables. These wonders are brought to our own door. You also are a man. Man and woman, and their social life, poverty, labor, sleep, fear, fortune, are known to you. Learn that none of these things is superficial, but that each phenomenon hath its roots in the faculties and affections of the mind. Whilst the abstract question occupies your intellect, nature brings it in the concrete to be solved by your hands. It were a wise inquiry for the closet, to compare, point by point, especially at remarkable crises in life, our daily history, with the rise and progress of ideas in the mind.

So shall we come to look at the world with new eyes. It shall answer the endless inquiry of the intellect,—What is truth? and of the affections,—What is good? by yielding itself passive to the educated Will. Then shall come to pass what my poet said; 'Nature is not fixed but fluid. Spirit alters, moulds, makes it. The immobility or bruteness of nature, is the absence of spirit; to pure spirit, it is fluid, it is volatile, it is obedient. Every spirit builds itself a house; and beyond its house, a world; and beyond its world, a heaven. Know then, that the world exists for you. For you is the phenomenon perfect. What we are, that only can we see. All that Adam had, all that Cœsar could, you have and can do. Adam called his house, heaven and earth; Cœsar called his house, Rome; you perhaps call yours, a cobbler's trade; a hundred acres of ploughed land; or a scholar's garret [small room]. Yet line for line and point for point, your dominion is as great as theirs, though without fine names. Build, therefore your own world. As fast as you conform your life to the pure idea in your mind, that will unfold its great proportions. A correspondent revolution in things will attend the influx of the spirit. So fast will disagreeable appearances, swine, spiders, snakes, pests, mad-houses, prisons, enemies, vanish; they are temporary and shall be no more seen. The sordor and filths of nature the sun shall dry up, and the wind exhale. As when the summer comes from the south, the snow-banks melt, and the face of the earth becomes green before it, so shall the advancing spirit create its ornaments along its path, and carry with it the beauty it visits, and the song which enchants it; it shall draw beautiful faces, and warm hearts, and wise discourse, and heroic acts, around its way, until evil is no more seen. The kingdom of man over nature, which cometh not with observation, — a dominion such as now is beyond his dream of God, — he shall enter without more wonder than the blind man feels who is gradually restored to perfect sight.'

Henry David Thoreau

Perhaps more than any of the other Transcendentalists, Henry David Thoreau (1817-1862) explored the radically individualistic, almost anarchic, implications of Transcendentalist thinking. Thoreau was a senior at Harvard University when Emerson's "Nature" appeared, and it moved him profoundly. For the next twenty-five years Thoreau viewed Emerson as a mentor and friend, and although their relationship finally ended in frustration, Emerson delivered a eulogy at Thoreau's funeral.

On July 4, 1845, Thoreau tried to turn Transcendentalist ideas into an "experiment in living," and he moved into a cabin by himself near Walden Pond in Concord, Massachusetts. He lived there, for two years, two months, and two days. The result of this experiment, the book Walden, or Life in the Woods, *remains a classic expression of American individuality.*

Like a child rebelling against a parent, Thoreau had become impatient with Emerson for telling Americans to develop a new relationship with nature, while not living off the land himself. Thoreau once caustically said of his mentor: "I doubt if Emerson could trundle a wheelbarrow through the streets." Through his experiments at Walden Pond, Thoreau turned rebellion into a quest for personal integrity.

Thoreau also challenged the political status quo more than Emerson. In the selection below, excerpted from Civil Disobedience, *originally published in 1849 as* Resistance to Civil Government, *Thoreau theo-*

rizes about when the individual conscience dictates the rejection of society's unjust laws. For Thoreau, the United States's declaration of war on Mexico in 1846 constituted a grave injustice. Thoreau refused to pay his taxes to protest the war. More significantly, Thoreau came to regard the whole basis of the American government as immoral because its founding document, the Constitution, permitted slavery. Thoreau's theories and acts of civil disobedience proved inspirational to many, including Martin Luther King, Jr.

Taken from Henry David Thoreau, Civil Disobedience *(Westwood, New Jersey, 1964), 11-18, 21-22, 27-31, 33, 46-47, 49-50, 55-56.*

I heartily accept the motto, "That government is best which governs least," and I should like to see it acted up to more rapidly and systematically. Carried out, it finally amounts to this, which also I believe—"That government is best which governs not at all;" and when men are prepared for it, that will be the kind of government which they will have. . . . The government itself, which is only the mode which the people have chosen to execute their will, is equally liable to be abused and perverted before the people can act through it. Witness the present Mexican war, the work of comparatively a few individuals using the standing government as their tool; for, in the outset, the people would not have consented to this measure. . . .

After all, the practical reason why, when the power is once in the hands of the people, a majority are permitted, and for a long period continue, to rule is not because they are most likely to be in the right, nor because this seems fairest to the minority, but because they are physically the strongest. But a government in which the majority rule in all cases cannot be based on justice, even as far as men understand it. Can there not be a government in which majorities do not virtually decide right and wrong, but conscience?—In which majorities decide only those questions to which the rule of expediency is applicable? Must the citizen ever for a moment, or in the slightest degree, resign his conscience to the legislator? Why has every man a conscience, then? I think that we should be men first, and subjects afterward. It is not desirable to cultivate a respect for the law, so much as for the right. The only obligation which I have a right to assume is to do at any time what I think right. It is truly enough said that a corporation has no conscience; but a corporation of conscientious men is a corpora-

Walden Pond, the site of Thoreau's experiment in solitude and self-sufficiency, is now a popular state park, located outside Boston. (Courtesy of AP/Wide World Photos.)

tion *with* a conscience. Law never made men a whit more just; and by means of their respect for it even the well-disposed are daily made the agents of injustice. A common and natural result of an undue respect for law is that you may see a file of soldiers—colonel, captain, corporal, privates, powder-monkeys, and all—marching in admirable order over hill and dale to the wars against their wills . . . against their common sense and consciences, which makes it very steep marching indeed, and produces a palpitation of the heart. They have no doubt that it is a damnable business in which they are concerned; they are all peaceably inclined. Now, what are they? Men at all? or small movable forts and magazines, at the service of some unscrupulous man in power? . . .

The mass of men serve the state thus, not as men mainly but as machines, with their bodies. They are the standing army, and the militia, jailers, constables, posse comitatus, etc. In most cases there is no free exercise whatever of the judgement or of the moral sense; but they put themselves on a level with wood and earth and stones, and wooden men can perhaps be manufactured that will serve the purpose as well. Such command no more respect than men of straw or a lump of dirt. They have the same sort of worth only as horses and dogs. Yet such as these even are commonly esteemed good citizens. Others—as most legislators, politicians, lawyers, ministers, and office-holders—serve the state chiefly with their heads; and as they rarely make any moral distinctions, they are as likely to serve as Devil, without *intending* it, as God. . . .

How does it become a man to behave toward this American government today? I answer, that he cannot without disgrace be associated with it. I cannot for an instant recognize that political organization as *my* government which is the *slave's* government also.

All men recognize the right of revolution; that is, the right to refuse allegiance to and to resist, the government, when its tyranny or its inefficiency are great and unendurable. But almost all say that such is not the case now. But such was the case, they think, in the Revolution of '75 [American Revolution]. . . . All machines have their friction, and possibly this does enough good to counterbalance the evil. . . . But when the friction comes to have its machine, and oppression and robbery are organized, I say, let us not have such a machine any longer. In other words, when a sixth of the population of a nation which has undertaken to be the refuge of liberty are slaves, and a whole country [Mexico] is unjustly overrun and conquered by a foreign army and subjected to military law, I think that it is not too soon for honest men to rebel and revolutionize. . . .

. . . There are thousands who are *in opinion* opposed to slavery and to the war [Mexican-American War], who yet in effect do nothing to put an end to them; who, esteeming themselves children of Washington and Franklin, sit down with their hands in their pockets, and say that they know not what to do, and do nothing; who even postpone the question of freedom to the question of free-trade, and quietly read the price-current along with the latest advices from Mexico after dinner, and, it may be, fall asleep over them both. What is the price-current of an honest man and patriot today? They hesitate, and they regret, and sometimes they petition; but they do nothing in earnest and with effect. They will wait, well disposed, for others to remedy the evil, that they may no longer have it to regret. At most, they give only a cheap vote. . . .

All voting is a sort of gaming, like checkers or backgammon, with a slight moral tinge to it, a playing with right and wrong, with moral questions; and betting naturally accompanies it. The character of the voters is not staked. I cast my vote, perchance, as I think right; but I am not vitally concerned that the right should prevail. I am willing to leave it to the majority. Its obligation, therefore, never exceeds that of expediency. Even voting *for the right* is *doing* nothing for it. It is only expressing to men feebly your desire that it should prevail. A wise man will not leave the right to the mercy of chance, nor wish it to prevail through the power of the majority. There is but little virtue in the action of masses of men. When the majority shall at length vote for the abolition of slavery, it will be because they are indifferent to slavery, or because there is but little slavery left to be abolished by their vote. *They* will then be the only slaves. Only *his* vote can hasten the abolition of slavery who asserts his own freedom by his vote. . . .

Unjust laws exist: shall we be content to obey them or shall we endeavor to amend them, and obey them until we have succeeded, or shall we transgress them at once? Men generally, under such a government as this, think that they ought to wait until they have persuaded the majority to alter them. They think that, if they should resist, the remedy would be worse than the evil. But it is the fault of the government itself that the remedy is worse than the evil. *It* makes it worse. Why is it not more apt to anticipate and provide for reform? Why does it not cherish its wise minority? Why does it cry and resist before it is hurt? Why does it not encourage its citizens to be on the alert to point out its faults, and *do* better than it would have them? Why does it always crucify Christ, and excommunicate Copernicus and Luther, and pronounce Washington and Franklin rebels? . . .

. . . If the injustice . . . is of such a nature that it requires you to be the agent of . . . injustice to another, then, I say, break the law. Let your life be the counter-friction to stop the machine. What I have to do is to see, at any rate, that I do not lend myself to the wrong which I condemn. . . .

I do not hesitate to say that those who call themselves Abolitionists should at once effectually withdraw their support, both in person and property, from the government of Massachusetts, and not wait till they constitute a majority of one, before they suffer the right to prevail through them. I think that it is enough if they have God on their side, without waiting for that other one. Moreover, any man more right than his neighbors constitutes a majority of one already.

. . . I know this well, that if one thousand, if one hundred, if ten men whom I could name—if ten *honest* men only—aye, if *one* HONEST man in this State of Massachusetts, *ceasing to hold slaves,*

Henry David Thoreau (1817–1862), was one of Emerson's devoted proteges. Emerson delivered the eulogy at Thoreau's funeral. (Courtesy of The Library of Congress.)

were actually to withdraw from this copartnership, and be locked up in the county jail therefore, it would be the abolition of slavery in America. For it matters not how small the beginning may seem to be; what is once well done is done forever. . . .

. . . A minority is powerless while it conforms to the majority; it is not even a minority then; but it is irresistible when it clogs by its whole weight. If the alternative is to keep all just men in prison, or give up war and slavery, the State will not hesitate which to choose. If a thousand men were not to pay their tax-bills this year, that would not be a violent and bloody measure as it would be to pay them and enable the State to commit violence and shed innocent blood. This is, in fact, the definition of a peaceable revolution, if any such is possible. . . .

I have never declined paying the highway tax, because I am as desirous of being a good neighbor as I am of being a bad subject; and as for supporting schools, I am doing my part to educate my fellow countrymen now. It is for no particular item in the tax-bill that I refuse to pay it. I simply wish to refuse allegiance to the State, to withdraw and stand aloof from it effectually. I do not care to trace the course of my dollar, if I could, till it buys a man or a musket to shoot one with—the dollar is innocent—but I am concerned to trace the effects of my allegiance. In fact, I quietly declare war with the State, after my fashion, though I will still make what use and get what advantage of her I can, as is usual in such cases. . . .

This, then, is my position at present. . . .

I do not wish to quarrel with any man or nation. I do not wish to split hairs, to make fine distinctions, or set myself up as better than my neighbors. I seek rather, I may say, even an excuse for conforming to the laws of the land. I am but too ready to conform to them. Indeed, I have reason to suspect myself on this head; and each year, as the tax-gatherer comes round, I find myself disposed to review the acts and position of the general and State governments, and the spirit of the people, to discover a pretext for conformity. . . .

I believe that the State will soon be able to take all my work of this sort out of my hands, and then I shall be no better a patriot than my fellow countrymen. Seen from a lower point of view, the Constitution, with all its faults, is very good; even this State and this American government are in many respects very admirable and rare things to be thankful for, such as a great many have described them; but seen from a point of view a little higher, they are what I have described them; seen from a higher still, and the highest, who shall say what they are, or that they are worth looking at or thinking of at all? . . .

The authority of government, even such as I am willing to submit to—for I will cheerfully obey those who know and can do better than I, and in many things even those who neither know nor can do so well—is still an impure one: to be strictly just, it must have the sanction and consent of the governed. It can have no pure right over my person and property but what I concede to it. The progress from an absolute to a limited monarchy, from a limited monarchy to a democracy, is a progress toward a true respect for the individual. . . . Is a democracy, such as we know it, the last improvement possible in government? Is it not possible to take a step further toward recognizing and organizing the rights of man? There will never be a really free and enlightened State until the State comes to recognize the individual as a higher and independent power, from which all its own power and authority are derived, and treats him accordingly. I please myself with imagining a State at last which can afford to be just to all men, and to treat the individual with respect as a neighbor; which even would not think it inconsistent with its own repose if a few were to live aloof from it, not meddling with it nor embraced by it, who fulfilled all the duties of neighbors and fellow men. A State which bore this kind of fruit, and suffered it to drop off as fast as it ripened, would prepare the way for a still more perfect and glorious State, which also I have imagined, but not yet anywhere seen.

Margaret Fuller

Edgar Allen Poe divided the world into three categories: men, women, and Margaret Fuller. Fuller (1810-1850) was in many ways the most dynamic of Emerson's disciples and among his closest friends, at least for a time. It was from Emerson, Fuller wrote, that she "first learned what is meant by an inward light."

Well-educated by any standards, male or female, Fuller served as the first editor of the journal The Dial *from 1840 to 1842. It was through* The Dial *that many Transcendentalist writings reached the public.*

While she participated in the activities of the Transcendental Club, Fuller also gathered together a group of educated women to engage in intellectual conversation and exploration. These meetings served as the backdrop for Fuller's most sensational and controversial publication, Woman in the Nineteenth Century, *which was the first fully developed feminist book to appear in the United States. It laid the intellectual groundwork for the Seneca Falls Convention of 1848, where those gathered issued their own call for gender equality.*

In the essay, Fuller argues that both men and women have been damaged by the unequal status of women in society. She proposes equality as a method of social healing. Much as Emerson describes Americans as having an incomplete relationship with nature, Fuller envisions a new relationship between men and women that will lead to greater "harmony."

As the 1840s progressed, Fuller's own political commitments became increasingly radical, and she grew frustrated with those Transcendentalists who did not engage in the great struggles of the day. She spent much of the end of her life in Europe, reporting on the revolution in Italy. Coming back from Europe, she died in a shipwreck.

Excerpted from Margaret Fuller Ossoli, Woman in the Nineteenth Century . . . *(Boston, 1855), 168-78.*

Man is a being of two-fold relations, to nature beneath, and intelligences above him. The earth is his school, if not his birthplace; God his object; life and thought his means of interpreting nature, and aspiring to God.

Only a fraction of this purpose is accomplished in the life of any one man. Its entire accomplishment is to be hoped only from the sum of the lives of men, or Man considered as a whole.

As this whole has one soul and one body, any injury or obstruction to a part, or to the meanest member, affects the whole. Man can never be perfectly happy or virtuous, till all men are so.

To address Man wisely, you must not forget that his life is partly animal, subject to the same laws with Nature.

But you cannot address him wisely unless you consider him still more as soul, and appreciate the conditions and destiny of soul.

The growth of Man is two-fold, masculine and feminine.

So far as these two methods can be distinguished, they are so as

Energy and Harmony;
Power and Beauty;
Intellect and Love;

or by some such rude classification; for we have not language primitive and pure enough to express such ideas with precision.

Those two sides are supposed to be expressed in Man and Woman, that is, as the more and the less, for the faculties have not been given pure to either, but only in preponderance. There are also exceptions in great number, such as men of far more beauty than power, and the reverse. But, as a general rule, it seems to have been the intention to give a preponderance on the one side, that is called masculine, and on the other, one that is called feminine.

There cannot be a doubt that, if these two developments were in perfect harmony, they would correspond to and fulfil[l] one another, like hemispheres, or the tenor and bass in music.

But there is no perfect harmony in human nature; and the two parts answer one another only now and then; or, if there be a persistent consonance, it can only be traced at long intervals, instead of discoursing an obvious melody.

What is the cause of this?

Man, in the order of time, was developed first; as energy comes before harmony; power before beauty.

Woman was therefore under his care as an elder. He might have been her guardian and teacher.

But, as human nature goes not straight forward, but by excessive action and then reäction in an undulated course, he misunderstood and abused his advantages, and became her temporal master instead of her spiritual sire.

On himself came the punishment. He educated Woman more as a servant than a daughter, and found himself a king without a queen. . . .

. . . [H]e did not clearly see that Woman was half himself; that her interests were identical with his; and that, by the law of their common being, he could never reach his true proportions while she remained in any wise shorn of hers.

And so it has gone on to our day; both ideas developing, but more slowly than they would under a clearer recognition of truth and justice, which would have permitted the sexes their due influence on one another, and mutual improvement from more dignified relations.

Wherever there was pure love, the natural influences were, for the time, restored.

Wherever the poet or artist gave free course to his genius, he saw the truth, and expressed it in worthy forms, for these men especially share and need the feminine principle. The divine birds need to be brooded into life and song by mothers.

Wherever religion (I mean the thirst for truth and good, not the love of sect and dogma) had its course, the original design was apprehended in its simplicity. . . .

I have aimed to show that no age was left entirely without a witness of the equality of the sexes in function, duty, and hope. . . .

That now the time has come when a clearer vision and better action are possible—when Man and Woman may regard one another as brother and sister, the pillars of one porch, the priests of one worship.

I have believed and intimated that this hope would receive an ampler fruition, than ever before, in our own land.

And it will do so if this land carry out the principles from which sprang our national life.

I believe that, at present, women are the best helpers of one another.

Let them think; let them act; till they know what they need.

We ask of men to remove arbitrary barriers. Some would like to do more. But I believe it needs that Woman show herself in her native dignity, to teach them how to aid her; their minds are so encumbered by tradition. . . .

You ask, what use will she make of liberty, when she has so long been sustained and restrained?

I answer; in the first place, this will not be suddenly given. I read yesterday a debate of this year on the subject of enlarging women's rights over property. It was a leaf from the class-book that is preparing for the needed instruction. The men learned visibly as they spoke. The champions of Woman saw the fallacy of arguments on the opposite side, and were startled by their own convictions. . . .

But, were this freedom to come suddenly, I have no fear of the consequences. Individuals might commit excesses, but there is not only in the sex a reverence for decorums and limits inherited and enhanced from generation to generation, which many years of other life could not efface, but a native love, in Woman as Woman, . . . which would create immediately a restraining party, the natural legislators and instructors of the rest, and would gradually establish such rules as are needed to guard, without impeding, life. . . .

But if you ask me what offices they may fill, I reply—any. I do not care what case you put; let them be sea-captains, if you will. I do not doubt there are women well fitted for such an office, and, if so, I should be as glad to see them in it. . . .

I think women need, especially at this juncture, a much greater range of occupation than they have, to rouse their latent powers. A party of travelers lately visited a lonely hut on a mountain. There they found an old woman, who told them she and her husband had lived there forty years. "Why," they said, "did you choose so barren a spot?" She "did not know; *it was the man's notion*."

And, during forty years, she had been content to act, without knowing why, upon "the man's notion." I would not have it so.

In families that I know, some little girls like to saw wood, others to use carpenters' tools. Where these tastes are indulged, cheerfulness and good-humor are promoted. Where they are forbidden, because "such things are not proper for girls," they grow sullen and mischievous. . . .

I have no doubt, however, that a large proportion of women would give themselves to the same employments as now, because there are circumstances that must lead them. Mothers will delight to make the nest soft and warm. Nature would take care of that; no need to clip the wings of any bird that wants to soar and sing, or finds in itself the strength of pinion for a migratory flight unusual to its kind. The difference would be that *all* need not be constrained to employments for which *some* are unfit.

Sarah Margaret Fuller (1810–1850), one of the most extraordinary women of the nineteenth century. She regarded Emerson both as a teacher and as a soulmate, though her "Transcendentalism" led her to increasingly radical political views. (Courtesy of The Library of Congress.)

I have urged upon the sex self-subsistence in its two forms of self-reliance and self-impulse, because I believe them to be the needed means of the present juncture.

I have urged on Woman independence of Man, not that I do not think the sexes mutually needed by one another, but because in Woman this fact has led to an excessive devotion, which has cooled love, degraded marriage, and prevented either sex from being what it should be to itself or the other.

I wish Woman to live, first for God's sake. Then she will not make an imperfect man her god, and thus sink into idolatry. Then she will not take what is not fit for her from a sense of weakness and poverty. Then, if she knows what she needs in Man embodied, she will know how to love, and be worthy of being loved.

By being more a soul, she will not be less Woman, for nature is perfected through spirit.

Now there is no woman, only an overgrown child. . . .

A profound thinker has said, "No married woman can represent the female world, for she belongs to her husband. The idea of Woman must be represented by a virgin."

But that is the very fault of marriage, and of the present relation between the sexes, that the woman *does* belong to the man, instead of forming a whole with him. . . .

Woman, self-centred, would never be absorbed by any relation; it would be only an experience to her as to man. It is a vulgar error that love, *a* love, to Woman is her whole existence; she also is born for Truth and Love in their universal energy. Would she but assume her inheritance, Mary would not be the only virgin mother. Not Manzoni alone would celebrate in his wife the virgin mind with the maternal wisdom and conjugal affections. The soul is ever young, ever virgin. . . .

. . . It is not Woman, but the law of right, the law of growth, that speaks in us, and demands the perfection of each being in its kind—apple as apple, Woman as Woman. Without adopting your theory, I know that I, a daughter, live through the life of Man; but what concerns me now is, that my life be a beautiful, powerful, in a word, a complete life in its kind. Had I but one more moment to live I must wish the same. . . .

I stand in the sunny noon of life. Objects no longer glitter in the dews of morning, neither are yet softened by the shadows of evening. Every spot is seen, every chasm revealed. Climbing the dusty hill, some fair effigies that once stood for symbols of human destiny have been broken; those I still have with me show defects in this broad light. Yet enough is left, even by experience, to point distinctly to the glories of that destiny; faint, but not to be mistaken streaks of the future day. I can say with the bard,

> "Though many have suffered shipwreck, still beat noble hearts."

Questions

1. *How would you summarize "Nature" in a short paragraph? There is no right way to do this, but what did you take away as the most important insights?*
2. *How does Thoreau justify civil disobedience? Where does this argument lead for a whole society? How would you refute it?*
3. *How does Fuller see the differences between men and women? What has resulted from these differences, and how does she propose to fix it?*

FURTHER READING

To understand Transcendentalism you must tackle the transcendentalists' own writings. Emerson and Thoreau are widely available in print, but for some of the lesser known writers and lesser known essays, Perry Miller's two anthologies The Transcendentalists: An Anthology *(Cambridge, Massachusetts, 1950) and* The American Transcendentalists: Their Prose and Poetry *(Garden City, New York, 1957) are good sources. For more on the relationship between Unitarianism and Transcendentalism see William Hutchison,* The Transcendentalist Ministers: Church Reform in the New England Renaissance *(New Haven, Connecticut, 1959). Another way to approach this subject is through the biographies of participants. See, for example, Robert D. Richardson, Jr.* Emerson: The Mind on Fire, a Biography *(Berkeley, 1995); Henry Stephen Salt,* The Life of Henry David Thoreau, *edited by George Hendrick, Willene Hendrick, and Fritz Oehlschlaeger (Urbana, Illinois, 1993); and Charles Capper,* Margaret Fuller: An American Romantic Life *(New York, 1992).*

Manifest Destiny

Peter L. Hahn and Michael J. Hogan

INTRODUCTION

During the 1840s, the United States acquired control over vast tracts of land in Texas, the southwest, including California, and the Oregon Territory. Some of the land was acquired by diplomacy and some by force; all of it has remained an integral part of the country. Some Americans advocated and celebrated such enormous territorial growth by rallying behind a sense of national mission and exceptionalism called "Manifest Destiny" and supporting war against Mexico as a means to continental empire. Others opposed this expansionism on political, economic, strategic, and moral grounds. Such controversy over expansionism has persisted since the 1840s.

THE CONTEMPORARY DEBATE OVER CONTINENTAL EXPANSION

The following documents reveal many aspects of the debate on expansionism that began in the 1830s and persisted into the 1840s. The first two documents offer contrasting views of the general question of expansionism. The remaining documents reveal the parameters of debate as it focused on specific issues: whether to annex Texas in 1844, whether to wage war on Mexico in 1846–1848, and whether to permit slavery to spread into the territories acquired. Collectively, these records demonstrate that the American people reached no consensus either in favor of, or in opposition to, the expansionism that occurred.

John L. O'Sullivan Advocates Manifest Destiny

An intellectual atmosphere conducive to expansionism stood behind the United States's drive across the continent in the 1840s. Some of the strongest advocates of expansion and conquest were writers of editorials in the popular press, and of these perhaps the most famous was John L. O'Sullivan, editor of The United States Magazine and Democratic Review. *The selection printed below, comprised of parts of two O'Sullivan editorials published in 1839 and 1845, conveys the themes and tone of O'Sullivan's advocacy. The editorials originally appeared in* The United States Magazine and Democratic Review, *6 (November 1839):426–27, 429–30; and 17 (July 1845):5, 7–8.*

[1839]

The American people having derived their origin from many other nations, and the Declaration of National Independence being entirely based on the great principle of human equality, these facts demonstrate at once our disconnected position as regards any other nation; that we have, in reality, but little connection with the past history of any of them, and still less with all antiquity, its glories, or its crimes. On the contrary, our national birth was the beginning of a new history, the formation and progress of an untried political system, which separates us from the past and connects us with the future only; and so far as regards the entire development of the natural rights of man, in moral, political, and national life, we may confidently assume that our country is destined to be *the great nation* of futurity. . . .

We have no interest in the scenes of antiquity, only as lessons of avoidance of nearly all their examples. The expansive future is our arena, and for our history. We are entering on its untrodden space, with the truths of God in our minds, beneficent objects in our hearts, and with a clear conscience unsullied by the past. We are the nation of human progress, and who will, what can, set limits to our onward march? Providence is with us, and no earthly power can. We point to the everlasting truth on the first page of our national declaration, and we proclaim to the millions of other lands, that "the gates of hell"—the powers of aristocracy and monarchy—"shall not prevail against it."

The far-reaching, the boundless future will be the era of American greatness. In its magnificent domain of space and time, the nation of many nations is destined to manifest to mankind the excellence of divine principles; to establish on earth the noblest temple ever dedicated to the worship of the Most High—the Sacred and the True. Its floor shall be a hemisphere—its roof the firmament of the star-studded heavens, and its congregation an Union of many Republics, comprising hundreds of happy millions, calling, owning no man master, but governed by God's natural and moral law of equality, the law of brotherhood—of "peace and good will amongst men.". . .

Yes, we are the nation of progress, of individual freedom, of universal enfranchisement. Equality of rights is the cynosure of our union of States, the grand exemplar of the correlative equality of individuals; and while truth sheds its effulgence, we cannot retrograde, without dissolving the one and subverting the other.

We must onward to the fulfilment of our mission—to the entire development of the principle of our organization—freedom of conscience, freedom of person, freedom of trade and business pursuits, universality of freedom and equality. This is our high destiny, and in nature's eternal, inevitable decree of cause and effect we must accomplish it. All this will be our future history, to establish on earth the moral dignity and salvation of man—the immutable truth and beneficence of God. For this blessed mission to the nations of the world, which are shut out from the life-giving light of truth, has America been chosen; and her high example shall smite unto death the tyranny of kings, hierarchs, and oligarchs, and carry the glad tidings of peace and good will where myriads now endure an existence scarcely more enviable than that of beasts of the field. Who, then, can doubt that our country is destined to be *the great nation* of futurity?

[1845]

It is time now for opposition to the Annexation of Texas to cease, all further agitation of the waters of bitterness and strife, at least in connexion with this question,—even though it may perhaps be required of us as a necessary condition of the freedom of our institutions, that we must live on for ever in a state of unpausing struggle and excitement upon some subject of party division or other. But, in regard to Texas, enough has now been given to Party. It is time for the common duty of Patriotism to the Country to succeed;—or if this claim will not be recognized, it is at least time for common sense to acquiesce with decent grace in the inevitable and the irrevocable.

Texas is now ours. Already, before these words are written, her Convention has undoubtedly ratified the acceptance, by her Congress, of our proffered invitation into the Union; and made the requisite changes in her already republican form of constitution to adopt it to its future federal relations. Her star and her stripe may already be said to have taken their place in the glorious blazon of our common nationality; and the sweep of our eagle's wing already includes within its circuit the wide extent of her fair and fertile land. She is no longer to us a mere geographical space—a certain combination of coast, plain, mountain, valley, forest and stream. She is no longer to us a mere country on the map. She comes within the dear and sacred designation of Our Country; no longer a *"pays,"* [country] she is part of *"la patrie;"*

[the nation] and that which is at once a sentiment and a virtue, Patriotism, already begins to thrill for her too within the national heart. . . .

Why, were other reasoning wanting, in favor of now elevating this question of the reception of Texas into the Union, out of the lower region of our past party dissensions, up to its proper level of a high and broad nationality, it surely is to be found, found abundantly, in the manner in which other nations have undertaken to intrude themselves into it, between us and the proper parties to the case, in a spirit of hostile interference against us, for the avowed object of thwarting our policy and hampering our power, limiting our greatness and checking the fulfilment of our manifest destiny to overspread the continent allotted by Providence for the free development of our yearly multiplying millions. This we have seen done by England, our old rival and enemy; and by France. . . .

. . . Texas has been absorbed into the Union in the inevitable fulfilment of the general law which is rolling our population westward; the connexion of which with that ratio of growth in population which is destined within a hundred years to swell our numbers to the enormous population of *two hundred and fifty millions* (if not more), is too evident to leave us in doubt of the manifest design of Providence in regard to the occupation of this continent. It was disintegrated from Mexico in the natural course of events, by a process perfectly legitimate on its own part, blameless on ours; and in which all the censures due to wrong, perfidy and folly, rest on Mexico alone. And possessed as it was by a population which was in truth but a colonial detachment from our own, and which was still bound by myriad ties of the very heartstrings to its old relations, domestic and political, their incorporation into the Union was not only inevitable, but the most natural, right and proper thing in the world—and it is only astonishing that there should be any among ourselves to say it nay.

W. E. Channing Denounces Expansion

Of course, not all Americans endorsed the annexation of Texas or the general pattern of continental expansion. Many Americans opposed this territorial growth on the grounds that it would undermine democratic institutions at home, estrange relations with foreign states, encourage the spread of slavery, and violate the country's deepest values, such as peace and the rule of law. Boston minister William Ellery Channing emerged as a leading anti-expansionist spokesman during the national debate on the Republic of Texas's request for annexation in 1837, a request that, at first, was denied. The selection below is taken from Channing's letter of August 1837 to Henry Clay. Excerpted from The Works of William E. Channing, D.D., *6th edition, (Boston, 1846), 2:183–87, 204–8, 210, 217–18, 220, 231–32, 240.*

MY DEAR SIR,

. . . It is with great reluctance that I enter on the topic of this letter. . . . I desire nothing so much as to devote what remains of life to the study and exposition of great principles and universal truths. But the subject of Texas weighs heavily on my mind, and I cannot shake it off. To me, it is more than a political question. It belongs eminently to morals and religion. . . . Should Texas be annexed to our country, I feel that I could not forgive myself, if, with my deep, solemn impressions, I should do nothing to avert the evil. I cannot easily believe, that this disastrous measure is to be adopted, especially at the present moment. The annexation of Texas, under existing circumstances, would be more than rashness; it would be madness. That opposition to it must exist at the South, as well as at the North, I cannot doubt. Still, there is a general impression, that great efforts will be made to accomplish this object at the approaching session of Congress, and that nothing but strenuous resistance can prevent their success. I must write, therefore, as if the danger were real and imminent; and if any should think that I am betrayed into undue earnestness by a false alarm, they will remember that there are circumstances, in which excess of vigilance is a virtue. . . .

We have a strong argument against annexing Texas to the United States, in the Criminality of the revolt which threatens to sever that country from Mexico. On this point our citizens need light. The Texan insurrection is seriously regarded by many among us as a struggle of the oppressed for freedom. The Texan revolution is thought to resemble our own. Our own is contaminated by being brought into such relationship, and we owe to our fathers and ourselves a disclaimer of affinity with this new republic. The Texan revolt, if regarded in its causes and its means of success, is criminal; and we ought in no way to become partakers in its guilt. . . .

Having unfolded the argument against the annexation of Texas from the criminality of the revolt, I proceed to a second very solemn consideration, namely, that by this act our country will enter on a career of encroachment, war, and crime, and will merit and incur the punishment and woe of aggravated wrong-doing. The seizure of Texas will not stand alone. It will darken our future history. It will be linked by an iron necessity to long-continued deeds of rapine and blood. Ages may not see the catastrophe of the tragedy, the first scene of which we are so ready to enact. It is strange that nations should be so much more rash than individuals; and this, in the face of experience, which has been teaching, from the beginning of society, that, of all precipitate and criminal deeds, those perpetrated by nations are the most fruitful of misery.

Did this country know itself, or were it disposed to profit by self-knowledge, it would feel the necessity of laying an immediate curb on its passion for extended territory. It would not trust itself to new acquisitions. It would shrink from the temptation to conquest. We are a restless people, prone to encroachment, impatient of the ordinary laws of progress, less anxious to consolidate and perfect than to extend our institutions, more ambitious of spreading ourselves over a wide space than of diffusing beauty and fruitfulness over a narrower field. We boast of our rapid growth, forgetting that, throughout nature, noble growths are slow. Our people throw themselves beyond the bounds of civilization, and expose themselves to relapses into a semi-barbarous state, under the impulse of wild imagination, and for the name of great possessions. . . .

It is full time, that we should lay on ourselves serious, resolute restraint. Possessed of a domain, vast enough for the growth of ages, it is time for us to stop in the career of acquisition and conquest. Already endangered by our greatness, we cannot advance without imminent peril to our institutions, union, prosperity, virtue, and peace. . . .

Even were the dispositions of our government most pacific and opposed to encroachment, the annexation of Texas would almost certainly embroil us with Mexico. This territory would be overrun by adventurers; and the most unprincipled of these, the proscribed, the disgraced, the outcasts of society, would, of course, keep always in advance of the better population. These would represent our republic on the borders of the Mexican States. The history of the connexion of such men with the Indians, forewarns us of the outrages which would attend their contact with the border inhabitants of our southern neighbour. . . .

Hitherto I have spoken of the annexation of Texas as embroiling us with Mexico; but it will not stop here. It will bring us into collision with other states. It will, almost of necessity, involve us in hostility with European powers. . . .

I proceed now to a consideration of what is to me the strongest argument against annexing Texas to the United States. . . . The annexation of Texas, I have said, will extend and perpetuate slavery. It is fitted, and, still more, intended to do so. On this point there can be no doubt. . . .

I now ask, whether, as a people, we are prepared to seize on a neighbouring territory for the end of extending slavery? I ask, whether, as a people, we can stand forth in the sight of God, in the sight of the nations, and adopt this atrocious policy? Sooner perish! Sooner be our name blotted out from the record of nations! . . .

I now proceed to another important argument against the annexation of Texas to our country, the argument drawn from the bearings of the measure on our National Union. Next to liberty, union is our great political interest, and this cannot but be loosened, it may be dissolved, by the proposed extension of our territory. . . .

I proceed now to the last head of this communication. I observe, that the cause of Liberty, of free institutions, a cause more sacred than union, forbids the annexation of Texas. It is plain from the whole preceding discussion, that this measure will exert a disastrous influence on the moral sentiments and principles of this country, by sanctioning plunder, by inflaming cupidity, by encouraging lawless speculation, by bringing into the confederacy a community whose whole history and circumstances are adverse to moral order and wholesome restraint, by violating national faith, by proposing immoral and inhuman ends, by placing us as a people in opposition to the efforts of philanthropy, and the advancing movements of the civilized world. It will spread a moral corruption, already too rife among us, and, in so doing, it will shake the foundations of freedom at home, and bring reproach on it abroad. It will be treachery to the great cause which has been confided to this above all nations.

Polk Asks for War on Mexico

Nine months after the Senate rejected the annexation treaty, lame-duck President John Tyler pushed through Congress a joint resolution authorizing the admission of Texas into the Union. That move provoked tension between the United States and Mexico, a country that felt cheated by the annexation of Texas and that contested American claims regarding Texas's border. Perhaps eager to provoke a war of conquest, President James K. Polk ordered the U.S. Army deep into the contested land. Fighting erupted between U.S. and Mexican soldiers in April 1846, and in early May, Polk asked Congress, in the message printed below, to issue a declaration of war. The message is taken from A Compilation of the Messages and Papers of the Presidents. . ., *ed. James D. Richardson (New York, 1897), 6:2287, 2291–93.*

WASHINGTON, May 11, 1846.

To the Senate and House of Representatives:

The existing state of the relations between the United States and Mexico renders it proper that I should bring the subject to the consideration of Congress. . . .

The Army moved from Corpus Christi on the 11th of March, and on the 28th of that month arrived on the left bank of the Del Norte opposite to Matamoras, where it encamped on a commanding position, which has since been strengthened by the erection of field works. . . .

The Mexican forces at Matamoras assumed a belligerent attitude, and on the 12th of April General Ampudia, then in command, notified General Taylor to break up his camp within twenty-four hours and to retire beyond the Nueces River, and in the event of his failure to comply with these demands announced that arms, and arms alone, must decide the question. . . .

The grievous wrongs perpetrated by Mexico upon our citizens throughout a long period of years remain unredressed, and solemn treaties pledging her public faith for this redress have been disregarded. A government either unable or unwilling to enforce the execution of such treaties fails to perform one of its plainest duties.

. . . Our forbearance has gone to such an extreme as to be mistaken in its character. Had we acted with vigor in repelling the insults and redressing the injuries inflicted by Mexico at the commencement, we should doubtless have escaped all the difficulties in which we are now involved.

Instead of this, however, we have been exerting our best efforts to propitiate her good will. Upon the pretext that Texas, a nation as independent as herself, thought proper to unite its destinies with our own, she has affected to believe that we have severed her rightful territory, and in official proclamations and manifestoes has repeatedly threatened to make war upon us for the purpose of reconquering Texas. In the meantime we have tried every effort at reconciliation. The cup of forbearance had been exhausted even before the recent information from the frontier of the Del Norte. But now, after reiterated menaces, Mexico has passed the boundary of the United States, has invaded our territory and shed American blood upon the American soil. She has proclaimed that hostilities have commenced, and that the two nations are now at war.

As war exists, and, notwithstanding all our efforts to avoid it, exists by the act of Mexico herself, we are called upon by every consideration of duty and patriotism to vindicate with decision the honor, the rights, and the interests of our country. . . .

In further vindication of our rights and defense of our territory, I invoke the prompt action of Congress to recognize the existence of the war, and to place at the disposition of the Executive the means of prosecuting the war with vigor, and thus hastening the restoration of peace.

JAMES K. POLK

Abraham Lincoln Challenges Polk's Justification for War

The war against Mexico went well for the United States, which eventually occupied Mexico City and forced Mexico to cede approximately one-third of its land. Yet from the earliest days of fighting, many in the United States questioned the legal and moral grounds for conducting what they viewed as an aggressive war of conquest. The following address, delivered by Representative Abraham Lincoln, Whig of Illinois, in Congress on 12 January 1848, raised such concerns. The speech is reprinted from Complete Works of Abraham Lincoln, *ed. John G. Nicolay and John Hay (New York, 1905), 1:329–30, 338–41.*

[T]aking for true all the President states as facts, he falls far short of proving his justification.... The President, in his first war message of May, 1846, declares that the soil was ours on which hostilities were commenced by Mexico, and he repeats that declaration almost in the same language in each successive annual message, thus showing that he deems that point a highly essential one. In the importance of that point I entirely agree with the President. To my judgment it is the very point upon which he should be justified, or condemned....

... I propose to state my understanding of the true rule for ascertaining the boundary between Texas and Mexico. It is that wherever Texas was exercising jurisdiction was hers; and wherever Mexico was exercising jurisdiction was hers; and that whatever separated the actual exercise of jurisdiction of the one from that of the other was the true boundary between them. . . . The extent of our territory in that region depended not on any treaty-fixed boundary (for no treaty had attempted it), but on revolution....

... In my view, just so far as she carried her resolution by obtaining the actual, willing or unwilling, submission of the people, so far the country was hers, and no farther. Now, sir, for the purpose of obtaining the very best evidence as to whether Texas had actually carried her revolution to the place where the hostilities of the present war commenced, let the President answer the interrogatories I proposed, as before mentioned, or some other similar ones. Let him answer fully, fairly, and candidly.... And if, so answering, he can show that the soil was ours where the first blood of the war was shed,—that it was not within an inhabited country, or, if within such, that the inhabitants had submitted themselves to the civil authority of Texas or of the United States, and that the same is true of the site of Fort Brown,—then I am with him for his justification.... But if he can not or will not do this,— if on any pretense or no pretense he shall refuse or omit it—then I shall be fully convinced of what I more than suspect already—that he is deeply conscious of being in the wrong; that he feels the blood of this war, like the blood of Abel, is crying to Heaven against him; that originally having some strong motive—what, I will not stop now to give my opinion concerning—to involve the two countries in a war, and trusting to escape scrutiny by fixing the public gaze upon the exceeding brightness of military glory,—that attractive rainbow that arises in showers of blood—that serpent's eye that charms to destroy,—he plunged into it, and has swept on and on till, disappointed in his calculation of the ease with which Mexico might be subdued, he now finds himself he knows not where. How like the half-insane mumbling of a fever dream is the whole war part of his late message!

The Expansion of Slavery Justified

The acquisition of vast territory in the southwest raised the question of whether slavery would be permitted to expand there. Representative David Wilmot, a Pennsylvania Democrat, provoked furious debate by proposing in August 1846 a prohibition against slavery in lands acquired in the war. The so-called Wilmot Proviso repeatedly passed the House, where northerners enjoyed a majority, but died in the Senate, where southerners and other Democrats blocked it. The document that follows, an editorial condemning the Wilmot Proviso, first appeared in The United States Magazine and Democratic Review *(October 1847), 21:292.*

All the territory of the Union is the common property of all the states—every member, new or old, of the Union, admitted to partnership under the constitution, has a perfect right to enjoy the territory, which is the common property of all. Some of the territory was acquired by treaty from England—much of it by cession from the older states; yet more by treaties with Indians, and still greater quantities by purchase from Spain and France;—large tracts again by the annexation of Texas—and the present war will add still more to the quantity yet to be entered by citizens of the United States, or of those of any of the countries of Europe that choose to migrate thither. All this land, no matter whence it was derived, belongs to all the states jointly. . . . [N]o citizen of the United States can be debarred from moving thither with his property, and enjoying the liberties guaranteed by the constitution. . . .

Any law or regulation which interrupts, limits, delays or postpones the rights of the owner to the immediate command of his service or labor, operates a discharge of the slave from service, and is a violation of the constitution. . . . To set up therefore a pretence that if they adhere to the property they possess, they shall be deprived of their rights in the states to be formed in any acquired territory, is an unprincipled violation of a solemn treaty, an attack upon the constitution, and a gross injustice to the rights of neighboring states. If the constitution is respected, then the rights of no member in the common property can be impaired, because it is possessed of other property distasteful to other members.

The Expansion of Slavery Condemned

Among the most strident supporters of the Wilmot Proviso stood the noted abolitionist Charles Sumner of Massachusetts. In this treatise, written for the Massachusetts legislature in April 1847, Sumner criticizes the war against Mexico on anti-slavery and other grounds. Taken from "Report on the War with Mexico," in Old South Leaflets, *no. 132 (Boston, n.d.), 150–53, 155–56 [separately paginated as 14–17, 19–20].*

It can no longer be doubted that this is a war of conquest. . . .

A war of conquest is bad; but the present war has darker shadows. It is a war for the extension of slavery over a territory which has already been purged, by Mexican authority, from this stain and curse. Fresh markets of human beings are to be established; further opportunities for this hateful traffic are to be opened; the lash of the overseer is to be quickened in new regions; and the wretched slave is to be hurried to unaccustomed fields of toil. It can hardly be believed that now, more than eighteen hundred years since the dawn of the Christian era, a government, professing the law of charity and justice, should be employed in war to extend an institution which exists in defiance of these sacred principles.

It has already been shown that the annexation of Texas was consummated for this purpose. The Mexican war is a continuance, a prolongation, of the same efforts; and the success which crowned the first emboldens the partisans of the latter, who now, as before, profess to extend the area of freedom, while they are establishing a new sphere for slavery. . . . But it is not merely proposed to open new markets for slavery: it is also designed to confirm and fortify the "Slave Power."... Regarding it as a war to strengthen the "Slave Power," we are conducted to a natural conclusion, that it is virtually, and in its consequences, a war against the free States of the Union.... Nor should we be indifferent to the enormous expenditures which have already been lavished upon the war, and the accumulating debt which will hold in mortgage the future resources of the country. It is impossible to estimate the exact amount of these. At this moment the cost of the war cannot be less than seventy millions. It may be a hundred millions.

This sum is so vast as to be beyond easy comprehension. It may be estimated, partly, by reference to the cost of other objects of interest. It is far more than all the funds for common schools throughout the United States. It is ample for the endowment of three or more institutions like Harvard College in every State. It would plant churches in all the neglected valleys of the land. It would bind and interlace every part of the country by new railroads. It would make our broad and rude soil blossom like a garden....

... The war is a crime, and all who have partaken in the blood of its well-fought fields have aided in its perpetration. It is a principle of military law that the soldier shall not question the orders of his superior. If this shall exonerate the army from blame, it will be only to press with accumulated weight upon the government, which has set in motion this terrible and irresponsible machine.

Questions

1. *On what grounds did some Americans advocate expansion into Texas, Oregon, and other regions? Why did other Americans oppose such steps? In your judgment, which side made the most compelling arguments on political, legal, and moral grounds?*
2. *Was the U.S. war against Mexico justified?*
3. *How did slavery and the emerging sectional dispute influence the debate over expansion? How did the acquisition of territory, in turn, aggravate the sectional conflict?*

FURTHER READING

Scholarship has diversified remarkably since Justin H. Smith published The War With Mexico *(New York, 1919), a patriotic account of U.S. expansionism in the 1840s. Norman A. Graebner,* Empire on the Pacific: A Study in American Continental Expansion *(New York, 1955), and David M. Pletcher,* The Diplomacy of Annexation: Texas, Oregon, and the Mexican War *(Columbia, Missouri, 1973), chronicle and critically analyze the westward surge of the American domain. Reginald Horsman,* Race and Manifest Destiny: The Origins of American Racial Anglo-Saxonism *(Cambridge, Massachusetts, 1981), probes the racism underlying expansionism, while Gene Brack,* Mexico Views Manifest Destiny, 1821–1845: An Essay on the Origins of the Mexican War *(Albuquerque, 1975), offers a view from south of the border.*

The World of the Slaves: The Roots of Modern African American Culture

Marshall F. Stevenson, Jr.
and Warren R. Van Tine

Introduction

For nearly two and a half centuries, Africans were enslaved on the North American continent. The system of racial slavery that developed in colonial America and the United States had a distinct impact on the nation's development. It helped shape the unique social and economic system of the South; it was a significant force propelling westward expansion; it was the underlying factor leading to the trauma of the Civil War; it generated the ideology of Black inferiority that led to Jim Crowism and African American economic impoverishment for well over a century after emancipation; and it established the racial tensions and divisions under which our nation still suffers.

Generations of enslavement also had a profound impact on African American culture. The practice of slavery in North America, it must be remembered, lasted for more years than the United States has yet been in existence. During this time of enslavement, Blacks shaped a distinctive culture by combining their African heritage with acquired European practices in a manner that allowed them to enjoy meaningful lives within the confines of bondage. The culture that emerged was one that not only enabled the enslaved Africans to survive but one that gave them a sense of dignity, self-worth, and hope under the most bleak of circumstances.

The world the slaves made continues to influence African American life in the present, although developments since emancipation have caused a continual evolution of Black culture. One of the most important of these developments was the mass movement of African Americans from the rural, agrarian South to the urban, industrial North during the great migration that began at the end of the nineteenth century. Another critical development has been the more recent struggle for Black equality, with its diverse themes of integration, Black Power, and Afrocentrism. Yet despite ongoing historical developments, scholars can still discern that the world the slaves made—the attitudes and practices developed while enslaved—still carries great meaning for all Americans.

The Culture of the Enslaved

While they shared a common heritage, slaves' experiences varied widely. Throughout the South, Blacks toiled on large plantations, small farms, and in urban areas. For a fortunate few, the opportunity for education and perhaps manumission existed. Most, however, were doomed to a life of bondage, in which old age set in before age fifty. All slaves, however, contributed to the development of a culture that allowed them to survive and find meaning for their life in servitude, and also provided a foundation for acts of resistance, both small and large.

The Voices of the Enslaved

Much of what scholars know about slavery is derived from the records and letters that have survived from the white slave owners, their family members, the local governments and courts that they controlled, or from northern or European whites touring the South and writing on their observations. The institution of slavery created major barriers to slaves generating sources that could later inform historians. Foremost among these barriers was a general prohibition against teaching enslaved Africans to read or write, which limited their ability to create a record for posterity. Fortunately, during the Depression-plagued 1930s, as part of the New Deal's relief work efforts, the Federal Writers' Project employed a number of interviewers to seek out and question the few thousand aged African Americans who had been born into slavery and had subsequently

---

Excerpts from "Interviews with Former Slaves," reprinted from *Bullwhip Days: The Slaves Remember, An Oral History,* James Mellon, editor. Published by Avon Books by arrangement with Weidenfeld & Nicholson.

been freed at the close of the Civil War. These "slave narratives," while somewhat tinted by the passage of six decades from the events being described, nonetheless have proved to be an invaluable source for understanding what the "peculiar institution" of slavery meant to those enslaved, how it influenced their attitudes and behavior, and how they built a culture of dignity while under its yoke. These passages are written in Black dialect, itself a heritage of generations of bondage without access to formal education. Many of the interviewers of the former slaves, moreover, were particularly interested in speech patterns and went out of their way to transcribe their subject phonetically. These excerpts are taken from Bullwhip Days: The Slaves Remember, An Oral History *(New York, 1988), 42, 47–48, 92–93, 197–98.*

Anna Wright

You wants ter know 'bout some ole slavery foods? Well, I'll tell you what I knows.

Did you ever hear of kush? Kush wus corn bread cooked on de big griddle in de fireplace, mashed up with raw onions an' ham gravy poured over it. You might think dat hit ain't good, but hit am.

Fried chicken wus seasoned, drapped in flour, an' den simmered in a big pan of ham gravy wid de lid on hit, till hit wus tender. Den, de lid wus tuck off, an' de chicken wus fried a golden brown, as quick as possible.

De griddle cakes wus flour an' meal mixed, put on a big ole iron griddle in de fireplace an' flipped over two times.

Ash cake wus made of either meal or flour, wrapped in a damp cloth an' cooked in de hot ashes on de ha'th. Taters wus cooked in de ashes, too, an' dey wus good like dat.

Fish, dem days, wus dipped in meal 'fore dey wus cooked, 'cept catfish, an' dey wus stewed wid onions.

Cornmeal dumplin's wus biled in de turnip greens, collards, cabbages, an' so on, even ter snap beans, an' at supper de potlicker wus eat wid de dumplin's. Dat's why de folks wus so healthy.

Speakin' 'bout sweets de blackberry or other kind of pie wus cooked in a big pan wid two crusts. Dat made more an' wus better to boot. Cakes wus mostly plain or had jelly fillin', 'cept fer special company.

Annie Reed

Way back in de old days, when de creatures was all people, Br'er Fox give a log-rollin' and invite all de neighborhood. Br'er Possum was dere, and Br'er Rabbit, and all de rest. Old Sis' Fox and some de neighbor women was fixin' de dinner. Dey done de churnin' too, and Sis' Fox go sat de bucket of butter in de spring where it be good and cool for de big dinner.

Br'er Rabbit, he keep cuttin' he eye roun' all de time, and he see Sis' Fox put de butter in de spring. At dat, he grin to hisse'f and lick his mouf. When dey start rollin' de logs, Br'er Rabbit was right dar wid he shoulder down, jest a-gruntin'. But he ain't do no wuk.

'Long up in de mornin', when de sun get hot, Br'er Rabbit, he let out a big holler: "Hooee, Br'er Fox got to run back home a li'l while!"

"What de matta now, Br'er Rabbit?"

"My wife gwine bring me a new heir."

Den, Br'er Rabbit, he run over in de woods like he takin' de shawtcut home. But he jest creep roun' to de spring and take up dat bucket of butter and eat it all. Den, he wipe he mouf and he hands and lay down in de shade to take a nap.

Jest 'fore dinner time, he git up and come out of de woods walkin' slow and proud.

Br'er Fox see him and holler, "Well, has you got de new heir, Br'er Rabbit?"

Br'er Rabbit say, "Uhuh, got a new heir."

Br'er Fox say, " What you name dis-un?"

Br'er Rabbit say, "He name 'Lickbottom.'" Br'er Rabbit tole dat 'cause he done lick de bottom of de butter bucket.

Br'er Fox say, "Well, dat sho' is fine; sho' hope he does well. And now, it's 'bout de middle of de day, so le's knock off and git dinner."

So dey all go up to de house, and Br'er Fox, he go down to de spring to git de butter. When he git dere, he find all de butter gone.

Br'er Fox, he go back to de house and he say, "Somebody done been to de spring and et all de butter. Any of you-all de one what done it?"

Dey all say dey ain't seen no butter. Den, Br'er Fox, he say, "Well, ain't nobody else been roun' heah, so somebody tole a lie. On'y way we kin find out is to hold ever'body up to de fiah [fire] and make de butter run out de one what done it."

Dey all 'greed to dat, and den dey start holdin' one 'nother up to de fiah, startin' off wid Br'er Possum. So dey keep on till dey git to Br'er Rabbit, and when dey hold him up, here come all de butter runnin' out.

Den, dey all say, "Uhuh, Br'er Rabbit got de butter. What us gwine do wid him?"

Some say to th'ow him in de fiah, and some say th'ow him in de brierpatch. Br'er Rabbit, he don't say nothin'.

Den, Br'er Fox, say, "Br'er Rabbit, which one you ruther us do?"

Br'er Rabbit, he say, "Th'ow me in de fiah, please, Br'er Fox; dem ole briers jest tear my eyes out, if you th'ow me in de brierpatch."

So dey tuk him and th'owed him in de brierpatch. And Br'er Rabbit, he shook he'se'f and jump 'way up on de hill and laugh and say, "Thank you, Br'er Fox. I was bred and born in a brierpatch."

Henry Lewis

One time, dey was two boys what went out to git hick'ry nuts. Some of 'em was white—dem dat had de hulls off—and dem what had de hulls on was black. When dey gwine back home, dey drap a couple out de bag by de gate of de graveyard. Warn't long befo' a nigger come by, and he hear 'em sortin' out de nuts, jis' inside de gate. He ain't see 'em, but he hear 'em say, "You tek de black ones and I'll tek de white ones." He t'ink it were de Lord and de Debil tekin' de souls of the white folks and cullud folks what been bury dere, and he lit out and run home and tell de marster.

Marster, he say he gwine see 'bout dat, and if dat nigger lyin' he gwine give him hundred lashes. So he go back wid de nigger, and when dey git to de gate de boys inside was done 'vidin' up deir nuts. Den, one say, "How 'bout dem two at de gate?" And de other say, "You tek de white one and I tek de black one." Wid dat, de white marster say, "I'm damned iffen you kin tek me. Tek de nigger. I'm gone." And he lit out. But when he git where he gwine de nigger git dere jis' a leedle bit ahead of him.

Sarah Wilson

I's larned to read de Bible, an' my chillun larned to read an' write, but our white folks didn't believe in niggers larnin' anything. Dey thought hit would make de niggers harder to keep slaves, an' to make dem wuk. All de slaves dat I knowed couldn't read nor write.

Mandy Jones

De slaves would run away, sometimes, an' hide out in de big woods. Dey would dig pits an' kivver de spot wid bushes an' vines, an' mebbe lay out fer a whole year. An' dey had pit schools, in slave days, too—way out in de woods. Dey *was* woods den, an' de slaves would slip out o' de quarters at night an' go to dese pits, an' some niggah dat had some learnin' would have a school.

De way de cullud folks would learn to read was from de white chillun. De white chillun thought a heap of de cullud chillun, an' when dey come out o' school wid deir books in deir han's, dey take de cullud chillun, an' slip off somewhere, an' learns de cullud chillun deir lessons what deir teacher has jus' learned dem.

Culture and Resistance to Slavery

While the distinctive culture that African American slaves created helped them endure the hardships and brutality of slavery, it also helped them actively resist their mistreatment. Frederick Douglass, perhaps the most famous of all antebellum African Americans, was born a slave in 1818 on the Eastern Shore of Maryland. Over the course of the next twenty years, Douglass's life was filled with experiences that were both typical and atypical for most slaves during this time. One of the more uncommon was his being taught to read by his master's wife and children, eventually figuring out the meaning of "abolition," and hearing of slaves running away to the North. By the mid-1830s, Douglass reached a point in his life where he decided to rebel against his oppressors. In 1834 Douglass was hired out by his master, Thomas Auld, to Edward Covey, a farmer with a reputation for "breaking" unruly slaves. The following passage vividly describes the blending of black culture and resistance.

Taken from his autobiography, Narrative of the Life of Frederick Douglass, An American Slave, Written by Himself, *ed. David W. Blight (Boston, 1993), 75–79.*

I have already intimated that my condition was much worse, during the first six months of my stay at Mr. Covey's, than in the last six. The circumstances leading to the change in Mr. Covey's course toward me form an epoch in my humble history. You have seen how a man was made a slave; you shall see how a slave was made a man. On one of the hottest days of the month of August, 1833, Bill Smith, William Hughes, a slave named Eli, and myself, were engaged in fanning wheat. Hughes was clearing the fanned wheat from before the fan, Eli was turning, Smith was feeding, and I was carrying wheat to the fan. The work was simple, requiring strength rather than intellect; yet, to one entirely unused to such work, it came very hard. About three o'clock of that day, I broke down; my strength failed me; I was seized with a violent aching of the head, attended with extreme dizziness; I trembled in every limb. Finding what was coming, I nerved myself up, feeling it would never do to stop work. I stood as long as I could stagger to the hopper with grain. When I could stand no longer, I fell, and felt as if held down by an immense weight. The fan of course stopped; every one had his own work to do; and no one could do the work of the other, and have his own go on at the same time.

Mr. Covey was at the house, about one hundred yards from the treading-yard where we were fanning. On hearing the fan stop, he left immediately, and came to the spot where we were. He hastily inquired what the matter was. Bill answered that I was sick, and there was no one to bring wheat to the fan. I had by this time crawled away under the side of the post and rail-fence by which the yard was enclosed, hoping to find relief by getting out of the sun. He then asked where I was. He was told by one of the hands. He came to the spot, and, after looking at me awhile, asked me what was the matter. I told him as well as I could, for I scarce had strength to speak. He then gave me a savage kick in the side, and told me to get up. I tried to do so, but fell back in the attempt. He gave me another kick, and again told me to rise. I again tried, and succeeded in gaining my feet; but, stooping to get the tub with which I was feeding the fan, I again staggered and fell. While down in this situation, Mr. Covey took up the hickory slat with which Hughes had been striking off the half-bushel measure, and with it gave me a heavy blow upon the head, making a large wound, and the blood ran freely; and with this again told me to get up. I made no effort to comply, having now made up my mind to let him do his worst. In a short time after receiving this blow, my head grew better. Mr. Covey had now left me to my fate. At this moment I resolved, for the first time, to go to my master, enter a complaint, and ask his protection. In order to [do] this, I must that afternoon walk seven miles; and this, under the circumstances, was truly a severe undertaking. . . . [A]fter a journey of about seven miles, occupying some five hours to perform it, I arrived at master's store. I then presented an appearance enough to affect any but a heart of iron. From the crown of my head to my feet, I was covered with blood. My hair was all clotted with dust and blood; my shirt was stiff with blood. My legs and feet were torn in sundry places with briers and thorns, and were also covered with blood. I suppose I looked like a man who had escaped a den of wild beasts, and barely escaped them. In this state I appeared before my master, humbly entreating him to interpose his authority for my protection. I told him all the circumstances as well as I could, and it seemed, as I spoke, at times to affect him. He would then walk the floor, and seek to justify Covey by saying he expected I deserved it. He asked me what I wanted. I told him, to let me get a new home; that as sure as I lived with Mr. Covey again, I should live with but to die with him; that Covey would surely kill me; he was in a fair way for it. Master Thomas ridiculed the idea that there was any danger of Mr. Covey's killing me, and said that he knew Mr. Covey; that he was a good man, and that he could not think of taking me from him; that, should he do so, he would lose the whole year's wages; that I belonged to Mr. Covey for one year, and that I must go back to him, come what might; and that I must not trouble him with any more stories, or that he would himself *get hold of me.* After threatening me thus, he gave me a very large dose of salts, telling me that I might remain in St. Michael's [town] that night, (it being quite late,) but that I must be off back to Mr. Covey's early in the morning; and that if I did not, he would *get hold of me,* which meant that he would whip me. I remained all night, and, according to his orders, I started off to Covey's in the morning, (Saturday morning,) wearied in body and broken in spirit. I got no supper that night, or breakfast that morning. I reached Covey's about nine o'clock; and just as I was getting over the fence that divided Mrs. Kemp's fields from ours, out ran Covey with his cowskin [bullwhip], to give me another whipping. Before he could reach me, I succeeded in getting to the cornfield; and as the corn was very high, it afforded me the means of hiding. He seemed very angry, and searched for me a long time. My behavior was altogether unaccountable. He finally gave up the chase, thinking, I suppose, that I must come home for something to eat; he would give himself no further trouble in looking for me. I spent that day mostly in the woods, having the alternative before me,—to go home and be whipped to death, or stay in the woods and be starved to death. That night, I fell in with Sandy Jenkins, a slave with whom I was somewhat acquainted. Sandy had a free wife who lived about four miles from Mr. Covey's; and it being Saturday, he was on his way to see her. I told him my circumstances, and he very kindly invited me to go home with him. I went home with him, and talked this whole matter over, and got his advice as to what course it was best for me to pursue. I found Sandy an old adviser. He told me, with great solemnity, I must go back to Covey; but that before I went, I must go with him into another part of the woods, where there was a certain *root,* which, if I would take some of it with me, carrying it *always on my right side,* would render it impossible for Mr. Covey, or any other white man, to whip me. He said he had carried it for years; and since he had done so, he had never received a blow, and never expected to while he carried it. I at first rejected the idea, that the simple carrying of a root in my pocket would have any such effect as he had said, and was not disposed to take it; but Sandy impressed the necessity with much earnestness, telling me it could do no harm, if it did no good. To please him, I at length took the root, and, according to his direction, carried it upon my right side. This was Sunday morning. I immediately started for home; and upon entering the yard gate, out came Mr. Covey on his way to meeting. He spoke to me very kindly, made me drive the pigs from a lot near by, and passed on towards the church. Now, this singular conduct of Mr. Covey really made me begin to think that there was something in the root which Sandy had given me; and had it been on any other day than Sunday, I could have attributed the conduct to no other cause than the influence of that root; and as it was, I was half inclined to think the root to be something more than I at first had taken it to be. All went well till Monday morning. On this morning, the virtue of the *root* was fully tested. Long before daylight, I was called to go and rub, curry, and feed, the horses. I obeyed, and was glad to obey. But whilst thus engaged, whilst in the act of throwing down some blades from the loft, Mr. Covey entered the stable with a long rope; and just as I was half out of the loft, he caught hold of my legs, and was about tying me. As soon as I found what he was up to, I gave a sudden spring, and as I did so, he holding to my legs, I was brought sprawling on the stable floor. Mr. Covey seemed now to think he had me, and could do what he pleased; but at this moment—from whence came the spirit I don't know—I resolved to fight; and, suiting my action to the resolution, I seized Covey hard by the throat; and as I did so, I rose. He held on to me, and I to him. My resistance was so entirely unexpected, that Covey seemed taken all aback. He trembled like a leaf. This gave me assurance, and I held him uneasy, causing the blood to run where I touched him with the ends of my fingers. Mr. Covey soon called out to Hughes for help. Hughes came, and, while Covey held me, attempting to tie my right hand. While he was in the act of doing so, I watched my chance, and gave him a heavy kick close under the ribs. This kick fairly sickened Hughes, so that he left me in the hands of Mr. Covey. This kick had the effect of not only weakening Hughes, but Covey also. When he saw Hughes bending over with pain, his courage quailed. He asked me if I meant to persist in my resistance. I told him I did, come what might; that he had used me like a brute for six months, and that I was determined to be used so no longer. With that, he strove to drag me to a stick that was lying just out of the stable door. He meant to knock me down. But just as he was leaning over to get the stick, I seized him with both hands by his collar, and brought him by a sudden snatch to the ground. By this time, Bill came. Covey called upon him for assistance. Bill wanted to know what he could do. Covey said, "Take hold of him, take hold of him!" Bill said his master hired him out to work, and not to help to whip me; so he left Covey and myself to fight our own battle out. We were at it for nearly two hours. Covey at length let me go, puffing and blowing at a great rate, saying that if I had not resisted, he would not have whipped me half so much. The truth was, that he had not whipped me at all. I considered him as getting entirely the worst end of the bargain; for he had drawn no blood from me, but I had from him. The whole six months afterwards, that I spent with Mr. Covey, he never laid the weight of his finger upon me in anger. He would occasionally say, he didn't want to get hold of me again. "No," thought I, "you need not; for you will come off worse than you did before."

This battle with Mr. Covey was the turning-point in my career as a slave. It rekindled the few expiring embers of freedom, and revived within me a sense of my own manhood. It recalled the departed self-confidence, and inspired me again with a determination to be free. The gratification afforded by the triumph was a full compensation for whatever else might follow, even death itself. He only can understand the deep satisfaction which I experienced, who has himself repelled by force the bloody arm of slavery. I felt as I never felt before. It was a glorious resurrection, from the tomb of slavery, to the heaven of freedom. My long-crushed spirit rose, cowardice departed, bold defiance took its place; and I now resolved that, however long I might remain a slave in form, the day had passed forever when I could be a slave in fact. I did not hesitate to let it be known of me, that the white man who expected to succeed in whipping, must also succeed in killing me.

Questions

1. *How can the folktales by Annie Reed and Henry Lewis be interpreted as "tales of personal empowerment"?*
2. *What functions did conjuring and spells have in a slave's life? In particular, how did conjuring aid Frederick Douglass in his resistance to slavery?*
3. *How were the pit schools described by Mandy Jones and the case of Sarah Wilson teaching her children to read and write everyday forms of resistance?*

FURTHER READING

Among the growing list of excellent studies that explore the culture of enslaved African Americans are John W. Blassingame, The Slave Community: Plantation Life in the Antebellum South *(New York, 1979); Herbert G. Gutman,* The Black Family in Slavery and Freedom, 1750–1925 *(New York, 1976); Lawrence W. Levine,* Black Culture and Black Consciousness: Afro-American Folk Thought from Slavery to Freedom *(New York, 1977); Albert J. Raboteau,* Slave Religion: The "Invisible Institution" in the Antebellum South *(New York, 1978); Sterling Stuckey,* Slave Culture: Nationalist Theory and the Foundations of Black America *(New York, 1987); William D. Pierson,* Black Yankees: The Development of an Afro-American Subculture in Eighteenth-Century New England *(Amherst, Massachusetts, 1988);* Africanisms in American Culture, *ed. Joseph E. Hollowey (Bloomington, Indiana, 1990); and Gwendolyn Mildo Hall,* Africans in Colonial Louisiana: The Development of Afro-Creole Culture in the Eighteenth Century *(Baton Rouge, 1992).*

Abolitionism

Merton L. Dillon

Introduction

Opposition to slavery in North America was as old as the institution itself. Africans—after being transported forcibly from their homes—resisted their enslavement from the day they reached American shores. At an early date, a few sympathetic whites joined them in condemning bondage. A religiously inspired movement aimed at abolishing slavery began in the middle of the eighteenth century when Quakers made opposition to slavery a condition of membership in their sect. Soon after, during the revolutionary period, a new concern for Natural Rights helped end slavery in the northern states. Some southerners also freed their slaves at that time, but antislavery sentiment in the South never became general enough to lead any southern state to abolish the institution.

Most early opponents of slavery assumed that it would be ended gradually by state legislative action, and that abolition would be accompanied by colonization—the removal of at least some of the freed men and women from the United States. But around 1830 a younger, more determined, more spirited group of abolitionists rejected each of these assumptions. Their demand for the immediate end of slavery and the abandonment of all plans for the expatriation of African Americans ushered in a new, exceedingly contentious phase of the antislavery movement. African Americans heartily endorsed the new "immediatist" program and joined in promoting it. They focused on the plight of their race in the northern states more consistently than did most of their white colleagues and were more intent than were most whites on working against such evidences of prejudice as segregated schools and discriminatory laws. Nonetheless, from beginning to end, the antislavery movement was a partnership, albeit an unequal one, of white and African American abolitionists.

Abolitionists condemned slavery as a cruel and sinful institution that ought to be ended at once. They argued, first, that it violated the principles set forth in the Declaration of Independence upon which the nation was founded, and, second, that it conflicted with such fundamental biblical teachings as the Golden Rule.

The majority of Americans at the time, patriotic and religious though they may have been, did not find these arguments persuasive. Abolitionists always comprised only a minority in the northern population and typically were both scorned and feared as dangerous fanatics. Their campaign to end slavery aroused fierce opposition throughout the north as well as the south. Abolitionist lecturers were regularly mobbed, their printing presses were wrecked, and one abolitionist editor, Elijah P. Lovejoy, was murdered.

A later generation may find such resistance to a call for freedom, justice, and equality hard to understand because the abolitionists' program and their point of view now form part of the American consensus: They are taken for granted. But we should remember that this achievement came only at the cost of a horrendous civil war and, a century later, the painful social and political upheaval incident to the civil rights struggles of the1960s.

ABOLITIONISM: ACTION AND RESPONSE

Abolitionists tried to publicize their program through lectures, newspapers, and pamphlets. Opposition to this effort by a resistant and sometimes enraged public (one abolitionist was mobbed two hundred times) inevitably raised the issue of civil rights for white Americans as well as for blacks and brought in to the open this important question: Should public opinion be allowed to stifle the rights of free speech, free assembly, and free press simply because a majority finds certain ideas or expressions objectionable or judges them dangerous? Abolitionist activism and rhetoric highlighted the debate on the proper limits of free speech, including the extent to which a community is obliged to tolerate speech that it deems offensive.

In order to consider these issues with respect to the abolitionists, it is necessary to examine their program, their rhetoric, and their mode of agitation, as well as the opposition to them.

The American Anti-Slavery Society Declares its Sentiments

At its founding in 1833, the American Anti-Slavery Society adopted this Declaration of Sentiments. In his characteristically impassioned rhetoric, William Lloyd Garrison condemned slavery and set forth the new organization's principles and proposed activities. Excerpted from William Lloyd Garrison, Selections from the Writings and Speeches of William Lloyd Garrison *(Boston, 1852), 66-71.*

More than fifty-seven years have elapsed, since a band of patriots convened in this place, to devise measures for the deliverance of this country from a foreign yoke. The corner-stone upon which they founded the Temple of Freedom was broadly this—'that all men are created equal; that they are endowed by their Creator with certain inalienable rights; that among these are life, LIBERTY, and the pursuit of happiness.' At the sound of their trumpet-call, three millions of people rose up as from the sleep of death, and rushed to the strife of blood; deeming it more glorious to die instantly as freemen, than desirable to live one hour as slaves. They were few in number—poor in resources; but the honest conviction that Truth, Justice and Right were on their side, made them invincible.

We have met together for the achievement of an enterprise, without which that of our fathers is incomplete; and which, for its magnitude, solemnity, and probable results upon the destiny of the world, as far transcends theirs as moral truth does physical force. . . .

Their principles led them to wage war against their oppressors, and to spill human blood like water, in order to be free. Ours forbid the doing of evil that good may come, and lead us to reject, and to entreat the oppressed to reject, the use of all carnal weapons for deliverance from bondage; relying solely upon those which are spiritual, and mighty through God to the pulling down of strong holds.

Their measures were physical resistance—the marshalling in arms—the hostile array—the mortal encounter. Ours shall be such only as the opposition of moral purity to moral corruption—the destruction of error by the potency of truth—the overthrow of prejudice by the power of love—and the abolition of slavery by the spirit of repentance.

Their grievances, great as they were, were trifling in comparison with the wrongs and sufferings of those for whom we plead. Our fathers were never slaves—never bought and sold like cattle—never shut out from the light of knowledge and religion—never subjected to the lash of brutal taskmasters.

But those, for whose emancipation we are striving—constituting at the present time at least one-sixth part of our countrymen—are recognized by law, and treated by their fellow-beings, as marketable commodities, as goods and chattels, as brute beasts; are plundered daily of the fruits of their toil without redress;

really enjoy no constitutional nor legal protection from licentious and murderous outrages upon their persons; and are ruthlessly torn asunder—the tender babe from the arms of its frantic mother—the heart-broken wife from her weeping husband—at the caprice or pleasure of irresponsible tyrants. For the crime of having a dark complexion, they suffer the pangs of hunger, the infliction of stripes, the ignominy of brutal servitude. They are kept in heathenish darkness by laws expressly enacted to make their instruction a criminal offence.

These are the prominent circumstances in the condition of more than two millions of our people, the proof of which may be found in thousands of indisputable facts, and in the laws of the slaveholding States.

Hence we maintain—that, in view of the civil and religious privileges of this nation, the guilt of its oppression is unequalled by any other on the face of the earth; and, therefore, that it is bound to repent instantly, to undo the heavy burdens, and to let the oppressed go free.

We further maintain—that no man has a right to enslave or imbrute his brother—to hold or acknowledge him, for one moment, as a piece of merchandize—to keep back his hire by fraud—or to brutalize his mind, by denying him the means of intellectual, social and moral improvement.

The right to enjoy liberty is inalienable. To invade it is to usurp the prerogative of Jehovah. Every man has a right to his own body—to the products of his own labor—to the protection of law—and to the common advantages of society. It is piracy to buy or steal a native African, and subject him to servitude. Surely, the sin is as great to enslave an American as an African.

Therefore we believe and affirm—that there is no difference, in principle, between the African slave trade and American slavery:

That every American citizen, who detains a human being in involuntary bondage as his property, is, according to Scripture, (Ex. xxi. 16,) a man-stealer:

That the slaves ought instantly to be set free, and brought under the protection of law:

That if they had lived from the time of Pharaoh down to the present period, and had been entailed through successive generations, their right to be free could never have been alienated, but their claims would have constantly risen in solemnity:

That all those laws which are now in force, admitting the right of slavery, are therefore, before God, utterly null and void . . .

We further believe and affirm—that all persons of color, who possess the qualifications which are demanded of others, ought to be admitted forthwith to the enjoyment of the same privileges, and the exercise of the same prerogatives, as others; and that the paths of preferment, of wealth, and of intelligence, should be opened as widely to them as to persons of a white complexion.

We maintain that no compensation should be given to the planters emancipating their slaves:

Because it would be a surrender of the great fundamental principle, that man cannot hold property in man:

Because slavery is a crime, and therefore is not an article to be sold:

Because the holders of slaves are not the just proprietors of what they claim; freeing the slave is not depriving them of property, but restoring it to its rightful owner; it is not wronging the master, but righting the slave—restoring him to himself:

Because immediate and general emancipation would only destroy nominal, not real property; it would not amputate a limb or break a bone of the slaves, but by infusing motives into their breasts, would make them doubly valuable to the masters as free laborers; and

Because, if compensation is to be given at all, it should be given to the outraged and guiltless slaves, and not to those who have plundered and abused them.

We regard as delusive, cruel and dangerous, any scheme of expatriation which pretends to aid, either directly or indirectly, in the emancipation of the slaves or to be a substitute for the immediate and total abolition of slavery.

We fully and unanimously recognise the sovereignty of each State, to legislate exclusively on the subject of the slavery which is tolerated within its limits; we concede that Congress, under the present national compact, has no right to interfere with any of the slave States, in relation to this momentous subject:

But we maintain that Congress has a right, and is solemnly bound, to suppress the domestic slave trade between the several States, and to abolish slavery in those portions of our territory which the Constitution has placed under its exclusive jurisdiction. . . .

These are our views and principles—these our designs and measures. With entire confidence in the overruling justice of God, we plant ourselves upon the Declaration of our Independence and the truths of Divine Revelation, as upon the Everlasting Rock.

We shall organize Anti-Slavery Societies, if possible, in every city, town and village in our land.

We shall send forth agents to lift up the voice of remonstrance, of warning, of entreaty, and of rebuke.

We shall circulate, unsparingly and extensively, anti-slavery tracts and periodicals.

We shall enlist the pulpit and the press in the cause of the suffering and the dumb.

We shall aim at a purification of the churches from all participation in the guilt of slavery.

We shall encourage the labor of freemen [free African Americans] rather than that of slaves, by giving a preference to their productions: and

We shall spare no exertions nor means to bring the whole nation to speedy repentance.

Our trust for victory is solely in God. We may be personally defeated, but our principles never! Truth, Justice, Reason, Humanity, must and will gloriously triumph. Already a host is coming up to the help of the Lord against the mighty, and the prospect before us is full of encouragement.

The Influence of Slavery

In the following excerpt, Garrison claims that slaveholders virtually controlled national policy and politics and exerted a governing influence on ideas and institutions even in the North. According to this analysis, ending slavery would do much more than restore freedom to the slaves. It also would destroy the base of the slaveholders' power and thus bring revolutionary change to power relationships throughout the country. With this insight, Garrison accounted for the intense opposition that abolitionists encountered. Abridged from William Lloyd Garrison, Selections from the Writings and Speeches of William Lloyd Garrison *(Boston, 1852), 137-39.*

For more than two centuries, slavery has polluted the American soil. It has grown with the growth, and strengthened with the strength of the republic. Its victims have multiplied, from a single cargo of stolen Africans, to three millions of native-born inhabitants. In our colonial state, it was deemed compatible with loyalty to the mother country. In our revolutionary struggle for independence, it exchanged the sceptre of monarchy for the star-spangled banner of republicanism, under the folds of which it has found ample encouragement and protection. From the days of the Puritans down to the present time, it has been sanctified by the religion, and upheld by the patriotism of the nation. From the adoption of the American Constitution, it has declared war and made peace, instituted and destroyed national banks and tariffs, controlled the army and navy, prescribed the policy of the government, ruled in both houses of Congress, occupied the Presidential chair, governed the political parties, distributed offices of trust and emolument among its worshippers, fettered Northern industry and enterprise, and trampled liberty of speech and of conscience in the dust.

It has exercised absolute mastery over the American Church. In her skirts is found 'the blood of the souls of the poor innocents.' With the Bible in their hands, her priesthood have attempted to prove that slavery came down from God out of heaven. . . .

If slavery be thus entwined around the civil, social, and pecuniary interests of the republic—if the religious sects and political parties are banded together for its safety from internal revolt and external opposition—if the people, awed by its power and corrupted by its influence, are basely bending their knees at its foot-

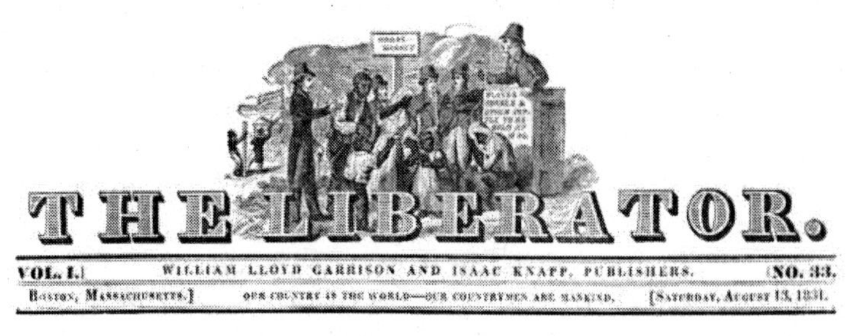

The masthead of the abolitionist Liberator *newspaper from 1833 features an illustration of a slave auction alongside the name of editor William Lloyd Garrison. (Courtesy of The Library of Congress.)*

stool—is it wonderful that Church and State are shaken to their foundations by the rallying cry of Liberty? . . .

Slavery must be overthrown. No matter how numerous the difficulties, how formidable the obstacles, how strong the foes to be vanquished—slavery must cease to pollute the land. . . . No matter, though, to effect it, every party should be torn by dissensions, every sect dashed into fragments, the national compact dissolved, the land filled with the horrors of a civil and a servile war—still, slavery must be buried in the grave of infamy, beyond the possibility of a resurrection.

If the State cannot survive the anti-slavery agitation, then let the State perish. If the Church must be cast down . . . to be free, then let the Church fall. . . . If the American Union cannot be maintained . . . then let the American Union be consumed by a living thunderbolt, and no tear be shed over its ashes.

A Call for Women to Become Abolitionists

Women helped organize the American Anti-Slavery Society, held fundraising antislavery bazaars, circulated antislavery petitions, and otherwise promoted the abolitionist cause. This essay is one of the earliest appeals to women. It also shows that women's participation in the movement was sometimes opposed even by women themselves. This excerpt is a response to a woman who objected to other women publicly advocating emancipation. Taken from Elizabeth Margaret Chandler, The Poetical Works of Elizabeth Margaret Chandler *(Philadelphia, 1836), 21-23.*

We have been so long accustomed to consider the duty of the female sex, with regard to slavery, as entirely plain, that we had almost imagined it must be equally so to any unprejudiced thinker upon the subject. Not that we expected to find no difference of feeling, or contrariety of sentiment; apathy and prejudices we were prepared for; but we certainly had not thought that the interference of woman in behalf of suffering humanity, could be seriously objected to, as improper, and at variance with right principles. Yet this we are sorry to find is the light in which it is regarded by one of our own sex—a lady, whose talents and char-

The declaration of the American Anti-Slavery Society from its founding convention in Philadelphia, Pennsylvania in 1833. (Courtesy of The Library of Congress.)

acter we respect very highly, and whose approbation of the course we are pursuing, we should be proud to have obtained. But as this is withheld, and it is probable she may not be singular in her opinions, we have taken the liberty of quoting some of her sentiments, and appending to them a statement of our own ideas on the same subject.

"Should you inquire why I do not devote myself more sedulously to promote the cause of emancipation?—I would tell you, that I think it is a work which requires the energies of *men*."

And so it does; but it requires also the *influence of woman*. She was given to man 'to be a helpmeet [helpmate] for him;' and it is therefore her duty, whenever she can do so, to lend him her aid in every great work of philanthropy. In *this* her cooperation may be of essential service, without leading her one step beyond her own proper sphere. . . .

"It is a subject so connected with those of government, of law and politics, that I should fear the direct or even apparent interference of my own sex, would be a departure from that propriety of character which nature, as well as society, imposes on woman."

It is true that it is a question of government and politics, but it also rests upon the broader basis of humanity and justice; and it is on *this* ground only, that we advocate the interference of women. We have not the least desire to see our own sex transformed into a race of politicians; but we do not think that in this case such consequences are in the least to be apprehended. To plead for the miserable, to endeavour to alleviate the bitterness of their destiny, and to soften the stern bosoms of their oppressors into gentleness and mercy, can never be unfeminine or unbefitting the delicacy of woman! She does not advocate Emancipation because slavery is at variance with the political interests of the state, but because it is an outrage against *humanity* and *morality* and *religion;* because it is *criminal*, and because her own supineness makes her a *sharer in the crime;* and because a great number of *her own sex* are among its victims. It is therefore, that she should steadily and conscientiously rank among the number of its opponents, and refuse to be benefited by its advantages. She does not by this become a partizan of any system of policy—she seeks only to shield from outrage all that is most holy in her religion! She does not seek to direct, or share with men, the government of the state; but she entreats them to lift the iron foot of despotism from the neck of her sisterhood; and this we consider not only quite within the sphere of her privileges, but also of her positive duties.

A Northern Woman Condemns Prejudice

This passage was one of the most powerful early critiques of slavery and the prejudice that supported it. The author is nearly as critical of the racial prejudice exhibited by Northerners as she is of slavery itself. Excerpted from Lydia Maria Child, An Appeal in Favor of that Class of Americans Called Africans *(Boston, 1833), 208-9, 211, 232.*

While we bestow our earnest disapprobation on the system of slavery, let us not flatter ourselves that we are in reality any better than our brethren of the South. Thanks to our soil and climate, and the early exertions of the Quakers, the *form* of slavery does not exist among us; but the very *spirit* of the hateful and mischievous thing is here in all its strength. The manner in which we use what power we have, gives us ample reason to be grateful that the nature of our institutions does not intrust us with more. Our prejudices against colored people is [are] even more inveterate than it is at the South. The planter is often attached to his negroes, and lavishes caresses and kind words upon them, as he would on a favorite hound; but our cold-hearted, ignoble prejudice admits of no exception—no intermission.

The Southerners have long continued habit, apparent interest and dreaded danger, to palliate the wrong they do; but we stand without excuse. They tell us that Northern ships and Northern capital have been engaged in this wicked business; and the reproach is true. Several fortunes in this city [Boston] have been made by the sale of negro blood. If these criminal transactions are still carried on, they are done in silence and secrecy, because public opinion has made them disgraceful. But if the free States wished to cherish the system of slavery forever, they could not take a more direct course than they now do. Those who are kind and liberal on all other subjects, unite with the selfish and the proud in their unrelenting efforts to keep the colored population in the lowest state of degradation; and the influence they unconsciously exert over children early infuses into their innocent minds the same strong feelings of contempt.

The intelligent and well informed have the least share of this prejudice; and when their minds can be brought to reflect upon it, I have generally observed that they soon cease to have any at all. But such a general apathy prevails and the subject is so seldom brought into view, that few are really aware how oppressively the influence of society is made to bear upon this injured class of the community. . . .

. . . [A]n unjust law exists in this Commonwealth [Massachusetts], by which marriages between persons of different color is [are] pronounced illegal. I am perfectly aware of the gross ridicule to which I may subject myself by alluding to this particular; but I have lived too long, and observed too much, to be disturbed by the world's mockery. In the first place, the government ought not to be invested with power to control the affections, any more than the consciences of citizens. A man has at least as good a right to choose his wife, as he has to choose his religion. His taste may not suit his neighbors; but so long as his deportment is correct, they have no right to interfere with his concerns. . . .

There is among the colored people an increasing desire for information, and a laudable ambition to be respectable in manners and appearance. Are we not foolish as well as sinful, in trying to repress a tendency so salutary to themselves, and so beneficial to the community? Several individuals of this class are very desirous to have persons of their own color qualified to teach something more than mere reading and writing. But in the public schools, colored children are subject to many discouragements and difficulties; and into the private schools they cannot gain admission. A very sensible and well-informed colored woman in a neighboring town, whose family have been brought up in a manner that excited universal remark and approbation, has been extremely desirous to obtain for her eldest daughter the advantages of a private school; but she has been resolutely repulsed, on account of her complexion. . . .

By publishing this book I have put my mite into the treasury [expressed my thoughts]. The expectation of displeasing all classes has not been unaccompanied with pain. But it has been strongly impressed upon my mind that it was a duty to fulfil this task; and earthly considerations should never stifle the voice of conscience.

An Abolitionist Lecturer's Instructions

In 1834 the American Anti-Slavery Society commissioned Theodore Dwight Weld to serve as an abolitionist agent in Ohio. These are his instructions. Abridged from Letters of Theodore Dwight Weld, Angelina Grimké Weld and Sarah Grimké, *1822-1844, vol. 1, ed. Gilbert H. Barnes and Dwight L. Dumond (New York, 1934), 125-27.*

Dear Sir—You have been appointed an Agent of the American Anti-Slavery Society; and will receive the following instructions from the Executive Committee. . . .

The general principles of the Society are set forth in the Declaration, signed by the members of the Convention which formed it at Philadelphia, Dec. 7, 1833. Our object is, the overthrow of American slavery, the most atrocious and oppressive system of bondage that has ever existed in any country. We expect to accomplish this, mainly by showing to the public its true character and legitimate fruits, its contrariety to the first principles of religion, morals, and humanity, and its special inconsistency with our pretensions, as a free, humane, and enlightened people. In this way, by the force of truth, we expect to correct the common errors that prevail respecting slavery, and to produce a just public sentiment, which shall appeal both to the conscience and love of character, of our slave-holding fellow-citizens, and convince them that both their duty and their welfare require the immediate abolition of slavery.

You will inculcate every where, the great fundamental principle of IMMEDIATE ABOLITION, as the duty of all masters, on the ground that slavery is both unjust and unprofitable. Insist principally on the SIN OF SLAVERY, because our main hope is in the consciences of men, and it requires little logic to prove that it is always safe to do right. To question this, is to impeach the superintending Providence of God.

We reprobate the idea of compensation to slave holders, because it implies the right of slavery. It is also unnecessary, because the abolition of slavery will be an advantage, as free labor is found to be more profitable than the labor of slaves. We also reprobate all plans of expatriation, by whatever specious pretences covered, as a remedy for slavery, for they all proceed from prejudice against color; and we hold that the duty of the whites in regard to this cruel prejudice is not to indulge it, but to repent and overcome it.

The people of color ought at once to be emancipated and recognized as citizens, and their rights secured as such, equal in all respects to others, according to the cardinal principle laid down in the American Declaration of Independence. . . .

Do not allow yourself to be drawn away from the main object, to exhibit a detailed PLAN of abolition; for men's consciences will be greatly relieved from the feeling of present duty, by any objections or difficulties which they can find or fancy in your plan. Let the *principle* be decided on, of immediate abolition, and the plans will easily present themselves. What ought to be done can be done. . . .

You will make yourself familiar with FACTS, for they chiefly influence reflecting minds. Be careful to use only facts that are well authenticated, and always state them with the precision of a witness under oath. You cannot do our cause a greater injury than by overstating facts. . . .

In traversing your field, you will generally find it wise to visit first several prominent places in it, particularly those where it is known our cause has friends. In going to a place, you will naturally call upon those who are friendly to our objects, and take advice from them. Also call on ministers of the gospel and other leading characters, and labor specially to enlighten them and secure their favor and influence. Ministers are the hinges of community, and ought to be moved, if possible. If they can be gained, much is gained. . . .

Form Auxiliary Societies, both male and female, in every place where it is practicable. Even if such societies are very small at the outset, they may do much good as centres of light, and means of future access to the people. Encourage them to raise funds and apply them in purchasing and circulating anti-slavery publications gratuitously. . . .

You are not to take up collections in your public meetings, as the practice often prevents persons from attending, whom it might be desirable to reach.

The Attorney General of Illinois Defends a Mob

In Alton, Illinois, in 1837 a mob destroyed Elijah P. Lovejoy's printing press while a group of armed men attempted to defend it. During the confrontation, Lovejoy was shot and killed. Some mob members were brought to trial and defended by Usher Linder, the state's attorney general. This portion of Linder's remarks to the jury is abridged from William S. Lincoln, Alton Trials: of Winthrop S. Gilman, Who Was Indicted . . . For the Crime of Riot . . . *(New York, 1838), 72-77.*

I ask you to travel along with me as I relate to you the facts in this case. Last August [1837], the first press was destroyed: the "boys" broke it to pieces and threw it into the river. Another was brought here, and after repeated failures to establish a press by which they [abolitionists] could disseminate their fiendish doctrines, another course was adopted. A convention [to form a state antislavery society] was called at Upper Alton. Alton was chosen as the scene of their operations. Alton was to be made the theatre of their preachings—and all their presses, and all their preachings, and all their conventions were to be held in the poor, devoted city of Alton. . . . [T]hese people thought they were going to have it all their own way. But it happened that these Western boys knew a thing or two: knew a trick worth two of that; and so they got together and out-voted them, and the convention blew up in smoke. It was a farce. Not satisfied with this; not satisfied with the blowing up of this farce; not satisfied with the result of this convention, headed by interlopers from other states, headed by an alien to our laws and our country, they issued their handbills, they made proclamation in the streets, of their intention to preach their doctrines in the Church. They posted up placards, notifying the world that Dr. [Edward] Beecher would preach upon this damning doctrine of abolition. . . . [Linder then criticizes the abolitionists' decision to protect themselves with arms.]

. . . So that you see, gentlemen, when all other sources fail . . . the doctrines of abolition are to be forced down our throats. . . . And was not all this calculated to disturb the peace? was not this calculated to excite terror? to stir up the feelings? to rouse the passions, and to provoke an attack? . . .

But the press came at last: the press which was intended to preach insurrection, and to disseminate the doctrines which must tend to disorganization and disunion. With what delight they caught the first glimpse of their new-born child; with what joy they hugged it to their hearts! . . .

. . . Suppose this press had not been guarded; suppose that, taking advantage of the absence of those who had assembled for its protection, the mob had destroyed it. Had these people [the abolitionists] no remedy? Is there no law which would have given them redress? They talk of being friends to good order; lovers of law!! Have they not taken the law into their own hands, and violated the laws of man and of God in depriving man of life? And for what? For a press! a printing press! A press brought here to teach rebellion and insurrection to the slave; to excite servile war; to preach murder in the name of religion; to strike dismay to the hearts of the people, and spread desolation over the face of this land. Society esteems good order more than such a press: sets higher value upon the lives of its citizens than upon a thousand such presses. I might depict to you the African, his passions excited by the doctrines intended to have been propagated by that press. As well might you find yourself in the fangs of a wild beast. I might portray to you the scenes which would exist in our neighbor states from the influence of that press: the father aroused to see the last gasp of his dying child, as it lays in its cradle, weltering in its blood; and the husband awakened from his last sleep by the shrieks of his wife as she is brained to the earth. I might paint to you a picture which would cause a demon to start back with affright, and still fall short of the awful reality which would be caused by the promulgation of the doctrines which this press was intended to disseminate.

[The jury found the defendants not guilty.]

Questions

1. *What might account for the anti-abolitionist sentiment of rural and small-town people in northern Ohio, who owned no slaves and who did not live among African Americans? The remarks of Usher Linder provide an explicit explanation for opposition in Alton, Illinois. What is it? Did it have any validity?*
2. *In what ways may abolitionism have especially appealed to women? Why did some oppose their participation?*
3. *Describe the tactics adopted by the abolitionists. Why did they select these? Might different tactics have been more effective?*
4. *Why did abolitionists focus so much of their attention on ministers and church members? Would present-day advocates of fundamental change adopt the same mode of operation? Why or why not?*

FURTHER READING

James Brewer Stewart, *Holy Warriors: The Abolitionists and American Slavery* (New York, 1976), is a concise account of abolitionism. Benjamin Quarles, *Black Abolitionists* (New York, 1969), traces the antislavery activities of African Americans. Merton L. Dillon, *Slavery Attacked: Southern Slaves and Their Allies, 1619-1865* (Baton Rouge, 1990), shows how African Americans, both slave and free, influenced abolitionism. Biographies especially pertinent to these readings are James Brewer Stewart, *William Lloyd Garrison and the Challenge of Emancipation* (Arlington Heights, 1992); Merton L. Dillon, *Elijah P. Lovejoy, Abolitionist Editor* (Urbana, 1961); and Robert H. Abzug, *Passionate Liberator: Theodore Dwight Weld and the Dilemma of Reform* (New York, 1980).

Why Union Soldiers Fought

Mark Grimsley

Introduction

The Civil War was by far the bloodiest conflict in American history. During its four years more than 620,000 men lost their lives. Of these, only about one third died in battle. The rest succumbed to the many diseases that stalked military encampments. If you were a Union soldier, the odds were one in five that you would not survive the war. For Confederate soldiers, the odds rose to one in three. What motivated Civil War soldiers to endure such peril?

"The Union Must Stand": The Diary of a Union Soldier

It is relatively rare for ordinary people to preserve a record of their own lives. Much of what we know about ordinary people in other centuries comes indirectly, through study of census returns, court records, voting patterns, and so on. From such sources we can infer a great deal, but seldom do we hear the voices of common people speak plainly and directly.

The Civil War years form a major exception to this rule. One of the best sources of insight into mid-nineteenth-century American life are the thousands of letters and diaries kept by soldiers and families during that conflict. These collections, lovingly preserved by descendants and often donated to archives and historical societies, speak eloquently, not just about the fighting but also about the attitudes and values of people from that era.

One such diary was kept by John Quincy Adams Campbell, a twenty-three-year-old Union soldier. A native of Brown County, Ohio, Campbell had only recently moved to Iowa when the firing on Fort Sumter led him to enlist in the Fifth Iowa Volunteer Infantry Regiment. Throughout his more than three years of military service, Campbell kept an extensive daily record of his experiences. His diary vividly describes life in the Union army: camp life, marches, battles. It also tells us much about Campbell's own views on the war, particularly the reasons he risked wounds and death to fight for the Union. Excerpts from the John Q. A. Campbell Civil War Diaries, Western Reserve Historical Society, Cleveland, Ohio [unpaginated].

Tuesday, July 9, 1861.

I left Newton, Jasper County, Iowa this day in Captain Samuel H. Chapman's Company (B), of the Fifth Regiment of Iowa Volunteers. Our company was drawn up in line in the Court-House yard and relatives of the volunteers bade them "farewell." It was the most affecting scene I ever witnessed.

I have volunteered to fight in this war for the Union and *a government.* I have left the peaceful walks of life and "buckled on the harness of war" not from any feeling of en-thusiasm, nor incited by any hopes of honor [or] glory, but because I believe that duty to my country and my *God,* bid me assist in crushing this wicked rebellion against our government, which rebellious men have instigated to secure their own promotion . . . and to secure the extension of that blighting curse—*slavery*—o'er our fair land. The name of our co[mpany] is "The Jasper Greys."

Campbell's regiment served the next thirteen months in Missouri, Tennessee, and Mississippi, but scarcely heard a shot fired in anger. Meanwhile other Union troops overran western Tennessee and much of northern Mississippi. Not until 19 September 1862 did the men of the 5th Iowa finally see combat. Then, at Iuka and Corinth, two small towns in northern Mississippi, they fought a brace of desperate battles to prevent a Confederate army from recapturing the region.

Friday, September 19, 1862.

At sunrise we took up our line of march towards Iuka, where [Confederate General Sterling] Price was said to be with his army, having captured the place a few days before. About 10 o'clock our cavalry came upon the enemy's pickets, and drove them in. We kept steadily advancing and at noon, came upon the enemy's infantry pickets.

Our skirmishers steadily drove back the enemy's pickets, for better than four miles, with occasional losses on both sides. About sundown, our skirmishers got *into a hornet's nest!* They came upon the enemy in force, and were compelled to fall back. At the same time, the rebels opened on us with artillery and attempted to flank us, on the left. Our Colonel immediately got our regiment into line, and prepared to meet the enemy. We waited (but only for a few moments) for the enemy. Soon the enemy appeared and opened a fire on us. The Fifth replied with a will and an effect that was admirable. Nobly the boys stood up to the work—loading

---

Excerpts reprinted from John Quincy Adams Campbell Diaries, courtesy: The Western Reserve Historical Society.

and firing amid a storm of lead, as if they were drilling—only showing much more enthusiasm and earnestness once we made a charge and the rebels gave way before us. But the nature of the ground, and the darkness prevented us following, farther than the brow of the ridge. We then fell back to our original line, and resumed our fire. The enemy was strong and bold, and their leaden hail swept our ranks with a broom of destruction. The boys flinched not, but stood over their dead & dying comrades and beat back thrice and quadruple their numbers, for more than an hour, until darkness had enveloped the field. Again and again the rebels charged upon us, but again and again they reeled and broke before the steady fire of Iowa's sons. At times, they came so close to us, that in a few instances, the bayonet was used. We had to stand before the steady fire of the rebels besides the heavy *volleys* which . . . the rebels poured into us at intervals from another ridge. . . .

The rebels gained our flank and we were subjected to a terrible cross fire. At length, after fighting an hour and a quarter, when our ranks were almost *annihilated,* when most of the men had fired all their cartridges away, the *remnant* of the Fifth, fell back before the superior force of the rebels. . . . After a half hour's further fighting, the rebels were repelled from the field, and our forces occupied our original ground. . . . Our loss is great but our *honor* is safe. I cannot particularize instances of daring, or bravery, for all did well.

Saturday, September 20, 1862.

This morning our forces moved on Price but found [that he had] skedaddled during the night. [Union General William S.] Rosecrans followed as far as Iuka. Iuka is full of wounded rebels, left behind, by Price, in his flight. Our regiment was halted on the battlefield as we marched out this morning and details were made to bury the dead. Most of the wounded were brought off the field, last night, but a few were found there this morning. The loss on both sides was great in the battle, yesterday, but only from the official report can we gain exact returns. Our company lost six killed on the field, and two mortally wounded, who died at the hospital. They died as the brave die—at the post of duty. Twenty-one others were wounded.

The conduct of our officers (regimental and company) was highly praiseworthy. They showed themselves fit officers for their regiment of *braves*. Our regiment fought (during the engagement) the 11th and 37th Alabama, the 5th Missouri, 3d Louisiana, and 38th Mississippi regiments. No wonder our loss was heavy, when we fought such odds. The battlefield, however, showed that while we suffered, our foe suffered equally with us. At times the contest was a hand to hand one. Rice, of our company, received three bayonet wounds. Col. Matthies recieves the highest praise for his bearing during the battle. Our regiment is the object of praise from all our generals. It is styled "the plucky Fifth."

During the battle, I was acting as Lieutenant. My duty was to cheer and encourage the men, and aid the company commmander in managing the company. For a time I turned *exhorter* and plead[ed] and cheered with an earnestness (I perhaps might say enthusiasm) that seriously affected my throat. I was utterly unconscious of danger, and although the dead and dying were dropping at my feet, I felt no emotion nor sorrow—there was a strange, unaccountable, lack of *feeling* with me, that followed me through the entire action. Out of a battle and in a battle, I find myself two different beings.

Saturday, September 27, 1862.

Papers came last evening containing President Lincoln's Emancipation Proclamation. The 1st of January 1863 is to be the day of our nation's second birth. God bless and help Abraham Lincoln—help him to "break every yoke and let the oppressed go free." The President has placed the Union pry under the corner stone of the Confederacy and the structure *will* fall.

Friday, October 3, 1862.

We were aroused this morning at 2 o'clock and at sunrise we marched into Corinth. As we marched into Corinth, we could hear the reports of our cannon—our forces eng[ag]ing Price's army, which was advancing upon Corinth from the west. Price having been joined by Generals [Earl] Van Dorn and [Mansfield] Lovell, with their commands, has marched upon this place expecting to capture it. He will meet a foe worthy of his steel. After our division marched into town, our regiment was sent to the North of town, to guard the road. . . . The position was assigned us by Gen. Rosecrans who said he wanted a regiment there that would hold the position. It was a post of honor for us. We ensconced ourselves behind the old earthworks of the enemy, where we remained without molestation, during the day.

Saturday, October 4, 1862.

During all of last night, there was noise of busy preparation in Corinth. At 2 o'clock this morning, we joined our brigade in Corinth. Our brigade was placed in position as a reserve. Shortly before daybreak, the big guns in our forts commenced shelling the enemy. The noise made by our 64-pound howitzers was terrible, and must have made many a poor rebel quake like an aspen. . . . We expected and were ready for a fierce attack from the rebels at dawn, but nothing (excepting the artillery firing) was done till nine o'clock. . . . We began to think Price had given us the slip during the night, but our delusion was soon apparent. Price had received 15,000 reinforcements during the night, and had no notion of skedaddling. At nine o'clock the battle began on our left, and the conflict there was terrific. After nearly an hour's fighting there the rebels seemed to give way or slacken their fire. We then had a short cessation—the lull before the storm.

At *ten* o'clock the rebels came sweeping down upon our right and center with the design of sweeping us before them by a grand charge. They came charging upon our lines—into the very mouths of our cannon—with a bravery and desperation that threatened calamity to our army. Our first line was compelled to fall back, and the enemy gained our breastworks and captured one of our big forts. Success seemed lighting upon their banners. Bravery and might seemed to be giving away before daring and desperation. But the enemy is taken in his toils. His desperation is to prove his destruction. Now Gen. Rosecrans generalship becomes manifest. He has permitted the enemy to come within the "death circle" and now the work of destruction commences. Our second line offers a terrible fire of musketry and our field batteries which had been silent, scatter death and destruction through the rebel ranks, with their fire of grape, shell and canister. Now the 5th Iowa, 4th Minnesota, and 26th Missouri, with the 11th Ohio [Artillery], start forth upon the double-quick and flank the rebels on their left. They give way. Their line wavers. Our [line] charges upon them with the bayonet and they break—they fly. It becomes a rout, and the *victory* is ours. Thanks be to God. But the work of destruction still continues. Our batteries continue their terrible fire, and hundreds of rebels fall before their death-hail. Our big guns are double-shotted with grape and the rebels fall by fifties at each discharge. The work is continued until distance intervenes between the foe and danger, when our forces return to their original position. The part played by our regiment was important, but we suffered no loss. Our double-quicking was very fatiguing. After the battle, the wounded were cared for and the dead buried (or rather preparations made to bury them). At sundown, Gen. [James B.] McPherson arrived with reinforcements, 5,000 [men] having made a forced march to join us in time for the fight, but without avail. We have achieved a great victory, at which the Nation may rejoice.

Tuesday, October 28, 1862.

Weather cool, but pleasant. Speaking of the weather being pleasant, reminds me that the weather has been favorable for any movements our army could wish to make, but the opportunity has not been improved. This fact is discouraging. The result of the elections in the North is also discouraging. Much, very much, there is to discourage the soldier, but I still trust that God will enable us to overthrow the armies of the Confederacy and reestablish the Supremacy of our law, over every foot of Southern Soil. I trust (now, that we are fighting for *Liberty* and Union and not Union and *Slavery*) that the God of battles will be with us. I feel confident that I am fighting for a righteous case, from true motives and whether successful or not, I will fight on and leave the result to God—in acting well *my* part, is where all honor lies.

In November 1862 the Fifth Iowa—now a regiment in the Union Army of the Tennessee, commanded by General Ulysses S. Grant—took part in an autumn campaign against Vicksburg, Mississippi. At Vicksburg the Confederates had built a fortress whose cannon blocked passage of the Mississippi River. Capture of the city formed an important Union objective.

On this march, Campbell noticed for the first time that large numbers of soldiers were vandalizing the property of Southern civilians.

Tuesday, November 4, 1862.

We marched 18 miles today. The march has been very fatiguing owing to the dust. All along the line of our march, fences and houses have been ruthlessly burned by straggling soldiers. Such deeds are disgraceful to our army, and the offenders merit the severest punishment.

Thursday, November 6, 1862.

Stringent orders from Gen. Grant were read today. They speak, in terms of strongest condemnation of the acts of vandalism, committed by our troops, and prohibit all foraging by the troops. All house burners will be severely punished if found out.

Saturday, November 15, 1862.

On dress parade this evening, the finding and sentence of a general court-martial in the cases of two houseburners (from the 4th Minnesota) were read. They are to be imprisoned in the Alton Penitentiary during the war and forfeit all their pay.

By early December, Grant's army had advanced about seventy miles toward Vicksburg and had occupied the town of Oxford, Mississippi. There some Southerners chose to take the oath of allegiance to the United States government. Throughout the war, a large number of Southern civilians took this step. Some did so from sincere feelings of loyalty toward the Union, but most did so in order to trade with the Union army, to avoid being exiled beyond Union lines, or in hopes of preserving their crops from confiscation by Northern soldiers. This seizure of crops was called "foraging," and through most of the war both sides did it regularly as a way to augment their usual rations.

Monday, December 8, 1862.

Several citizens passed through our lines today into town, to be "cussed" into the United States again. Among others, was one old man from Indiana, who has always been true to the old flag, though his sons have been pressed into the rebel army. His secesh neighbors bear testimony to his *treason* (loyalty). After "taking the oath," the butternuts returned to their homes, with light hearts and easy consciences.

Wednesday, December 10, 1862.

Our regiment accompanied the Division train, on a "foraging" expedition, as escort, today. We went eight miles southeast of town, and foraged on the plantation of a Mr. Porter, who has run off to Alabama, with his slaves. One or two old darkies are left on the place "to see to things."

"De massa run, ha! ha!
De darkey stay, ho! ho!"

About sixty bales of cotton were taken on Mr. Porter's plantation yesterday, by "our folks." We reached camp, on our return at 4 o'clock, P.M., tired and hungry.

Saturday, December 13, 1862.

I came across a genuine Mississippi *Union* man today. He was one of the *poor whites,* but was a man of good sense, and some information. He had been conscripted into the rebel army, but deserted three times. He wouldn't take Secesh *scrip*! He says there are a number of Union men living near here—*poor whites*.

Sunday, December 14, 1862.

I was detailed as Lieutenant of a fatigue party (for repairing the road across the river bottom) this morning. While at work, I met a *poor white* who lives just across the river. He is bitter against slavery and slaveholders—says they have caused all the trouble, and have always oppressed the poor white man. He is for the *Union,* and has been throughout. He says many of the poor whites are going to move North from this neighborhood. He remarked that the road, which we were repairing, was getting better *worked* than it had been, for many a year.

Wednesday, December 24, 1862.

Our Division marched today to Lumpkin's Mill where we camped. "On the march." Who, that never marched, knows the meaning of that phrase? What an interesting thing a regiment, a company is, when "on the march." Watch a company, see its characters, hear them talking, laughing and joking—and catch their spirit. There they go, merrily, jogging along—some laughing and joking at each other, at everybody and everything they pass—others spouting politics, talking of the elections, of the probabilities of war and the possibilities of peace—others singing—others looking about, eyes wide open, "viewing the landscape o'er." Here you have a man laughing, "fit to split his sides," at the humor of his "file leader." At his side, some mischief is relating his adventures while pursuing butternut hogs, and digging for rebel potatoes. There you see a man, plodding along, with his head down, brooding over the reverses of our army, and muttering "good for my three *years,*" while by his side his more hopeful comrade is singing "Hail Columbia" or "There's a good time coming." Just behind him a pensive lad is humming the air of "Home, Sweet Home," while *his* "right hand man" is munching a hard cracker, and greasing his throat with a piece of rusty bacon. There you see a man, whose "ideal" is a good Iowa farm, laughing at the farms and farming of the Southern nabobs, occasionally joining an ex-Supervisor in the imprecations on southern roads and southern mud-holes. So they go. "A company on the march." Look on them, and you see, in reflection, the human race, on the journey of life.

Grant's first campaign against Vicksburg failed when Confederate cavalry destroyed his main supply dump. His army withdrew into Tennessee, then part of it went down the Mississippi River to strike at Vicksburg from another direction. Campbell's regiment stayed behind to guard a strategic railroad near Memphis. The nearness of the bustling river port tempted many Union soldiers there in search of liquor, gambling, and prostitutes. Among the latter were African American women who had fled slavery and, penniless, turned in desperation to prostitution.

A highly upright man, Campbell strongly believed in temperance and attended church services regularly—frequently two or three times a week. He had a strong reaction upon learning that several of his comrades had visited Memphis.

Monday, February 9, 1863.

Several of our company returned to camp, from Memphis, this evening, *drunk*. This is an everyday occurrence, not confined to our company, or our regiment, however. Our proximity to Memphis is taken advantage of, by many, to indulge in the grossest and lowest dissipation. Men(?) whom I had *before* considered men of principle and mind, have given way to their passions and sunk the *man* into a mere animal, disgracing themselves, their company, their regiment, their friends, and *their race*. The presence of temptation is no excuse. He is no *man*, that is one only when he has no opportunity to be otherwise. The *man* shines the brightest through trials and temptations—the *creature* bows to every adverse wind. He is only the true sailor, who braves the storm, and rides upon the ocean's roughest billows. "A diamond sparkles brightest in the mine." The being who is a man merely because those around him are men is but a parrot mimicking his suspicions. Such creatures demand our pity. The true man challenges our admiration. He alone who puts his trust in God, is certain that he will be able to avoid the vices of this world and live, *a man*.

Tuesday, February 10, 1863.

While in town, yesterday, I heard a rumor, to the effect that we would leave here for Vicksburgh, next Thursday. This passes for what it is worth, but it suggests to me the fact that Vicksburgh is not yet *ours.* When I think of what *might* have been done and what has been done, since last February, it causes a gloomy feeling to creep o'er my mind. And when I see the discontent that exists in our army, and the *treason* that is showing itself in the North, that gloom grows darker and heavier. When I hear of traitors boldly proclaiming their hostility to our government, in the legislative halls of the North—and when I hear *so many* privates, in our army, express a desire to have the war closed *on any terms,* my faith in the American people is much shaken, and I have at times my *misgivings* as to the final result of our struggle for nationality. But the contest must be continued and directed by the *true patriots* of the land. The *sheet lightning patriotism* of our country has spent itself, but those who will not fight as *patriots* must fight as *subjects.* The Union must stand, undivided, entire, triumphant. Many sacrifices will have to be made, many trials endured, and perhaps many temporary reverses met. But what is a success, unless obtained over difficulties? The end, *I believe,* will be the complete triumph of our cause. And such an end is worth the sacrifices and sufferings of a generation.

The rumors of a renewed advance on Vicksburg proved correct. By early spring, the Fifth Iowa was aboard a transport steaming down the Mississippi River to rejoin Grant's army.

Wednesday, April 1, 1863.

Our fleet started this morning at 8 o'clock. Owing to rumors of "guerrillas ahead," the troops on all the boats were ordered to prepared for action. Half of each regiment has stood to arms all day. We passed quite a number of plantations on which we saw some fields of excellent looking wheat, apparently within two weeks of *"heading."* The "improvements" on most of these plantations might more appropriately be called some other name. On one or two plantations, however, we saw improvements that were very creditable. The *negro-cabins* are the same all over the south;—A small one story frame (or log) with a chimney at one end and a door in the middle—no window, and but one little room.

Sunday, April 5, 1863.

We met two boats today, one of them reported being fired into by guerrillas about two miles above. The boys were instantly on the alert but we saw no guerrillas. We, however, passed the ruins of a house that had been burned by those on the boat that had been fired into. The family were sitting around in the yard, looking very disconsolate, as well they might. This is severe retribution, but guerrilla warfare *must* be stopped.

Friday, April 17, 1863.

Last night, about 12 o'clock, a fleet of five gunboats, and two transports, ran the blockade at Vicksburgh. One transport was burned by the carelessness of our men (her crew). The casualties on the blockade runners were trivial. We could hear very distinctly the reports of the enemy's heavy guns, as they thundered away at the yankee boats. The rebels had large bonfires burning while the fleet was passing to light up the river and render their firing effective. This morning, our Division was reviewed by Adjutant General [Lorenzo] Thomas. After review, Gen. Thomas, and others, made speeches proclaiming and advocating the policy the Administration has adopted, with regard to arming the contrabands [freed slaves]. The plan meets with favor and will (at least) be *earnestly* carried out. This afternoon our regiment was mustered—preparations to being filled up with conscripts. I am on guard today.

Thursday, April 30, 1863.

A very warm day. We have marched 15 miles down the river, mostly along the shore of Lake St. Joseph. On this land there are some of the finest plantations in Louisiana. On one of these (Dr. Bowie's) there is a splendid dwelling home or mansion, that far surpasses anything I have seen in the South. All these plantations were deserted, on the approach of the yankees—the planters fleeing with their families and "chattel," to Mississippi and Red river, leaving only the *"worthless niggers"* behind.

The fine furniture left in these houses had been mostly destroyed, by the *vandals* of our army, before we came. After looking upon these plantations and seeing the despotic sway that these few planters wielded over this whole section, I am not surprised that they should be aristocrats, nor do I wonder that they cling to their "pet institution." Where their treasures, there will their heart be also." "Give me, neither poverty nor riches."

At the beginning of May 1863, Grant launched a brilliant, daring offensive against Vicksburg. His troops marched hard, fought several pitched battles with Confederate forces, and by mid-month had completely surrounded the Confederate fortress. Its surrender was now a matter of time. Hoping to speed its capture, however, he ordered his troops to try fighting their way directly through the Confederate fortifications.

Friday, May 22, 1863.

This morning, at 7 o'clock, our brigade was moved forward over a ridge, in our advance to a ravine within 400 yards of the rebels works. We were there drawn up in line and ordered to "*rest.*" Thus far we knew nothing of the *meaning* of our move, but the riddle was soon solved by [General John B.] Stevenson's brigade of [General John A.] Logan's division coming up and passing us with twenty or thirty *ladders.* There was no mistaking this sign—the rebel works were to be *stormed.*

We soon moved to a position, at the brow of the ridge in our front. Along this our brigade was posted in two lines. Stevenson's brigade was assigned the task of charging the rebel works. They advanced steadily up the slope, with "bayonets fixed" and orders not to fire guns. The 7th Missouri was in the advance. No rebels were to be seen, until our force had approached close up to the rebel works, when their breastworks and forts swarmed with butternuts, who poured volley after volley into our advancing columns. Our brigade and our batteries opened fire on the rebels as soon as they showed themselves, and with considerable effect. Most of our brigade, whoever, was unable to fire from the position we were in. Our company was exposed to the fire of the enemy, but was unable to return the fire, without endangering the lives of our own men. We were compelled to lie flat on the ground for protection and the heat was so great that our suffering became almost intolerable. Several men were sun-struck and carried off. I never suffered more from heat at any time and I think, never as much. By some blunder, the 10th Iowa was moved over the brow of the hill, and by the time it could be brought back to the proper position, their loss was quite heavy.

Stevenson's brigade moved steadily on, till they reached the rebel works when they found their ladders were too short and after standing awhile under a withering fire, they were ordered back. Their loss was very heavy. In our company, Isaac

Courtwright and Charles Morris were wounded—the former severely. I have learned since the charge, that our brigade was ordered to follow Gen. Stevenson's but (fortunately for us) Col. [George B.] Boomer did not so understand the orders he received. After remaining in our position for several hours after the charge, we were ordered down off the hill, and marched to the rear. We supposed we were going back to camp, but we were only "getting out of the frying pan into the fire." Our Division was ordered to reinforce Carr's Division which had been partially successful in a charge on our left—the 22nd Iowa having succeeded in driving the rebels out of one fort and planted their flag on it, although they could not occupy the fort as the rebels could command it from the rear. But the brave fellows of the 22nd, occupying the rifle pits and ditches of the enemy, held their position and kept the enemy at bay. To complete their success, reinforcements were ordered to their relief, but unfortunately much too late. Reinforcements that might have made the success certain at noon, were powerless for good at 5 o'clock in the evening. Each of our brigades was sent to a different point and operated separately. Our brigade marched around to the left and took position to the right of the railroad within 500 yds of the enemy's works. We could then see the flag of the 22nd Iowa, proudly waving on the rebel fort, and the boys of the 22nd (and other regiments of the brigade) stubbornly holding their position. Our position was formed, under cover, preparatory to a charge, in two lines—the 5th Iowa and 93d Illinois in the front line, and the 26th Missouri and 10th Iowa in the 2nd line. Col. Boomer took his position between the two lines. In front of us were two ravines and over this ridge, we were ordered to charge, in order to reach the rebel works.

About half past seven o'clock, (as soon after our arrival as our dispositions could be made) Col. Boomer commanded "Right shoulder shift arms!" "Forward, common time, march!" and our brigade moved forward in perfect line. As soon as we reached the top of the rise in our front, we came in plain view of the rebels, and they instantly opened fire on us, with musketry and artillery, from our front and flanks. We moved steadily down the slope in our front, at common time, presenting a perfect line, until we were half way down, when the line was broken by the nature of the ground, and we "double-quicked" the remainder of the distance into the ravine. We were not under fire for more than a minute, but the balls flew about us like hail, and our loss was considerable.

George L. Jones, of our company, one of the "bravest of the brave," was shot through the heart. Wm. Adamson was knocked down and slightly wounded in the head. Sergeant Heron was struck by three spent balls and knocked down. Just as we reached the ravine, the rebels (who had been reinforced from some other point in their line) drove our men from their positions around the fort, and captured the flag of the 22nd Iowa. By the use of "hand grenades" they drove our men from the rifle pits without exposing themselves, and thus regained their fort. Although the purpose for which our brigade was ordered to charge was thus already thwarted, Col. Boomer immediately reformed the brigade to continue our charge. We advanced to the brow of the hill that lay between us and the rebel works, when the brigade was formed in mass—our regiment and the 26th Missouri forming in rear of the 10th Iowa and 93d Illinois. While Col. Boomer was forming our brigade, in this manner, he was mortally wounded, by a ball from the rebel fort, on our left flank. He lived but a few moments, and his last words were: *"Tell Col. [Holden] Putnam* (of the 93d [Illinois]—our next senior Colonel) *not to go over that hill."* It was then dusk, and Col. Boomer well knew that a further advance would incur a fearful sacrifice of life, without the possibility of accomplishing ought. Col. Putnam then sent an orderly back to Gen. Carr to report these facts. Gen Carr immediately sent an order back for the brigade to hold their position until it was fairly dark, and then retire to the position where our brigade first formed. After falling back, we gathered in our wounded and dead. We then threw ourselves on the ground, wearied, and exhausted for a night's rest—not knowing what the morrow might bring forth. The results of today's fighting are heavy losses and small gains on our side.

Having failed in his bid to gain a quick victory, Grant now accepted a prolonged siege of Vicksburg. For the next six weeks his infantry held the lines ringing the city while dozens of cannon bombarded it day and night. Campbell, in the meantime, had an unhappy personal experience.

Wednesday, June 24, 1863.

[O]ur company [has] held an election to fill the office of Captain made vacant by the resignation of Capt. Tait. The election resulted in the choice of W.C. Pennywitt, 2nd Sergeant, as Captain of the company. This result was brought about by various influences. I did not expect nor desire the election to the office, nor did I expect a candidate from the ranks to be elected over my head. However, I abide by the decision of the company. Sergeant Pennywitt will make a very good officer. . . . The vote of the company has unmistakably indicated a lack of confidence in me as an officer and I shall embrace the first opportunity (after termination of our present Vicksburg campaign) to remove "my obnoxious presence" from the company.

This afternoon, Colonel Sampson [commander of the 5th Iowa] gave in his decision, with regards to the election of Captain in our company—the result of the election having been made known to him by a committee from the company. He stated that Lieutenants McKee and Campbell were officers who had been tried on the field of battle and never found wanting and that the promotion of a Sergeant to the office of Captain, over them, would be an act of gross injustice, and he would, therefore, recommend Lieut. McKee for Captain, and Lieut. Campbell for 1st Lieutenant and Sergeant Pennywitt for 2nd Lieutenant of the company. Although this expression of confidence on the part of the Colonel is especially gratifying, I shall nevertheless abide by my original resolution to put *distance* between myself and the company. Lieut. McKee will accept the position of Captain. We look through different glasses.

On 3 July the Confederate garrison commander at Vicksburg requested an armistice. The following day he agreed to surrender his more than thirty thousand soldiers. It was the greatest Union victory, to that point, of the entire war.

Saturday, July 4, 1863.

"The glorious Fourth" made doubly *"glorious"* by the confirmation of the news of the capture of Vicksburg. At 10 oclock this morning the surrender was completed and at 10 1/4 [10:15] the rebel army marched out and stacked arms, and then marched back as prisoners of war. The number surrendered is not yet known. The news was received in camp very coolly, but little excitement being manifested. Some looked upon the report as a *canard,* but I determined from the first, to believe it, and *feel good over it* as it was *the 4th* and I wanted to enjoy it. I celebrated *"the 4th"* by *putting on a clean paper collar.* This afternoon we received the official announcement of the capture of Vicksburg from Gen. [William T.] Sherman. The great stronghold has fallen! To Him who hath crowned our arms with victory be all the glory. Our victory is an important one and the questions naturally arises to our minds "what will be its effects?" Can we see the end of war any nearer than when the rebel stronghold defiantly denied our navigation of the Mississippi? The victory is too important to not be followed by important results but I can not recognize the fall of Vicksburg as the fall of the Confederacy. Many hard battles are yet to be fought, and months, perhaps years, of fighting stand between us and peace. To me it appears that the chastisements of the Almighty are not yet ended—that the nation has not yet been brought down into the dust of humility and will not *let the oppressors go free.* My firm conviction is that the Almighty has taken up the cause of the oppressed and that he will deny us peace until we "break every yoke" and sweep every vestige of the cursed institution from our land.

Campbell served in the Union army for another eighteen months and fought in several more battles. In the autumn of 1864, learning that his father had died and that his family needed him, he returned to civilian life. After the war he became a newspaper editor in Ohio. He died in 1913.

Questions

1. *With few ties to the community in which the "Jasper Greys" were raised, and a priggish disposition that evidently made him unpopular with his comrades, Campbell seems to have been motivated more by his ideological convictions than by a sense of kinship with his fellow soldiers. What were these convictions?*
2. *What did Campbell think of slavery? What did he think of African Americans? Do you notice any apparent contradiction in his views? If so, how would you account for it?*
3. *Many Northerners saw a connection between slavery and the existence of an antidemocratic "slaveholding aristocracy" in the South. Did Campbell believe this? What can you infer about his beliefs concerning Southern society compared with his own society?*
4. *In a study of Civil War soldiers entitled Embattled Courage, historian Gerald F. Linderman suggests that many soldiers believed that in order to possess the military virtue of courage, a soldier must be virtuous in other ways as well. Does Campbell's diary provide support for this view? What virtues did Campbell regard as important? How widely shared were his views among his fellow soldiers?*

Further Reading

For more on the ideological motivations of Civil War soldiers see James M. McPherson, What They Fought For, 1861–1865 *(Baton Rouge, 1994). Gerald F. Linderman presents a contrasting perspective in* Embattled Courage: The Experience of Combat in the American Civil War *(New York, 1987). Another good recent book is Reid Mitchell,* Civil War Soldiers: Their Expectations and Their Experiences *(New York, 1988). The most detailed surveys of soldier life in the Civil War are two older but still useful works by Bell I. Wiley:* The Life of Billy Yank: The Common Soldier of the Union *(Indianapolis and New York, 1952) and* The Life of Johnny Reb: The Common Soldier of the Confederacy *(Indianapolis and New York, 1943).*

The Struggle for Black Rights during Reconstruction

Michael Les Benedict

Introduction

The Civil War and Reconstruction era witnessed a desperate fight for equal civil and political rights for African Americans. The legal position of black Americans had deteriorated in the first part of the nineteenth century, with racism actually growing in the North and South as slavery was rejuvenated by the development of cotton agriculture. The growth of the antislavery movement in the 1840s and 1850s, however, led some Northerners to argue that African Americans were entitled to the rights of citizenship. The Supreme Court's Dred Scott decision was a watershed that dashed black Americans' claims to citizenship. Black hopes and expectations brightened with the passage of the Thirteenth Amendment, but they were dimmed once more by the adoption of restrictive southern Black Codes. Seeing the codes as an attempt to salvage key aspects of slavery, Republicans urged the passage of the Civil Rights Act of 1866 to ensure that all Americans, regardless of color, received the basic rights of citizenship. Congress passed the bill, only to be rebuffed by President Andrew Johnson's veto. Overriding the president's veto, Republicans then passed the Fourteenth Amendment in an effort to secure African-American citizenship and rights beyond constitutional doubt.

While blacks embraced their new citizenship, they continued to demand suffrage. Among the most eloquent was Frederick Douglass, one of the greatest orators of his day. The clamor for black enfranchisement aroused apprehension among southern whites that black voters might overturn the traditional social order. The white people of Alabama were among those who voiced their fears of black dominance in a petition to Congress. Nonethe-

less, Congress imposed black suffrage on the South in the Reconstruction Act of 1867, and in 1870 the requisite number of states ratified the Fifteenth Amendment, which extended the change throughout the nation and made it permanent.

But Republicans proved unable to secure equal civil and political rights for African Americans over bitter southern white resistance. A series of Supreme Court decisions narrowed the definition of federal citizenship and limited Congress's power to protect these rights. The court proclaimed that the postwar constitutional amendments authorized the federal government to protect rights only against violations by state authorities, leaving African Americans to rely on unsympathetic state and local officials to protect them against all other invasions of their rights.

Securing Equal Rights: The Documentary Record

As slaves, most African Americans had been denied nearly all fundamental rights. But for much of the time before the Civil War, the civil status of free African Americans was uncertain. Many Northern states considered them citizens entitled to basic rights; most of the New England states conceded them political rights as well. Other states denied or limited the basic rights of free blacks to travel, to associate with others, and to sue and testify in court, without making clear whether they were citizens or not. It was uncertain how state citizenship related to United States citizenship. Not until the case of Dred Scott v. Sandford did the Supreme Court answer that question. In this case, the Supreme Court distinguished United States citizenship from state citizenship and held that African Americans were not citizens of the United States, whether they were citizens of individual states or not.

White southerners refused to accept the legitimacy of state governments elected by black voters, and they engaged in systematic violence to resubordinate African Americans and to paralyze the Republican state officials in the South. From 1868 to 1871 much of the violence was instigated by the Ku Klux Klan, loosely organized gangs of white terrorists that sprang up in various southern localities. From 1874 to 1876 the Democratic party organized "White Leagues," "Red Shirts," and less formal armed auxiliaries to break up the Republican party. Both white and black Republicans were victimized.

Most of the southern states passed vagrancy laws that prohibited freedpeople from buying or leasing land or homes, except in towns, and then authorized towns to make their own regulations.

The following documents will introduce you to the legislation and arguments associated with the effort to secure equal rights after the Civil War, as well as to the practical effect on the lives of ordinary people. Read them in light of the questions that follow this section, particularly considering how far Republicans intended to change the American system of government in order to protect citizens' rights.

The Thirteenth Amendment

Congress passed the Thirteenth Amendment in January 1865 and it was ratified by December of that same year. The amendment abolished slavery throughout the United States.

Section 1 - Neither slavery nor involuntary servitude, except as a punishment for crime whereof the party shall have been duly convicted, shall exist within the United States, or any place subject to their jurisdiction.

Section 2 - Congress shall have power to enforce this article by appropriate legislation.

The Black Codes

Under President Andrew Johnson's plan of reconstruction, southern state governments, elected by white men who had taken an oath pledging loyalty to the United States, passed laws specifying the rights of the freedpeople. Some were more restrictive than others. All gave freedpeople the right to make contracts and to buy, own, and sell property. Some subjected them to the same criminal laws and punishments that covered white people; others subjected them to the harsher criminal laws that had covered free black people before the war. None of the codes extended political rights or the right to serve on juries. Local communities also passed regulations that limited freedpeople's rights. The following are examples of restrictive state and local provisions that convinced Republicans to intervene.

Selections from the Mississippi Black Code conferring civil rights on freedmen and defining vagrancy are from Laws of the State of Mississippi . . . *(1866), 82-84, 91 92.*

Mississippi Black Code

An Act to confer Civil Rights on Freedmen . . .

Section 1. . . . [A]ll freedmen, free negroes and mulattoes may sue and be sued . . . in all the courts of law and equity of this State, and may acquire personal property . . . by descent or purchase, and may dispose of the same, in the same manner, and to the same extent that white persons may: Provided that the provisions of this section shall not be so construed as to allow any freedman, free negro or mulatto to rent or lease any lands or tenements, except in incorporated towns or cities in which places the corporate authorities shall control the same. . . .

Sec. 5. . . . [E]very freedman, free negro and mulatto, shall . . . have a lawful home or employment, and shall have written evidence thereof. . . .

Sec. 7. . . . [E]very civil officer shall, and every person may arrest and carry back to his or her legal employer any freedman, free negro or mulatto, who shall have quit the service of his or her employer before the expiration of his or her term of service without good cause. . . .

Mississippi Vagrancy Law

Sec. 2. . . . [A]ll freedmen, free negroes and mulattoes in this State, over the age of eighteen years, found on the second Monday in January, 1866, or thereafter, with no lawful employment or business, or found unlawfully assembling themselves together either in the day or night time, and all white persons so assembling with freedmen, free negroes or mulattoes, or usually associating with freedmen, free negroes or mulattoes on terms of equality, or living in adultery or fornication with a freedwoman, free negro, or mulatto, shall be deemed vagrants, and on conviction thereof, shall be fined in the sum of not exceeding, in the case of a freedman, free negro, or mulatto, fifty dollars, and a white man two hundred dollars, and imprisoned at the discretion of the court, the free negro not exceeding ten days, and the white man not exceeding six months. . . .

Sec. 5. . . . [I]n case any freedman, free negro or mulatto, shall fail . . . after the imposition of any fine . . . to pay the same, . . . it shall be, and is hereby made the duty of the sheriff of the proper county to hire out said freedman, free negro or mulatto, to any person who will, for the shortest period of service, pay said fine . . . .

Debate over African American Rights: The Civil Rights Act

Republicans insisted that all Americans, regardless of color, were entitled to the basic rights of citizenship. In response to the black codes and other deprivations of rights in many states, North and South, they proposed a civil rights act.

Congress passed the Civil Rights bill on 15 March 1866, with southern congressmen still not permitted to take their seats. The bill made it a crime for anyone acting "under the color of law" or "custom" to deny the rights specified in Section 1. It also allowed those denied their rights in the states to transfer civil and criminal cases to the federal courts.

President Johnson vetoed the Civil Rights bill, giving his reasons in the message excerpted below from The Congressional Globe, *39th Congress, 1st Session, 1679-81 (27 March 1866).*

To the Senate of the United States:

I regret that the bill which has passed both Houses of Congress . . . contains provisions which I cannot approve, consistently with my sense of duty to the whole people and my obligations to the Constitution of the United States. . . .

By the first section of the bill, all persons born in the United States, and not subject to any foreign Power, excluding Indians not taxed, are declared to be citizens of the United States. This provision comprends the Chinese of the Pacific States, Indians subject to taxation, the people called Gypsies, as well as the entire race designated as blacks, people of color, negroes, mulattoes, and persons of African blood. . . .

The right of Federal citizenship thus to be conferred on the several excepted races before mentioned, is now, for the first time, proposed to be given by law. If, as is claimed by many, all persons who are native-born already are, by virtue of the Constitution, citizens of the United States, the passage of the pending bill cannot be necessary to make them such. If, on the other hand, such persons are not citizens, as may be assumed from the proposed legislation to make them such, the grave question presents itself, whether when eleven of the thirty-six States are unrepresented in Congress, at this time it is sound policy to make our entire colored population and all other excepted classes citizens of the United States? Four millions of them have just emerged from slavery into freedom. Can it be reasonably supposed that they possess the requisite qualifications to entitle them to all the privileges and immunities of citizens of the United States? . . .

Thus a perfect equality of the white and black races is attempted to be fixed by Federal law in every State of the Union, over the vast field of State jurisdiction covered by these enumerated rights. . . . In the exercise of State policy over matters exclusively affecting the people of each State, it has frequently been thought expedient to discriminate between the two races. By the statutes of some of the States, northern as well as southern, it is enacted, for instance, that no white person shall intermarry with a negro or mulatto. . . .

Hitherto every subject embraced in the enumeration of rights contained in this bill has been considered as exclusively belonging to the States. They all relate to the internal policy and economy of the respective States. . . .

In all our history, in all our experience as a people living under Federal and State law, no such system as that contemplated by the details of this bill has ever before been proposed or adopted. They establish, for the security of the colored race, safeguards which go infinitely beyond any that the General Government has ever provided for the white race. In fact, the distinction of race and color is, by the bill, made to operate in favor of the colored and against the white race. They interfere with the municipal legislation of the States, with the relations existing exclusively between a State and its citizens, or between inhabitants of the same State_an absorption and assumption of power by the General Government which, if acquiesced in, must sap and destroy our federative system of limited powers, and break down the barriers which preserve the rights of the States. It is another step, or rather stride, towards centralization and the concentration of all legislative powers in the national Government. The tendency of the bill must be to resuscitate the spirit of rebellion, and to arrest the progress of those influences which are more closely drawing around the States the bonds of union and peace.

Senator Trumbull's Response

Republican senator from Illinois Lyman Trumbull, managing the bill in the Senate, successfully argued for passage of the Civil Rights Act of 1866 over the president's veto. Taken from The Congressional Globe, *39th Congress, 1st Session (4 April 1866), 1756-58, 1760-61.*

What is the bill? It declares that there shall be no distinction in civil rights between any other race or color and the white race. It declares that there shall be no different punishment inflicted on a colored man in consequence of his color than that which is inflicted on a white man for the same offense. Is that a discrimination in favor of the negro and against the foreigner—a bill the only effect of which is to preserve equality of rights?

... Why, sir, the very object ... is to prevent discrimination, and language, it seems to me, could not more plainly express that object and effect. It may be said that it is for the benefit of the black man because he is now in some instances discriminated against by State laws; but that is the case with all remedial statutes. They are for the relief of the persons who need the relief, not for the relief of those who have the right already; and when those needing the relief obtain it, they stand upon the precise footing of those who do not need the benefit of the law.

... The bill neither confers nor abridges the rights of any one, but simply declares that in civil rights there shall be an equality among all classes of citizens. ... Each State, so that it does not abridge the great fundamental rights belonging, under the Constitution, to all citizens, may grant or withhold such civil rights as it pleases; all that is required is that, in this respect, its laws shall be impartial.

... This bill in no manner interferes with the municipal regulations of any State which protects all alike in their rights of person and property. ... How preposterous, then, to charge that unless some State can have and exercise the right to punish somebody, or to deny somebody a civil right on account of his color, its rights as a State will be destroyed.

The Fourteenth Amendment

To secure African-American citizenship and rights beyond constitutional doubt, Congress passed the Fourteenth Amendment later in 1866.

Section 1. All persons born or naturalized in the United States, and subject to the jurisdiction thereof, are citizens of the United States and of the State wherein they reside. No State shall make or enforce any law which shall abridge the privileges or immunities of citizens of the United States; nor shall any State deprive any person of life, liberty, or property, without due process of law; nor deny to any person within its jurisdiction the equal protection of the laws. . . .

Section 5. The Congress shall have power to enforce, by appropriate legislation, the provisions of this article.

Frederick Douglass Argues in Favor of Black Suffrage

Even before the Civil War ended, African-American leaders and radical Republicans were insisting that the national government secure the freedmen the right to vote. By 1867 most Republicans agreed, and by 1869 they were considering a constitutional amendment to bar racial tests for voting. Frederick Douglass, the great African-American orator and newspaper editor, explained "What the Black Man Wants" to a Boston audience in 1865. Note Douglass's allusion to the fact that women did not have the right to vote at this time. Note also his brief appeal to the anti-Irish prejudices of his Republican audience.

Excerpted from The Frederick Douglass Papers—Series One: Speeches, Debates, and Interviews, Volume 4: 1864-80, *ed. John W. Blassingame and John R. McKivigan (New Haven, 1991), 62-63, 66-68.*

I have had but one idea for the last three years to present to the American people. . . . I am for the "immediate, unconditional and universal" enfranchisement of the black man, in every State of the Union. (Loud applause.) Without this, his liberty is a mockery; without this, you might as well almost retain the old name of slavery for his condition; for, in fact, if he is not the slave of the individual master, he is the slave of society, and holds his liberty as a privilege, not as a right. . . .

It may be asked, "Why do you want it? Some men have got along very well without it. Women have not this right." Shall we justify one wrong by another? That is a sufficient answer. Shall we at this moment justify the deprivation of the negro of the right to

A photograph of Frederick Douglass, ex-slave and prominent African-American political activist. (Courtesy the Library of Congress)

vote because some one else is deprived of that privilege? I hold that women as well as men have the right to vote (applause), and my heart and my voice go with the movement to extend suffrage to woman. But that question rests upon another basis than that on which our right rests. We may be asked, I say, why we want it. I will tell you why we want it. We want it because it is our right, first of all. (Applause.) No class of men can, without insulting their own nature, be content with any deprivation of their rights. We want it, again, as a means for educating our race. Men are so constituted that they derive their conviction of their own possibilities largely from the estimate formed of them by others. If nothing is expected of a people, that people will find it difficult to contradict that expectation. By depriving us of suffrage, you affirm our incapacity to form an intelligent judgment respecting public men and public measures; you declare before the world that we are unfit to exercise the elective franchise, and by this means lead us to undervalue ourselves, to put a low estimate upon ourselves, and to feel that we have no possibilities like other men. . . . [H]ere, where universal suffrage is the rule, where that is the fundamental idea of the government, to rule us out is to make us an exception, to brand us with the stigma of inferiority, and to invite to our heads the missiles of those about us. Therefore I want the franchise for the black man.

. . . It is said that we are ignorant; I admit it. But if we know enough to be hung, we know enough to vote. If the negro knows enough to pay taxes to support the Government, he knows enough to vote—taxation and representation should go together. If he knows enough to shoulder a musket and fight for the flag, fight for the Government, he knows enough to vote. If he knows as much when he is sober as an Irishman knows when drunk, he knows enough to vote, on good American principles. (Laughter and applause.)

. . . What have you asked the black men of the South, the black men of the whole country to do? Why, you have asked them to incur the deadly enmity of their masters, in order to befriend you and to befriend this government. You have asked us to call down, not only upon ourselves, but upon our children's children, the deadly hate of the entire Southern people. You have called upon us to turn our backs upon our masters, to abandon their cause and espouse yours; to turn against the South and in favor of the North; to shoot down the Confederacy and uphold the flag—the American flag. . . . And now, what do you propose to do when you come to make peace? To reward your enemies, and trample in the dust your friends? . . . Do you mean to give your enemies the right to vote, and take it away from your friends? . . . In time of trouble we are citizens. Shall we be citizens in war, and aliens in peace? Would that be just?

. . . What I ask for the negro is not benevolence, not pity, not sympathy, but simply justice.

The Nation Supports Black Suffrage

The weekly journal The Nation *was founded in 1865 to support radical solutions to the problem of restoring the Union. The journal endorsed black suffrage.*

Excerpted from "Universal Suffrage And Universal Amnesty," The Nation *(29 November 1866), 430.*

[T]he Federal Government is bound by every consideration of justice, honor, and decency either to see that the freedmen enjoy complete security or to furnish them with the means of protecting themselves. In other words, we are bound either to give the freedmen a police—to see that every man of whom we claim allegiance can eat or sleep in peace—or we are bound to see that he enjoys a fair share in the making of the laws and the selection of the officers who are to execute them. . . . The former of these courses is not strictly in accordance with the spirit of our institutions; the latter is. . . .

[T]he ballot will do for the negro what it does for the poor ignorant Irishman, or German, or Englishman, but no more. It will secure him against flagrant class legislation, or cruel or unusual punishments, and against all oppression which is on its face oppressive. It will do more than this; it will cause politicians and public men—sheriffs, policemen, and the whole race of functionaries, actual and expectant—to treat him with civility, even with deference. It will put a stop to outrages and assaults of various kinds on negroes, and to all open expressions of contempt for them or dislike of them. . . .

But more than this the ballot will not do for the negro. It will not make him a good judge of the value or importance of measures not bearing directly and patently on his personal comfort or convenience; it will not enable him to tell the difference between statesmen and demagogues; between honest public men and knavish public men; between his own real friends and his real enemies; to distinguish laws contrived by scoundrels for his spoliation, under a show of immediate benefit, and schemes contrived by statesmen for his permanent advantage.

Opposition to Black Suffrage

The Reconstruction Act of 1867 enfranchised both black and white southerners, with the exception of those whites who as officeholders had sworn to uphold the Constitution of the United States and then joined the rebellion. It put the southern states back under military control temporarily. In exchange for restoration to normal relations in the Union, the Reconstruction Act required each southern state to frame a new constitution that would secure equal civil and political rights regardless of race. In the following document, a number of white Alabamans protested against the process.

Excerpted from the Petition and Memorial File, Records of the House of Representatives, 40th Cong., Record Group 233, National Archives, Washington, D.C.

The White people of Alabama send this their humble petition.

We beseech your Honorable Bodies to withdraw yourselves from the influence of the passions and contests of the hour, and contemplate for a brief period, our miserable condition . . . .

. . . [I]t is well known by all who have knowledge on the subject,—that while the negroes of the South may be more intelligent and of better morals than those of the same race in any other part of the world . . . —yet they are in the main, ignorant generally, wholly unacquainted with the principles of free Governments, improvident, disinclined to work, credulous yet suspicious, dishonest, untruthful, incapable of self-restraint, and easily impelled by want or incited by false and specious counsels, into folly and crime. . . .

Are these the people in whom should be vested the high governmental functions of establishing institutions and enacting and enforcing laws, to prevent crime, protect property, preserve peace and order in society, and promote industry, enterprise and civilization in Alabama, and the power and honor of the United States? Without property, without industry, without any regard for reputation, without controul over their own caprices and strong passions, and without fear of punishment under laws, by courts and through juries which are . . . created by and composed of . . . themselves, or of those whom they elect,—how can it be otherwise than that they will bring, to the great injury of themselves as well as of us and our children,—blight, crime, ruin and barbarism on this fair land? . . .

Will you, nearly three years after the war has ended, . . . suffer a whole State full of your kindred civilized white inhabitants, not only those who had opposed the Government, but women, children, and loyal men who had adhered to it,—to be thus consigned over to the horrid rule of barbarian negroes! . . .

. . . [D]o not, we implore you, abdicate your own rule over us, by transferring us to the blighting, brutalizing and unnatural dominion of an alien and inferior race: A race which has never shown sufficient administrative capacity for the good government of even the tribes, into which it has always been broken up in its native seats; and which in all ages, has itself furnished slaves for all the other races of the earth.

The Fifteenth Amendment

To make black enfranchisement permanent and to extend it to the north, Congress passed the Fifteenth Amendment in 1869 and sent it to the states for ratification. The required number of states ratified it in 1870.

Section 1. The right of citizens of the United States to vote shall not be denied or abridged by the United States or by any

The Fifteenth Amendment gave African Americans the right to vote for the first time; however, the end of Reconstruction, followed by the rise of Jim Crow laws in the South, largely marked the end of black suffrage until the Civil Rights movement almost a century later. (Courtesy of HarpWeek.)

State on account of race, color, or previous condition of servitude.

Section 2. The Congress shall have power to enforce this article by appropriate legislation.

Violent Resistance to Equal Rights in the South

The following documents describe Klan activities from several perspectives. Amzi Rainey, a black South Carolina sharecropper, described how the Klan terrorized his family in testimony excerpted from Proceedings in the Ku Klux Trials, at Columbia, S. C. in the United States Circuit Court, November Term, 1871 *(Columbia, S.C., 1872) 279-80.*

Former Senator James Chesnut of South Carolina testified before a congressional committee investigating the Klan. Simpson Bobo, a white lawyer and jack-of-all-trades, testified before the same committee. Their testimony is excerpted from Testimony Taken by the Joint Select Committee to Inquire into the Condition of Affairs in the Late Insurrectionary States, *vol. 1 and 2,* South Carolina *(Washington, D.C., 1872) 1:446, 449, 2:796-97.*

[Amzi Rainey's Testimony]

I looked out of the window, and I see some four or five disguised men coming up, and I ran up in the loft, and they came on; come to the door; and when they come to the door, they commenced beating and knocking. "God damn you, open the door! open the door! open the door!" . . . and my wife run to one of the doors and they knocked the top hinges off of the first, and she run across the house to the other, and agin that time they got the two hinges knocked off the other door, and the bolt held the door from falling, and she got it open . . . and when they come in, they struck her four or five licks before they said a word . . . .

They asked her who lived here. She said, "Rainey—Amzi Rainey." "What Amzi Rainey? What Amzi Rainey?" And she said, "Amzi Rainey," and he struck her another lick, and says: "Where is he? God damn him, where is he?" And she says: "I don't know."

The chief organization violently opposed to equal rights for African Americans was the Ku Klux Klan, which began in 1866 and relied on intimidation, terror, and murder to enforce white supremacy. (Courtesy the Library of Congress.)

And one said: "O, I smell him, God damn him; he has gone up in the loft." He says: "We'll kill him, too," and they come up then. . . .

I was in a box, and they said: "Oh, he is in this box, God damn him, I smell him; we'll kill him!" and the other says: "Don't kill him yet;" and they took me down. This man that struck my wife first, ran back to her and says: "God damn her, I will kill her now; I will kill her out;" and the one that went after me, he says: "Don't kill her;" and he commenced beating her then; struck her some four or five more licks, and then run back and struck me; he run back to her then, and drawed his pistol, and says: "Now, I am going to blow your damn brains out;" and the one by me threw the pistol up, and says: "Don't kill her." He aimed to strike me over the head, and struck me over the back and sunk me right down. Then, after he had done that, my little daughter—she was back in the room with the other little children—he says: "I am going to kill him;" and she runs out of the room, and says: "Don't kill my pappy; please don't kill my pappy!" He shoved her back, and says; "You go back in the room, you God damned little bitch; I will blow your brains out!" and fired and shot her . . . .

. . . [A]nd then they took me . . . [o]ff up the road, about a hundred and fifty yards; and they wanted to kill me up there, and one said, "No, don't kill him, let's talk a little to him first." Then, he asked me which way did I vote. I told him I voted the Radical [Republican] ticket. "Well," he says, "now you raise your hand and swear that you will never vote another Radical ticket, and I will not let them kill you." And he made me stand and raise my hand before him and my God, that I never would vote another Radical ticket . . . .

[Ex-Senator Chesnut's Testimony]

There is a deep dissatisfaction . . . in the hearts of the people of this State. . . . Three hundred thousand white people here around us, who had been accustomed to self-government, who had had an orderly government and had participated in that government, whose property had been taxed only by those who paid the taxes, beheld the whole thing suddenly subverted and themselves placed at the mercy of ignorance and of corruption . . . . These people are under an absolute despotism, and you will find that the countries where governments are most despotic are precisely those in which secret associations appear; small associations of parties ardent and seeking redress for real or fancied wrongs which they think cannot be avenged through the government. That is the true secret of this thing.

[Simpson Bobo's Testimony]

We have gone through one of the most remarkable changes in our relations to each other that has been known, perhaps, in the history of the world. The negro that was our slave has become our master suddenly . . . ; the bottom rail has got on top . . .—any one living here and knowing all about it, will be surprised that there has been as little disturbance as there has been. If the Government had give us a good government; if it had let us remain under a military government, none of these troubles would have been in this country. . . . There have been a great many . . . cases of the whipping of negroes in this county and some of the adjoining counties, some for one purpose and some for another. I think some of them have been political, and some of them have been with a view of answering special ends. . . . [T]he lower class of white people have a great prejudice against the negro, because he is a competitor for common labor, and wherever they come into collision, these fellows form themselves into a Klan, and take up negroes that come in their way, and punish them. . . . [F]or instance, a white man rents a tract of land to a negro. Some white man wants to get the land. The owner prefers giving it to the negro. For the purpose of punishing the negro, he will then get up a parcel of neighbors, and in disguise they will go and whip the negro half to death.

The Supreme Court Limits the Ability of the Federal Government to Protect Rights

In a series of cases interpreting the Fourteenth Amendment, the justices of the Supreme Court made it difficult for the federal government to protect the rights of American citizens in the south. In the Slaughter-House Cases, the Court distinguished between the rights people held as citizens of the United States and those they held as citizens of their states. The rights Americans thought of as basic to citizenship were those they held as state citizens, not as citizens of the United States. The Fourteenth Amendment, the justices said, only authorized the federal government to protect the latter.

Abridged from the Slaughter-House Cases, *83 U.S. 36, at 72-78 (1873).*

The Slaughter-House Cases

The first section of the fourteenth article . . . opens with a definition of citizenship—not only citizenship of the United States, but citizenship of the States. . . . It declares that persons may be citizens of the United States without regard to their citizenship of a particular State, and it overturns the Dred Scott decision by making all persons born within the United States and subject to its jurisdiction citizens of the United States. . . .

It is quite clear, then, that there is a citizenship of the United States, and a citizenship of a State, which are distinct from each other, and which depend upon different characteristics or circumstances in the individual.

We think this distinction and its explicit recognition in this amendment of great weight in this argument, because the next paragraph of this same section . . . speaks only of privileges and immunities of citizens of the United States, and does not speak of those of citizens of the several States. . . .

The language is, "No State shall make or enforce any law which shall abridge the privileges or immunities of citizens of the United States." It is a little remarkable, if this clause was intended as a protection to the citizen of a State against the legislative power of his own State, that the word citizen of the State should be left out when it is so carefully used, and used in contradistinction to citizens of the United States, in the very sentence which precedes it. It is too clear for argument that the change in phraseology was adopted understandingly and with a purpose.

Of the privileges and immunities of the citizen of the United States, and of the privileges and immunities of the citizen of the State, . . . it is only the former which are placed by this clause under the protection of the Federal Constitution . . . .

The latter must rest for their security and protection where they have heretofore rested . . . .

[The Court then quoted an earlier lower court decision that defined the privileges and immunities of state citizenship:]

"What are the privileges and immunities of citizens of the several states? We feel no hesitation in confining these expressions to those privileges and immunities which are fundamental; which belong of right to the citizens of all free governments, and which have at all times been enjoyed by citizens of the several states which compose this Union. . . . They may all . . . be comprehended under the following general heads: protection by the government, with the right to acquire and possess property of every kind, and to pursue and obtain happiness and safety, subject, nevertheless, to such restraints as the government may prescribe for the general good of the whole."

. . . Was it the purpose of the 14th Amendment, by the simple declaration that no state should make or enforce any law which shall abridge the privileges and immunities of citizens of the United States, to transfer the security and protection of all the civil rights which we have mentioned, from the states to the Federal government? And where it is declared that Congress shall have the power to enforce that article, was it intended to bring within the power of Congress the entire domain of civil rights heretofore belonging exclusively to the states?

. . . We are convinced that no such results were intended by the Congress which proposed these amendments, nor by the legislatures of the states, which ratified them.

Civil Rights Cases

In the Civil Rights Cases, the Court ruled that the Fourteenth Amendment only authorized the federal government to protect people against deprivations of their rights by state officials or people acting under color of state authority.

Abridged from Civil Rights Cases, *109 U.S. 3, at 10-11 (1883).*

The first section of the Fourteenth Amendment . . . is prohibitory in its character, and prohibitory upon the States. It declares that:

"No State shall make or enforce any law which shall abridge the privileges or immunities of citizens of the United States; nor shall any State deprive any person of life, liberty, or property without due process of law; nor deny to any person within its jurisdiction the equal protection of the laws."

It is State action of a particular character that is prohibited. Individual invasion of individual rights is not the subject-matter of the amendment. . . . [T]he last section of the amendment invests Congress with power to enforce it by appropriate legislation. To enforce what? To enforce the prohibition. . . . This is the legislative power conferred upon Congress, and this is the whole of it. It does not invest Congress with power to legislate upon subjects which are within the domain of State legislation; but to provide modes of relief against State legislation, or State action, of the kind referred to. It does not authorize Congress to create a code of municipal law for the regulation of private rights. . . .

The Effect of "Redemption" on Black Southerners

The Supreme Court's narrow interpretation of the Fourteenth Amendment made it difficult to prosecute southern violence. Between 1873 and 1875, the resolve of the federal government to protect the rights of citizens in the south waned. By 1877, southern white Democrats regained control of southern state governments. Southern whites referred to their success as "redemption," and they used fraud in many states to prevent Republicans from regaining power. The following plea from

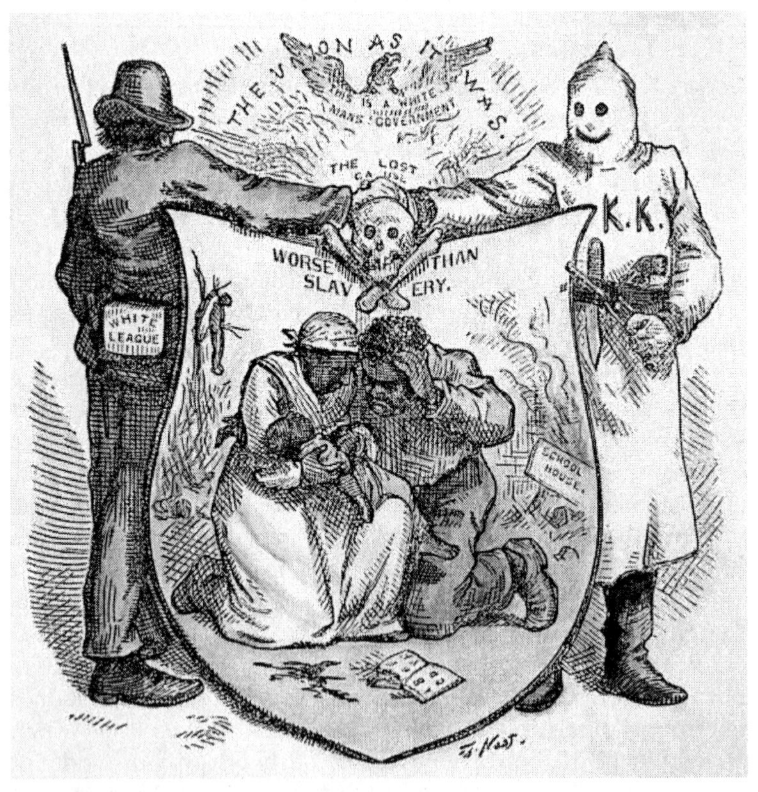

The return of control of state government to southern white Democrats resulted in conditions that, according to this Thomas Nast cartoon, were worse than slavery for American blacks. (Courtesy of the Library of Congress.)

Wilson H. Williams for help from the national government suggests how the change affected African Americans in the South. It had been illegal to teach slaves to read or write, so Williams's literacy, with all its spelling errors, was quite an accomplishment.

From Wilson H. Williams to Senator John Sherman, care of Rev. John D. Haynes, 15 January 1879, John Sherman papers, Manuscript Division, Library of Congress, Washington, D.C.

We poor coul[ored] men have got no more show then a good Dog. The White people is tareing all over the land picking up the poor coul men acreing [forcing] them back to thar old Homes giving them no triel but butchering them up for things that [got] don in 20 and 30 years a go. God hoe [who] made the wourld knows that it is not rite and we know you all ought to do sum thing for ous for we are healpletts cant do eney thing nor say eney thing [P]lease you all stop that thing for it has been going on long anuffe. . . .

Questions

1. *Describe the issues of social justice that affected the lives of free African Americans at the time the Civil War broke out.*
2. *Why did President Andrew Johnson oppose the Civil Rights Act? Did it discriminate in favor of African Americans, as he charged?*
3. *What reasons did proponents of African-American suffrage give for supporting it? Aside from the racism of the petition, did the petitioners have a point about enfranchising former slaves so soon after emancipation? How would Frederick Douglass have answered? Given the hostility of white southerners toward equal civil rights for African Americans, what would you have done to secure their rights?*
4. *To what degree were the Supreme Court decisions interpreting the Fourteenth Amendment consistent with the spirit in which they were passed?*
5. *Over all, to what degree did the civil status of African Americans change during the era of Reconstruction? How much did their status improve? What were the limitations of the change?*

FURTHER READING

The standard, prize-winning work on Reconstruction in general, providing a wealth of information about the effort to restore the Union on the basis of equality of rights, is Eric Foner's *Reconstruction: America's Unfinished Revolution, 1863-1877* (New York, 1988). A briefer and more focused work is Foner's "Rights and the Constitution in Black Life during the Civil War and Reconstruction," *Journal of American History* 74 (December 1987): 863-83. Herman Belz addresses constitutional questions more directly than Foner in *Emancipation and Equal Rights: Politics and Constitutionalism in the Civil War Era* (New York, 1978). Peyton McCrary offers another argument for the radicalism of Republican Reconstruction policy in "Republican Ideas about Politics and Social Change," *Civil War History* 30 (December 1984): 330-50. Robert J. Kaczorowski criticizes the Supreme Court for retreating from the Republican commitment to rights in *The Politics of Judicial Interpretation: The Federal Courts, Department of Justice, and Civil Rights, 1866-1876* (New York, 1985).

The Rise of Big Business and the Persistence of Small Business in American Industry, 1850–1920

Mansel G. Blackford

INTRODUCTION

In 1901, J. P. Morgan, America's best-known and most powerful investment banker, combined Carnegie Steel with other firms to form United States Steel, capitalized at over $1.4 billion. The establishment of the world's first billion-dollar corporation was a signal that big business had achieved a permanent institutional status on the American scene. Morgan organized United States Steel from firms that had earlier competed in the marketplace. Now those firms could cooperate; and through their combined size, control of iron ore, and efficiencies of production, Morgan expected that they would dominate the nation's steel industry, reducing price competition. A key element in modern America had been created: in 1860 no single American company was valued at $10 million, but by 1904 some three hundred were.

Giant firms clustered in just a few fields. Nearly all were in industry. Of the 278 American companies with assets of $20 million or more, in 1917, some 236 were manufacturing companies. By way of contrast, only five were agricultural firms (one each in ranching, the growing of sugar cane, and the harvesting of crude rubber, and two diversified multinationals, the United Fruit Company and its competitor, the Atlantic Fruit and Sugar Company). Of the manufacturing businesses, 171 firms, or nearly three-quarters, were in just six groups: 39 in primary metals, 34 in food processing, 29 in transportation equipment, 24 in manufacturing machinery, 24 in oil refining, and 21 in chemicals. These companies shared certain characteristics. Most had combined production with distribution—previously, these two business functions had been carried out by separate companies—by the time of World War I. Nearly all were multi-unit enterprises with factories spread across the United States.

The share of America's industrial output coming from small businesses dropped as large manufacturing ventures rose to prominence. Corporations—the legal form assumed by most big businesses, but relatively few small businesses (most small firms were single-owner proprietorships or partnerships)—accounted for three-quarters of America's industrial production by 1904. Small businesses also became less important as employers. By 1914, nearly a third of all industrial workers found employment in plants with 500 or more in their labor forces, and another third in those with 100 to 499. As large companies arose in manufacturing, a growing share of industrial workers found employment in companies operating more than one plant; at least a third of the nation's workers did so by 1923.

Small businesses did not, however, disappear from the industrial scene in the United States. The same set of census statistics alluded to above show that in 1914 a third of America's industrial workforce found employment in firms with 100 or fewer laborers. If small businesses are defined as those with 250 or fewer workers, 54 percent of those employed by manufacturing concerns worked for small firms. Moreover, some fifty-four thousand little businesses, those with six to twenty workers, were still in operation on the eve of the First World War. Those small businesses that survived and prospered in manufacturing did so by following several strategies. In some fields—such as leather working, furniture making, and lumber milling—few economies of scale existed, and big businesses did not develop. That is, the cost of production per number of goods made did not decline as the number of products turned out increased. In these areas, small manufacturers continued to make goods much as they had in earlier years. In those realms in which big businesses did emerge, small industrialists had to adapt to the presence of their larger counterparts, and many small firms were quite successful in doing so. [Portions of this introduction have been previously published in Mansel G. Blackford, A History of Small Business in America *(New York, 1991), 28–37.]*

The Search for Order, The Struggle to Survive

The selections below offer contemporary perspectives on major trends in American business during the late nineteenth and early twentieth centuries. The first two sources provide first-hand explanations of specific organizational innovations in big business: bureaucratic management, pioneered by the nation's railroads, and vertical integration, exemplified by Andrew Carnegie's steel empire. The concluding documents present contrasting accounts of how smaller companies fared in the era of big business. The first business failed when it attempted to compete directly with the powerful Standard Oil trust. The experience of the second, however, illustrates how some smaller businesses flourished by finding a "niche" in the market, by utilizing advanced technology, and by adopting some of the accounting and managerial techniques perfected by their larger counterparts.

Railroads Change Their Management Methods

The New York & Erie Railroad and the Chicago, Burlington & Quincy were among America's leading trunk-line railroads of the mid- and late-nineteenth century. As they grew in size and complexity, railroads developed modern bureaucratic management methods, as this report from the superintendent of the New York & Erie Railroad illustrates. Selected from The Railroads: The Nation's First Big Business, Sources and Readings, *ed. Alfred D. Chandler, Jr. (New York, 1965), 101–3, 108, 118–20.*

Superintendent's Report

Office General Sup't N. Y. & Erie R. R.
New York, March 25, 1856

Homer Ramsdell, Esq.
PRESIDENT OF THE NEW YORK AND ERIE RAILROAD COMPANY:

Sir:

. . . *Theoretically*, other things being equal, a long road should be operated for a less cost per mile than a short one. This position is so clearly evident and so generally admitted, that its truth may be assumed without offering any arguments in support of it; and, notwithstanding the reverse so far as *practical* results are considered, has generally been the case, we must look to other causes than the mere difference in length of roads for a solution of the difficulty.

A Superintendent of a road fifty miles in length can give its business his personal attention, and may be almost constantly upon the line engaged in the direction of its details. . . . In the government of a road five hundred miles in length a very different state of things exists. Any system which might be applicable to the business and extent of a short road, would be found entirely inadequate to the wants of a long one; and I am fully convinced, that in the want of a system perfect in its details, properly adapted and vigilantly enforced, lies the true secret of their failure; and that this disparity of cost per mile in operating long and short roads, is not produced by *a difference in length*, but is in proportion to the perfection of the system adopted. . . .

In my opinion a system of operations, to be efficient and successful, should be such as to give to the principal and responsible head of the running department a complete daily history of details in all their minutiae. Without such supervision, the procurement of a satisfactory annual statement must be regarded as extremely problematical. . . . [I]t will scarcely be expected that we can at once adopt any plan of operations which will not require amendment and a reasonable time to prove its worth. A few general principles, however, may be regarded as settled and necessary in its formation, amongst which are:

1. A proper division of responsibilities.
2. Sufficient power conferred to enable the same to be fully carried out. . . .

3. The means of knowing whether such responsibilities are faithfully executed.

4. Great promptness in the report of all derelictions of duty, that evils may be at once corrected.

5. Such information, to be obtained through a system of daily reports and checks that will not embarrass principal officers, nor lessen their influence with their subordinates.

6. The adoption of a system, as a whole, which will not only enable the General Superintendent to detect errors immediately, but will also point out the delinquent.

Organization

The following comprises a list of the principal officers acting directly under the General Superintendent, with powers and duties arranged with reference to obtaining the results proposed.

1. Division and Branch Superintendents.
2. Masters of Engine and Car Repairs.
3. Car Inspectors.
4. General Freight Agent.
5. General Ticket Agent.
6. General Wood Agent.
7. Superintendent of Telegraph.
8. Foreman of Bridge Repairs.

For the more convenient working of the road it is now separated into Divisions. . . . The several Divisions and Branches are in charge of Superintendents, who are held responsible for the successful working of their respective Divisions, and for the maintenance of proper discipline and conduct of all persons employed thereon, except such as are in the employment of other officers acting under directions from this office. . . . They possess all the powers delegated by the organization to the General Superintendent, except in matters pertaining to the duties of General Ticket Agent, General Freight Agent, General Wood Agent, Telegraph management, and Engine and Car Repairs. . . .

All that is required to render the efforts of railroad companies in every respect equal to that of individuals, is a rigid system of personal accountability through every grade of service.

[DANIEL C. MCCALLUM]

Organization of Railroads (1885)

[A memorandum from Charles E. Perkins, president of the Chicago, Burlington & Quincy Railroad]

IN DECIDING the question of organization it will be necessary to consider two stages, so to speak, of railroad development. The first stage where the volume of traffic is not sufficient to make necessary or to warrant the highest degree of physical efficiency; and the second stage where the volume of traffic is so great as not only to warrant the expenditure, but also to make it economical to maintain the physical efficiency at the highest point.

Ordinarily the second stage will come only with increased mileage and while there are exceptional cases where roads of small fixed mileage acquire a large business by reason of their forming a link in a through line, or being in direct competition with one or more other roads between two commercial centers, they are so rare that it is best in considering the general question of organization to assume that a road in the second stage will be one of 500 miles or more in length. . . .

The responsible head of the operations of a road in the first stage is usually the general superintendent, a general manager only becoming necessary when the road has grown and business has so increased as to make it desirable to confine the general superintendent to the care of the machine alone. In the first stage he can and will himself look closely after his track and rolling stock as well as the traffic. In the second stage with the increase of traffic he will find his time and mind largely occupied with business questions, and also that he can draw the straight line of perfection to work to, and can safely trust to educated experts most of the questions relating to the efficient maintenance of the machine. The proper economical maintenance of a road in the first stage is not an exact science, while that of a road in the second stage is, and scientific methods which would be unnecessary and extravagant on the one may become necessary and economical on the other.

An organization for the management of a road in the first stage is comparatively simple. The duties of the president will be to advise the chief financial and accounting officer and the chief operating officer and also the purchasing and supply agents, to supervise and execute all important contracts, to conduct the most important negotiations, to specifically approve all expenditures chargeable to capital account before they are incurred, to supervise and direct the most important purchases of material and equipment, and to watch closely the results by means of reports from the heads of the two great departments of accounts and operations. . . .

An organization for the management of a large road in the second stage is on the other hand more complex. Here the duties of the president will be the same as in the first stage of development, but the amount of expenditure, the number of contracts, negotiations, reports, interviews, new schemes, etc., will have so largely increased that the president may require the aid of one vice president to assist him generally and possibly two or three personal assistants with fixed duties besides.

The departments of accounts and finances will also have grown so that a second vice president may be needed to look after the treasurer, the auditor and the secretary, three offices which in the first stage would be so combined as to be held by one, or at the most two, persons.

So of the departments of operation and construction. If the mileage is large it will be found expedient probably to put a third vice president at the head of this great department, which controls so largely the income and outgo. Under him again will be a general manager in direct charge of the daily details and taking the position occupied by the general superintendent in the first stage. The purchasing agent will act under the 3rd vice president and also especially in making large purchases of rails, rolling stock etc. directly under the president.

Andrew Carnegie and Carnegie Steel

Carnegie Steel was the largest industrial enterprise in the world in its day and formed the basis for the establishment of United States Steel. Vertical integration—the linking of all the steps in making steel in one company—gave Carnegie Steel production cost advantages over its less-well-integrated rivals. In his autobiography, Carnegie discussed how he organized his firm and some of the reasons he was successful. He stressed the importance of vertical integration, especially owning his own supplies of raw materials and his own pig iron furnaces (pig iron was then made into steel). Excerpt from Autobiography of Andrew Carnegie *(Boston, 1920), 220–22, 226–27.*

THE one vital lesson in iron and steel that I learned in Britain was the necessity for owning raw materials and finishing the completed article ready for its purpose. Having solved the steel-rail problem at the Edgar Thomson Works, we soon proceeded to the next step. The difficulties and uncertainties of obtaining regular supplies of pig iron compelled us to begin the erection of blast furnaces. Three of these were built. . . .

. . . We were the second firm in the United States to manufacture our own spiegel [a combination of iron, magnesium, and carbon], and the first, and for years the only, firm in America that made ferro-manganese. We had been dependent upon foreigners for a supply of this indispensable article, paying as high as eighty dollars a ton for it. . . .

We continued to develop our blast-furnace plant, every new one being a great improvement upon the preceding, until at last we thought we had arrived at a standard furnace. . . . The blast-furnace department was no sooner added than another step was seen to be essential to our independence and success. The supply of superior coke was a fixed quantity—the Connellsville field being defined. We found that we could not get on without a supply of the fuel essential to the smelting of pig iron; and a very thorough investigation of the question led us to the conclusion that the Frick Coke Company had not only the best coal and coke property, but that it had in Mr. Frick himself a man with a positive genius for its management. He had proved his ability by starting as a poor railway clerk and succeeding. In 1882 we purchased one half of the stock of this company, and by subsequent purchases from other holders we became owners of the great bulk of the shares.

There now remained to be acquired only the supply of iron stone. If we could obtain this we should be in the position occupied by only two or three of the European concerns. We thought at one time we had succeeded in discovering in Pennsylvania this last remaining link in the chain. We were misled, however, in our investment in the Tyrone region, and lost considerable sums as the result of our attempts to mine and use the ores of that section. . . .

To make a ton of steel one and a half tons of iron stone has to be mined, transported by rail a hundred miles to the Lakes, carried by boat hundreds of miles, transferred to cars, transported by rail one hundred and fifty miles to Pittsburgh; one and a half tons of coal must be mined and manufactured into coke and carried fifty-odd miles by rail; and one ton of limestone mined and carried one hundred and fifty miles to Pittsburgh. How then could steel be manufactured and sold without loss at three pounds for two cents? This, I confess, seemed to me incredible, and little less than miraculous, but it was so.

Opposition to Standard Oil

Not all Americans favored the development of big business; many saw large firms as threats to economic and political independence in the United States. Standard Oil, one of the first large industrial concerns, became the butt of much criticism. Independent refiners feared the competition from Standard Oil, whose costs of production were lower, resulting in lower consumer prices for goods such as kerosene. No independent producer was more outspoken than George Rice, who refined crude oil in Marietta, Ohio. Rice believed Standard Oil was using unethical means to destroy his business. In particular, Rice thought railroads colluded with Standard against him—charging less to carry Standard Oil's products than they charged him. Rice also accused Standard of undercutting his prices in an unethical fashion. Selected from "Testimony of George Rice, November 11, 1899" in the Industrial Commission: Preliminary Report on Trusts and Industrial Combinations *(Washington, 1900), 1:687, 704.*

"I am a citizen of the United States, born in the State of Vermont. Producer of petroleum for more than 30 years, and a refiner of same for 20 years, but my refinery has been shut down during the past 3 years, owing to the powerful and all-prevailing machinations of the Standard Oil Trust, in criminal collusion and conspiracy with the railroads to destroy my business of 20 years of patient industry, toil, and money in building up, wholly by and through unlawful freight discriminations. I have been driven from pillar to post, from one railway line to another, for 20 years, in the absolutely vain endeavor to get equal and just freight rates with the Standard Oil Trust, so as to be able to run my refinery at anything approaching a profit, but which I have been utterly unable to do. I have had to consequently shut down, with my business absolutely ruined and my refinery idle. . . .

Outside of rebates or freight discriminations I had no show with the Standard Oil trust, because of their unlawfully acquired monopoly, by which they could temporarily cut only my customers' prices, and below cost, leaving the balance of the town, nine-tenths, uncut. This they can easily do without any appreciable harm to their general trade, and thus effectually wipe out all competition, as fully set forth. Standard Oil prices generally were so high that I could sell my goods 2 to 3 cents a gallon below their prices and make a nice profit, but these savage attacks and cuts upon my customers' goods, and their consequent loss, plainly showed to them their power for evil, and the uselessness to contend against such odds. . . ."

A Smaller Manufacturer: The Buckeye Steel Castings Company

The success of small firms in the iron and steel industries was not limited to the Pittsburgh region. Buckeye Steel Castings Company of Columbus, Ohio, was formed as a partnership in 1881. It was one of some two hundred companies producing a variety of cast-iron goods for the local market in central Ohio. Buckeye did not produce a specialty product, which might have given it an advantage over its competitors, and it came very close to failing during the hard times of the mid-1880s. Buckeye Steel, however, was saved by the development of a specialty product for a niche market—an automatic railroad car coupler. Originally made out of cast iron in the 1890s, and later out of stronger cast steel, this technologically sophisticated coupler gave Buckeye an edge over its competitors and allowed the company to break into the national market. New management techniques, especially new cost accounting practices, also made Buckeye more competitive.

In his approach to cost accounting, Buckeye's plant superintendent was among the most advanced managers of his day, pioneering in the inclusion of indirect and overhead expenses as part of his costs of produc-

tion, as illustrated by the following April 1905 financial report. Taken from Mansel G. Blackford, A Portrait Cast in Steel: Buckeye International and Columbus, Ohio, 1881–1980 *(Westport, Connecticut, 1982), 56–57.*

Costs of Production for April 1905

Metal in mould	$ 49,266
Moulding	17,730
Core-making	4,873
Annealing and cleaning	3,419
Fitting and finishing	15,725
Patterns and drafting	414
Repairs to plant and equipment	5,266
Locomotive service, heat, light, and power	2,779
Selling expense	2,755
Shipping expense	989
Office expense	698
Superintendence	527
Miscellaneous expenses	2,691
Salary of officers	838
Advertising	250
Insurance and taxes	350
Freight	2,347
Testing	259
Total	$ 111,179
Add for defective castings	2,241

. . . While not engaging in true capital accounting (few businesses had reached this level of sophistication), Buckeye's superintendent was figuring monthly charges for furnace repairs, building repairs, machinery repairs, and building depreciation as production costs as early as 1903. He explained his accounting methods in that year:

> For instance, we produced 18,500 tons of castings from the beginning of operations to Dec. 31, 1903. Total cost furnace repairs $12,129 = 70¢ per ton. Repairs of buildings about $3,000 = 20¢ per ton. Repairs of machinery about $6,000 = 35¢ per ton. Depreciation of buildings figures at 3% per year. Buildings are worth $200,000. Depreciation is $5,000 or 35¢ per ton.

Depreciation of machinery is figured at 10% per year. Machinery is worth $250,000. So depreciation comes to $25,000 or $1.40 per ton.

Questions

1. *What unique problems did managing a large railroad network entail? How did the New York & Erie Railroad attempt to meet these challenges?*
2. *How did Andrew Carnegie pursue vertical integration in his steel empire? In what ways did such a policy bring "order" and "efficiency" to Carnegie's operations?*
3. *Why, according to George Rice, did his oil refining business fail? Do you think his judgment of Standard Oil's business practices is fair? Why or why not? What specific techniques and strategies used by Buckeye Steel Castings allowed that company to survive? Explain.*

FURTHER READING

Alfred D. Chandler, Jr., Visible Hand: The Managerial Revolution in American Business *(Cambridge, 1977), examines the emergence of big businesses. Two good studies of Andrew Carnegie are Harold Livesay,* Andrew Carnegie and the Rise of Big Business *(Boston, 1975); and Joseph Frazier Wall,* Andrew Carnegie *(New York, 1970). Allan Nevins,* John D. Rockefeller: The Heroic Age of American Enterprise *(New York, 1940), and Ralph and Muriel Hidy,* Pioneering in Big Business, 1882–1921 *(New York, 1955), look at the history of Standard Oil. John N. Ingham,* Making Iron and Steel: Independent Mills in Pittsburgh, 1820–1920 *(Columbus, Ohio, 1991), and Philip Scranton,* Proprietary Capitalism: The Textile Manufacture at Philadelphia, 1800–1885 *(Cambridge, 1983), present industry studies emphasizing the roles smaller firms played in manufacturing.*

The Age of Industrial Violence

Warren R. Van Tine

Introduction

The year 1877 is a significant turning point in American history. On the one hand, the federal government abandoned efforts to reconstruct the South, bringing the Civil War era to a close. On the other hand, the Railroad Strike of 1877—the first nationwide strike in American history, one that left at least one hundred people dead and $109 million worth of property in rubble—alerted Americans that an age of industrial violence was at hand. The issues that had dominated several decades of American politics and social life—sectionalism, states' rights, slavery, and the preservation of the Union—were replaced by new concerns linked to industrialism, particularly those popularly lumped under the vague heading "The Labor Question"—urban squalor, massive immigration, ethnic diversity, and class conflict.

For the next three-quarters of a century, until the 1950s, the United States experienced massive labor unrest. Indeed, in the judgment of two highly respected scholars, Philip Taft and Philip Ross, America "has had the bloodiest and most violent labor history of any industrial nation in the world." This development seems rather ironic, first because for much of the antebellum period native-born Americans took pride in believing that their country was unique and would avoid the class strife that plagued other industrializing nations, and second because workers in America did not flock to unions in massive numbers. When they did, the organizations they joined were essentially cautious ones—wanting to preserve working conditions, reduce hours of work, and gain better pay, but not to take over the means of production or dominate the political and economic system.

Why violence became such a dominant feature of industrial relations in America is subject to debate. Some of the factors contributing to industrial turmoil are the same ones that contributed to America being such a violent nation in general: unstable communities as a consequence of high levels of geographic mobility; ethnic and racial tensions as a result of the heterogeneity of the population; the far more rapid and disruptive rate of industrializing here than in Western Europe; segments of the population trapped in poverty while most people experienced material abundance; a creed of masculine individualism that prized aggressiveness; and the widespread ownership of firearms.

Other factors are more directly tied to the way industrial capitalism developed in the United States. Deeply planted Protestant values that associated economic success with God's blessings combined with laissez faire thought to create a business culture approving of possessive individualism. This culture was embraced by a political system that eagerly sought to stimulate business growth through tariffs, internal improvements, loans, and outright grants of money and land, while moving extremely cautiously to regulate socially disruptive and inhumane business practices (the United States, for example, trailed far behind European nations in outlawing child labor or establishing safety standards). In the post-Civil War era, moreover, the courts said that the Constitution granted private corporations rights guaranteed by the Constitution to individuals, but no agency of the government protected workers against the power of corporations to deprive them of similar rights in the workplace. Nor did the courts review government action against striking workers with anything like the rigor with which it reviewed government regulation of business. Consequently, until the 1930s, far more often than not, the state intervened in labor-management disputes on the side of the employer.

Indeed, the high level of industrial violence did not recede in America until the early 1950s. Instrumental in producing this decline was a shift in the government's role in labor disputes, stimulated by the passage of the Wagner Act in 1935. It gave workers the legal right to join labor organizations of their own choosing, mandated that employers bargain collectively with them, and forbade a whole set of practices employers previously used to break unions. Equally important in reducing the level of industrial violence, however, was the extraordinary prosperity that most of the nation experienced in the decades following World War II. With foreign competition temporarily eliminated by the war and its destructive consequences, American corporations were making healthy earnings and were gladly passing on some of the gains to their workers in order to maintain production and profits. Today, with the waning of American affluence in the 1980s and '90s, working-class and many middle-class Americans are experiencing deteriorating standards of living, while more and more employers are resisting dealing with unions, two developments that raise the probability of increased industrial violence in America.

THE PULLMAN BOYCOTT OF 1894: A CASE STUDY OF INDUSTRIAL STRIFE

Of the many industrial disturbances of the late nineteenth and early twentieth centuries, few had such national impact as the Pullman Boycott of 1894. Not only did the strike disrupt transportation across the nation, but it brought into focus many of the issues associated with industrial strife—the right of workers to form unions and pursue collective bargaining; the right of employers to form associations to collectively resist employee demands; the nature of company towns; the moral and legal right of workers to take actions in sympathy with other striking workers; the right of public utility employees to strike; and the nature, scope, and fairness of Federal intervention in labor disputes.

George Pullman, whose company manufactured and rented Pullman railroad cars, had built a "model" town near Chicago for his factory and workforce. Workers lived in company houses, bought in company stores, attended churches built and controlled by the company. By 1894, most of the Pullman workers were members of the American Railway Union (ARU), led by Eugene Victor Debs, while Pullman was a member of the General Managers' Association (GMA), an organization of twenty-four railroads linked to Chicago which, among other things, tried to establish uniform wage policies. A confrontation was almost certain when, in response to the depression of the 1890s, Pullman cut wages 25 percent. When a workers' committee asked Pullman for a corresponding cut in the rents in company houses and the prices in company stores, he responded by firing three of the committee members, causing the rest of Pullman's workers to walk out. Debs tried to get Pullman to arbitrate the dispute, but when the industrialist refused, the ARU called upon its members not to move any train with a Pullman car attached. After receiving advice from U.S. Attorney General Richard Olney, a former

Chicago railroad lawyer, the GMA called upon its affiliates to attach Pullman cars to every train, particularly those carrying the U.S. mail. Olney then obtained from various federal judges injunctions forbidding the union or any individual from engaging in any activity that might impede railroad operations. Quickly, thousands of U.S. marshals were in the Chicago area to see that the injunctions were obeyed. President Grover Cleveland used minor outbreaks of violence as the justification for ordering in additional federal troops, which only stimulated more violence. Finally, the arrest of Eugene Debs and other ARU officials for violating the injunctions, combined with the massive military presence, caused the strike to crumble. Yet the debate about the activities of the strikers, management, the president, and the courts would linger on for decades, as the following documents reveal.

Cost and Crimes Associated with the Pullman Boycott

In the aftermath of the Pullman Boycott, President Cleveland appointed a commission to investigate its causes and consequences. The following section from the commission's report summarizes the financial losses and the range of crimes associated with the strike. Taken from The United States Strike Commission Report on the Chicago Strike of June–July 1894 . . . *(Washington, 1895), xviii-xix.*

According to the testimony the railroads lost in property destroyed, hire of United States deputy marshals, and other incidental expenses, at least $685,308. The loss of earnings of these roads is estimated at $4,672,916. Some 3,100 employees at Pullman lost in wages, as estimated, at least $350,000. About 100,000 employees upon the 24 railroads centering at Chicago, all of which were more or less involved in the strike, lost in wages, as estimated, at least $1,389,143. Many of these employees are still adrift and losing wages.

Beyond these amounts very great losses, widely distributed, were incidentally suffered throughout the country. The suspension of transportation at Chicago paralyzed a vast distributive center, and imposed many hardships and much loss upon the great number of people whose manufacturing and business operations, employment, travel, and necessary supplies depend upon and demand regular transportation service to, from, and through Chicago.

During the strike the fatalities, arrests, indictments, and dismissals of charges for strike offenses in Chicago and vicinity were as follows:

Number shot and fatally wounded 12
Number arrested by the police 515
Number arrested under United States statutes
and against whom indictments were found 71
Number arrested against whom indictments
were not found 119

The arrests made by the police were for murder, arson, burglary, assault, intimidation, riot, inciting to riot, and lesser crimes. The cases passed upon by the special United States grand jury, which convened on July 10, 1894, related to obstruction of the mail, forbidden by section 3995 of the United States Revised Statutes; conspiracy to commit offenses against the United States, forbidden by section 5440 of the Revised Statutes; conspiracy in restraint of trade or commerce among the several States, forbidden by chapter 647 of the United States, laws of 1890; conspiracy to injure, oppress, threaten, or intimidate citizens in the free exercise and enjoyment of their rights and privileges under the constitution and laws of the United States, forbidden by section 5508 of the United States Revised Statutes.

Several indictments were found against Eugene V. Debs, George W. Howard, L. W. Rogers, and Sylvester Keliher, officers of the American Railway Union, under these different statutes. Neither indictments nor proceedings were had under the act to regulate commerce, approved February 4, 1887, as has been sometimes stated.

These great losses and many crimes; the vast numbers, strength, and resources of the labor that contended under the leadership of the American Railway Union upon the one side and Pullman's Palace Car Company and the General Managers' Association upon the other; the attitude of labor toward capital, disclosed in its readiness to strike sympathetically; the determination of capital to crush the strike rather than to accept any peaceable solution through conciliation, arbitration, or otherwise; the certainty with which vast strikes let loose the disreputable to burn, plunder, and even murder; the conversion of industrious and law-abiding men into idlers, lawbreakers, or associates of criminals; the want brought to many innocent families; the transformation of railroad yards, tracks, and stations, as well as the busy marts of trade, into armed camps; the possibilities of future strikes on more extended lines of union against even greater combinations of capital—are all factors bearing upon the present industrial situation which need to be thoroughly understood by the people and to be wisely and prudently treated by the government.

Troops, Military, etc.

For the protection of city, state, and federal property, for the suppression of crime and the preservation of order, the city, county, State, and federal forces were utilized as shown in the following statement:

From July 3 to July 10 the number of United States troops sent to and used in Chicago to protect the United States mail service and federal buildings, and to sustain the execution of the orders of the United States courts was	1,936
Between July 6 and July 11 the State militia was ordered on duty at Chicago and remained so as long as needed, to the number of about	4,000
Extra deputy marshals, about	5,000
Extra deputy sheriffs	250
Police force of Chicago	3,000
Total	14,186

Lessons of the Pullman Boycott from a Union Perspective

Shortly after the Pullman Boycott ended, Samuel Gompers, president of the American Federation of Labor (AFL), tried to convey to the middle- and upper-class readership of The North American Review *how labor viewed the recent upheaval. It should be kept in mind that the ARU was not affiliated with the AFL, and that the AFL did not participate in the strike. The following passage is excerpted from* The North American Review *159 (August 1894): 201–06.*

ON Decoration Day, May 30, 1894, Judge Grosscup, of the United States Courts, in his oration commemorative of the day, took occasion to say that "the growth of labor organizations must be checked by law," yet when the sounds of his voice had scarcely died away we had in the midst of us the greatest and most extensive labor struggle that has ever taken place among the wage-workers of America, and possibly of the world.

Thousands of miles of railroads in all directions have been at a standstill, and nearly a hundred thousand workmen in voluntary idleness to secure what they regard as justice to their fellow workmen. It has been questioned whether the boycott or strike was wise or whether it was justifiable. On the first question there may be some difference of opinion. It may sincerely be doubted whether it was wise for an organization such as the American Railway Union, within a year of its formation, to attempt to inaugurate a movement which, in its inception, of necessity, assumed gigantic proportions.

The policy or wisdom of entering into so great a movement without consultation with, or against the advice of, the older railroad and *bona-fide* labor organizations of the country is open, to serious question. Nor will I attempt from the usual standpoint of trade dispute to justify the strike. Sufficient for me are the facts which provoked it and to which I shall allude later; but that the railroadmen deliberately entered a contest which entailed many sacrifices and dangers in an attempt to redress grievances not of their own, but of other workmen, who, having become thoroughly enervated and impoverished, without organization or previous understanding, in sheer desperation threw down their work, is indeed to their credit.

A little more than twenty years ago George M. Pullman conceived the idea of starting, in connection with his car shops, a town—one that should bear his name and hand down to posterity a monument of his enterprise and philanthropy. He built houses for his employees to live in, stores to make their purchases in, and churches to do their praying in. The workers were told their interests and Mr. Pullman's were one and the same, that what would bring him a greater prosperity would redound to their

AFL President Samuel Gompers. (Courtesy of The Library of Congress.)

advantage. They were warned that to belong to a trade-union would be inimical to their *joint* enterprise, hence workmen who would [propose] forming a union among them would be discharged, regarded as a common enemy, and driven out of town. They were to depend entirely upon Mr. Pullman's generosity and foresight in all things.

The result was that the workers at Pullman were huddled together in the (outwardly) neat houses, for which they were required to pay higher rents than are paid for similar accommodations in Chicago. They were reduced in wages as often as the seasons would recur and opportunities either arose or were made. This was carried on until last February, when a reduction in wages was offered varying from 25 to 33 1/3 and in a few instances 50 per cent.

Here are a few figures which may be taken as a fair criterion of the extent of the reduction in wages offered:

	Price per piece, 1893	Price offered, 1894
Making trolley roofs	$2.25	$1.40
Framework car seat	1.25	.79
Cutting carpets	3.00	1.50
Making mattresses double	.25	.15
Cutting brussels carpet	2.50	1.10
Blacksmith work, platform	4.00	2.65
Truck setting	.45	.16
Sleeping car bodies	180.00	115.50

The workmen being driven to desperation, a meeting was

held. Who called it no one knows; how it came about not a vestige of evidence is at hand. It was held and a committee appointed to wait upon Mr. Pullman or a representative of the company, to show that it was absolutely impossible to live on the wages offered; that a middle ground should be sought; that if wages were to be reduced the rents should also come down. Instead of the request of the men being considered by Mr. Pullman, the committee was summarily dismissed and discharged almost instantly. Is it surprising that these men in their rude awakening, finding themselves injured and insulted and their spokesmen discharged and blacklisted, and themselves without an organization to protect or defend them, without the means of properly laying their grievances before organized labor of the country, struck work, declaring that they might as well remain idle and starve as work and slowly meet that fate?

Organized labor of Chicago becoming aware of the unusual commotion at Pullman did not hold against the workers of that town their previous refusals to organize. It was readily appreciated that these men had been wholly misled by false promises and covert threats. Relief committees were at once formed, and it is firmly declared that the average workmen of that town have fared better since they engaged in the contest and fraternized with their fellow-workmen than they have for the past two years while working.

It was during this time, when relief committees from the Pullman strikers were making their visits to organizations, that the American Railway Union was holding its first convention in Chicago, and a committee called upon it for its financial and moral assistance. A committee from the convention was appointed to wait upon the company with the request that the matter in dispute might be submitted to arbitration. The committee was told that there was nothing to arbitrate and that the company refused to discuss the matter at all. Insulted, humiliated by the manner their disinterested efforts at restoring amicable relations between Mr. Pullman and his former servile employees were received, the committee made its report. The convention in a moment reflected the feelings of the committee, and though at first sullen, silent, and indignant they resolved amidst the wildest enthusiasm that unless the Pullman company either adjusted the matter in controversy with their employees or submitted it to arbitration the members of the American Railway Union would not handle Pullman cars and would ask all workmen to act likewise. No heed was given to the request, resolution, or threat (call it what you will), and the great boycott (strike) was on.

I can scarcely bring myself to the belief that the convention imagined that the movement would be as extended as it became into, nor that it would last as long as it did. Be that as it may, we certainly found ourselves in the midst of one of the greatest labor struggles.

Now comes the question repeated: Was the strike wise or justifiable? the answer to which must always depend upon the character and position of the party giving it. As to the wisdom, time only can tell. Since "nothing succeeds so well as success" in all efforts of life, I presume this element will finally set its *quietus* upon this consideration of the subject. But was it justifiable? From the standpoint of the employer, No. From the standpoint of a labor organization having an agreement with an employer whose provisions a strike would violate, No. From the standpoint of the A. R. U., having no agreement with either of the railroad companies involved, and expressing the inarticulate protest of the masses against the wrongs inflicted upon any of their brothers and their yearning for justice to all mankind, Yes; a thousand times yes.

It is something not yet fully understood how thoroughly organized labor stands as the sturdy pioneer of all the hopes of the masses for justice and humane conditions, of their aspirations for a nobler manhood resultant from an equality of opportunities. It is in consequence of these facts that organized labor feels itself frequently called upon to espouse the cause of those who have neglected their own interests, and who have even antagonized any effort to bring them within the fold of organization. Laboring men feel and know that the wealth producers would certainly avail themselves of their only means of defending and advancing their position in life were it not that they in many instances had their prejudices aroused and their ignorance of actual conditions preyed upon by the instruments of their oppression in the hands of the corporate and employing class. But the men are on strike, the police armed to the teeth are on guard to protect life and property, the militia are called out ostensibly for the same purpose, and the regular army of the United States are marshalled into the fields by order of the President to enforce injunctions, restraining "everybody" from even writing a letter, issued by the Judge who only a few days before expressed the firm conviction that the growth of labor organizations must be checked by law.

Is it not somewhat strange that the provisions of the Interstate Commerce Law, a law passed by Congress in compliance with the demand of the people of our country to protect them against the greed and outrageous discriminations of the railroads, can be distorted to such a degree as to appall its authors and promoters, and should be perverted from its true purpose, and made to do service as an instrument to oppress the parties to whom it was never intended to apply, workingmen engaged in a contest to redress grievances. One may look almost in vain for the restraint the law has put upon the avarice and injustice practised by the railroad corporations. The reform elements in our country seem to have unconsciously created their own Frankenstein, the breath of life being injected into it by plutocracy in the shape of ill-gotten gains.

There is no desire nor even a tendency on the part of organized labor to have its movement go beyond the limits of the law, but I submit that there is a standpoint from which this great problem should be considered other than a judge's injunction, a policeman's club, or the point of the bayonet. The fact of the matter is that industrial conditions have changed to a wonderful extent within the past thirty years, that wealth has been accumulated as never before, that new forces are at play in the production and transportation of wealth, and that the civil law of our States and country has simply not kept pace in becoming accommodated to the altered conditions. Do what you will, declaim as you may, industrial and commercial development cannot be confined within the limits of laws enacted to fit past decades the theories of which are sought to be applied to modern conditions.

Civilization of the past and present is based upon labor, and yet the laborer has no standing nor protection in the economy of our life. It may well be asked, if the state refuses to deal out some degree of justice and guarantee protection to labor, what interest has the laborer in the state? As a matter of fact the organizations of labor are endeavoring to secure that protection and guaranty to the workingmen which the state has failed to take cognizance of. Without organization the workmen would simply be reduced to a much worse condition than the slaves in ante-bellum days, and all attempts to strain the law, construing the exercise of natural rights to be criminal, will only react upon the heads of the legal prestidigitators.

If in monarchical England, with its old and effete traditions and crusty customs, Parliament can afford to liberalize its laws and legalize the action of workingmen engaged in the maintenance of their organizations and their effort to obtain better conditions, certainly the Republic of these United States should not only keep pace with that spirit, but advance beyond it, and not bring the entire military and civil forces to aid the strong and help crush out the weak.

Labor cannot, and will not if it could, utilize the process of securing legislation by the use of money; it relies upon the justice of its cause, the nobility of its purposes, the humanizing influences of its efforts.

Mr. Pullman, it is said, is willing to spend millions of dollars if necessary to bring his former employees "to their senses." That is to say, he is willing to spend millions of dollars to bring his workmen to the sense of their utter dependence upon him.

This is evidently his purpose. It is the purpose of many another corporation king. He and a few others may possibly win for the present, but the people of America, when once aroused to a sense of the wrong inflicted upon them, will not be slow in so shaping our laws and industrial conditions as to surprise their most supercilious critics.

We insist upon the right to organize, the right to think, to act; to protect ourselves, our homes, and our liberties, and work out our emancipation. We are confident we shall secure them, and that the world will stand surprised that they were accomplished through the means of an enlightened public opinion and by peaceful means.

Lessons of the Pullman Boycott from a Business Perspective

In the same issue of The North American Review *in which Samuel Gompers's article appeared was an assessment of the strike by Wade Hampton, a former South Carolina senator and governor, serving as United States commissioner of railroads. Hampton had close ties to the business community and reflected the values of middle- and upper-class America. The following passage is excerpted from* The North American

Review *159 (August 1894): 190–94.*

There can be no possible excuse for conduct such as that which has characterized the acts of the lawless mobs, who, in defiance of all laws, divine and human, blindly and madly struck at the very foundation of all organized society, seemingly only intent on involving the whole country in common ruin. There can be no palliation for outrages such as they have committed, and their conduct has been as senseless as it is inexcusable, for if in their mad rage they bring about a war of labor against capital, there can be but one result to it—a disastrous one to the originators. Should such a fearful conflict occur, the misguided men, who, under the influence of evil counsels, seek to remedy their grievances by unlawful means, would inevitably be the severest sufferers, for not only would all their means of livelihood be swept away, but hundreds, perhaps thousands, of them would lose their lives.

I have said that this strike was inexcusable. The ostensible reason given for it by the strikers is that Mr. Pullman did not pay his employees sufficient wages. In answer to this charge, Mr. Pullman says that he cannot pay more for the manufacture of a car than the price he can obtain for it from the railroads. Every business man must admit that this answer is conclusive and logical. But admitting, for the sake of argument, that his employees were right in their contention, does that justify a resort on their part, not only against him and his property, but against all property, private as well as public? What justification can be offered for the order of the leaders of all the labor organizations in the country, connected in any manner with the railroads, that each member should at once throw up his position as evidence of sympathy with the Pullman employees?

And above all other inexplicable questions suggested by the action of the Pullman employees, what semblance of right had these men, who had voluntarily left their employment, to combine unlawfully with men whose object was the destruction of the railroads and of property of all other descriptions? The workmen of the Pullman company were not connected with railroads in any manner; their sole business was in the construction of sleeping cars, and yet, when they threw up their position, they joined in the work of wrecking the roads, obstructing travel, stopping the mails, and defying the laws of the land. Another strange feature in this matter is the action taken by A. R. U., an organization in no wise connected with the Pullman company, but, notwithstanding this fact, this body of railroad employees decreed that no railroad should use Pullman cars! The railroads, many of which were under contract to use these cars, naturally and properly paid no respect to this order emanating as it did from an irresponsible source, whereupon these sympathetic strikers of the A. R. U. became enemies of the public peace, and resorted to violence, robbery, and bloodshed, to enforce their lawless demands. And these things are done on our own soil, where it has been the proud boast that the laws were supreme, guaranteeing to every citizen equal rights! But it seems that the new doctrine announced by the A. R. U. puts the railroads of the country outside of the pale of the law, leaving the vast interests of these corporations, as well as those of their bondholders, at the mercy of any mob of ignorant or vicious men. To our shame, too, there are men in high position who uphold these careless proceedings and who defend the perpetrators. We have surely fallen on strange and evil times, and conservative men of all sections and of all parties should devote all efforts to the restoration of order and the maintenance of law. There is not one present vested right of individuals, of corporations, or one of government ownership of property that would be safe if the criminal acts recently committed by riotous mobs in several of the States are permitted to go unpunished. Life itself would no longer be safe, for in more than one instance murder was added to the long list of atrocities which marked the carnival of crime that held mad sway of late in many portions of our country. And the hollow pretence given by those strikers for the outrages they committed is the assertion that they were endeavoring to aid the former workmen of the Pullman company. Every interest of the country is to be sacrificed, every vested right is to be trampled upon, every principle of law and of morals is to be violated, simply because workmen engaged in a particular business cannot obtain the wages they demand. How could these workmen be possibly benefited by the lawless and indiscreet conduct of such misguided sympathizers? No right, no principle, can be established by the commission of a wrong.

For this unholy alliance between unemployed workmen and the disreputable and worst elements of our population to succeed would, indeed, be the consecration of a crime. The President has been criticised, even denounced, because he attempted to prevent the consummation of the crimes contemplated against the peace, the honor, and the welfare of the country; and the ground upon which this attack on him is based is that his action has been in violation of the rights of States. No one upholds whatever of State's rights is left to us more earnestly than myself, but I can see no force in the charge that the President has, by his course, exceeded the authority conferred on him by the Constitution and the laws made in pursuance of that instrument. Those who hold that the President has, by sending Federal troops to the scenes of disorder, exceeded his power predicate their opinion on Sec. 4, Article 4, of the Constitution, which authorizes Congress to send troops to any State "to protect it against invasion, and, on application of the legislature (or of the executive when the legislature cannot be convened), against domestic violence." The meaning of this provision is perfectly clear. Congress is authorized to send troops to any State on the call of the legislature, or of the governor, under certain conditions, when the authorities of such State are unable to repel invasion or to repress domestic violence. But those who criticise the acts of the President forget that Congress has enacted laws which confer on the chief magistrate larger and wider powers than those given to Congress by the Constitution. The authority for the exercise of those powers is found in Sections 5298 and 5299 of the Revised Statutes. A reference to these laws will prove that the President not only has absolute power to call on the Federal forces to suppress "any insurrection, violence, unlawful combination or conspiracy" occurring in any State, and indeed it is made "his duty to take such measures, by the employment of the militia, or the land and naval forces of the United States, or of either, or by other means, as he may deem necessary, for the suppression of such insurrection, domestic violence or combinations." These quotations from Section 5299 are sufficient to show how ample is the authority of the President to deal with such cases as those confronting him now, and it should be a source of heart-felt congratulation to all law-abiding citizens that the executive chair is now filled by one, who, knowing what his duty demanded of him, had the courage to discharge it promptly, fully, and fearlessly. There is another potent reason why the Federal authorities should have been called on to intervene in suppressing the riots which occurred, and why the shield of Federal authority should have been interposed for the protection of property. The government has millions of dollars invested in the trans-continental railroads, secured by mortgages on these roads, and it was the clear duty of the President to use all the means in his power to guard this immense property from destruction, for the whole country is interested in its preservation. Lawless mobs have not only stopped traffic and travel on these roads, thus cutting off the legitimate revenue due to the Government, but they have in many instances destroyed the roads and burned the bridges on them. If such outrages are permitted to go unpunished, our laws are a farce, for they give protection neither to life nor to property. Every consideration of duty, self-respect, honor, interest, demands that the majesty of the law should be vindicated whatever the cost of doing so may be. Every humane man must feel profound sympathy for all honest toilers where labor does not yield proper remuneration; but no legislation, no government, no earthly power, can rectify the immutable law by which the gifts of fortune are distributed with an unequal hand. It has been so since the beginning of the world and it will probably so continue to the end, or to the millennium, for our Divine Master said, "The poor ye have always with you."

Questions

1. *In terms of the "costs" of the strike, what groups were the winners and losers? Were there factors in evaluating "costs" that the commission report failed to note?*
2. *Why did Samuel Gompers believe the strike occurred? Did he feel it was justified? In his opinion, what role did the courts and military play in the dispute? Did he give any explanation, directly or indirectly, for the violence and disruption that occurred?*
3. *Why did Wade Hampton believe the strike occurred? Did he feel it was justified? What was his attitude toward the sympathy action by the A.R.U.? Why did he feel that violence occurred? How did his view of the workers and their place in society differ from Gompers's view?*
4. *What arguments used by Gompers and Hampton are still in vogue today to justify or condemn labor militancy?*

FURTHER READING

There are numerous studies of particular strikes in American history. Among the best are Robert V. Bruce, 1877: Year of Violence *(Indianapolis, 1959); Almont Lindsay,* The Pullman Strike *(Chicago, 1942); Leon Wolff,* Lockout: The Story of the Homestead Strike of 1892, A Study of Violence, Unionism and the Carnegie Steel Empire *(New York, 1965); and David Brody,* Labor in Crisis: The Steel Strike of 1919 *(New York, 1965). Studies that try to deal more broadly with labor violence include Jeremy Brecher,* Strike! *(San Francisco, 1972), and Rhodri Jeffreys-Jones,* Violence and Reform in American History *(New York, 1978).*

The Debate over Annexing the Philippines, 1898–1900

Peter L. Hahn, Michael J. Hogan,
and Rowland Brucken

Introduction

When the United States government declared war on Spain in the spring of 1898, most Americans believed that its purpose was to liberate Cuba from oppressive Spanish imperialism. The first battle of the Spanish-American War, however, occurred thousands of miles to the west, in the Philippine Islands, another Spanish colony where U.S. Navy ships under the command of Admiral George Dewey defeated a Spanish fleet on 1 May 1898. Three months after the victory in Manila harbor, President William McKinley ordered the U.S. Army to occupy the Philippines. In October 1898, McKinley ensured that the peace treaty with Spain authorized U.S. annexation of the archipelago.

Although it surprised many contemporary observers, the acquisition of the Philippines actually fit tightly in a pattern of late-nineteenth-century U.S. expansionism across the Pacific. Driven by a variety of intellectual, political, economic, and strategic motives, the United States purchased Alaska and occupied Midway Island (1867), acquired a naval base in Samoa (1878), annexed Hawaii (1898), and opened Japan and Korea to trade. After the acquisition of the Philippines (as well as Guam and Wake Island) in 1898-99, the United States would compete with other imperialist powers for economic, political, and security interests in China.

Conflict and controversy accompanied the annexation of the Philippines. In the islands themselves, U.S. occupation forces met stiff military resistance by Filipino warriors led by Emilio Aguinaldo, a revolutionary who had battled for years for national independence from Spain. In 1901, after an enormous military effort, prolonged guerrilla warfare, and massive casualties on both sides, U.S. troops captured Aguinaldo and smashed the Filipino insurrection. In the United States, meanwhile, McKinley's policy on the Philippines provoked a heated political debate. Imperialists identified strategic, economic, and intellectual reasons to acquire the islands, and anti-imperialists countered that annexation would undermine the military, political, and moral foundations of the country. Although the Senate approved annexation in February 1899, the American-Filipino war and the approaching presidential election stimulated additional debate. Only President McKinley's decisive defeat of Democratic challenger William Jennings Bryan in November 1900 silenced the anti-imperialists.

The Contemporary Debate on Expansionism

The documents compiled in this section reveal the extensive debate within the United States over the wisdom and justification of U.S. expansionism in general and annexation of the Philippines in particular. Most of the selections record the arguments made by various imperialist and anti-imperialist spokesmen from the war of 1898 to the presidential election of 1900. The fundamental conflict between the United States and Filipino leader Emilio Aguinaldo is also illustrated.

The imperialists advocated American acquisition of the islands for economic and nationalistic reasons. Some also believed that the United States could play a "civilizing" role by bringing democracy, Christianity, and American culture to the Filipinos. The anti-imperialists denounced Philippine annexation and argued that U.S. control of the islands would corrupt American ideals of liberty and democracy. Many also rejected annexation on racist grounds, objecting to the potential addition of non-Anglo Saxons to the American populace. Emilio Aguinaldo, a native of the Philippines and a staunch advocate of its political independence, also criticized President McKinley's decision to assume political control over the islands, though for different reasons than the anti-imperialists.

Beveridge Advocates American Expansionism

In the late nineteenth century, many Americans adhered to a belief, known as Manifest Destiny, that their country had a divinely sanctioned mission to expand and to civilize foreign peoples. In a famous address entitled "The March of the Flag," delivered in September 1898, Indiana Republican politician Albert Beveridge conveyed such ideas to justify the recent occupation of the Philippines and to call for its annexation. Beveridge encouraged his audience to elect to Congress Republicans who would ensure retention of the islands. Excerpted from The Library of Oratory, Ancient and Modern, *ed. Chauncey M. Depew (New York, 1902), 14:426-27, 435–39, 445–46, 448–49.*

FELLOW CITIZENS,—It is a noble land that God has given us; a land that can feed and clothe the world; a land whose coast lines would enclose half the countries of Europe; a land set like a sentinel between the two imperial oceans of the globe, a greater England with a nobler destiny. It is a mighty people that he has planted on this soil; a people sprung from the most masterful blood of history; a people perpetually revitalized by the virile, man-producing workingfolk of all the earth; a people imperial by virtue of their power, by right of their institutions, by authority of their heaven-directed purposes—the propagandists and not the misers of liberty. It is a glorious history our God has bestowed upon his chosen people; a history whose keynote was struck by Liberty Bell; a history heroic with faith in our mission and our future; a history of statesmen who flung the boundaries of the Republic out into unexplored lands and savage wildernesses; a history of soldiers who carried the flag across the blazing deserts and through the ranks of hostile mountains, even to the gates of sunset; a history of a multiplying people who overran a continent in half a century; a history of prophets who saw the consequences of evils inherited from the past and of martyrs who died to save us from them; a history divinely logical, in the process of whose tremendous reasoning we find ourselves to-day.

Therefore, in this campaign, the question is larger than a party question. It is an American question. It is a world question. Shall the American people continue their resistless march toward the commercial supremacy of the world? Shall free institutions broaden their blessed reign as the children of liberty wax in strength, until the empire of our principles is established over the hearts of all mankind?

Have we no mission to perform, no duty to discharge to our fellow-man? . . .

. . . William McKinley is continuing the policy that Jefferson began, Monroe continued, Seward advanced, Grant promoted, Harrison championed, and the growth of the republic has demanded. Hawaii is ours; Porto Rico is to be ours; at the prayer of the people Cuba will finally be ours; in the islands of the East, even to the gates of Asia, coaling-stations are to be ours; at the very least the flag of a liberal government is to float over the Philippines, and I pray God it may be the banner that Taylor unfurled in Texas and Fremont carried to the coast—the Stars and Stripes of glory.

And the burning question of this campaign is, whether the American people will accept the gifts of events; whether they will rise as lifts their soaring destiny; whether they will proceed upon the lines of national development surveyed by the statesmen of our past; or whether, for the first time, the American people doubt their mission, question fate, prove apostate to the spirit of their race, and halt the ceaseless march of free institutions.

The Opposition tells us that we ought not to govern a people without their consent. I answer, The rule of liberty that all just government derives its authority from the consent of the governed, applies only to those who are capable of self-government. I answer, We govern the Indians without their consent, we govern our territories without their consent, we govern our children without their consent. I answer, How do you assume that our government would be without their consent? Would not the people of the Philippines prefer the just, humane, civilizing government of this republic to the savage, bloody rule of pillage and extortion from which we have rescued them? . . .

And, regardless of this formula of words made only for enlightened, self-governing peoples, do we owe no duty to the world? Shall we turn these peoples back to the reeking hands from which we have taken them? Shall we abandon them to their fate, with the wolves of conquest all about them—with Germany, Russia, France, even Japan, hungering for them? Shall we save them from those nations, to give them a self-rule of tragedy? It would be like giving a razor to a babe and telling it to shave itself. It would be like giving a typewriter to an Eskimo and telling him to publish one of the great dailies of the world. . . .

They ask us how we will govern these new possessions. I answer: Out of local conditions and the necessities of the case methods of government will grow. If England can govern foreign lands, so can America. If Germany can govern foreign lands, so can America. . . .

. . . Will you remember that we do but what our fathers did—we but pitch the tents of liberty further westward, further southward—we only continue the march of the flag.

The march of the flag! . . .

And, now . . . William McKinley plants the flag over the islands of the seas, outposts of commerce, citadels of national security, and the march of the flag goes on! . . .

. . . [T]o-day, we are raising more than we can consume. To-day, we are making more than we can use. To-day, our industrial society is congested; there are more workers than there is work; there is more capital than there is investment. We do not need more money—we need more circulation, more employment. Therefore we must find new markets for our produce, new occupation for our capital, new work for our labor. . . .

Ah! as our commerce spreads, the flag of liberty will circle the globe, and the highways of the ocean—carrying trade of all mankind, be guarded by the guns of the republic. And, as their thunders salute the flag, benighted peoples will know that the voice of Liberty is speaking, at last, for them; that civilization is dawning, at last, for them—Liberty and Civilization, those children of Christ's gospel, who follow and never precede, the preparing march of commerce! . . .

Fellow Americans, we are God's chosen people. . . . His great purposes are revealed in the progress of the flag, which surpasses the intentions of Congresses and Cabinets. . . . We cannot retreat from any soil where Providence has unfurled our banner; it is ours to save that soil for Liberty and Civilization. For Liberty and Civilization and God's promise fulfilled, the flag must henceforth be the symbol and the sign to all mankind—the flag!

Sumner Denounces American Imperialism

William Graham Sumner, a Yale University professor, sharply criticized the course of imperialism that Beveridge and others advocated. In an address delivered in late 1898, Sumner acknowledged that the United States ranked as an exceptional nation in human history but warned that imperialism would corrupt its ideals, endanger its security, and undermine its political and social order. He urged the government to grant the Philippines independence. Selected from War and Other Essays by William Graham Sumner, *ed. Albert Galloway Keller (New Haven, Connecticut 1911), 297–98, 304–5, 311–12, 314–15, 322, 325–26, 334.*

Spain was the first, for a long time the greatest, of the modern imperialistic states. The United States, by its historical origin, its traditions, and its principles, is the chief representative of the revolt and reaction against that kind of a state. I intend to show that, by the line of action now proposed to us, which we call expansion and imperialism, we are throwing away some of the most important elements of the American symbol and are adopting some of the most important elements of the Spanish symbol. We have beaten Spain in a military conflict, but we are submitting to be conquered by her on the field of ideas and policies. Expansionism and imperialism are nothing but the old philosophies of national prosperity which have brought Spain to where she now is. Those philosophies appeal to national vanity and national cupidity. They are seductive, especially upon the first view and the most superficial judgment, and therefore it cannot be denied that they are very strong for popular effect. They are delusions, and they will lead us to ruin unless we are hard-headed enough to resist them. . . .

. . . We assume that what we like and practice, and what we think better, must come as a welcome blessing to Spanish-Americans and Filipinos. This is grossly and obviously untrue. They hate our ways. They are hostile to our ideas. Our religion, language, institutions, and manners offend them. They like their own ways, and if we appear amongst them as rulers, there will be social discord in all the great departments of social interest. The most important thing which we shall inherit from the Spaniards will be the task of suppressing rebellions. . . . If we believe in liberty, as an American principle, why do we not stand by it? Why are we going to throw it away to enter upon a Spanish policy of dominion and regulation? . . .

. . . [I]t is unwisdom to take into a State like this any foreign element which is not congenial to it. Any such element will act as a solvent upon it. Consequently we are brought by our new conquests face to face with this dilemma: we must either hold them as inferior possessions, to be ruled and exploited by us after the fashion of the old colonial system, or we must take them in on an equality with ourselves, where they will help to govern us and to corrupt a political system which they do not understand and in which they cannot participate. From that dilemma there is no escape except to give them independence and to let them work out their own salvation or go without it. . . .

The question of imperialism, then, is the question whether we are going to give the lie to the origin of our own national existence by establishing a colonial system of the old Spanish type, even if we have to sacrifice our existing civil and political system to do it. I submit that it is a strange incongruity to utter grand platitudes about the blessings of liberty, etc., which we are going to impart to these people, and to begin by refusing to extend the Constitution over them, and still more, by throwing the Constitution into the gutter here at home. If you take away the Constitution, what is American liberty and all the rest? Nothing but a lot of phrases. . . .

Another phenomenon which deserves earnest attention from the student of contemporaneous history and of the trend of political institutions is the failure of the masses of our people to perceive *the inevitable effect of imperialism on democracy*. . . .

Now what will hasten the day when our present advantages will wear out and when we shall come down to the conditions of the older and densely populated nations? The answer is: war, debt, taxation, diplomacy, a grand governmental system, pomp, glory, a big army and navy, lavish expenditures, political jobbery—in a word, imperialism. . . .

The great foe of democracy now and in the near future is plutocracy. Every year that passes brings out this antagonism more distinctly. It is to be the social war of the twentieth century. In that war militarism, expansion and imperialism will all favor plutocracy. In the first place, war and expansion will favor jobbery, both in the dependencies and at home. In the second place, they will take away the attention of the people from what the plutocrats are doing. In the third place, they will cause large expenditures of the people's money, the return for which will not go into the treasury, but into the hands of a few schemers. In the fourth place, they will call for a large public debt and taxes, and these things especially tend to make men unequal, because any social burdens bear more heavily on the weak than on the strong, and so make the weak weaker and the strong stronger. Therefore expansion and imperialism are a grand onslaught on democracy.

The point which I have tried to make in this lecture is that expansion and imperialism are at war with the best traditions, principles, and interests of the American people, and that they will plunge us into a network of difficult problems and political perils, which we might have avoided, while they offer us no corresponding advantage in return. . . .

. . . [Y]et there are people who are boasting of their patriotism, because they say that we have taken our place now amongst the nations of the earth by virtue of this war. My patriotism is of the kind which is outraged by the notion that the United States never was a great nation until in a petty three months' campaign it knocked to pieces a poor, decrepit, bankrupt old state like Spain. To hold such an opinion as that is to abandon all American standards, to put shame and scorn on all that our ancestors tried to build up here, and to go over to the standards of which Spain is a representative.

The Decision to Annex the Philippines

Rejecting reservations such as Sumner's, President McKinley decided that the United States should acquire the entire Philippines archipelago. His reasons for this decision were conveyed to American commissioners at the peace conference with Spain in a telegram sent on 28 October 1898 by Secretary of State John Hay. The telegram, excerpted below, is from U.S. Department of State, Foreign Relations of the United States, 1898 *(Washington, 1901), 937–38.*

Mr. Hay to Mr. Day.

DEPARTMENT OF STATE,
Washington, October 28, 1898.

While the Philippines can be justly claimed by conquest, which position must not be yielded, yet their disposition, control, and government the President prefers should be the subject of negotiation, as provided in the protocol. It is imperative upon us that as victors we should be governed only by motives which will exalt our nation. Territorial expansion should be our least concern; that we shall not shirk the moral obligations of our victory is of the greatest. It is undisputed that Spain's authority is permanently destroyed in every part of the Philippines. To leave any part in her feeble control now would increase our difficulties and be opposed to the interests of humanity. The sentiment in the United States is almost universal that the people of the Philippines, whatever else is done, must be liberated from Spanish domination. In this sentiment the President fully concurs. Nor can we permit Spain to transfer any of the islands to another power. Nor can we invite another power or powers to join the United States in sovereignty over them. We must either hold them or turn them back to Spain.

Consequently, grave as are the responsibilities and unforeseen as are the difficulties which are before us, the President can see but one plain path of duty—the acceptance of the archipelago. Greater difficulties and more serious complications, administrative and international, would follow any other course. . . . [The president] has been influenced by the single consideration of duty and humanity.

Aguinaldo Declares Philippines Independence

As McKinley demanded, the peace treaty provided for U.S. annexation of the Philippines, and the Senate ratified the compact in February 1899, although by a slim margin of 57 to 27, only two votes more than the two-thirds required for approval. As U.S. intentions became clear in the weeks preceding the Senate vote, Filipino leader Emilio Aguinaldo declared the independence of his country and ordered his soldiers to fight American troops. Portions of two of Aguinaldo's manifestos, dated 5 January and 4 February 1899, appear below. Abridged from Report of Major-General E. S. Otis, U.S. Volunteers, on Military Operations and Civil Affairs in the Philippine Islands *(Washington, 1899), 78, 95.*

Emilio Aguinaldo, leader of the Filipino resistance.

Malolos, *January 5, 1899.*

. . . A proclamation of Mr. E. S. Otis, major-general of the United States Volunteers, appeared in Manila papers yesterday, compelled me to issue the present, with a view to expose to all who read and understand the present document my most solemn protest against the whole contents of the said proclamation, the duties of my conscience toward God, my political compromises toward my beloved people, and my private and official relationship with the United States nation, all of which forced me to do so.

The General Otis called himself in the said proclamation military governor of the Philippine Islands. I protest one and a thousand times, with all the energy of my soul, against such authority.

I solemnly declare that neither at Singapore, Hongkong, nor here in the Philippines did I ever agree, by word or in writing, to recognize the sovereignty of America in this our lovely country. On the contrary, I declare that I return to these islands, transported by the United States man-of-war, on the 19th of May last, with the decided and firm intention to fight the Spaniards in order to reconquer our liberty and independence. . . . I in the name of God, the root and fountain of all justice, and that of all the right which has been visibly granted to me to direct my dear brothers in the difficult work of our regeneration, protest most solemnly against this intrusion of the United States Government on the sovereignty of these islands.

I equally protest in the name of the Filipino people against the said intrusion, because as they have granted their vote of confidence appointing me president of the nation, although I don't consider that I deserve such, therefore I consider it my duty to defend to death its liberty and independence. . . .

GENERAL ORDER TO THE PHILIPPINE ARMY.

[MALOLOS, *February 4, 1899.*]

Nine o'clock p. m., this date, I received from Caloocan station a message communicated to me that the American forces, without prior notification or any just motive, attacked our camp at San Juan del Monte and our forces garrisoning the blockhouses around the outskirts of Manila, causing losses among our soldiers, who in view of this unexpected aggression and of the decided attack of the aggressors, were obliged to defend themselves until the firing became general all along the line.

No one can deplore more than I this rupture of hostilities. I have a clear conscience that I have endeavored to avoid it at all costs, using all my efforts to preserve friendship with the army of occupation, even at the cost of not a few humiliations and many sacrificed rights.

But it is my unavoidable duty to maintain the integrity of the national honor and that of the army so unjustly attacked by those who, posing as our friends and liberators, attempted to dominate us in place of the Spaniards, as is shown by the grievances enumerated in my manifest of January 8 last; such as the continued outrages and violent exactions committed against the people of Manila, the useless conferences, and all my frustrated efforts in favor of peace and concord.

Summoned by this unexpected provocation, urged by the duties imposed upon me by honor and patriotism and for the defense of the nation intrusted to me, calling on God as a witness of my good faith and the uprightness of my intentions—

I order and command:

1. Peace and friendly relations between the Philippine forces and the American forces of occupation are broken, and the latter will be treated as enemies, with the limits prescribed by the laws of war.

2. American soldiers who may be captured by the Philippine forces will be treated as prisoners of war.

3. This proclamation shall be communicated to the accredited consuls of Manila, and to congress, in order that it may accord the suspension of the constitutional guaranties and the resulting declaration of war.

Given at Malolos February 4, 1899.

EMILIO AGUINALDO,
General-in-Chief.

Beveridge Urges Retention of the Islands

The costly civil war that ensued from Aguinaldo's defiance of U.S. rule kept the issue of the Philippines at the forefront of debate in the United States. Albert Beveridge, elected to the U.S. Senate in 1899, remained a passionate and persistent advocate of American empire. In a speech to the Senate on 9 January 1900, excerpted below, Beveridge defended U.S. control of the Philippines with a combination of intellectual, economic, political, and racial arguments. Taken from Congressional Record, *56th Cong., 1st sess., 1900; 33, pt. 1: 704–5, 709, 711–12.*

The Philippines are ours forever, "territory belonging to the United States," as the Constitution calls them. And just beyond the Philippines are China's illimitable markets. We will not retreat from either. We will not repudiate our duty in the archipelago. We will not abandon our opportunity in the Orient. We will not renounce our part in the mission of our race, trustee. [,] under God, of the civilization of the world. And we will move forward to our work, not howling out regrets like slaves whipped to their burdens, but with gratitude for a task worthy of our strength, and thanksgiving to Almighty God that He has marked us as His chosen people, henceforth to lead in the regeneration of the world. . . .

. . . Our largest trade henceforth must be with Asia. The Pacific is our ocean. . . . China is our natural customer. . . . The Philippines give us a base at the door of all the East. . . . The power that rules the Pacific, therefore, is the power that rules the world. And, with the Philippines, that power is and will forever be the American Republic. . . .

But if they did not command China, India, the Orient, the whole Pacific for purposes of offense, defense, and trade, the Philippines are so valuable in themselves that we should hold them. . . . I have ridden hundreds of miles on the islands, every foot of the way a revelation of vegetable and mineral riches.

No land in America surpasses in fertility the plains and valleys of Luzon. Rice and coffee, sugar and cocoanuts, hemp and tobacco, and many products of the temperate as well as the tropic zone grow in various sections of the archipelago. I have seen hundreds of bushels of Indian corn lying in a road fringed with banana trees. The forests of Negros, Mindanao, Mindora, Paluan, and parts of Luzon are invaluable and intact. The wood of the Philippines can supply the furniture of the world for a century to come. . . . 40 miles of Cebu's mountain chain are practically mountains of coal. . . . [I]t is better steamer fuel than the best coal of Japan.

I have a nugget of pure gold picked up in its present form on the banks of a Philippine creek. I have gold dust washed out by crude processes of careless natives from the sands of a Philippine stream. Both indicate great deposits at the source from which they come. In one of the islands great deposits of copper exist untouched. The mineral wealth of this empire of the ocean will one day surprise the world. . . . And the wood, hemp, copra, and other products of the Philippines supply what we need and can not ourselves produce. . . .

. . . They are a barbarous race, modified by three centuries of contact with a decadent race. The Filipino is the South Sea Malay, put through a process of three hundred years of superstition in religion, dishonesty in dealing, disorder in habits of industry, and cruelty, caprice, and corruption in government. It is barely possible that 1,000 men in all the archipelago are capable of self-government in the Anglo-Saxon sense.

My own belief is that there are not 100 men among them who comprehend what Anglo-Saxon self-government even means, and there are over 5,000,000 people to be governed. . . .

Example for decades will be necessary to instruct them in American ideas and methods of administration. Example, example; always example—this alone will teach them. As a race, their general ability is not excellent. . . . [T]hey are, as a people, dull and stupid. In showy things, like carving and painting or embroidery or music, they have apparent aptitude, but even this is superficial and never thorough. . . .

. . . Our fathers . . . founded no paralytic government, incapable of the simplest acts of administration. They planted no sluggard people, passive while the world's work calls them. They established no reactionary nation. They unfurled no retreating flag.

GOD'S HAND IN ALL.

That flag has never paused in its onward march. Who dares halt it now—now, when history's largest events are carrying it forward; now, when we are at last one people, strong enough for any task, great enough for any glory destiny can bestow? . . . Blind indeed is he who sees not the hand of God in events so vast, so harmonious, so benign.

The Anti-Imperialist League Denounces U.S. Policy

Many individuals who rejected Beveridge's arguments rallied to establish the Anti-Imperialist League. Founded in 1898, the league counted thirty thousand members and five hundred thousand donors, including prominent Americans such as journalist Carl Schurz, industrialist Andrew Carnegie, unionist Samuel Gompers, and Democratic politician William Jennings Bryan. At its convention in Chicago in October 1899, the league published a platform of its principles. Excerpted from Speeches, Correspondence and Political Papers of Carl Schurz, *vol. 6,* January 1, 1899–April 8, 1906, *ed. Frederic Bancroft (New York, 1913), 77–79.*

We hold that the policy known as imperialism is hostile to liberty and tends toward militarism, an evil from which it has been our glory to be free. We regret that it has become necessary in the land of Washington and Lincoln to reaffirm that all men, of whatever race or color, are entitled to life, liberty and the pursuit of happiness. We maintain that governments derive their just powers from the consent of the governed. We insist that the subjugation of any people is "criminal aggression" and open disloyalty to the distinctive principles of our Government.

We earnestly condemn the policy of the present National Administration in the Philippines. It seeks to extinguish the spirit of 1776 in those islands. We deplore the sacrifice of our soldiers and sailors, whose bravery deserves admiration even in an unjust war. We denounce the slaughter of the Filipinos as a needless horror. We protest against the extension of American sovereignty by Spanish methods.

We demand the immediate cessation of the war against liberty, begun by Spain and continued by us. We urge that Congress be promptly convened to announce to the Filipinos our purpose to concede to them the independence for which they have so long fought and which of right is theirs. . . .

Imperialists assume that with the destruction of self-government in the Philippines by American hands, all opposition here will cease. This is a grievous error. Much as we abhor the war of "criminal aggression" in the Philippines, greatly as we regret that the blood of the Filipinos is on American hands, we more deeply resent the betrayal of American institutions at home. The real firing line is not in the suburbs of Manila. The foe is of our own household. The attempt of 1861 was to divide the country. That of 1899 is to destroy its fundamental principles and noblest ideals.

Whether the ruthless slaughter of the Filipinos shall end next month or next year is but an incident in a contest that must go on until the Declaration of Independence and the Constitution of the United States are rescued from the hands of their betrayers. . . .

We propose to contribute to the defeat of any person or party that stands for the forcible subjugation of any people. We shall oppose for reëlection all who in the White House or in Congress betray American liberty in pursuit of un-American ends. We still hope that both of our great political parties will support and defend the Declaration of Independence in the closing campaign of the century. . . .

We cordially invite the coöperation of all men and women who remain loyal to the Declaration of Independence and the Constitution of the United States.

Senator Daniel Opposes Annexation on Racist Grounds

Not all anti-imperialists were motivated by the altruism manifest in the Anti-Imperialist League platform. Some of them, such as Senator John Warwick Daniel, a Virginia Democrat, shared Beveridge's racist assumptions about Filipino people but concluded from such beliefs that the United States should not annex the islands. Daniel conveyed his views in a speech to the Senate on 3 February 1899. Selected from Congressional Record, *55th Cong., 3d sess., 1899; 32, pt. 2: 1429–30.*

We are breaking down our history, repudiating and belittling our principles, and seeking to subvert the who[l]e theory and settled tenure of American progress and of American rule, just to get and embody in our commonwealth some scattered, barbarous, or savage islands and peoples of a mixed and nondescript race.

. . . In the first place, we are to have 25,000 Negritos, aborigines. They have no fixed occupation. They are American citizens, or will be, out of a job, but ready for one. They are dwarfish as a rule, 4 feet 8 inches in average height; negroid features, hair, and color; tattoed; nearly naked. Their religion is pagan.

In the next place, we have 3,000,000 Tagals and 2,500,000 Visayos. They are Catholic. They are field hands, day laborers, servants, agriculturists, small traders. They are tall and well formed, round head, flat nose, low brow, large dark eyes.

Then we have the Moros, of whom there are 300,000. They are Mohammedans. . . .

Then come the Igorrotes. They are pagan. There are 500,000 of them. They live in the mountainous districts. They are dirty and repulsive in appearance, industrious, monogamists, distinct from Malays and Negritos. They are probably of Japanese origin. Then come scattered tribes, 2,000,000, mixed (pagan, Catholic, Mohammedan) altogether. . . .

Then come the Spanish Mestizos, descendants of Spanish fathers and native mothers, 50,000, Catholic. Then come the Chinese, 200,000, Buddhists. They are in every city and town. John Chinaman is everywhere. . . .

Then come the Chinese Mestizos, or mixed breed, 400,000; double the number of the pure and genuine article. They are Buddhists and Catholics. . . .

We are asked to annex to the United States a witch's caldron—

> Black spirits and white, red spirits and gray,
> Mingle, mingle, mingle, you that mingle may.

We are not only asked to annex the caldron and make it a part of our great, broad, Christian, Anglo-Saxon, American land, but we are asked also to annex the contents and take this brew—mixed races, Chinese, Japanese, Malay Negritos—anybody who has come along in three hundred years, in all of their concatenations and colors; and the travelers who have been there tell us and have written in the books that they are not only of all hues and colors, but there are spotted people there, and, what I have never heard of in any other country, there are striped people there with zebra signs upon them.

This mess of Asiatic pottage, 7,000 miles from the United States, in a land that we can not colonize and can not inhabit, we are told to-day by the fortune of a righteous war waged for liberty, for the ascendency of the Declaration of Independence, for the gift of freedom to an adjoining State, we must take up and annex and combine with our own blood and with our own people, and consecrate them with the oil of American citizenship.

Mr. President, there has never been since time began such a fatuous notion in the breast of a nation. There has never been such condescension from a high ideal and from a noble and manifest destiny.

Root Defends McKinley's Policy

The contemporary debate on McKinley's policy toward the Philippines peaked during the presidential election campaign of 1900. Secretary of War Elihu Root, among other Republican officials, vigorously defended the president. In an address delivered at Canton, Ohio, on 24 October 1900, Root rebutted two major criticisms lodged against the administration. Abridged from Elihu Root, The Military and Colonial Policy of the United States: Addresses and Reports, *ed. Robert Bacon and James Brown Scott (Cambridge, Massachusetts, 1916), 35–37, 42–44, 47.*

The charge is that President McKinley has been guilty of something called imperialism, in his treatment of the people of the Philippine Islands. . . .

What President McKinley has done in the Philippines has been to defend and assert the sovereignty of the United States thus acquired with the assent of both parties and of both candidates for the presidency, with the means thus placed in his hands by Congress. What is charged against him is that he did not yield or procure Congress to authorize him to yield the sovereignty of the United States acquired by the cession of Spain with the assent of both parties, to the force of armed Tagalogs whose hands were red with the blood of American soldiers; place in their hands the government of the Philippine Islands, lower the American flag upon the walls of Manila and hurry away with our wounded and our dead from the bay made glorious by Dewey's victory.

The first specification under the charge is that it was unjust to the Filipinos not to do this. Of course it was impossible to do it. Self-respect forbade it, national honor forbade it; the whole world would have contemned and despised us if we had done it; the whole country would have risen in indignant protest against any President who dared to do it. . . .

But we are told that, irrespective of agreements, irrespective of anything said or done by the Filipino leaders, or by ourselves, we ought to transfer to them sovereignty over the Philippine Islands, because government derives its just powers from the consent of the governed, and our maintenance of sovereignty is a violation of that great principle of the Declaration of Independence.

"Take Your Choice" Color lithograph. Cartoon from Judge, *Vol. 38, pages 298–299, May 12, 1900. McKinley raises the flag over the Philippines while William Jennings Bryan tries to chop it down.*

Nothing can be more misleading than a principle misapplied. . . . The doctrine that government derives its just powers from the consent of the governed was applicable to the conditions for which Jefferson wrote it, and to the people to whom he applied it. It is true wherever a people exist capable and willing to maintain just government, and to make free, intelligent and efficacious decision as to who shall govern. . . .

The true question in the Philippines was . . . whether the humble and peaceable inhabitants, who constituted the great mass of the population, were competent to protect themselves; . . . or whether, on the other hand, the people, incapable of governing themselves, would become the subjects of a dictatorship, or the prey of bloody discord. . . .

. . . [T]he people inhabiting the Philippine Archipelago are incapable of self-government, and . . . the fate here described would have befallen these islands of the tropics had American sovereignty been withdrawn. There is no Philippine people. The hundreds of islands which compose the Archipelago are inhabited by more than eighty different tribes, speaking more than sixty different languages. They have no common medium of communication, and they never had a government except the arbitrary rule of Spain. Most of them have not the first conception of what self-government means, or the first qualification for its exercise. Many of them have the capacity to learn, but they have never learned. . . .

The second specification under the charge of imperialism is, in substance, that the exercise of government must be over the people of the Philippine Islands as subjects, if not as citizens, and that this exercise of power over others will be destructive to our national character and institutions. A republic cannot have subjects and live, it is said. . . . The true proposition is the precise reverse of the charge which is made. The government of the Philippine Islands will not affect the character of our institutions, but the character of our institutions will determine and mould the government of the Philippine Islands. To govern as a despot would be fatal to the character of a republic, but to govern as Congress always has and always will govern in territory outside of the limits of the States, in accordance with the spirit of our institutions, subject to all the great rules of liberty and right, and responsible for every act to a great liberty-loving people can but extend and strengthen our institutions.

Bryan Rejects Imperialists' Arguments

William Jennings Bryan, the Democratic nominee for president in 1900, based part of his campaign against McKinley on criticism of the annexation of the Philippines. In a speech to his party's convention in Indianapolis, delivered on 8 August 1900, Bryan attacked major arguments advanced by imperialists and vowed to grant the Philippines immediate independence. McKinley's comfortable victory in the November election, of course, prevented such a step from taking place. Taken from William Jennings Bryan, Speeches of William Jennings Bryan *(New York, 1909), 2:39–46.*

The principal arguments . . . advanced by those who enter upon a defense of imperialism are:

First—That we must improve the present opportunity to become a world power and enter into international politics.

Second—That our commercial interests in the Philippine Islands and in the Orient make it necessary for us to hold the islands permanently.

Third—That the spread of the Christian religion will be facilitated by a colonial policy.

Fourth—That there is no honorable retreat from the position which the nation has taken.

The first argument is addrest [addressed] to the nation's pride and the second to the nation's pocket-book. The third is intended for the church member and the fourth for the partizan [partisan].

It is sufficient answer to the first argument to say that for more than a century this nation has been a world power. For ten decades it has been the most potent influence in the world. Not only has it been a world power, but it has done more to shape the politics of the human race than all the other nations of the world combined. Because our Declaration of Independence was promulgated others have been promulgated. Because the patriots of 1776 fought for liberty others have fought for it. Because our Constitution was adopted other constitutions have been adopted. . . .

It is not necessary to own people in order to trade with them. We carry on trade today with every part of the world, and our commerce has expanded more rapidly than the commerce of any

European empire. We do not own Japan or China, but we trade with their people. We have not absorbed the republics of Central and South America, but we trade with them. It has not been necessary to have any political connection with Canada or the nations of Europe in order to trade with them. Trade cannot be permanently profitable unless it is voluntary. . . .

The religious argument varies in positiveness from a passive belief that Providence delivered the Filipinos into our hands, for their good and our glory, to the exultation of the minister who said that we ought to "thrash the natives (Filipinos) until they understand who we are," and that "every bullet sent, every cannon shot and every flag waved means righteousness."

We cannot approve of this doctrine in one place unless we are willing to apply it everywhere. If there is poison in the blood of the hand it will ultimately reach the heart. It is equally true that forcible Christianity, if planted under the American flag in the faraway Orient, will sooner or later be transplanted upon American soil.

If true Christianity consists in carrying out in our daily lives the teachings of Christ, who will say that we are commanded to civilize with dynamite and proselyte with the sword? He who would declare the divine will must prove his authority either by Holy Writ or by evidence of a special dispensation. . . .

The argument made by some that it was unfortunate for the nation that it had anything to do with the Philippine Islands, but that the naval victory at Manila made the permanent acquisition of those islands necessary, is also unsound. We won a naval victory at Santiago, but that did not compel us to hold Cuba. . . .

There is an easy, honest, honorable solution of the Philippine question. It is set forth in the Democratic platform and it is submitted with confidence to the American people. This plan I unreservedly indorse. If elected, I will convene Congress in extraordinary session as soon as inaugurated and recommend an immediate declaration of the nation's purpose, first, to establish a stable form of government in the Philippine Islands, just as we are now establishing a stable form of government in Cuba; second, to give independence to the Filipinos as we have promised to give independence to the Cubans; third, to protect the Filipinos from outside interference while they work out their destiny.

Questions

1. *What were the major assumptions of imperialists and anti-imperialists about America's mission in the world and about the people of the Philippines? How did differences between their assumptions account for their varying positions in the debate over American policy?*
2. *What were the major reasons imperialists cited to justify annexation and retention of the Philippines? Why did anti-imperialists oppose such steps?*
3. *In your judgment, were the arguments of the imperialists or the anti-imperialists more persuasive and credible? What should the United States have done with the Philippines?*

FURTHER READING

Recent examinations of the diplomatic and military dimensions of the Spanish-American War include John L. Offner, An Unwanted War: The Diplomacy of the United States and Spain over Cuba, 1895–1898 *(Chapel Hill, North Carolina, 1992); and David Trask,* The War with Spain in 1898 *(New York, 1981). William Appleman Williams,* The Tragedy of American Diplomacy *(Cleveland, 1959) and Walter LaFeber,* The New Empire: An Interpretation of American Expansion, 1860–1898 *(Ithaca, New York, 1963), stress economic motives behind overall U.S. expansionism; Stuart Creighton Miller,* "Benevolent Assimilation": The American Conquest of the Philippines, 1899–1903 *(New Haven, Connecticut, 1982), examines racism in U.S. policy; and Charles S. Campbell,* The Transformation of American Foreign Relations, 1865–1900 *(New York, 1976), provides a multicausal explanation. Philip Foner,* The Spanish-Cuban-American War and the Birth of American Imperialism, 1895–1902 *(New York, 1972), sharply criticizes McKinley. Regarding the anti-imperialists, see Robert Beisner,* Twelve Against Empire *(New York, 1968), and Thomas J. Osborne,* Empire Can Wait: American Opposition to Hawaiian Annexation, 1893–1898 *(Kent, Ohio, 1981).*

Clash of Cultures in the 1910s and 1920s

William R. Childs

INTRODUCTION

From the colonial times until the present, Americans have had a peculiar ability to look backward and forward at the same time. Tradition and progress have stood side-by-side in the American mind. In the 1910s and 1920s, this paradox interacted with a variety of economic, social, and intellectual forces in a manner that suggested that Americans, for the very first time, were really trying to define themselves as a culture, as a civilization distinct from others. Cultural tensions—conflicts between opposing views of how the world should be and how Americans should define themselves—more intensely and widely engaged Americans between 1915 and 1930 than ever before. The debates took place in the mass media and in the state and national legislatures. At times the conflicts resulted in violence. The next comparable period would be the 1960s and early 1970s.

The explosive nature of the 1910s and 1920s had been building for nearly one-half a century. Expansion of industrialism had by the 1910s set the stage for a number of conflicts. A consumer society that exalted immediate consumption undermined the older producer economy that was based on delayed gratification. Economic expansion attracted more and more immigrants from Eastern and Southern Europe, areas that had not sent many immigrants to the United States before, and that had languages, religions, and cultures different from the White Anglo-Saxon Protestant (WASP) culture that dominated American society in the nineteenth century. At the same time, "modern" ideas from science challenged religious truths that had been held for several centuries. Discoveries in biology, particularly the ideas of Darwinian evolutionism, joined new concepts from physics, such as

Einstein's relativity principles, to challenge older ideas. The new ideas stressed uncertainty and relativism and thus conflicted with older Victorian ideas of stability and predictability. Conflicts between old and new appeared to separate older generations from the younger one. New sexual mores challenged older Victorian beliefs.

The World War I experience enhanced the tensions between old and new. It sharpened Americans' awareness that they were different from Europe, even though many of the American traditions and peoples hailed from Europe. It stimulated more citizens to move from the country to the city, even though the city had a greater number of temptations and vices that challenged many rural beliefs. It showed that national advertising campaigns could stimulate sales of goods. (During the war, the government used national advertising to promote bond sales that financed much of the war effort.) It showed that technological change could greatly affect a war effort—with the result that more soldiers and civilians were affected.

Many Americans did not like the changes being wrought, and they challenged the emerging modern order. While it is too simplistic to say that country folk battled city folk for the power to define the American civilization, it is not too simplistic to argue that people who held traditionally rural values battled those who held modern values. This conflict between city and country appeared more directly in the evolving Democratic party than in the majority Republican party.

Between 1915 and 1930, with the World War I experience accelerating the trend, more and more a number of Americans challenged directly the move toward a modern world. Their challenges took on a variety of forms and encompassed a large number of issues. Some people promoted the idea of restricting the number of new immigrants and "Americanizing" those already here. The infamous Sacco and Vanzetti trial in Massachusetts reflected American fears of "outsiders." Immigration restriction laws targeted such outsiders specifically. Some Americans tried to force others to follow their value systems. Prohibition was in large measure an attempt to control the drinking habits of the working class, comprised mostly of immigrants from Eastern and Southern

Europe. The second Ku Klux Klan, while designed to be a money-making enterprise, also directly challenged the immorality of the cities. Prime targets of KKK violence included not only blacks and immigrants, but also those who participated in the new sexual mores. Much of the conflict of cultures centered around religion and science. Indeed, although the number of churches declined in the 1920s, the number of Americans participating in organized religion increased. The John Scopes trial of 1925—the "monkey trial"—became a national cause celebre, as fundamentalists battled modernists for the power to shape the education of young Americans.

By the early 1930s, the major manifestations of the clash of cultures—Prohibition, immigration restrictions, the KKK, the battle between fundamentalism and scientific inquiry—had decreased in intensity. Opponents of the new values had lost many of the battles. In fact, the Democratic party was clearly evolving away from its Southern and Western roots towards becoming a political organization with an urban base of supporters. But the older values were not totally lost. Later societal eras—the Depression, World War II, and the postwar era—continued to refine what it meant to be "American." And as the clashes of the 1960s and 1970s, and of the 1990s, illustrate, Americans are still capable of noisily debating—sometimes violently—the nature of their culture.

CONTEMPORARY ANALYSES OF THE KKK AND THE "MONKEY TRIAL"

Prohibition and immigration restriction were two aspects of the clash of cultures that manifested themselves in the national political arena. Both utilized the national government to promote the shaping of the American culture. Although two other movements—the second KKK and the Scopes trial—drew national attention, both took place for the most part in the local and state government arenas. Like prohibition, but unlike immigration restriction, both were momentary crusades that did not sustain government support for their causes. All four movements, however, reasserted themselves throughout the rest of the twentieth century.

The Second KKK

Ironically, the KKK used modern business techniques to stem the tide of modernism. The KKK drew on Americans' anxieties with the changes occurring in society to build membership and thus enhance the coffers of the institution. The Klan did try—and in a few cases succeeded for a short time—to use government to foster its goals of returning Americans to older values.

The following extract, written in 1931 by journalist Frederick Lewis Allen, presents, on one level, the facts behind the rise and decline of the Klan. On another level, however, the selections reveal where Allen stood in the clash of cultures that the Klan embodied. Only recently have historians begun to re-evaluate the Klan phenomenon in order to obtain a better understanding of why people joined the Klan. Taken from Frederick Lewis Allen, Only Yesterday: An Informal History of the Nineteen-Twenties *(New York, 1964), 54–57.*

The Klan had been founded as far back as 1915 by a Georgian named Colonel William Joseph Simmons, but its first five years had been lean. When 1920 arrived, Colonel Simmons had only a few hundred members in his amiable patriotic and fraternal order, which drew its inspiration from the Ku-Klux Klan of Reconstruction days and stood for white supremacy and sentimental Southern idealism in general. But in 1920 Simmons put the task of organizing the Order into the hands of one Edward Y. Clarke of the Southern Publicity Association. Clarke's gifts of salesmanship . . . were prodigious. The time was ripe for the Klan, and he knew it. Not only could it be represented to potential members as the defender of the white against the black, of Gentile against Jew, and of Protestant against Catholic, and thus trade on all the newly inflamed fears of the credulous small-towner, but its white robe and hood, its flaming cross, its secrecy, and the preposterous vocabulary of its ritual could be made the vehicle for all that infantile love of hocus-pocus and mummery, that lust for secret adventure, which survives in the adult whose lot is cast in drab places. Here was a chance to dress up the village bigot and let him be a Knight of the Invisible Empire. The formula was perfect. And there was another inviting fact to be borne in mind. Well organized, such an Order could be made a paying proposition.

The salesmen of memberships were given the entrancing title of Kleagles; the country was divided into Realms headed by King Kleagles, and the Realms into Domains headed by Grand Goblins; Clarke himself, as chief organizer, became Imperial Kleagle, and the art of nomenclature reached its fantastic pinnacle in the title bestowed upon Colonel Simmons: he became the Imperial Wizard. A membership cost ten dollars; and as four of this went into the pocket of the Kleagle who made the sale, it was soon apparent that a diligent Kleagle need not fear the wolf at the door. Kleagling became one of the profitable industries of the decade. The King Kleagle of the Realm and Grand Goblin of the Domain took a small rake-off from the remaining six dollars of the membership fee, and the balance poured into the Imperial Treasury at Atlanta.

... [In 1921] Simmons was succeeded as Imperial Wizard by a Texas dentist named Hiram Wesley Evans, who referred to himself, perhaps with some justice, as "the most average man in America"; but a humming sales organization had been built up and the Klan continued to grow. It grew, in fact, with such inordinate rapidity that early in 1924 its membership had reached ... the staggering figure of nearly four and a half millions. It came to wield great political power, dominating for a time the seven states of Oregon, Oklahoma, Texas, Arkansas, Indiana, Ohio, and California. Its chief strongholds were the New South, the Middle West, and the Pacific coast, but it had invaded almost every part of the country and had even reached the gates of that stronghold of Jewry, Catholicism, and sophistication, New York City. So far had Clarke's genius and the hospitable temper of the times carried it.

The objects of the Order as stated in its Constitution were "to unite white male persons, native-born Gentile citizens of the United States of America, who owe no allegiance of any nature to any foreign government, nation, institution, sect, ruler, person, or people; whose morals are good, whose reputations and vocations are exemplary ... to cultivate and promote patriotism toward our Civil Government; to practice an honorable Klanishess toward each other; to exemplify a practical benevolence; to shield the sanctity of the home and the chastity of womanhood; to maintain forever white supremacy, to reach and faithfully inculcate a high spiritual philosophy through an exalted ritualism, and by a practical devotion to conserve, protect, and maintain the distinctive institutions, rights, privileges, principles, traditions and ideals of a pure Americanism."

Thus the theory. In practice the "pure Americanism" varied with the locality. At first, in the South, white supremacy was the Klan's chief objective, but as time went on and the organization grew and spread, opposition to the Jew and above all to the Catholic proved the best talking point for Kleagles in most localities. Nor did the methods of the local Klan organizations usually suggest the possession of a "high spiritual philosophy." These local organizations were largely autonomous and beyond control from Atlanta. They were drawn, as a rule, mostly from the less educated and less disciplined elements of the white Protestant community. ("You think the influential men belong here?" commented an outspoken observer in an Indiana city. "Then look at their shoes when they march in parade. The sheet doesn't cover the shoes.") Though Imperial Wizard Evans inveighed against lawlessness, the members of the local Klans were not always content with voting against allowing children to attend parochial schools, or voting against Catholic candidates for office, or burning fiery crosses on the hilltop back of the town to show the niggers that the whites meant business. The secrecy of the Klan was an invitation to more direct action.

If a white girl reported that a colored man had made improper advances to her—even if the charge were unsupported and based on nothing more than a neurotic imagination—a white-sheeted band might spirit the Negro off to the woods and "teach him a lesson" with tar and feathers or with the whip. If a white man stood up for a Negro in a race quarrel, he might be kidnapped and beaten up. If a colored woman refused to sell her land at an arbitrary price which she considered too low, and a Klansman wanted the land, she might receive the K. K. K. ultimatum—sell or be thrown out. Klan members would boycott Jewish merchants, refuse to hire Catholic boys, refuse to rent their houses to Catholics. A hideous tragedy in Louisiana, where five men were kidnapped and later found bound with wire and drowned in a lake,

A parade of Ku Klux Klan members march along Pennsylvania Avenue in the nation's capital in 1926. (Courtesy of The Library of Congress.)

was laid to Klansmen. R. A. Patton, writing in *Current History*, reported a grim series of brutalities from Alabama: "A lad whipped with branches until his back was ribboned flesh; a Negress beaten and left helpless to contract pneumonia from exposure and die; a white girl, divorcée, beaten into unconsciousness in her own home; a naturalized foreigner flogged until his back was a pulp because he married an American woman; a Negro lashed until he sold his land to a white man for a fraction of its value."

Even where there were no such outrages, there was at least the threat of them. The white-robed army paraded, the burning cross glowed across the valley, people whispered to one another in the darkness and wondered "who they were after this time," and fear and suspicion ran from house to house. Furthermore, criminals and gangs of hoodlums quickly learned to take advantage of the Klan's existence: if they wanted to burn someone's barn or raid the slums beyond the railroad tracks, they could do it with impunity now: would not the Klan be held responsible? Anyone could chalk the letters K. K. K. on a fence and be sure that the sheriff would move warily. Thus, as in the case of the Red hysteria, a movement conceived in fear perpetuated fear and brought with it all manner of cruelties and crimes.

Slowly, as the years passed and the war-time emotions ebbed, the power of the Klan waned, until in many districts it was dead and in others it had become merely a political faction dominated by spoilsmen: but not until it had become a thing of terror to millions of men and women.

Rescued Self-Esteem

In this extract from sociologist John Moffatt Mecklin, we see a somewhat different approach to understanding the motivations behind the rise of the KKK. Extracted from John Moffatt Mecklin, The Ku Klux Klan: A Study of the American Mind *(New York, 1924), 107–8.*

He is tossed about in the hurly-burly of our industrial and so-called democratic society. Under the stress and strain of social competition he is made to realize his essential mediocrity. Yet according to traditional democratic doctrine he is born free and the equal of his fellow who is outdistancing him in the race. Here is a large and powerful organization offering to solace his sense of defeat by dubbing him a knight of the Invisible Empire for the small sum of ten dollars. Surely knighthood was never offered at such a bargain!

The Monkey Trial and the *New York Times*

The so-called "monkey trial" in Dayton, Tennessee, in mid-summer 1925, attracted a lot of media attention across the U.S. and in Europe. The New York Times included coverage every day during the month of July, sometimes including several stories. Although the New York Times included copy on both sides of the issue, the newspaper's editorial stance clearly favored one side: modernism over fundamentalism.

While there were many actors in this media event, several were central to the drama that unfolded in the hot summer of 1925. John Scopes was the teacher accused of violating the state's law that forbade the teaching of evolution in the schools. Clarence Darrow was a prominent civil liberties lawyer who led the defense. William Jennings Bryan, a candidate for president in 1896 and several times thereafter, Woodrow Wilson's secretary of state, and most recently a traveling fundamentalist preacher and huckster for Florida real estate, lent his prestige to the prosecution. For both Darrow and Bryan, the trial was not over whether or not Scopes violated the law, but rather over what values should define American culture. Darrow reflected "modernist" views that encompassed the new sciences and freedom of thought and speech. Bryan reflected some Americans' desires that Protestant religious principles should anchor American culture.

What follows is a chronological sampling of coverage from the New York Times. *Often the headlines alone indicated the content of the story that followed. Other times the text filled in necessary detail. The presentation of these primary sources draws from a technique that the novelist John Dos Passos employed in his USA trilogy, three novels on the 1920s written in the 1930s. It is intended to convey the breadth, and sometimes*

Opposing attorneys Clarence Darrow and William Jennings Bryan chat during the Scopes Trial. (Courtesy of AP/Wide World Photos.)

depth(s), of the story that caught Americans' attention in 1925. The issues embraced include science versus religion; state versus national law; the separation of church and state; city versus country; and, always, the fight over who would define American culture. Students are encouraged to find the original stories (generally available in newspaper microfilm collections in university and public libraries) and read them for more detail.

JULY 4, 1925, PAGE 2

Scopes Attorneys Fight Dayton Trial

To Ask Federal Court Monday for Injunction Based on Law's Unconstitutionality.

SHUN CIRCUS ATMOSPHERE

Darrow Says Case Is Too Serious to Be Made a Jest, as Other States May Ban Evolution.

JULY 4, 1925, PAGE 10 (EDITORIAL PAGE)

More Than Scopes Is on Trial.

Being a man of ability, CLARENCE DARROW sees much more in the Scopes case than the trial of a young school teacher on the charge of breaking an absurd law. To MR. DARROW it is a much larger thing than that, and for him it is larger by the fact that two other States already have passed similar laws, while in two others like laws have been beaten by the narrowest of majorities, and in some twenty more the enemies of evolution are actively engaged in preaching to the ignorant and fanatical the taking of like action. This he sees as only a beginning of an effort to enslave the human mind and as something to be met and fought at once. . . .

But these questions are not at all involved in the indictment of MR. SCOPES, or they are involved only indirectly and in a way to which it seems impossible for a Judge ... to consider. And it will not be for them to decide whether the law is constitutional or not. Power to do that will lie in higher courts on appeal. . . .

It is to be regretted that the affair has so many amusing features and that it lies under some suspicion, probably unjust, of being an advertising dodge invented by the inhabitants of Dayton.

[The *New York Times* was incorrect in its assumption! Scopes had agreed to go on trial when business leaders of Dayton approached him to institute a test court case.]

JULY 5, 1925, SECTION 4, PAGE 1 (MAGAZINE SECTION)

The Evolution Arena At Dayton

Circus Sideshows and Curious Visitors Descend Upon Tennessee Mountain Town, but Legal Struggle Will Involve Christian Faith, Science, Free Speech, and the Constitution

JULY 5, 1925, SECTION 2, PAGE 1

Fights Evolution To Uphold Bible

Author of Tennessee Law Tells Motives That Led Him to Frame It.

Fears For The Children

Believes Statute, if Enforced, Will Prevent Them From Becoming Infidels.

HAS SPENT LIFE ON FARM

J. W. Butler Is a Primitive Baptist Who Believes Government Is Founded on Scripture.

. . . [John W. Butler:] "For some time it has been against the law of Tennessee to teach the Bible in the public schools or to allow the teaching of any system of religion, although the Bible can be read in such schools without comment. If this law can be upheld, I am satisfied that a law which, in my opinion and those of thousands of other Tennessee parents, would tend to prevent the making of infidels of our children can be equally enforced."

JULY 6, 1925, PAGE 2

Doubts Scopes Violated The Law

Chattanooga Bar Association Head Says It Doesn't Prohibit Teaching of Evolution.

Explains Act's Meaning

John C. Cantrill Disapproved Use of Court Proceeding as Background for Personal Publicity.

... "Many people outside the State who have become excited over the case of John T. Scopes, the Dayton teacher indicted for violation of the law prohibiting the teaching of evolution in the public schools, have expressed surprise that Tennessee lawyers, as a rule, have seemed to consider the case as of little importance.

... [The Tennessee lawyers] are justified in this ... because:

"First, the so-called anti-evolution law is very narrow in its scope, and does not prohibit the teaching of evolution as is generally supposed.

"Second, I do not believe ... that Professor Scope, or any other Tennessee teacher, has actually violated the act by affirmatively teaching 'that man has descended from a lower order of animals.' Any teacher may teach that there was no divine creation of anything, that everything in Nature happened by chance, and that the Bible teaching on every subject is false from Genesis to Revelation and he will not violate this law, unless he also affirmatively teaches 'that man has descended from a lower order of animals.' ["]

JULY 7, 1925, PAGE 1

Scopes Fails To Get Federal Injunction; State Trial Friday

Judge Gore Rules Tennessee Officers Are Acting in the Only Way They Are Authorized.

Two Petitions Presented

Teacher Charges Violation of Liberty—Parent Asserts Right to Educate His Children.

Appeal To Be Taken Later

Darrow Says He Fears the State Court May Limit the Case to

Whether Law Was Violated.

JULY 8, 1925, PAGE 1

Bryan In Dayton, Calls Scopes Trial Duel To The Death

If Evolution Wins, He Declares, Chrisitianity Goes, for Both Cannot Survive.

Sees The Bible At Stake

Trying to Destroy It, He Asserts, on Evidence That Would Not Convict a Habitual Criminal.

CROWD CHEERS HIS ARRIVAL

. . . Altogether, Mr. Bryan was in good humor. He had been met at the station by about 300 people, 50 of whom were reporters and photographers, had been paraded up the main street in an automobile, had shaken hands with all those on the side of the prosecution and some interested in the defense, had had a long talk with the lawyers with whom he will be associated, had been interviewed, had an ice cream soda in the drug store, and made a speech at a dinner in his honor. It was Bryan day, for there was no other distinguished visitor in town. He even looked at the court house where he will declaim against evolution, sitting far back from the road behind a green lawn and trees, and pronounced it good.

JULY 9, 1925, PAGE 1

Bryan Threatens National Campaign To Bar Evolution

Warns That if Defeated in the Courts the Bible Will Be Put Into the Constitution.

Sees Morality Imperiled

He Declares There Is a Majority in Every State to Push Through Federal Amendment.

DAYTON READY FOR TRIAL

JULY 10, 1925, PAGE 1

Dayton Keyed Up For Opening Today Of Trial Of Scopes

Intense Excitement Grips Town as Principals Reach Scene of Battle on Evolution.

JUDGE GIVES HIS ATTITUDE

Says He Wants Inquiry for "Eternal Truth" and Warns Against Personal Ambitions.

STATE'S CASE TO BE BRIEF

Defense Will Then Produce Scientists and Educators—Catholics Offer Help to Bryan.

Trial Attracts Many Cranks.

People have come from all over the South to Dayton. What they hope to get out of it is a problem. One negro drifted in from Georgia today, having got leave from his employer to come here and work for his employer's relatives for the duration of the trial. He wanted to see the show. One or two women, with obvious mental irregularities of a religious tendency, have come to town, and chatter volubly to any one who will listen to them.

A man who calls himself the greatest authority on the Bible, proclaimed by a large sign on his back on which is printed inversions of Bible phrases, trots up and down indefatigably. He is willing to exhort anybody at any time on any subject.

"Independent," the only proponent of evolution to appear so far, is James Pollock Kohler of 350 Fulton Street, Brooklyn. He announced he came "on his own hook to combat the influence of Bryan on the outside." He said he was ready to hire a hall and speak to the people on "evils of accepting the Bible literally."

"Monkey town" is the name of Dayton in the rest of Tennessee. Whatever the deep significance of this trial, if it has any, there is no doubt that it has attracted some of the world's champion freaks.

JULY 11, 1925, PAGE 1

Who's Who and What's What in Scopes Trial

Plaintiff—The People of the State of Tennessee through their legal officers, who have the aid of volunteer outside counsel.

Defendant—John Thomas Scopes, 24 years old, native of Paducah, Ky., teacher of biology in the Rhea County High School at Dayton.

The Charge—That Scopes taught his pupils that man descended from a lower order of animals, in violation of a State statute forbidding such teaching.

Penalty—A fine of not less than $100 nor more than $500 for each offense.

Counsel for Prosecution—William Jennings Bryan, ex-presidential candidate and ex-Secretary of State; General Ben McKenzie, ex-District Attorney of Dayton; J. Gordon McKenzie, his son; Sue and Herbert Hicks, young Dayton lawyers; E. T. Stewart, Circuit Attorney General; Walter White, Superintendent of Schools and County Prosecutor; W. C. Haggard, Dayton attorney; William Jennings Bryan Jr.

Counsel for Defense—Clarence Darrow of Chicago, noted criminal lawyer; John R. Neal, Knoxville, former acting Dean of the University of Tennessee Law School; Dudley Field Malone, New York attorney.

The Jury—W. F. Robertson, tenant farmer; J. W. Dagley, farmer; James Riley, farmer; W. J. Taylor, farmer; R. L. Gentry, farmer and teacher; J. R. Thompson, farm owner (retired); W. D. Smith, farmer; W. J. Day, retired farmer; Jesse Goodrich, shipping clerk; J. S. Wright, farmer; J. H. Bowman, farmer; R. L. West, farmer.

Trial before Judge J. T. Raulston of Winchester, Tenn., Judge of the Eighteenth Tennessee Circuit, in Rhea County Court House, Dayton.

The Law in the Case.

Be it enacted by the General Assembly of the State of Tennessee, That it shall be unlawful for any teacher in any of the universities, normals and all other public schools of the State which are supported in whole or in part by the public school funds of the State, to teach any theory that denies the story of the Divine creation of man as taught in the Bible, and to teach instead that man has descended from a lower order of animals.

Be it further enacted, That any teacher found guilty of the violation of this act, shall be guilty of a misdemeanor. * * *

JULY 11, 1925, PAGES 1-2

Europe Is Amazed By The Scopes Case

NOTED SCIENTISTS PROTEST

LONDON, July 10.—The Scopes trial at Dayton, Tenn., is attracting the widest attention of the British press, scientists and public men. All the published opinion strongly condemns the prosecution of the school teacher or expresses amazement that an American State should attempt to prevent the teaching of the known facts of evolution. . . .

Sir Arthur Shipley, Master of Christ College, Cambridge, one of the many prominent educators expressing views of the Dayton trial ... says the average American of the Middle and Southern States is a very "naive mammal."

"As a prominent citizen tells us in the current number of the National Review," he says, "the United States is a nation of adult children and certainly some things they do seem to older and more mature countries decidedly childish. And after all thought is free in spite of William Jennings Bryan. If one likes to think that man is descended from animals resembling man it will be very difficult to stop it.". . .

The Rev. Frank Ballard, Christian Evidence lecturer for the Wesleyan conference, writes:

"The assumptions of Fundamentalism are so preposterous, alike in theory and practice, I am not altogether surprised when I call to mind my experiences in America twenty-five years ago. It was pitifully manifest then that both the science and theology of many of those who posed as authorities were half a century behind the times. But one did hope the intervening years would have opened their eyes. The notion of a Judge's charge to the Grand Jury beginning with the reading of the First Chapter of Genesis as an account of creation which Tennessee teachers must adopt savors of sixteenth rather than the twentieth century.". . .

"To those who think of the United States as the extreme expression of modern spirit, the man or ape trial in Tennessee must come as a severe shock. To a smaller number of Englishmen who judge America not by its movies or its millionaires or motor cars or its schemes for regeneration, on a strictly dividend paying basis, of the Old World, but by its attitude toward abstract ideas there is nothing surprising, though there is much that is curious in that heresy hunt.

July 11, 1925, page 1

Scopes Jury Chosen With Dramatic Speed After Prayer Opens Picturesque Trial; State Fights Testimony By Scientists

FARMERS WILL TRY TEACHER

Jury Includes Ten, a Schoolmaster and a Shipping Clerk.

ONE IS UNABLE TO READ

None Believes in Evolution, but Darrow Says He Did Not Expect to Find Any Who Did.

July 12, 1925, page 1

Hostility Grows In Dayton Crowds; Champions Clash

Bryan and Darrow Gird for Monday's Battle, Contending Over Testimony by Scientists.

Sectional Feeling Raised

Bryan Scores 'Invasion of Outsiders'—Defense Counsel Tilts at Commoner's 'Chinese Wall.'

JULY 13, 1925, PAGE 1

Dayton's One Pro-Evolution Pastor Quits As Threat Bars Dr. Potter From Pulpit; Bryan's Sermons Anger Scopes Defense

Trial Stirs Local Storm

Preacher Is Told Church Would Be Wrecked Over New York 'Infidel.'

3,000 Listen to Commoner

JULY 13, 1925, PAGE 15

CALLS DAYTON TRIAL A SILLY PERFORMANCE

Evolution Does Not Contradict Fact of Creation, Says the Rev. W. B. Kinkead.

JULY 13, 1925, PAGE 15

Says Bryan Group Betrays Freedom

Trying to Put the State Behind a Religion of Authority, Warns Dr. Dieffenbach.

EVOLUTION MINOR MATTER

Real Issue Is Whether We Shall Return to Medievalism, He Tells Unitarians Here.

Says Tennessee Ignores Progress

Christians Need Not Believe in Genesis Literally, Declares Dean Mathews.

SHOULD USE INTELLIGENCE

Dean Cites Beliefs of Biblical Age Which Have Been Discarded Without Harm to Religion.

JULY 14, 1925 PAGE 1

Darrow Scores Ignorance And Bigotry, Seeking To Quash Scopes Indictment; State Argues For Its Police Power

DECISION TODAY IS LIKELY

Judge Will Also Decide on Whether He Will Hear Scientists.

FLOOD OF SATIRE LOOSENED

Darrow Denounces the Statute as Unconstitutional and the Indictment as Faulty.

STEWART DEFENDS BOTH

He Contends That the Legislature, Supporting the Schools, Has Right to Fix Curriculum.

JULY 14, 1925, PAGE 3

Streets Of Dayton Deserted For Shade

Concessionaires Fare Poorly as People Gather Under Trees to Hear Trial by Radio.

SOME EVANGELISTS DEPART

Peace and Good-Will Are Displayed After Sunday's Religious Turmoil.

JULY 15, 1925, PAGE 1

Stormy Scenes In The Trial Of Scopes As Darrow Moves To Bar All Prayers; 'Leak' Delays Indictment Decision

INTENSE BITTERNESS SHOWN

Heated Words Are Passed as Defense Calls Prayers Argumentative.

JUDGE OVERRULES DARROW

Defense Then Fails in Plan to Have Alternate Modernist and Fundamentalist Prayers.

PRESS WARNED BY COURT

Contempt Action Threatened on Premature Publication of Ruling on the Indictment.

July 15, 1925, page 1

TWO APES AND 'LINK' ARRIVE AT DAYTON

Wrath of Town Placated When It Is Said That They May Be Used to Disprove Evolution.

Bryan Visits Chimpanzee

'Wonderful!' He Exclaims, When Theory of Simian Degeneration From Man Is Explained to Him.

Special to The New York Times.

DAYTON, Tenn., July 14.—Two chimpanzees and a strange-appearing man who is called the "missing link" were brought today to Dayton. After flocking to view the monkeys, Dayton has decided that it was not man who evolved from the anthropoid, but the anthropoid which devolved from man; and it points now at the two chimpanzees and the "missing link" to prove the assertion. . . .

Bryan Meets the Chimpanzee.

. . . [William Jennings Bryan and scientist Hubbard Nye inspected the chimpanzee.] "I hate, even as Tennessee has already said, to think that we are descended from one of those beasts," said Mr. Nye. "I have studied them for years, and I have come to the conclusion, supported by scientific and demonstrable fact, that Darwin was wrong. We did not evolve upward from the anthropoid. Instead, the anthropoid is the product of man who went down—he devolved. It's devolution, and this chimpanzee is the refutation of the Darwinian theory."

Mr. Bryan's eyes sparkled as he gazed at the chimpanzee.

"Wonderful!" he said. "Wonderful!"

July 15, 1925, page 2

Mr. Bryan Protests Against A Dispatch

Did Not Say That He 'Would Put the Bible In the Constitution.'

REPORTER CONDENSED IT SO

What Bryan Did Say Which Led to the Belief That He Contemplated Such a Campaign.

JULY 16, 1925, PAGE 1

Darrow Puts First Scientist On Stand To Instruct Scopes Judge On Evolution; State Completes Its Case In An Hour

DEFENSE CASE IS OUTLINED

Malone Denies Any Conflict Between Evolution and Christianity.

"MILLIONS BELIEVE BOTH"

He Declares That His Side Will Prove That the Bible Teaches Various Theories of Creation.

QUOTES COMMONER'S WORDS

Bryan Declares He Will Reply in Full and Wants No Court Protection.

INDICTMENT IS SUSTAINED

Judge Also Upholds Constitutionality of the Tennessee Law.

STATE CALLS 4 WITNESSES

Puts Bible Into Record After Showing Scopes Taught Life Originated From One Cell.

MODERNIST PRAYER IN COURT

Decision Likely Today on Permitting the Jury To Hear Scientists' Testimony.

BRYAN NOW REGRETS BARRING OF EXPERTS

Says He Would Welcome Evidence, but That the Law Had to Be Obeyed.

DARROW TURNS ON HIM

Declares Commoner Did Not Dare to Test His Views In Court Against Scientists.

JULY 18, 1925, PAGE 12 (EDITORIAL PAGE)

The End In Sight At Dayton.

. . . It must not be forgotten that this prosecution was initiated by Tennessee citizens who do not believe in the anti-evolution law and who are confident that it will ultimately be declared null and void by the courts. A test case was deliberately made up for the express purpose of appealing from an expected conviction in the lower court to a higher tribunal.

JULY 19, 1925, SECTION 1, PAGE 2

JULY 18, 1925, PAGE 1

Judge Shatters The Scopes Defense By Barring Testimony Of Scientists; Sharp Clashes As Darrow Defies Court

[For purposes of appeal, Judge Raulston allowed the defense to read into the record scientific statements about evolution.]

JULY 18, 1925, PAGE 2

DAYTON HOSPITABLE TO CRITICAL GUESTS

Citizens Patiently Bear Intrusion of 'Foreigners' and Their 'Strange' Beliefs.

DAYTON, Tenn., July 18.—Rhea County's emotional stress during the anti-evolution trial has been impressive and remarked upon in the press of all the world. High religious feeling, intolerance, bigotry, fear, unfairness, ignorance, all these have been seen, felt and reported more or less accurately; but one of the most remarkable phases of this remarkable trial has been the courtesy shown by the people of East Tennessee to the writers and lawyers who have said to the world these things about them.

Dayton, an agricultural town of less than 500 families who for generations have never questioned the "literal inerrancy" of the Bible, was overrun in a day by a horde of persons whose ways and thoughts were strange; lawyers with a strange argument that the Bible was not revealed religion; free thinkers who insisted that the Bible was superstition; animal trainers with chimpanzees which they asserted were the fathers or the sons of men, and special writers who ridiculed them, their town, their habits and even their religion.

These have been trying days for a self-respecting independent people. Yet they have behaved with remarkable constraint and courtesy toward all who have criticized and ridiculed them and their beliefs so unrestrainedly.

. . . These persons who have called Dayton, Rhea County and Tennessee all these names have been living in the homes of the very people they criticized, but there has been no instance of where anything that has been said has been openly resented, no instance where a writer or a lawyer or a special advocate or a freak has been asked to desist save for his own safety among the irresponsible.

JULY 21, 1925, PAGE 1

[On Monday, July 20, 1925, the defense read into the record the evidence for evolution. In the afternoon the defense requested that Mr. Bryan take the stand for the purpose of showing that the Bible need not be taken literally; if that were so, then Mr. Scopes did not teach a theory that contradicted the Bible. The confrontation took place outside, for there were too many onlookers for the courthouse.]

. . . To the crowd spread under the trees watching the amazing spectacle on the platform the fight seemed a fair one. There was no pity for the helplessness of the believer come so suddenly and so unexpectedly upon a moment when he could not reconcile statements of the Bible with generally accepted facts. There was no pity for his admissions of ignorance of things boys and girls learn in high school, his floundering confessions that he knew practically nothing of geology, biology, philology, little of comparative religion, and little even of ancient history.

. . . These Tennesseans were enjoying a fight. That an ideal of a great man, a biblical scholar, an authority on religion, was being dispelled seemed to make no difference. They grinned with amusement and expectation, until the next blow by one side or the other came, and then they guffawed again. And finally, when Mr. Bryan, pressed harder and harder by Mr. Darrow, confessed he did not believe everything in the Bible should be taken literally, the crowd howled.

JULY 22, 1925, PAGE 1

Scopes Guilty, Fined $100, Scores Law; Benediction Ends Trial, Appeal Starts; Darrow Answers Nine Bryan Questions

FINAL SCENES DRAMATIC

Defense Suddenly Decides to Make No Plea and Accept Conviction.

BRYAN IS DISAPPOINTED

Loses Chance to Examine Darrow and His Long-Prepared Speech Is Undelivered.

HIS EVIDENCE IS EXPUNGED

Differences Forgotten in the End as All Concerned Exchange Felicitations.

[The $100 fine was about one-third of the court's cost in putting on the trial. The defense spent $25,000, even though the defense lawyers accepted no fee. The appeal was based on two considerations: First, the defense contended that the law was not constitutional. Second, even if it were constitutional, it was not violated by Mr. Scopes. The defense had been prevented during the trial from showing this.]

JULY 22, 1925, PAGE 2

Crowd At The End Surges To Darrow

Tennessee Fundamentalists Pay a Spontaneous Tribute to His Courage.

ALL CONGRATULATE HIM

It Is Only Later That Thought Is Given to Bryan and the Other Figures in the Trial.

Special to The New York Times.

DAYTON, Tenn., July 21.—When John Thomas Scopes, the young school teacher, was found guilty today of teaching the theory of evolution, as every one had expected, a strange thing happened in the Rhea County Court House, where so many strange things have happened since the strange trial started.

The so-called Fundamentalists of Tennessee, who had seemed so overwhelming in favor of the law, who had cheered the utterances of counsel defending faith in the Bible against the "heresies" of scientists, stormed Clarence Darrow, the agnostic, to shake his hand.

JULY 27, 1925, PAGE 1

W.J. Bryan Dies In His Sleep At Dayton, While Resting In Evolution Battle; Had Spoken Continuously Since Trial

APOPLEXY CAUSES HIS DEATH

Had Said He 'Never Felt Better' on His Return From Church.

SPOKE TO 50,000 SATURDAY

Full of Zeal to Take Cause to Country, He Was Thrilled by Crowds on Last Journey.

WIFE WAS APPREHENSIVE

Feared Anti-Evolution Fight Was Overtaxing His Strength, but Now Bears Loss Bravely.

Questions

1. *List the aspects of the KKK that reflect the clash of cultures. Can you rank-order these motivating factors in terms of significance? In what order?*
2. *KKK activities often turned violent. Except for a little rowdiness early on, the Dayton trial proceedings took place without violence. How do you explain this?*
3. *Why did the legal issue—whether or not Scopes had broken the law—not remain the focus of the judicial proceedings? Who was responsible for this development?*
4. *How do you think television news would have covered the Scopes trial?*

FURTHER READING

Andrew Sinclair, Prohibition: The Era of Excess *(Boston, 1962), is still one of the best overviews of this topic.* Nativism, Discrimination, and Images of Immigrants, *ed. George E. Pozzetta (New York, 1991) offers numerous essays that show the vast extent to which nativism and anti-immigrant actions have punctuated American history. Kathleen Blee,* Women of the Klan: Racism and Gender in the 1920s *(Berkeley, 1991), is one of numerous recent works that have focused on the second KKK.* Center of the Storm: Memoirs of John T. Scopes *(New York, 1967), by John T. Scopes and James Presley, furnishes an insider's view of the monkey trial. The 1998 Pulitzer Prize for History,* SUMMER FOR THE GODS: The Scopes Trial and America's Continuing Debate Over Science and Religion *(New York, 1997), by Edward J. Larson, presents a very balanced view of the trial and its place in the on-going clash between religion and science in American culture.*

United States Entry into World War II

Peter L. Hahn,
Michael J. Hogan, and Amy L. S. Staples

Introduction

World War II began in September 1939 when Nazi Germany invaded Poland and subsequently traded declarations of war with Great Britain and France. The European war ran parallel to a major Asian conflict that had started years earlier with a Japanese attack on China and continued with Japanese expansion into Southeast Asia. U.S. officials had opposed Japanese aggression but had done little to stop it. Nor did they rush to intervene in the European conflict. Many Americans believed that their country had been dragged into World War I by bankers and businessmen who had invested heavily in the Allied cause and by misleading British propaganda about German behavior. They were sadly disillusioned about the results of that conflict. It had failed to "make the world safe for democracy," as President Woodrow Wilson had predicted it would, and there was no reason to believe that involvement in a second world war would reach such an ideal objective. Other Americans believed that World War II, like World War I and earlier European conflicts, lacked real importance to the United States. They affirmed the principles of the Monroe Doctrine, which established America's realm of interest as the Western Hemisphere, and George Washington's Farewell Address, which warned of the dangers of entangling alliances with European powers. American isolationism was manifested in a series of neutrality laws, passed by Congress in the 1930s, designed to regulate public and private actions in order to avert involvement in the brewing European conflict.

Although he had earlier accepted the neutrality laws, President Franklin D. Roosevelt came to believe that German and Japanese aggression posed serious threats to America's national security and political and economic way of life. This conviction became stronger in 1940-41 after Germany conquered most of continental Europe and Japan continued its expansion into Southeast Asia. The president slowly chipped away at the neutrality laws and isolationist sentiment in the United States. He acted to aid the Allied powers of Britain and France, even though some of his actions violated international law and risked involving the United States in war. Despite Roosevelt's actions, however, only Japan's devastating attack on Pearl Harbor on 7 December 1941 would overcome isolationism in the United States and trigger American entry into World War II.

The Contemporary Debate about American Entry into World War II

The period preceding the attack on Pearl Harbor witnessed a vigorous debate between Americans who wished to remain isolated from the war and those who wished to enter the conflict. Historian Charles A. Beard and groups such as the America First Committee clearly articulated the isolationist position. On the other hand, President Franklin D. Roosevelt delivered a series of public addresses that progressively called for involvement in the war. His campaign culminated in an address to Congress on 8 December 1941 that asked for a declaration of war against Japan.

Beard Favors Neutrality

The prominent historian Charles A. Beard outspokenly opposed American intervention in any foreign conflict. He tried to influence public opinion through publications and testimony to Congress. The selection below, written by Beard in anticipation of the outbreak of war, clearly expresses the isolationists' view of history and current events. Abridged from Charles A. Beard, Giddy Minds and Foreign Quarrels: An Estimate of American Foreign Policy *(New York, 1939), 8, 12, 27–29, 45–47, 49–51, 53–59, 61–62, 64–65, 86–87.*

Since the foundation of the American Republic there has been an endless procession of foreign quarrels with which giddy minds could have been busied.... [T]he Government of the United States kept aloof from the aggressions, wars, and quarrels of Europe....

. . . [During the Great Depression] the American people had enough jitters at home to keep their giddy minds away from foreign affairs, and in a quest for relief they swept into office Franklin D. Roosevelt, who promised to get them out of the slough of economic despond. . . . The state of jitters in domestic economy has not been cured by the New Deal, despite the best of intentions. And Great Britain, after playing Germany off against France and treating Russia with studied contempt, has once more got . . . "the grizzly German terror" on her doorstep, and needs American help again. . . .

The return to constant jitters over European affairs came after the election of 1936. In the campaign of that year President Roosevelt gave no hint that he intended to take a strong hand in European quarrels. The Democratic platform, made in his own office, declared positively: "We shall continue to observe a true neutrality in the disputes of others; to be prepared resolutely to resist aggression against ourselves; to work for peace and to take the profits out of war; to guard against being drawn, by political commitments, international banking, or private trading, into any war which may develop anywhere." This looked like a pledge to keep out of foreign conflicts and wars. The pledge President Roosevelt confirmed in his Chautauqua address of August 14, 1936: "We can keep out of war if those who watch and decide have a sufficiently detailed understanding of international affairs to make certain that the small decisions of each day do not lead toward war and if, at the same time, they possess the courage to say 'no' to those who selfishly or unwisely would let us go to war." If words meant anything in 1936, those words confirmed an evident desire to avoid meddling with the incessant quarrels of Europe and Asia. . . .

. . . But on October 5, 1937, President Roosevelt went to Chicago and called, in effect, for collective action by all the "democracies" against Germany, Italy, and Japan. He declared that if a holocaust came the United States could not avoid it and appealed to "the peace loving nations" to put a quarantine on aggressors. The significance of this address was grasped immediately. Advocates of collective security and collaboration with Brit-

---

A newspaper reports the Japanese attack on Pearl Harbor. (Courtesy of The Library of Congress.)

ain and France hailed it as a sharp change of front on the part of the President. But the counter blast of criticism from all parts of the country was startling and for a few weeks President Roosevelt lapsed into silence. Nevertheless he had evidently made up his mind that he was going to take a big hand in European and Asiatic affairs anyway and that the country would have to bend to his will or break.

Additional proof of his resolve soon came. On January 28, 1938, President Roosevelt . . . demanded an enormous increase in naval outlays, with special emphasis on battleships, and called for a mobilization bill which had no meaning unless he wanted a huge army that could be used in Europe. . . .

. . . President Roosevelt renewed his battle in 1939. His message to Congress in January . . . asserted that the United States is directly menaced by "storms from abroad." These storms, the President said, challenge "three institutions indispensable to Americans. The first is religion. It is the source of the other two—democracy and international good faith." Evidently he was clearing a way to make the next war a real holy war. This clarion call President Roosevelt followed by another demand for an increase in armaments on a scale more vast. . . .

. . . In the summer of 1939 they [President Roosevelt and Secretary of State Hull] opened a public campaign to break down the provision of the Neutrality Act which imposed an embargo on munitions in case of a foreign war. . . . [T]hey were . . . resolved if possible to erase every line of the Neutrality Act that stood in the way of their running the foreign affairs of the United States on the basis of constant participation in the quarrels of Europe and Asia, with war as their *ultima ratio.*

Now President Roosevelt's foreign policy is clear as daylight. He proposes to collaborate actively with Great Britain and France in their everlasting wrangle with Germany, Italy, and Japan. He wants to wring from Congress the power to throw the whole weight of the United States on the side of Great Britain and France in negotiations, and in war if they manage to bungle the game. That using measures short of war would, it is highly probable, lead the United States into full war must be evident to all who take thought about such tactics.

From the point of view of the interest of the United States as a continental nation in this hemisphere, the Roosevelt policy is, in my opinion, quixotic and dangerous. . . . [I]t is not based upon a realistic comprehension of the long-time history of Europe and Asia and of the limited power which the United States has over the underlying economies and interests of those two continents. It assumes that the United States can in fact bring those continents into a kind of stable equilibrium, assure them the materials of a peaceful economic life, and close their history in a grand conference of the powers. . . . It assumes that somebody in the White House or State Department can calculate the consequences likely to come out of the explosive forces which are hidden in the civilizations of those immense areas. . . .

. . . [I]t seems to me, it would be wiser to suggest that those countries of Europe which are immediately menaced by Germany and Italy put aside their jealousies, quarrels, and enmities, and join in a combination of their own to effect control over the aggressors. If countries whose very existence seems at stake will not unite for self-protection, how can the United States hope to effect a union among them? . . .

On what then should the foreign policy of the United States be based? . . . It is the doctrine formulated by George Washington, supplemented by James Monroe, and followed by the Government of the United States until near the end of the nineteenth century, when the frenzy for foreign adventurism burst upon the country. This doctrine is simple. Europe has a set of "primary interests" which have little or no relation to us, and is constantly vexed by "ambition, rivalship, interest, humor, or caprice." The United States is a continental power separated from Europe by a wide ocean which, despite all changes in warfare, is still a powerful asset of defense. In the ordinary or regular vicissitudes of European politics the United States should not become implicated by any permanent ties. . . .

Those Americans who refuse to plunge blindly into the maelstrom of European and Asiatic politics are not defeatist or neurotic. They are giving evidence of sanity, not cowardice; of adult thinking as distinguished from infantilism. Experience has educated them and made them all the more determined to concentrate their energies on the making of a civilization within the circle of their continental domain. They do not propose to withdraw from the world, but they propose to deal with the world as it is and not as romantic propagandists picture it. They propose to deal with it in American terms, that is, in terms of national interest and security on this continent. Like their ancestors who made a revolution, built the Republic, and made it stick, they intend to preserve and defend the Republic, and under its shelter carry forward the work of employing their talents and resources in enriching American life. They know that this task will call for all the enlightened statesmanship, the constructive energy, and imaginative intelligence that the nation can command. America is not to be Rome or Britain. It is to be America.

Roosevelt's Fireside Chat after the Invasion of Poland, 3 September 1939

Roosevelt realized that public opinion strongly opposed U.S. intervention in World War II. In his first fireside chat, a nationwide radio broadcast, after the invasion of Poland, therefore, he declared American neutrality and expressed his determination to isolate the United States from the hostilities. But at the same time he clearly leaned toward the Allied powers of Britain and France and began to prepare the American people for future actions to support these nations. Excerpted from The Public Papers and Addresses of Franklin D. Roosevelt, 1939, War—and Neutrality, *comp. Samuel I. Rosenman (New York, 1941), 460–64.*

My fellow Americans and my friends:

. . . Until four-thirty this morning I had hoped against hope that some miracle would prevent a devastating war in Europe and bring to an end the invasion of Poland by Germany.

For four long years a succession of actual wars and constant crises have shaken the entire world and have threatened in each case to bring on the gigantic conflict which is today unhappily a fact. . . .

You must master at the outset a simple but unalterable fact in modern foreign relations between nations. When peace has been broken anywhere, the peace of all countries everywhere is in danger.

It is easy for you and for me to shrug our shoulders and to say that conflicts taking place thousands of miles from the continental United States, and, indeed, thousands of miles from the whole American Hemisphere, do not seriously affect the Americas—and that all the United States has to do is to ignore them and go about its own business. Passionately though we may desire detachment, we are forced to realize that every word that comes through the air, every ship that sails the sea, every battle that is fought, does affect the American future.

Let no man or woman thoughtlessly or falsely talk of America sending its armies to European fields. At this moment there is being prepared a proclamation of American neutrality. . . .

. . . And I trust that in the days to come our neutrality can be made a true neutrality. . . .

. . . Most of us in the United States believe in spiritual values. Most of us, regardless of what church we belong to, believe in the spirit of the New Testament—a great teaching which opposes itself to the use of force, of armed force, of marching armies and falling bombs. The overwhelming masses of our people seek peace—peace at home, and the kind of peace in other lands which will not jeopardize our peace at home.

We have certain ideas and certain ideals of national safety, and we must act to preserve that safety today, and to preserve the safety of our children in future years.

That safety is and will be bound up with the safety of the Western Hemisphere and of the seas adjacent thereto. We seek to keep war from our own firesides by keeping war from coming to the Americas. . . .

This nation will remain a neutral nation, but I cannot ask that every American remain neutral in thought as well. Even a neutral has a right to take account of facts. Even a neutral cannot be asked to close his mind or his conscience.

I have said not once, but many times, that I have seen war and that I hate war. I say that again and again.

I hope the United States will keep out of this war. I believe that it will. And I give you assurance and reassurance that every effort of your Government will be directed toward that end.

As long as it remains within my power to prevent, there will be no black-out of peace in the United States.

Roosevelt's "Arsenal of Democracy" Address, 29 December 1940

With France occupied by the Nazis and Britain anticipating a German invasion, Roosevelt in late 1940 urged the nation toward greater participation in the war. In a fireside chat broadcast on 29 December 1940, he defined Great Britain's continued ability to fight Germany as vital to America's national security. Despite continuing protests by isolationists, this speech ultimately inspired the passage of lend-lease legislation, which enabled Roosevelt "to sell, transfer title to, exchange, lease, lend, or otherwise dispose of war matériel to any country whose defense the President deems vital to the defense of the United States." Selected from The Public Papers and Addresses of Franklin D. Roosevelt, 1940, War—and Aid to Democracies, *comp. Samuel I. Rosenman (New York, 1941), 633–36, 638–41, 643–44.*

My friends:

This is not a fireside chat on war. It is a talk on national security; because the nub of the whole purpose of your President is to keep you now, and your children later, and your grandchildren much later, out of a last-ditch war for the preservation of

American independence and all the things that American independence means to you and to me and to ours. . . .

Never before since Jamestown and Plymouth Rock has our American civilization been in such danger as now.

For, on September 27, 1940, by an agreement signed in Berlin, three powerful nations, two in Europe and one in Asia, joined themselves together in the threat that if the United States of America interfered with or blocked the expansion program of these three nations—a program aimed at world control—they would unite in ultimate action against the United States.

The Nazi masters of Germany have made it clear that they intend not only to dominate all life and thought in their own country, but also to enslave the whole of Europe, and then to use the resources of Europe to dominate the rest of the world. . . .

In view of the nature of this undeniable threat, it can be asserted, properly and categorically, that the United States has no right or reason to encourage talk of peace, until the day shall come when there is a clear intention on the part of the aggressor nations to abandon all thought of dominating or conquering the world.

At this moment, the forces of the states that are leagued against all peoples who live in freedom, are being held away from our shores. The Germans and the Italians are being blocked on the other side of the Atlantic by the British, and by the Greeks, and by thousands of soldiers and sailors who were able to escape from subjugated countries. In Asia, the Japanese are being engaged by the Chinese nation in another great defense. . . .

Does anyone seriously believe that we need to fear attack anywhere in the Americas while a free Britain remains our most powerful naval neighbor in the Atlantic? Does anyone seriously believe, on the other hand, that we could rest easy if the Axis powers were our neighbors there?

If Great Britain goes down, the Axis powers will control the continents of Europe, Asia, Africa, Australasia, and the high seas—and they will be in a position to bring enormous military and naval resources against this hemisphere. It is no exaggeration to say that all of us, in all the Americas, would be living at the

---

point of a gun—a gun loaded with explosive bullets, economic as well as military.

We should enter upon a new and terrible era in which the whole world, our hemisphere included, would be run by threats of brute force. To survive in such a world, we would have to convert ourselves permanently into a militaristic power on the basis of war economy.

Some of us like to believe that even if Great Britain falls, we are still safe, because of the broad expanse of the Atlantic and of the Pacific.

But the width of those oceans is not what it was in the days of clipper ships. . . . Even today we have planes that could fly from the British Isles to New England and back again without refueling. And remember that the range of the modern bomber is ever being increased. . . .

The experience of the past two years has proven beyond doubt that no nation can appease the Nazis. No man can tame a tiger into a kitten by stroking it. There can be no appeasement with ruthlessness. There can be no reasoning with an incendiary bomb. We know now that a nation can have peace with the Nazis only at the price of total surrender.

Even the people of Italy have been forced to become accomplices of the Nazis; but at this moment they do not know how soon they will be embraced to death by their allies.

The American appeasers ignore the warning to be found in the fate of Austria, Czechoslovakia, Poland, Norway, Belgium, the Netherlands, Denmark, and France. . . .

With all their [the Nazis] vaunted efficiency, with all their parade of pious purpose in this war, there are still in their background the concentration camp and the servants of God in chains.

The history of recent years proves that shootings and chains and concentration camps are not simply the transient tools but the very altars of modern dictatorships. They may talk of a "new order" in the world, but what they have in mind is only a revival of the oldest and worst tyranny. In that there is no liberty, no religion, no hope.

The proposed "new order" is . . . not a Government based upon the consent of the governed. It is not a union of ordinary, self-respecting men and women to protect themselves and their freedom and their dignity from oppression. It is an unholy alliance of power and pelf to dominate and enslave the human race.

The British people and their allies today are conducting an active war against this unholy alliance. Our own future security is greatly dependent on the outcome of that fight. Our ability to "keep out of war" is going to be affected by that outcome.

Thinking in terms of today and tomorrow, I make the direct statement to the American people that there is far less chance of the United States getting into war, if we do all we can now to support the nations defending themselves against attack by the Axis than if we acquiesce in their defeat, submit tamely to an Axis victory, and wait our turn to be the object of attack in another war later on.

If we are to be completely honest with ourselves, we must admit that there is risk in any course we may take. But I deeply believe that the great majority of our people agree that the course that I advocate involves the least risk now and the greatest hope for world peace in the future.

The people of Europe who are defending themselves do not ask us to do their fighting. They ask us for the implements of war, the planes, the tanks, the guns, the freighters which will enable them to fight for their liberty and for our security. Emphatically we must get these weapons to them in sufficient volume and quickly enough, so that we and our children will be saved the agony and suffering of war which others have had to endure. . . .

Our national policy is not directed toward war. Its sole purpose is to keep war away from our country and our people.

Democracy's fight against world conquest is being greatly aided, and must be more greatly aided, by the rearmament of the United States and by sending every ounce and every ton of munitions and supplies that we can possibly spare to help the defenders who are in the front lines. It is no more unneutral for us to do that than it is for Sweden, Russia and other nations near Germany, to send steel and ore and oil and other war materials into Germany every day in the week. . . .

We must be the great arsenal of democracy. For us this is an emergency as serious as war itself. We must apply ourselves to our task with the same resolution, the same sense of urgency, the same spirit of patriotism and sacrifice as we would show were we at war.

We have furnished the British great material support and we will furnish far more in the future. . . .

We have no excuse for defeatism. We have every good reason for hope—hope for peace, hope for the defense of our civilization and for the building of a better civilization in the future.

I have the profound conviction that the American people are now determined to put forth a mightier effort than they have ever yet made to increase our production of all the implements of defense, to meet the threat to our democratic faith.

As President of the United States I call for that national effort. I call for it in the name of this nation which we love and honor and which we are privileged and proud to serve. I call upon our people with absolute confidence that our common cause will greatly succeed.

Roosevelt Justifies "Shoot on Sight," 11 September 1941

In 1941, German submarines attacked American merchant ships that were transporting war matériel to the British Empire and the U.S.S. Greer, *a destroyer that had provided the British navy with detailed information on German U-boat locations. In an address on 11 September 1941, Roosevelt publicized these incidents in order to enrage the public against Germany and thereby build support for American involvement in the war. In this speech, Roosevelt committed the United States Navy to escort convoys of merchant ships of all nations halfway across the Atlantic Ocean and to "shoot on sight" any German submarines. Taken from* The Public Papers and Addresses of Franklin D. Roosevelt, 1941, The Call to Battle Stations, *comp. Samuel I. Rosenman (New York, 1950), 384–91.*

THE Navy Department of the United States has reported to me that on the morning of September fourth the United States destroyer *Greer*, proceeding in full daylight toward Iceland, had

---

reached a point southeast of Greenland. She was carrying American mail to Iceland. She was flying the American flag. Her identity as an American ship was unmistakable.

She was then and there attacked by . . . a German submarine. The submarine deliberately fired a torpedo at the *Greer*, followed later by another torpedo attack. In spite of what Hitler's propaganda bureau has invented, and in spite of what any American obstructionist organization may prefer to believe, I tell you the blunt fact that the German submarine fired first upon this American destroyer without warning, and with deliberate design to sink her.

Our destroyer, at the time, was in waters which the Government of the United States had declared to be waters of self-defense— surrounding outposts of American protection in the Atlantic.

In the North of the Atlantic, outposts have been established by us in Iceland, in Greenland, in Labrador and in Newfoundland. Through these waters there pass many ships of many flags. They bear food and other supplies to civilians; and they bear matériel of war, for which the people of the United States are spending billions of dollars, and which, by Congressional action, they have declared to be essential for the defense of our own land.

The United States destroyer, when attacked, was proceeding on a legitimate mission. . . .

This was piracy—piracy legally and morally. It was not the first nor the last act of piracy which the Nazi Government has committed against the American flag in this war. For attack has followed attack.

A few months ago an American flag merchant ship, the *Robin Moor*, was sunk by a Nazi submarine in the middle of the South Atlantic, under circumstances violating long-established international law and violating every principle of humanity. The passengers and the crew were forced into open boats hundreds of miles from land, in direct violation of international agreements signed by nearly all Nations including the Government of Germany. No apology, no allegation of mistake, no offer of reparations has come from the Nazi Government.

In July, 1941, an American battleship in North American waters was followed by a submarine which for a long time sought to maneuver itself into a position of attack. The periscope of the submarine was clearly seen. No British or American submarines were within hundreds of miles of this spot at the time, so the nationality of the submarine is clear.

Five days ago a United States Navy ship on patrol picked up three survivors of an American-owned ship operating under the flag of our sister Republic of Panama—the *S.S. Sessa.* On August seventeenth, she had been first torpedoed without warning, and then shelled, near Greenland, while carrying civilian supplies to Iceland. It is feared that the other members of her crew have been drowned. In view of the established presence of German submarines in this vicinity, there can be no reasonable doubt as to the identity of the flag of the attacker.

Five days ago, another United States merchant ship, the *Steel Seafarer,* was sunk by a German aircraft in the Red Sea two hundred and twenty miles south of Suez. She was bound for an Egyptian port. . . .

It would be unworthy of a great Nation to exaggerate an isolated incident, or to become inflamed by some one act of violence. But it would be inexcusable folly to minimize such incidents in the face of evidence which makes it clear that the incident is not isolated, but is part of a general plan. . . .

. . . It is the Nazi design to abolish the freedom of the seas, and to acquire absolute control and domination of these seas for themselves.

For with control of the seas in their own hands, the way can obviously become clear for their next step—domination of the United States—domination of the Western Hemisphere by force of arms. . . .

To be ultimately successful in world mastery, Hitler knows that he must get control of the seas. He must first destroy the bridge of ships which we are building across the Atlantic and over which we shall continue to roll the implements of war to help destroy him, to destroy all his works in the end. He must wipe out our patrol on sea and in the air if he is to do it. He must silence the British Navy. . . .

Generation after generation, America has battled for the general policy of the freedom of the seas. And that policy is a very simple one—but a basic, a fundamental one. It means that no Nation has the right to make the broad oceans of the world at great distances from the actual theater of land war unsafe for the commerce of others.

That has been our policy, proved time and time again, in all our history. . . .

And I am sure that even now the Nazis are waiting to see whether the United States will by silence give them the green light to go ahead on this path of destruction. . . .

We have sought no shooting war with Hitler. We do not seek it now. But neither do we want peace so much, that we are willing to pay for it by permitting him to attack our naval and merchant ships while they are on legitimate business. . . .

But when you see a rattlesnake poised to strike, you do not wait until he has struck before you crush him.

These Nazi submarines and raiders are the rattlesnakes of the Atlantic. They are a menace to the free pathways of the high seas. They are a challenge to our sovereignty. They hammer at our most precious rights when they attack ships of the American flag—symbols of our independence, our freedom, our very life. . . .

The time for active defense is now. . . .

. . . Their very presence in any waters which America deems vital to its defense constitutes an attack.

In the waters which we deem necessary for our defense, American naval vessels and American planes will no longer wait until Axis submarines lurking under the water, or Axis raiders on the surface of the sea, strike their deadly blow—first.

Upon our naval and air patrol—now operating in large number over a vast expanse of the Atlantic Ocean—falls the duty of maintaining the American policy of freedom of the seas—now. That means, very simply, very clearly, that our patrolling vessels and planes will protect all merchant ships—not only American ships but ships of any flag—engaged in commerce in our defensive waters. They will protect them from submarines; they will protect them from surface raiders.

This situation is not new. The second President of the United States, John Adams, ordered the United States Navy to clean out European privateers and European ships of war which were infesting the Caribbean and South American waters, destroying American commerce.

The third President of the United States, Thomas Jefferson, ordered the United States Navy to end the attacks being made upon American and other ships by the corsairs of the Nations of North Africa.

My obligation as President is historic; it is clear. It is inescapable.

It is no act of war on our part when we decide to protect the seas that are vital to American defense. The aggression is not ours. Ours is solely defense.

But let this warning be clear. From now on, if German or Italian vessels of war enter the waters, the protection of which is necessary for American defense, they do so at their own peril.

The orders which I have given as Commander in Chief of the United States Army and Navy are to carry out that policy—at once.

America First Committee Charges Roosevelt with Fighting a One-Man War

Roosevelt's addresses convinced many Americans to endorse an interventionist policy toward the war in Europe. But diehard isolationists vigorously resisted what they perceived as an inexorable slide toward war by seeking to rally the public against the president. The isolationist America First Committee, in a treatise published on 13 September 1941, disputed Roosevelt's account of the American-German naval incidents and demanded that Congress check his war-making authority. Excerpted from the America First Committee's newsletter Did You Know 22 *(September 13, 1941): 1–5.*

In his speech on September 11, 1941, President Roosevelt informed the nation that, without consultation with, or approval by, the Congress of the United States, he had ordered our naval and air patrols to clear all German and Italian warships from any waters considered vital to American defense, and had, in effect, ordered our armed forces to "shoot on sight." . . . His asserted justification for this sudden move, admittedly involving danger of involvement in a "shooting war," arose out of the sinking of three merchant ships and attacks on two American warships. . . .

Reprinted from *Did You Know*, #22, prepared by America First Committee Research Bureau, September 13, 1941.

. . . [The] important criticisms of the President's speech are these: 1) shooting war is not justified; 2) it circumvents the spirit of the Neutrality Act and the Lease-Lend law; 3) the doctrine which the President calls "freedom of the seas" is really "freedom to aid one country at war without interference from that country's enemies"; 4) it takes the war-making power away from Congress.

Examination of the circumstances under which occurred the attacks upon American ships cited by the President, demonstrates clearly that they fail utterly to justify participation in a "shooting war." The three merchant ships were the Robin Moor, the Steel Seafarer and the Sessa. The Robin Moor was sunk in the South Atlantic while carrying contraband to British South Africa, a country at war. . . .

The Steel Seafarer was sunk without loss of life in the Red Sea, some 12,000 miles from the United States, while carrying war supplies for Britain, a country at war. . . .

The Sessa was not even sailing under the American flag when sunk. . . . [The ship] had been transferred to the flag of Panama in order that she might be used to carry supplies into war zones in clear violation of the intent of the Neutrality Act. . . .

The attacks upon the destroyer Greer . . . were of course unjustified. But those attacks arose because of the one-man policy pursued by the President of occupying Iceland (nearer to the heart of the European war zone . . . [than] to the United States) and of keeping American troops there along with the British. . . . That is a policy whose implementation requires the use of American naval vessels for patrol purposes in order to keep the surrounding waters clear. It is inevitable that they will come into conflict with Nazi warships which are seeking British ships in those waters, part of the Nazi-declared war zone. . . . Certainly these five attacks, resulting in no loss of American lives on any ship operating under the American flag, do not justify American participation in a "shooting" war. . . .

Nor can the President's "shoot on sight" order be justified, as he claims, as necessary to protect "freedom of the seas." It must be recalled that American armed protection is to be given, not only to American ships, but also to the ships of any flag, and that the waters in which that protection is to be given extend . . . to any waters the President chooses to declare vital to our "defense." This would enable our fleet to give what amounts to "convoy protection" to British ships or the ships of any other allied nation, as well as American ships, carrying war supplies for Britain or Russia or China. It would enable American patrols even to convoy British ships right into English ports. . . .

. . . But there is a remedy, a means of checking the drive towards an all-out shooting war. Congress still has the constitutional power to assert its control over the war power. . . . Congress can still assert its control over the pursestrings. . . . Congress can still investigate and bring to the public view the orders given our patrols and their implications. . . . Assertion by the American people of their will to remain out of war, and of their intention to retain our constitutional form of government, can compel the repudiation of Presidential war moves. It is late, but not yet too late.

Roosevelt's War Message, 8 December 1941

Isolationists who opposed Roosevelt's policy toward the war were overwhelmed by a surge of emotional public opinion favoring immediate entry into World War II, a surge triggered by the surprise Japanese attack on U.S. forces at Pearl Harbor and other locations in the Pacific Ocean on 7 December 1941. The next day, Roosevelt asked Congress to declare war on Japan, and Congress complied within an hour by votes of 82-0 in the Senate and 388-1 in the House. Days later the United States also traded declarations of war against Germany and Italy. Pearl Harbor thus ended the debate that had raged between isolationists and interventionists since the 1930s. Roosevelt's war address is taken from The Public Papers and Addresses of Franklin D. Roosevelt, 1941, The Call to Battle Stations, *comp. Samuel I. Rosenman (New York, 1950), 514–15.*

Mr. Vice President, and Mr. Speaker, and Members of the Senate and House of Representatives:

YESTERDAY, December 7, 1941—a date which will live in infamy—the United States of America was suddenly and deliberately attacked by naval and air forces of the Empire of Japan.

The United States was at peace with that Nation and, at the solicitation of Japan, was still in conversation with its Government and its Emperor looking toward the maintenance of peace in the Pacific. Indeed, one hour after Japanese air squadrons had commenced bombing in the American Island of Oahu, the Japanese Ambassador to the United States and his colleague delivered to our Secretary of State a formal reply to a recent American message. And while this reply stated that it seemed useless to continue the existing diplomatic negotiations, it contained no threat or hint of war or of armed attack.

It will be recorded that the distance of Hawaii from Japan makes it obvious that the attack was deliberately planned many days or even weeks ago. During the intervening time the Japanese Government has deliberately sought to deceive the United States by false statements and expressions of hope for continued peace.

The attack yesterday on the Hawaiian Islands has caused severe damage to American naval and military forces. I regret to tell you that very many American lives have been lost. In addition American ships have been reported torpedoed on the high seas between San Francisco and Honolulu.

Yesterday the Japanese Government also launched an attack against Malaya.

Last night Japanese forces attacked Hong Kong.

Last night Japanese forces attacked Guam.

Last night Japanese forces attacked the Philippine Islands.

Last night the Japanese attacked Wake Island.

And this morning the Japanese attacked Midway Island.

Japan has, therefore, undertaken a surprise offensive extending throughout the Pacific area. The facts of yesterday and today speak for themselves. The people of the United States have already formed their opinions and well understand the implications to the very life and safety of our Nation.

As Commander in Chief of the Army and Navy I have directed that all measures be taken for our defense.

But always will our whole Nation remember the character of the onslaught against us.

No matter how long it may take us to overcome this premeditated invasion, the American people in their righteous might will win through to absolute victory.

I believe that I interpret the will of the Congress and of the people when I assert that we will not only defend ourselves to the uttermost but will make it very certain that this form of treachery shall never again endanger us.

Hostilities exist. There is no blinking at the fact that our people, our territory, and our interests are in grave danger.

With confidence in our armed forces—with the unbounding determination of our people—we will gain the inevitable triumph—so help us God.

I ask that the Congress declare that since the unprovoked and dastardly attack by Japan on Sunday, December 7, 1941, a state of war has existed between the United States and the Japanese Empire.

Questions

1. *Do you think that Roosevelt was correct in believing that Nazi Germany posed a threat to the national security of the United States? Why or why not?*
2. *How do you explain the different views of the isolationists and the president about events and their significance to American security?*
3. *What dimension of the isolationists' arguments seem most convincing? What were President Roosevelt's most effective arguments for greater American involvement in the war?*

FURTHER READING

The isolationists' impact on American diplomacy during World War II is discussed in In Danger Undaunted: The Anti-Interventionist Movement of 1940–1941 as Revealed in the Papers of the America First Committee, *ed. Justus D. Doenecke (Stanford, 1990); Wayne S. Cole,* Roosevelt and the Isolationists, 1932–45 (*Lincoln, Nebraska, 1983); and Manfred Jonas,* Isolationism in America, 1935–1941 *(Ithaca, 1966). Charles A. Beard made a strong isolationist argument about Roosevelt's World War II diplomacy in* President Roosevelt and the Coming of the War, 1941: A Study in Appearances and Realities *(New Haven, 1948). Frederick W. Marks III developed a related argument in* Wind Over Sand: The Diplomacy of Franklin Roosevelt *(Athens, Georgia, 1988). For internationalist viewpoints see Herbert Feis,* The Road to Pearl Harbor: The Coming of the War Between the United States and Japan *(Princeton, 1950), and Roberta Wohlstetter,* Pearl Harbor: Warning and Decision *(Stanford, 1962). Historians who have produced more nuanced accounts include Akira Iriye,* Power and Culture: The Japanese-American War, 1941–1945 *(Cambridge, Massachusetts, 1981); and Waldo Heinrichs,* Threshold of War: Franklin D. Roosevelt and American Entry into World War II *(New York, 1988). An abridged version of Pearl Harbor investigations is Roland H. Worth, Jr.,* Pearl Harbor: Selected Testimonies, Fully Indexed, from the Congressional Hearings (1945–1946) and Prior Investigations of the Events Leading Up to the Attack *(Jefferson, North Carolina, 1993).*

The Expulsion and Relocation of Japanese Americans in World War II

Michael Les Benedict

Introduction

On 7 December 1941, following years of growing tension between Japan and the United States, Japan launched a surprise bombing of Pearl Harbor, the home port of the United States Pacific fleet. Japan's allies, Germany and Italy, quickly joined it in declaring war on the United States, bringing the Americans fully into World War II.

Claiming that Japanese and Japanese Americans on the Pacific coast were sympathetic to Japan and preparing to aid Japanese air raids and even invasion, many people there called for their expulsion from the coast. Within two months the government of the United States ordered all persons of Japanese ancestry—both aliens and "non-aliens" (that is, citizens)—to leave a large swath of territory along the Pacific coast. This included both Japanese immigrants (called Issei or "first generation") and their children (Nisei or "second generation"). The small number previously identified as pro-Japan by U.S. intelligence agencies were interned at special locations. Over 100,000 others who had nowhere to go and no means of support outside of their homes in California, western Oregon, and western Washington were expelled from the region and taken to "relocation" camps in a process military authorities called "controlled evacuation." While German Americans had been subject to harassment during World War I, and both German and Italian aliens were interned during World War II, the scope of the forced Japanese evacuation was unprecedented. Moreover, unlike German and Italian immigrants, who could acquire American citizenship after five years' residence, Japanese immigrants had been barred from acquiring American citizenship by laws that limited naturalization to white immigrants and those of African descent.

After the war, more and more Americans came to doubt the practical and legal justification for wrenching Japanese and Japanese Americans from their homes and sending them to the relocation camps. Many of the relocated Japanese were outraged; after the war some returned to Japan rather than continue to live in the United States. The vast majority who remained did little to protest their treatment after the war, but by the 1970s many Japanese Americans demanded apologies and restitution. After a long struggle, Congress passed the Civil Liberties Act of 1988, acknowledging the injustice of the "controlled evacuation" and making reparations. The readings that follow describe the evacuation and relocation program, the reaction of the people subjected to it, life in the camps, and the demand for redress.

The Japanese Relocation: Documents and First-Hand Accounts

After their release from the relocation camps, few of the residents were willing to describe their experiences. For some the memory was too painful. Many adult Japanese considered their time in the camps to be a mark of shame, to be hidden. Moreover, many Japanese and Japanese Americans had been taught not to express anger openly. But over time, Japanese Americans—especially the younger generation—began to describe their experiences and express their outrage. The following documents and first-hand accounts describe their experiences and the actions of the United States government.

Executive Order 9066

After several months of debate within his administration, on 19 February 1942, President Franklin D. Roosevelt signed an executive order authorizing the military to relocate the Japanese and Japanese Americans living on the West coast. Did the president allege any actual evidence of sabotage or disloyalty? Excerpted from U.S. House of Representatives, Report of the Select Committee Investigating National Defense Migration *(hereafter cited as* Tolan Committee*), House Report No. 2124, 77th Cong., 2d sess. (1942), 314.*

WHEREAS the successful prosecution of the war requires every possible protection against espionage and against sabotage to national defense material, national defense premises, and national defense utilities. . . .

NOW, THEREFORE, by virtue of the authority vested in me as President of the United States, and Commander in Chief of the Army and Navy, I hereby authorize and direct the Secretary of War, and the Military Commanders who he may from time to time designate, whenever he or any designated Commander deems such action necessary or desirable, to prescribe military areas in such places and of such extent as he or the appropriate Military Commander may determine, from which any or all persons may be excluded, and with respect to which, the right of any person to enter, remain in, or leave shall be subject to whatever restrictions the Secretary of War or the appropriate Military Commander may impose in his discretion. The Secretary of War is hereby authorized to provide for residents of any such area who are excluded therefrom, such transportation, food, shelter, and other accommodations as may be necessary, in the judgment of the Secretary of War or the said Military Commander, and until other arrangements are made, to accomplish the purpose of this order.

An Evacuation Order

The following was the first of the evacuation orders that forced over 100,000 Japanese Americans from their homes on the West coast and led to their relocation to camps in the interior. Abridged from Tolan Committee, House Report No. 2124, *332–33.*

CIVILIAN EXCLUSION ORDER NO. 1
HEADQUARTERS, WESTERN DEFENSE COMMAND AND FOURTH ARMY,
Presidio of San Francisco, California, March 24, 1942.

1. Pursuant to the provisions of Public Proclamations Nos. 1 and 2, this headquarters, dated March 2, 1942, and March 16, 1942, respectively, it is hereby ordered that all persons of Japanese ancestry, including aliens and nonaliens, be excluded from that portion of Military Area No. 1 described as "Bainbridge Island," in the State of Washington,

on or before 12 o'clock noon, P. W. T., of the 30th day of March 1942.

2. Such exclusion will be accomplished in the following manner:
   (a) Such persons may, with permission, on or prior to March 29, 1942, proceed to any approved place of their choosing beyond the limits of Military Area No. 1 and the prohibited zones established by said proclamations or hereafter similarly established, subject only to such regulations as to travel and change of residence as are now or may hereafter be prescribed by this headquarters and by the United States Attorney General. Persons affected hereby will not be permitted to take up residence or remain within the region designated as Military Area No. 1 or the prohibited zones heretofore or hereafter established. Persons affected hereby are required on leaving or entering Bainbridge Island to register and obtain a permit at the Civil Control Office to be established on said Island at or near the ferryboat landing.
   (b) On March 30, 1942, all such persons who have not removed themselves from Bainbridge Island in accordance with Paragraph 1 hereof shall, in accordance with instructions of the Commanding General, Northwestern Sector, report to the Civil Control Office referred to above on Bainbridge Island for evacuation in such manner and to such place or places as shall then be prescribed.
   (c) A responsible member of each family affected by this order and each individual living alone so affected will report to the Civil Control Office described above between 8 a. m. and 5 p. m. Wednesday, March 25, 1942.
3. Any person affected by this order who fails to comply with any of its provisions or who is found on Bainbridge Island after 12 o'clock noon, P. W. T., of March 30, 1942, will be subject to the criminal penalties provided by Public Law No. 503, 77th Congress, approved March 21, 1942, entitled "An Act to Provide a Penalty for Violation of Restrictions or Orders with Respect to Persons Entering, Remaining in, Leaving, or Committing Any Act in Military Areas or

Zone", and alien Japanese will be subject to immediate apprehension and internment.

J. L. DE WITT,
Lieutenant General,
U.S. Army, Commanding

The Uchida Family is Evacuated

Like many other community leaders, Yoshiko Uchida's father, Dwight Takashi Uchida, the manager of a leading department store serving the Japanese community in Berkeley, California, was arrested and interned immediately after the bombing of Pearl Harbor. His family, including his daughter Yoshiko, a student at the University of California, remained in Berkeley until ordered to evacuate on 21 April 1942. From Yoshiko Uchida, Desert Exile: The Uprooting of a Japanese American Family *(Seattle, 1982), 58–60, 62.*

Each day we watched the papers for the evacuation orders covering the Berkeley area. On April 21, the headlines read: "Japs Given Evacuation Orders Here." I felt numb as I read the front page story. "Moving swiftly, without any advance notice, the Western Defense Command today ordered Berkeley's estimated 1,319 Japanese, aliens and citizens alike, evacuated to the Tanforan Assembly Center by noon, May 1." (This gave us exactly ten days' notice.) "Evacuees will report at the Civil Control Station being set up in Pilgrim Hall of the First Congregational Church . . . between the hours of 8:00 A.M. and 5:00 P.M. next Saturday and Sunday."

This was Exclusion Order Number Nineteen, which was to uproot us from our homes and send us into the Tanforan Assembly Center in San Bruno, a hastily converted racetrack.

All Japanese were required to register before the departure date, and my sister, as head of the family, went to register for us.

She came home with baggage and name tags that were to bear our family number and be attached to all our belongings. From that day on we became Family Number 13453.

Although we had been preparing for the evacuation orders, still when they were actually issued, it was a sickening shock.

"Ten days! We have only ten days to get ready!" my sister said frantically. Each day she rushed about, not only taking care of our business affairs, but, as our only driver, searching for old crates and cartons for packing, and taking my mother on various errands as well.

Mama still couldn't seem to believe that we would have to leave. "How can we clear out in ten days a house we've lived in for fifteen years?" she asked sadly.

But my sister and I had no answers for her.

Mama had always been a saver, and she had a tremendous accumulation of possessions. Her frugal upbringing had caused her to save string, wrapping paper, bags, jars, boxes, even bits of silk thread left over from sewing, which were tied end to end and rolled up into a silk ball. Tucked away in the corners of her desk and bureau drawers were such things as small stuffed animals, wooden toys, *kokeshi* dolls, marbles, and even a half-finished pair of socks she was knitting for a teddy bear's paw. Many of these were "found objects" that the child in her couldn't bear to discard, but they often proved useful in providing diversion for some fidgety visiting child. These were the simple things to dispose of.

More difficult were the boxes that contained old letters from her family and friends, our old report cards from the first grade on, dozens of albums of family photographs, notebooks and sketch pads full of our childish drawings, valentines and Christmas cards we had made for our parents, innumerable guest books filled with the signatures and friendly words of those who had once been entertained. These were the things my mother couldn't bear to throw away. Because we didn't own our house, we could leave nothing behind. We had to clear the house completely, and everything in it had either to be packed for storage or thrown out.

We surveyed with desperation the vast array of dishes, lacquerware, silverware, pots and pans, books, paintings, porcelain and pottery, furniture, linens, rugs, records, curtains, garden tools, cleaning equipment, and clothing that filled our house. We put up a sign in our window reading, "Living room sofa and chair for sale." We sold things we should have kept and packed away foolish trifles we should have discarded. We sold our refrigerator, our dining room set, two sofas, an easy chair, and a brand new vacuum cleaner with attachments. Without a sensible scheme in our heads, and lacking the practical judgment of my father, the three of us packed frantically and sold recklessly. Although the young people of our church did what they could to help us, we felt desperate as the deadline approached. Our only thought was to get the house emptied in time, for we knew the Army would not wait.

Organizations such as the First Congregational Church of Berkeley were extremely helpful in anticipating the needs of the panic-stricken Japanese and provided immediate, practical assistance. Families of the church offered storage space to those who needed it, and we took several pieces of furniture to be stored in the basement of one such home. Another non-Japanese friend offered to take our books and stored more than eight large cartons for us. In typical Japanese fashion, my mother took gifts to express her gratitude to each person who helped us. . . .

By now I had to leave the university, as did all the other Nisei students. We had stayed as long as we could to get credit for the spring semester, which was crucial for those of us who were seniors. My professors gave me a final grade on the basis of my midterm grades and the university granted all Nisei indefinite leaves of absence.

During the last few weeks on campus, my friends and I became sentimental and took pictures of each other at favorite campus sites. The war had jolted us into a crisis whose impact was too enormous for us to fully comprehend, and we needed these small remembrances of happier times to take with us as we went our separate ways to various government camps throughout California.

A Description of a Camp

Minoru Yasui, a California-born lawyer and U.S. Army reserve officer, refused to report for relocation. He was taken from his home in Oregon, interned with 3,000 other Japanese Americans in Portland for five months, and then transported to the Minidoka camp in Idaho. Abridged

The belongings of relocated Japanese and Japanese-Americans, piled behind the barbed-wire fence at the Salinas Relocation Center. (Courtesy of The Library of Congress.)

from John Tateishi, And Justice for All: An Oral History of the Japanese American Detention Camps *(New York, 1984), 76–77.*

We arrived late afternoon, at some isolated siding in the desert area, north of Twin Falls, although we did not know where we were. No houses were in sight, no trees or anything green—only scrubby sagebrush and an occasional low catcus, and mostly dry, baked earth. There was a slight rise to the north, and one could not see to the horizon.

Baggage was unloaded and piled up next to the road, and Army trucks were rolling in, kicking up huge clouds of dust. People came off the train, were lined up and loaded into the trucks, and went off into the distance. The seats were hard planks, and after riding all day on the train, most were sore and tired.

We had left the dark, dank confines of a livestock barn hoping to breathe the fresh, open air. But because the virgin desert had been bulldozed and disturbed by men and machinery, instead of

---

fresh air, we got to breathe dust. I remember groups of women getting off the train, looking bewildered. After the lush greenness of the Willamette Valley, to see the sterile, dusty desert which was to be our home "for the duration," many sat on the baggage in the middle of nowhere and wept. . . .

We saw again the barbed-wire fences, the watchtowers, guard houses, the MP detachments, the administration housing, warehouse areas, and block after block of black, tar-paper barracks, about 120 feet long and about 20 feet wide. I remember that at least the mess halls and kitchens were completed, and that evening we had hot meals, perhaps spam and canned vegetables. The barracks were supplied with army cots with metal springs, and we got padding-filled ticks and a couple of army blankets. There was a potbellied stove, and each block had a coal depot. One bare bulb hung from the center of the room. There were real composition-board ceilings but the walls were unfinished with open two-by-four studs. The floor was wood, and single layered, so one could see the earth below, through the cracks. The smaller units for childless couples were on the end of the building, with two windows on each side, or a total of four windows. There was only one entrance to each unit. No chairs or tables were furnished; however, later the evacuees scrounged scrap lumber and built chairs, tables, bunk beds, dressers, and other things. But only those who were handy with tools could do this. The internee wives with small children were not always able to furnish their rooms comfortably. There was, however, a great deal of sharing and exchange going on.

The Loyalty Questionnaire

In February 1943 the government began to register the people it had relocated to camps. To facilitate the release of those considered loyal and to encourage loyal Japanese Americans to enlist in the armed forces, the government prepared a questionnaire to accompany registration. Question 27 asked Nisei men if they were willing to serve in the armed forces in combat wherever ordered. Question 28 amounted to a loyalty oath—asking respondents to reaffirm allegiance to the United States and renounce allegiance to Japan. In the camps, Japanese Americans divided bitterly about how to respond. In the end about 5,000 refused to take the oath of allegiance and refused to express a willingness to fight for the United States against "any or all" of its enemies, including Japan. Extremists among the refusers worked to foment resistance to American authorities among camp residents, resorting at times to violence and intimidation. The following describes how Frank Chuman, a California-born law student in the Manzanar camp in the California desert, anguished over what to do. Taken from John Tateishi, And Justice for All: An Oral History of the Japanese American Detention Camps, *230–32.*

I didn't get the full brunt of the anti-Japanese hostility which was a hell of a good thing, because when I went to Manzanar there was a delayed reaction for me. What the hell am I doing in camp? I thought. While I was very busy working in the hospital, I said to myself, Why should the United States Government doubt our loyalty to the United States? We haven't done anything to justify this kind of treatment. Certainly not myself and certainly none of the others that I know of. And yet here I am in a camp of ten thousand people—men, women, and children. So I began to think to myself, because I had studied law—constitutional law and constitutional rights and due process and equal protection and all the rest of it—Jesus Christ, we've been deprived of our constitutional rights. There's been no accusations against me, and yet I'm suspect and I'm arbitrarily told to go into a camp. It's completely in violation of my rights. . . . And I really got angry and very, very upset at the United States Government for doing this kind of thing to not only me, but all Japanese Americans. I really got upset.

The Army recruiting team came into Manzanar around the early part of 1943. We had a big meeting in this mess hall of all persons eligible for military duty with two white soldiers and a person of Japanese ancestry, and this guy was trying to persuade us all to volunteer for the Army, and I'm not too sure whether I got up and spoke back to him or whether I said it in my own mind, but I said, "Why should we fight for the United States Government as soldiers, when the United States Government distrusts us? Why do they now want us to serve when they consider us to be disloyal? Why do they want us to serve when they have taken us out of our homes and schools and businesses, and now they want us to become loyal to the United States? It doesn't make sense, and so far as I'm concerned I'm not going to do anything to go into the

United States Army until the United States Government does something to remedy this unjust situation." I cannot remember whether I stood up and said it or whether I felt it.

In any event, that's the way it was. In the latter part of 1943, this questionnaire came out sponsored by the WRA, and in that questionnaire it had something like "request for relocation" as well as the questionnaire. It was in two parts. And there were these questions 27 and 28, "Are you willing to foreswear any allegiance to any foreign potentate and say that you are loyal to the United States?" and, "Are you willing to bear arms for the United States?" The first answer that I gave to both questions was no. I was so goddamned mad at that questionnaire. It was insulting, impugning without any evidence, just from the top down that there was something that made us Japanese Americans suspect in loyalty, allegiance, that we wouldn't fight for the government and saying now you're going to fight. They don't have to push it down my throat—are you willing to bear arms to defend the United States? That's so goddamned obvious that I would do that that it just really made me angry. . . .

I did not remain a no-no, because all of a sudden I thought to myself, after I had said that, I regretted it, because it wasn't my true feelings. There was no way that I could hate the United States Government, but I was goddamned angry at them for doing things like that about us.

The Supreme Court Upholds Japanese Relocation: *Korematsu* v. *U.S.* (1944)

Several Japanese Americans resisted the government exclusion orders in order to challenge their constitutionality in the courts. In 1943 the Supreme Court sustained a curfew applying to all people of Japanese ancestry along the Pacific Coast. A year later, to the dismay of civil libertarians, it upheld Executive Order 9066 and the relocation program instituted under its authority. Abridged from Korematsu v. U.S.*, 323 US 214, (1944), 216, 218–20, 233–34, 240, 242.*

Opinion of the Court

It should be noted, to begin with, that all legal restrictions which curtail the civil rights of a single racial group are immediately suspect. That is not to say that all such restrictions are unconstitutional. It is to say that courts must subject them to the most rigid scrutiny. Pressing public necessity may sometimes justify the existence of such restrictions; racial antagonism never can. . . .

. . . [E]xclusion of those of Japanese origin was deemed necessary because of the presence of an unascertained number of disloyal members of the group, most of whom we have no doubt were loyal to this country. It was because we could not reject the finding of the military authorities that it was impossible to bring about an immediate segregation of the disloyal from the loyal that we sustained the validity of the curfew order as applying to the whole group. In the instant case, temporary exclusion of the entire group was rested by the military on the same ground. The judgment that exclusion of the whole group was for the same reason a military imperative answers the contention that the exclusion was in the nature of group punishment based on antagonism to those of Japanese origin. . . .

We uphold the exclusion order as of the time it was made and when the petitioner violated it. . . . In doing so, we are not unmindful of the hardships imposed by it upon a large group of American citizens. . . . Citizenship has its responsibilities as well as its privileges, and in time of war the burden is always heavier. Compulsory exclusion of large groups of citizens from their homes, except under circumstances of direst emergency and peril, is inconsistent with our basic governmental institutions. But when under conditions of modern warfare our shores are threatened by hostile forces, the power to protect must be commensurate with the threatened danger. . . .

MR. JUSTICE MURPHY, dissenting.

This exclusion of "all persons of Japanese ancestry, both alien and non-alien," from the Pacific Coast area on a plea of military necessity in the absence of martial law ought not to be approved. Such exclusion goes over "the very brink of constitutional power" and falls into the ugly abyss of racism. . . .

. . . [I]t is essential that there be definite limits to military discretion, especially where martial law has not been declared.

Individuals must not be left impoverished of their constitutional rights on a plea of military necessity that has neither substance nor support. . . .

. . . No one denies, of course, that there were some disloyal persons of Japanese descent on the Pacific Coast who did all in their power to aid their ancestral land. Similar disloyal activities have been engaged in by many persons of German, Italian and even more pioneer stock in our country. But to infer that examples of individual disloyalty prove group disloyalty and justify discriminatory action against the entire group is to deny that under our system of law individual guilt is the sole basis for deprivation of rights. . . . To give constitutional sanction to that inference in this case, however well intentioned may have been the military command on the Pacific Coast is to adopt one of the cruelest of the rationales used by our enemies to destroy the dignity of the individual and to encourage and open the door to discriminatory actions against other minority groups in the passions of tomorrow. . . .

. . . All residents of this nation are kin in some way by blood or culture to a foreign land. Yet they are primarily and necessarily a part of the new and distinct civilization of the United States. They must accordingly be treated at all times as the heirs of the American experiment and as entitled to all the rights and freedoms guaranteed by the Constitution.

The Government Reinvestigates

In response to agitation by Japanese Americans in the 1970s and renewed public interest in the events surrounding Japanese exclusion and relocation, Congress established a commission to investigate the subject. After taking testimony from those who organized and administered the program, those subjected to it, and historians of it, the Commission concluded that the exclusion and relocation had been unjustified and unjustifiable. It recommended a formal apology and restitution. Excerpted from Personal Justice Denied: Report of the Commission on Wartime Relocation and Internment of Civilians *(Washington, D.C., 1982), 2–3, 18.*

This policy of exclusion, removal and detention was executed against 120,000 people without individual review, and exclusion was continued virtually without regard for their demonstrated loyalty to the United States. Congress was fully aware of and supported the policy of removal and detention; it sanctioned the exclusion by enacting a statue which made criminal the violation of orders issued pursuant to Executive Order 9066. The United States Supreme Court held the exclusion constitutionally permissible in the context of war, but struck down the incarceration of admittedly loyal American citizens on the ground that it was not based on statutory authority.

All this was done despite the fact that not a single documented act of espionage, sabotage or fifth column activity was committed by an American citizen of Japanese ancestry or by a resident Japanese alien on the West Coast.

No mass exclusion or detention, in any part of the country, was ordered against American citizens of German or Italian descent. Official actions against enemy aliens of other nationalities were much more individualized and selective than those imposed on the ethnic Japanese.

The exclusion, removal and detention inflicted tremendous human cost. There was the obvious cost of homes and businesses sold or abandoned under circumstances of great distress, as well as injury to careers and professional advancement. But, most important, there was the loss of liberty and the personal stigma of suspected disloyalty for thousands of people who knew themselves to be devoted to their country's cause and to its ideals but whose repeated protestations of loyalty were discounted—only to be demonstrated beyond any doubt by the record of Nisei solders, who returned from the battlefields of Europe as the most decorated and distinguished combat unit of World War II, and by the thousands of other Nisei who served against the enemy in the Pacific, mostly in military intelligence. The wounds of the exclusion and detention have healed in some respects, but the scars of that experience remain, painfully real in the minds of those who lived through the suffering and deprivation of the camps.

The personal injustice of excluding, removing and detaining loyal American citizens is manifest. Such events are extraordinary and unique in American history. For every citizen and for American public life, they pose haunting questions about our country and its past. . . .

The promulgation of Executive Order 9066 was not justified by military necessity, and the decisions which followed from it—detention, ending detention and ending exclusion—were not driven by analysis of military conditions. The broad historical causes which shaped these decisions were race prejudice, war hysteria and a failure of political leadership. Widespread ignorance of Japanese Americans contributed to a policy conceived in haste and executed in an atmosphere of fear and anger at Japan. A grave injustice was done to American citizens and resident aliens of Japanese ancestry who, without individual review or any probative evidence against them, were excluded, removed and detained by the United States during World War II.

The Civil Liberties Act of 1988

In response to the report of the Commission on Wartime Relocation and Internment of Civilians, on 10 August 1988, Congress passed the Civil Liberties Act of 1988. The act requested the president to issue pardons to those convicted of violating the curfew, exclusion, and relocation orders; authorized restitution in the amount of $20,000 to every person expelled, interned, or relocated; and set up a fund to finance educational programs to inform the public about the expulsion and relocation "so as to prevent the recurrence of any similar event." Taken from U.S. Statutes at Large, *vol. 102, 1988 (1990), 903–4.*

Sec. 2. Statement of the Congress.

(a) With Regard to Individuals of Japanese Ancestry.—The Congress recognizes that, as described by the Commission on Wartime Relocation and Internment of Civilians, a grave injustice was done to both citizens and permanent resident aliens of Japanese ancestry by the evacuation, relocation, and internment of civilians during World War II. As the Commission documents, these actions were carried out without adequate security reasons and without any acts of espionage or sabotage documented by the Commission, and were motivated largely by racial prejudice, wartime hysteria, and a failure of political leadership. The excluded individuals of Japanese ancestry suffered enormous damages, both material and intangible, and there were incalculable losses in education and job training, all of which resulted in significant human suffering for which appropriate compensation has not been made. For these fundamental violations of the basic civil liberties and constitutional rights of these individuals of Japanese ancestry, the Congress apologizes on behalf of the Nation.

Questions

1. *Many non-Japanese tried to help their Japanese and Japanese American neighbors as they were forced to leave the Pacific Coast. Should they have done more? What more could they have done?*
2. *Should the Nisei have resisted the relocation program more forcefully? What might have inhibited such resistance?*
3. *Why did some of the Japanese and Japanese Americans in the relocation camps refuse to reaffirm their allegiance to the United States and refuse to agree to fight in the armed forces when presented with Questions 27 and 28 of the registration questionnaire in 1943? How would you have answered the questions?*
4. *On what basis did the Supreme Court sustain the constitutionality of Japanese expulsion and relocation in* Korematsu *v.* U.S.*? On what basis did Justice Murphy disagree? Do you think an occurrence similar to Japanese relocation could take place in a future time of war? Do you think the Supreme Court might intervene?*
5. *Do you think it was appropriate for Congress to apologize formally for the actions taken during World War II? Do you think the formal apology and the Civil Liberties Act might deter similar actions by government in the future? Explain.*

FURTHER READING

Page Smith, Democracy on Trial: The Japanese American Evacuation and Relocation in World War Two *(New York, 1995) is a balanced chronicle of the events leading up to the relocation of the Japanese and their experiences afterwards. Smith argues that perceived military necessity, rather than racism, motivated the government's decision. Roger Daniels takes the opposite view in* Concentration Camps USA: Japanese Americans and World War II *(New York, 1971). In* Justice at War *(New York, 1983), Peter H. Irons also argues that political considerations and the racism of the Pacific coast military leaders overcame the resistance to relocation on the part of some officials of the Roosevelt administration. John Tateishi compiled the remembrances of camp inmates in* And Justice for All: An Oral History of the Japanese American Detention Camps *(New York, 1984).* Righting a Wrong: Japanese Americans and the Passage of the Civil Liberties Act of 1988 *(Stanford, California, 1993), by Leslie T. Hatamiya, tells how crusaders secured compensation and the official apology of the United States government for its treatment of Japanese American citizens during World War II. Lillian Baker trenchantly defends the expulsion and relocation policy in* American and Japanese Relocation in World War II: Fact, Fiction & Fallacy *(Medford, Oregon, 1990).*

The Origins of the Cold War

Peter L. Hahn,
Michael J. Hogan, and Bruce Karhoff

Introduction

During World War II the United States and the Soviet Union overcame their traditional discord and cooperated to defeat Germany and Japan. The end of the war in 1945, however, eliminated the original reason for American-Soviet cooperation and opened an era of profound tension between the two victorious allies. The United States and the Soviet Union vied for political and economic influence in a postwar world beset by massive physical destruction, political instability, and vacuums of power in the regions formerly dominated by Germany and Japan. A series of conflicts and crises ensued over issues such as the form of government in Poland, the political and economic orientation of Germany, the level of U.S. and Soviet military involvement in Europe, the control of atomic weapons, and the outcome of civil wars in Greece, China, and Korea. By 1950, the great powers had divided Europe into eastern and western spheres of influence in political, economic, and military matters. Tensions escalated sharply after June 1950, when U.S. forces intervened to repulse a major offensive by Communist North Korea against non-Communist South Korea. Such conflicts caused the Cold War, an American-Soviet confrontation that lasted for nearly fifty years.

The Contemporary Debate over the Cold War

The documents printed in this section shed light on several dimensions of the early Cold War. They illustrate some of the ideas that gave birth to the United States's policy of containment of the Soviet Union and the evolution of that policy from 1946 to 1950. They also reveal some of the opposition to this policy on the American side and provide a glimpse of the Soviet view of global affairs in general and of the Truman Doctrine of 1947 in particular. Collectively, the records printed below demonstrate the multilayered and constantly changing dynamics of the early Cold War conflict.

Stalin Suggests that Conflict Is Inevitable

On February 9, 1946, Soviet leader Josef Stalin delivered a public address in which he blamed World War II on international capitalism and celebrated Soviet contributions to the defeat of Germany. Published during a time of mounting East-West tensions over territorial issues in Eastern Europe and the Middle East, the speech provoked substantial concern in the United States that Stalin was mobilizing his people for conflict—possibly even war—with the West. Excerpted from Text of a Speech Delivered By J. V. Stalin at an Election Rally in Stalin Electoral Area, Moscow, February 9, 1946 *(Washington, 1946), 3, 5–8, 13–15.*

Comrades!

. . . It would be wrong to think that the Second World War was a casual occurrence or the result of mistakes of any particular statesmen, though mistakes undoubtedly were made. Actually, the war was the inevitable result of the development of world economic and political forces on the basis of modern monopoly capitalism. Marxists have declared more than once that the capitalist system of world economy harbors elements of general crises and armed conflicts and that, hence, the development of world capitalism in our time proceeds not in the form of smooth and even progress but through crises and military catastrophes.

The fact is, that the unevenness of development of the capitalist countries usually leads in time to violent disturbance of equilibrium in the world system of capitalism, that group of capitalist countries which considers itself worse provided than others with raw materials and markets usually making attempts to alter the situation and repartition the "spheres of influence" in its favor by armed force. The result is a splitting of the capitalist world into two hostile camps and war between them.

... And so, what are the results of the war?

There is one chief result in which all other results have their source. This result is that in the upshot of the war our enemies were defeated and we, together with our Allies, emerged the victors. We concluded the war with complete victory over the enemies. That is the chief result of war. . . . In order to grasp the great historic importance of our victory we must examine the thing more concretely.

And so, how is our victory over our enemies to be understood? ...

Our victory means, first of all, that our Soviet social order has triumphed, that the Soviet social order has successfully passed the ordeal in the fire of war and has proved its unquestionable vitality.

... Second, our victory means that our Soviet state system has triumphed, that our multinational Soviet State has stood all the trials of war and has proved its vitality.

... Third, our victory means that the Soviet armed forces have triumphed, that our Red Army has triumphed, that the Red Army bore up heroically under all the trials of war, utterly routed the armies of our enemies and came out of the war as a victor.

... The war showed that the Red Army is not a "colossus with feet of clay," but a first-class contemporary army with fully mod-

---

Reprinted from *Information Bulletin:* Embassy of the Union of Soviet Socialist Republics, Washington, D.C., March 1946.

ern armaments, highly experienced commanding personnel and high moral and fighting qualities. It must not be forgotten that the Red Army is the army that utterly routed the German army which but yesterday was striking terror into the armies of the European states.

. . . Now a few words about the Communist Party's plans of work for the immediate future. As is known these plans are set forth in the new Five-Year Plan which is shortly to be endorsed. The principal aims of the new Five-Year Plan are to rehabilitate the ravaged areas of the country, to restore the prewar level in industry and agriculture, and then to surpass this level in more or less substantial measure. To say nothing of the fact that the rationing system will shortly be abolished *(stormy, prolonged applause)*, special attention will be devoted to extending the production of consumer goods, to raising the living standard of the working people by steadily lowering the prices of all goods *(stormy, prolonged applause)*, and to the widespread construction of all manner of scientific research institutions (*applause*) that can give science the opportunity to develop its potentialities. *(Stormy applause.)*

. . . As regards the plans for a longer period ahead, the Party means to organize a new mighty upsurge in the national economy, which would allow us to increase our industrial production, for example, three times over as compared with the prewar period. . . .

In conclusion, allow me to thank you for the confidence you have shown me *(prolonged, unabating applause. Shout from the audience: "Hurrah for the great captain of all victories, Comrade Stalin!")* in nominating me to the Supreme Soviet. You need not doubt that I shall do my best to justify your trust.

Kennan Warns of Russian Expansion

Alarmed by Stalin's speech, the State Department instructed its leading Soviet expert, George F. Kennan, chargé d'affaires at the U.S. embassy in Moscow, to assess the speech's significance and to predict future Soviet behavior. Kennan replied by sending the so-called long telegram, a secret cable that summarized the principles of Soviet foreign policy, anticipated substantial Soviet efforts to expand political and economic influence around the world by overt and covert methods, and suggested peaceful but firm U.S. resistance to such expansionism. Kennan's arguments, which he also published under a pseudonym in Foreign Affairs *in July 1947, formed the basis of President Truman's policy of containment of the Soviet Union. Excerpted from U.S. Department of State,* Foreign Relations of the United States, 1946 *(Washington, 1969), 6:697–99, 701–9.*

Basic Features of Post War Soviet Outlook, as Put Forward by Official Propaganda Machine, Are as Follows:

(a) USSR still lives in antagonistic "capitalist encirclement" with which in the long run there can be no permanent peaceful coexistence. As stated by Stalin in 1927 to a delegation of American workers:

> "In course of further development of international revolution there will emerge two centers of world significance: a socialist center, drawing to itself the countries which tend toward socialism, and a capitalist center, drawing to itself the countries that incline toward capitalism. Battle between these two centers for command of world economy will decide fate of capitalism and of communism in entire world."

(b) Capitalist world is beset with internal conflicts, inherent in nature of capitalist society. These conflicts are insoluble by means of peaceful compromise. Greatest of them is that between England and US.

(c) Internal conflicts of capitalism inevitably generate wars. Wars thus generated may be of two kinds: intra-capitalist wars between two capitalist states, and wars of intervention against socialist world. Smart capitalists, vainly seeking escape from inner conflicts of capitalism, incline toward latter.

(d) Intervention against USSR, while it would be disastrous to those who undertook it, would cause renewed delay in progress of Soviet socialism and must therefore be forestalled at all costs.

(e) Conflicts between capitalist states, though likewise fraught with danger for USSR, nevertheless hold out great possibilities for advancement of socialist cause, particularly if USSR remains militarily powerful, ideologically monolithic and faithful to its present brilliant leadership.

. . . So much for premises. To what deductions do they lead from standpoint of Soviet policy? To following:

(a) Everything must be done to advance relative strength of USSR as factor in international society. Conversely, no opportunity must be missed to reduce strength and influence, collectively as well as individually, of capitalist powers.

(b) Soviet efforts, and those of Russia's friends abroad, must be directed toward deepening and exploiting of differences and conflicts between capitalist powers. If these eventually deepen into an "imperialist" war, this war must be turned into revolutionary upheavals within the various capitalist countries.

(c) "Democratic-progressive" elements abroad are to be utilized to maximum to bring pressure to bear on capitalist governments along lines agreeable to Soviet interests.

(d) Relentless battle must be waged against socialist and social-democratic leaders abroad. . . .

Background of Outlook

Before examining ramifications of this party line in practice there are certain aspects of it to which I wish to draw attention.

First, it does not represent natural outlook of Russian people. . . . But party line is binding for outlook and conduct of people who make up apparatus of power—party, secret police and Government—and it is exclusively with these that we have to deal.

Second, please note that premises on which this party line is based are for most part simply not true. Experience has shown that peaceful and mutually profitable coexistence of capitalist and socialist states is entirely possible. . . .

Nevertheless, all these theses, however baseless and disproven, are being boldly put forward again today. What does this indicate? It indicates that Soviet party line is not based on any objective analysis of situation beyond Russia's borders: that it has, indeed, little to do with conditions outside of Russia; that it arises mainly from basic inner-Russian necessities which existed before recent war and exist today.

At bottom of Kremlin's neurotic view of world affairs is traditional and instinctive Russian sense of insecurity. Originally, this was insecurity of a peaceful agricultural people trying to live on vast exposed plain in neighborhood of fierce nomadic peoples. To this was added, as Russia came into contact with economically advanced West, fear of more competent, more powerful, more highly organized societies in that area. . . . For this reason they have always feared foreign penetration, feared direct contact between Western world and their own, feared what would happen if Russians learned truth about world without or if foreigners learned truth about world within. And they have learned to seek security only in patient but deadly struggle for total destruction of rival power, never in compacts and compromises with it. . . .

Projection of Soviet Outlook in Practical Policy on Official Level

. . . (a) Internal policy devoted to increasing in every way strength and prestige of Soviet state: intensive military-industrialization; maximum development of armed forces; great displays to impress outsiders; continued secretiveness about internal matters, designed to conceal weaknesses and to keep opponents in dark.

(b) Wherever it is considered timely and promising, efforts will be made to advance official limits of Soviet power. . . .

(c) Russians will participate officially in international organizations where they see opportunity of extending Soviet power or of inhibiting or diluting power of others. . . .

(d) Toward colonial areas and backward or dependent peoples, Soviet policy, even on official plane, will be directed toward weakening of power and influence and contacts of advanced Western nations, on theory that in so far as this policy is successful, there will be created a vacuum which will favor Communist-Soviet penetration. . . .

Basic Soviet Policies on Unofficial, or Subterranean Plane . . .

Agencies utilized for promulgation of policies on this plane are following:

1. *Inner central core of Communist Parties in other countries . . . tightly coordinated and directed by Moscow. . . .*
2. *Rank and file of Communist Parties. . . . no longer even taken into confidence about realities of movement. . . .*
3. *A wide variety of national associations or bodies which can be dominated or influenced. . . . These include: labor unions, youth*

leagues, women's organizations, racial societies, religious societies, social organizations, cultural groups, liberal magazines, publishing houses, etc.

4. *International organizations which can be similarly penetrated through influence over various national components. Labor, youth and women's organizations are prominent among them. . . .*

It may be expected that component parts of this far-flung apparatus will be utilized . . . as follows:

(a) To undermine general political and strategic potential of major western powers. Efforts will be made in such countries to disrupt national self confidence, to hamstring measures of national defense, to increase social and industrial unrest, to stimulate all forms of disunity. . . . Here poor will be set against rich, black against white, young against old, newcomers against established residents, etc.

(b) On unofficial plane particularly violent efforts will be made to weaken power and influence of Western Powers of [*on*] colonial backward, or dependent peoples. On this level, no holds will be barred. . . .

(c) Where individual governments stand in path of Soviet purposes pressure will be brought for their removal from office. . . .

(d) In foreign countries Communists will, as a rule, work toward destruction of all forms of personal independence, economic, political or moral. . . .

(e) Everything possible will be done to set major Western Powers against each other. . . .

(f) In general, all Soviet efforts on unofficial international plane will be negative and destructive in character, designed to tear down sources of strength beyond reach of Soviet control. . . . The Soviet regime is a police regime par excellence, reared in the dim half world of Tsarist police intrigue, accustomed to think primarily in terms of police power. This should never be lost sight of in gauging Soviet motives. . . .

Practical Deductions from Standpoint of U S Policy

In summary, we have here a political force committed fanatically to the belief that with US there can be no permanent *modus vivendi*, that it is desirable and necessary that the internal harmony of our society be disrupted, our traditional way of life be destroyed, the international authority of our state be broken, if Soviet power is to be secure. . . . This is admittedly not a pleasant picture. Problem of how to cope with this force in [*is*] undoubtedly greatest task our diplomacy has ever faced and probably greatest it will ever have to face. . . . I would like to record my conviction that problem is within our power to solve—and that without recourse to any general military conflict. And in support of this conviction there are certain observations of a more encouraging nature I should like to make:

(1) *Soviet power . . . does not take unnecessary risks. . . . For this reason it can easily withdraw—and usually does—when strong resistance is encountered at any point. Thus, if the adversary has sufficient force and makes clear his readiness to use it, he rarely has to do so. . . .*
(2) *Gauged against Western World as a whole, Soviets are still by far the weaker force. Thus, their success will really depend on degree of cohesion, firmness and vigor which Western World can muster. . . .*
(3) *Success of Soviet system, as form of internal power, is not yet finally proven. . . .*
(4) *All Soviet propaganda beyond Soviet security sphere is basically negative and destructive. It should therefore be relatively easy to combat it by any intelligent and really constructive program.*

For these reasons I think we may approach calmly and with good heart problem of how to deal with Russia. . . . [B]y way of conclusion, following comments:

(1) *Our first step must be to apprehend, and recognize for what it is, the nature of the movement with which we are dealing. . . .*
(2) *We must see that our public is educated to realities of Russian situation. . . .*
(3) *Much depends on health and vigor of our own society. World communism is like malignant parasite which feeds only on diseased tissue. . . .*
(4) *We must formulate and put forward for other nations a much more positive and constructive picture of sort of world we would like to see than we have put forward in past. . . .*
(5) *Finally we must have courage and self-confidence to cling to our own methods and conceptions of human society. After all, the greatest danger that can befall us in coping with this problem of*

Soviet communism, is that we shall allow ourselves to become like those with whom we are coping.

KENNAN

Wallace Questions Containment

Not all American officials approved of President Truman's policy of firm containment of the Soviet Union. In an address delivered September 12, 1946, in New York City, Secretary of Commerce Henry A. Wallace publicly encouraged Truman to reduce tensions with the Soviets through accommodation and compromise and thereby avoid a catastrophic military conflict. Truman rejected such advice and within weeks of Wallace's address fired him from the cabinet. Selected from Vital Speeches of the Day *12 (October 1, 1946): 738–40.*

Tonight I want to talk about peace—and how to get peace. Never have the common people of all lands so longed for peace. Yet, never in a time of comparative peace have they feared war so much.

Up till now peace has been negative and unexciting. War has been positive and exciting. Far too often, hatred and fear, intolerance and deceit have had the upper hand over love and confidence, trust and joy. Far too often, the law of nations has been the law of the jungle; and the constructive spiritual forces of the Lord have bowed to the destructive forces of Satan.

During the past year or so, the significance of peace has been increased immeasurably by the atom bomb, guided missiles and airplanes which soon will travel as fast as sound. Make no mistake about it—another war would hurt the United States many times as much as the last war. We cannot rest in the assurance that we invented the atom bomb—and therefore that this agent of destruction will work best for us. He who trusts in the atom bomb will sooner or later perish by the atom bomb—or something worse.

I say this as one who steadfastly backed preparedness

Excerpt from "The Way to Peace," speech by Henry A. Wallace, as it appeared in *Vital Speeches of the Day*, Vol. XII, No. 24, City News Publishing Company, October 1, 1946.

throughout the Thirties. We have no use for namby-pamby pacifism. But we must realize that modern inventions have now made peace the most exciting thing in the world—and we should be willing to pay a just price for peace. If modern war can cost us $400 billion, we should be willing and happy to pay much more for peace. But certainly, the cost of peace is to be measured not in dollars but in the hearts and minds of men.

The price of peace—for us and for every nation in the world—is the price of giving up prejudice, hatred, fear, and ignorance.

... I plead for an America vigorously dedicated to peace—just as I plead for opportunities for the next generation throughout the world to enjoy the abundance which now, more than ever before, is the birthright of man.

To achieve lasting peace, we must study in detail just how the Russian character was formed—by invasions of Tartars, Mongols, Germans, Poles, Swedes, and French; by the czarist rule based on ignorance, fear and force; by the intervention of the British, French and Americans in Russian affairs from 1919 to 1921; by the geography of the huge Russian land mass situated strategically between Europe and Asia; and by the vitality derived from the rich Russian soil and the strenuous Russian climate. Add to all this the tremendous emotional power which Marxism and Leninism gives to the Russian leaders—and then we can realize that we are reckoning with a force which cannot be handled successfully by a "Get tough with Russia" policy. "Getting tough" never bought anything real and lasting—whether for schoolyard bullies or businessmen or world powers. The tougher we get, the tougher the Russians will get.

... We most earnestly want peace with Russia—but we want to be met half way. We want cooperation. And I believe that we can get cooperation once Russia understands that our primary objective is neither saving the British Empire nor purchasing oil in the Near East with the lives of American soldiers....

The real peace treaty we now need is between the United States and Russia. On our part, we should recognize that we have no more business in the *political* affairs of Eastern Europe than Russia has in the *political* affairs of Latin America, Western Europe and the United States....

As for Germany, we all must recognize that an equitable settlement, based on a unified German nation, is absolutely essential to any lasting European settlement. This means that Russia must be assured that never again can German industry be converted into military might to be used against her—and Britain, Western Europe and the United States must be certain that Russia's Germany policy will not become a tool of Russian design against Western Europe.

The Russians have no more business in stirring up native communists to political activity in Western Europe, Latin America and the United States than we have in interfering in the politics of Eastern Europe and Russia. We know what Russia is up to in Eastern Europe, for example, and Russia knows what we are up to. We cannot permit the door to be closed against our trade in Eastern Europe any more than we can in China. But at the same time we have to recognize that the Balkans are closer to Russia than to us—and that Russia cannot permit either England or the United States to dominate the politics of that area.

. . . We are still arming to the hilt. Our excessive expenses for military purposes are the chief cause for our unbalanced budget. If taxes are to be lightened we must have the basis of a real peace with Russia—a peace that cannot be broken by extremist propagandists. . . .

Russian ideas of social-economic justice are going to govern nearly a third of the world. Our ideas of free enterprise democracy will govern much of the rest. The two ideas will endeavor to prove which can deliver the most satisfaction to the common man in their respective areas of political dominance. But by mutual agreement, this competition should be put on a friendly basis and the Russians should stop conniving against us in certain areas of the world just as we should stop scheming against them in other parts of the world. Let the results of the two systems speak for themselves.

Meanwhile, the Russians should stop teaching that their form of communism must, by force if necessary, ultimately triumph over democratic capitalism—while we should close our ears to those among us who would have us believe that Russian communism and our free enterprise system cannot live, one with another, in a profitable and productive peace.

Under friendly peaceful competition the Russian world and the American world will gradually become more alike. The Russians will be forced to grant more and more of the personal freedoms; and we shall become more and more absorbed with the problems of social-economic justice.

Russia must be convinced that we are not planning for war

against her and we must be certain that Russia is not carrying on territorial expansion or world domination through native communists faithfully following every twist and turn in the Moscow party line. But in this competition, we must insist on an open door for trade throughout the world. There will always be an ideological conflict—but that is no reason why diplomats cannot work out a basis for both systems to live safely in the world side by side.

The Truman Doctrine

President Truman's handling of an early 1947 crisis in Greece reflected his resolve to deal firmly with the Soviet Union. In February 1947, British officials explained to Truman that financial troubles would compel them to suspend their support of the monarchy of Greece, which was resisting an internal revolt by leftists. In a personal appearance at a joint session of Congress on March 12, Truman portrayed the rebellion in Greece as evidence of covert Soviet expansionism and vowed to resist it with massive financial assistance to the government in Athens. He also planned to provide aid to Turkey to encourage it to resist Soviet pressures for territorial and political concessions. Congress endorsed the president's policy, commonly called the Truman Doctrine, by allocating some $400 million in assistance to the two Mediterranean states. Truman's address, excerpted below, appears in Public Papers of the Presidents of the United States: Harry S. Truman, 1947 *(Washington, 1963), 176–80.*

The gravity of the situation which confronts the world today necessitates my appearance before a joint session of the Congress. The foreign policy and the national security of this country are involved. One aspect of the present situation, which I present to you at this time for your consideration and decision, concerns Greece and Turkey.

The United States has received from the Greek Government an urgent appeal for financial and economic assistance. . . . [A]ssistance is imperative if Greece is to survive as a free nation.

I do not believe that the American people and the Congress wish to turn a deaf ear to the appeal of the Greek Government. . . . The very existence of the Greek state is today threatened by the terrorist activities of several thousand armed men, led by Communists, who defy the government's authority at a number of points, particularly along the northern boundaries. . . .

. . . [T]he Greek Government is unable to cope with the situation. The Greek army is small and poorly equipped. It needs supplies and equipment if it is to restore authority to the government throughout Greek territory. Greece must have assistance if it is to become a self-supporting and self-respecting democracy. The United States must supply this assistance. . . .

President Harry S. Truman. (Courtesy of The Library of Congress.)

Greece's neighbor, Turkey, also deserves our attention. The future of Turkey as an independent and economically sound state is clearly no less important to the freedom-loving peoples of the world than the future of Greece. . . . Turkey now needs our support.

. . . I am fully aware of the broad implications involved if the United States extends assistance to Greece and Turkey, and I shall discuss these implications with you at this time.

One of the primary objectives of the foreign policy of the United States is the creation of conditions in which we and other nations will be able to work out a way of life free from coercion. This was a fundamental issue in the war with Germany and Japan. . . . At the present moment in world history nearly every nation must choose between alternative ways of life. The choice is too often not a free one.

One way of life is based upon the will of the majority, and is distinguished by free institutions, representative government, free elections, guarantees of individual liberty, freedom of speech and religion, and freedom from political oppression.

The second way of life is based upon the will of a minority forcibly imposed upon the majority. It relies upon terror and oppression, a controlled press and radio, fixed elections, and the suppression of personal freedoms.

I believe that it must be the policy of the United States to support free peoples who are resisting attempted subjugation by armed minorities or by outside pressures. I believe that we must assist free peoples to work out their own destinies in their own way. I believe that our help should be primarily through economic and financial aid which is essential to economic stability and orderly political processes.

. . . If Greece should fall under the control of an armed minority, the effect upon its neighbor, Turkey, would be immediate and serious. Confusion and disorder might well spread throughout the entire Middle East. Moreover, the disappearance of Greece as an independent state would have a profound effect upon those countries in Europe whose peoples are struggling against great difficulties to maintain their freedoms and their independence while they repair the damages of war. . . . The seeds of totalitarian regimes are nurtured by misery and want. They spread and grow in the evil soil of poverty and strife. They reach their full growth when the hope of a people for a better life has died.

We must keep that hope alive.

The free peoples of the world look to us for support in maintaining their freedoms. If we falter in our leadership, we may endanger the peace of the world—and we shall surely endanger the welfare of this Nation.

Soviets Denounce the Truman Doctrine

On March 14, 1947, the day after Truman's speech to Congress, the Moscow newspaper Izvestiia *printed a broadside of the Truman Doctrine that likely reflected official Soviet thinking. The statement suggested that neither Greece nor Turkey was threatened by external forces and that American aid would lead to American domination of both states. Abridged from* Izvestiia, *with English translation provided by Dr. Kurt Schultz of the staff of* The Russian Review.

On 12 March, U.S. President H. Truman addressed a message to Congress in which he requested $400 million for urgent aid to Greece and Turkey, and permission to send American civilian and military personnel to these countries and to provide "specially selected" Greek and Turkish personnel with training and instruction by Americans.

To justify his proposal, Truman declared that Greece's economic and political situation was desperate, and that England could no longer take care of the Greeks. "England," said Mr. Truman, "faces the necessity of reducing and liquidating its obligations in several parts of the world, including Greece."

Turkey, for its part, needs America's "immediate assistance." It is true that Turkey, unlike Greece, did not suffer from the Second World War, but she needed England's and America's financial aid, said Truman, "for implementing the modernization necessary to maintain her national integrity." And since the British government, "due to its own difficulties," is in this case not able to extend financial or other assistance to the Turks, then the United States, in Truman's opinion, "must" extend that assistance.

And thus the American Congress is asked to promptly sanction two "good deeds": to save Greece from internal disorders and to pay for the costs of "modernizing" Turkey, upon which, allegedly, her very existence depends.

There can be no doubt that the Tsaldaris administration's tearful pleas to the USA for help is clear evidence of the bankruptcy of Greece's internal political regime, which in Truman's address is portrayed flatteringly. What is key here is not only and not so much the mercenary Greek monarchists and their allies, who are being politely portrayed to American congressmen as the direct descendants of the legendary defender of Thermopylae, Tsar Leonid.

It is well known that the real masters of Greece have been and remain British military authorities. British troops have been on Greek territory since 1944. On Churchill's initiative, England took upon itself the responsibility for "stabilizing" political conditions in Greece. English authorities have not only assisted in perpetuating and nurturing the rule of reactionary and anti-democratic forces in Greece, showing at the same time an extreme indifference to and even supporting people who actively and consciously cooperated with the Germans. All the political and economic activities of every manner of coalition and short-lived Greek gov-

---

Excerpted from *Izvestia*, March 14, 1947, translated by Dr. Kurt Schultz.

ernments have been carried out under close English control and direction.

The result of this is now before us: complete bankruptcy. English troops have not brought peace and tranquillity to a tortured Greece. The Greek people have been cast into the abyss of new sufferings, hunger, and poverty. Instead of subsiding, the civil war is acquiring ever more fierce forms.

Has not the presence of foreign troops on Greek territory actually contributed to this sad situation? Doesn't England, which declared itself to be Greece's guardian, bear the responsibility for its ward's bankruptcy?

The American president's message skirts these perfectly natural questions. The reason for such delicacy is understandable: the United States does not wish to criticize English policy because it intends to follow the English example. No wonder the *Times* of London warmly welcomed Truman's address, while the *Daily Telegraph* noted that his speech "fully justifies English policy in Greece." It is clear from Truman's speech that the United States does not plan to change the course set by British policy in Greece. But in light of this, one cannot expect better results.

The American government has no intention whatsoever of dealing with the Greek question in a fashion that one might expect of a member of the United Nations that is concerned about the fate of another of its members. Clearly no one in Washington wishes to consider the obligations the U.S. government accepted with regard to the UN. Showing unusual nervousness, Truman didn't even consider it necessary to wait for the results of the work of a special commission of the Security Council that had been sent to Greece to investigate the situation on the spot. In vain, the American president remembered that "the United States took upon itself the leading role in creating the United Nations." In any event, it wasn't worth remembering this in order to now declare his desire to act through the head of the United Nations, not taking into account the existence of the international organization and forgetting that in New York there meets a continually active international organ—the Security Council.

Truman has ignored both the international organization as well as the sovereignty of Greece. Indeed, what will remain of Greek sovereignty when "American military and civilian personnel" are sitting on the head of the Greek government and when these "personnel" begin to run the show with the help of their 250 million American dollars? The sovereignty and independence of Greece above all else will be the victims of such peculiar "defense." The Greek people, who have been engaged in a heroic struggle for their independence and freedom, do not deserve this sort of attention. If this is what Messrs. Tsaldarises aim for, then so much the worse for them, since they're the ones who have led Greece into this situation.

The ever-suffering Greek people are now threatened with the replacement of one "master"—England—with another "master"—the United States of America. It is impossible to conceal American pretensions to American predominance in Greece by justifying those pretensions as defense of the freedom and independence of the Greek people.

American arguments for assisting Turkey are based on the existence of a threat to the integrity of Turkish territory, even though no one or nothing is threatening Turkey's integrity.

American "aid" to Turkey is clearly directed toward subordinating that country as well to U.S. control, after which point it will be impossible even to talk about independent domestic and foreign Turkish policy, since that policy will be under the control of American imperialism. Some American commentators are openly speaking of this. Walter Lippmann frankly points out in the *New York Herald Tribune* that the American "alliance with Turkey" would give the United States a "strategic position that is incomparably more favorable than any other from which to exercise authority in the Middle East." And the *New York Times*, commenting upon Truman's message to Congress, bombastically proclaims the advent of "the age of American responsibility."

But, the question arises, what else is this monopolistic "American responsibility" but a screen for expansionist plans?

Arguments that the U.S.A. "is obliged to save" Greece and Turkey from the expansion of so-called "totalitarian states" is not new. Hitler also relied on the Bolsheviks when he wanted to pave the way for his conquests. Now they want to subordinate Greece and Turkey, and they are trying to conceal their expansionist plans by raising a racket about "totalitarian states." This is even more attractive given that the United States is elbowing non-totalitarian Britain out of yet another one or two countries.

Mr. Truman's address could not help but attract the attention of the broad public in both the U.S.A. and abroad. One cannot say that it has not met serious criticism even within the circles of the

U.S. Congress. A group of 13 American congressmen tried to talk Truman out of making the address before he delivered it. As the Democratic Senator Taylor declared, "We would be disgusted by a proposal to vote for rendering financial aid to a monarchist government that is persecuting those who fought against the Nazis."

Another Democratic Senator, Johnson, expressed the same thought: "I wholeheartedly sympathize with giving food as aid, without political aims, but the president made no distinction between food and bullets, and that is the reason for my disappointment. I am not sympathetic to the dispatch of our military personnel to Greece and Turkey even as advisers. Military aid to Turkey and Greece could lead to military intervention in other parts of the world. I am ready to give millions in support of aid to hungry people, but not one cent for helping rotting monarchies."

The Democratic Senator Pepper declared that "Truman's recommendation, made without any consultation with the United Nations, constitutes a threat to the UN and lays unknown obligations upon the United States." Also characteristic was the observation of the chairman of the House of Representatives' Budget Committee, the Republican Knudson, who said that "the supporters of Truman's program apparently will not be satisfied until the United States goes bankrupt." Henry Wallace came out with a sharply negative judgment of Truman's address, as did several other leading American figures.

Before us is yet another intrusion by the United States into the affairs of another state. The pretensions of the United States to leadership in international affairs are growing along with the appetite of the interested American circles. But American leaders, operating in new historical circumstances, are not taking into account that the old methods of colonizers and hard-headed politicians have outlived their age and are doomed to failure.

This is the main weakness of Mr. Truman's address.

NSC-68 and the Enduring Cold War

American-Soviet tensions provoked by the Truman Doctrine were exacerbated in 1948-49 by such other Western initiatives as the Marshall Plan, the North Atlantic Treaty Organization, and by the communist coup d'etat in Czechoslovakia and the Soviet blockade of Berlin. In 1949, when Communists seized power in China after a long civil war and when the Soviets successfully tested an atomic device years before Western experts anticipated they would, American concerns escalated sharply. U.S. officials conducted a major re-examination of foreign policy and produced a top secret planning document called NSC-68. The document attributed to Moscow a concerted plan of global conquest and proposed a massive increase in U.S. defense preparations to deter Soviet aggression and thereby create opportunities to weaken the Soviet Union through political and economic means. Drafted in April 1950, NSC-68 was approved by President Truman as an official policy document after the outbreak of the Korean War in June. Excerpted from U.S. Department of State, Foreign Relations of the United States, 1950 *(Washington, 1977), 1:237–38, 240–41, 243–44, 263, 272, 282, 285–87, 292.*

During the span of one generation, the international distribution of power has been fundamentally altered. For several centuries it had proved impossible for any one nation to gain such preponderant strength that a coalition of other nations could not in time face it with greater strength. The international scene was marked by recurring periods of violence and war, but a system of sovereign and independent states was maintained, over which no state was able to achieve hegemony.

Two complex sets of factors have now basically altered this historical distribution of power. First, the defeat of Germany and Japan and the decline of the British and French Empires have interacted with the development of the United States and the Soviet Union in such a way that power has increasingly gravitated to these two centers. Second, the Soviet Union, unlike previous aspirants to hegemony, is animated by a new fanatic faith, antithetical to our own, and seeks to impose its absolute authority over the rest of the world. . . .

. . . [A]ny substantial further extension of the area under the domination of the Kremlin would raise the possibility that no coalition adequate to confront the Kremlin with greater strength could be assembled. It is in this context that this Republic and its citizens in the ascendancy of their strength stand in their deepest peril.

The issues that face us are momentous, involving the fulfillment or destruction not only of this Republic but of civilization itself. . . . The fundamental purpose of the United States . . . is to assure the integrity and vitality of our free society, which is founded upon the dignity and worth of the individual. . . . The fundamental design of those who control the Soviet Union and the international communist movement is to retain and solidify their absolute power, first in the Soviet Union and second in the areas now under their control. In the minds of the Soviet leaders, however, achievement of this design requires the dynamic extension of their authority and the ultimate elimination of any effective opposition to their authority. . . . Thus unwillingly our free society finds itself mortally challenged by the Soviet system. No other value system is so wholly irreconcilable with ours, so implacable in its purpose to destroy ours, so capable of turning to its own uses the most dangerous and divisive trends in our own society, no other so skillfully and powerfully evokes the elements of irrationality in human nature everywhere, and no other has the support of a great and growing center of military power. . . .

In a shrinking world, which now faces the threat of atomic warfare, it is not an adequate objective merely to seek to check the Kremlin design, for the absence of order among nations is becoming less and less tolerable. This fact imposes on us, in our own interests, the responsibility of world leadership. . . .

The Kremlin is able to select whatever means are expedient in seeking to carry out its fundamental design. . . . We have no such freedom of choice, and least of all in the use of force. Resort to war is not only a last resort for a free society, but it is also an act which cannot definitively end the fundamental conflict in the realm of ideas. . . .

Practical and ideological considerations therefore both impel us to the conclusion that we have no choice but to demonstrate the superiority of the idea of freedom by its constructive application, and to attempt to change the world situation by means short of war in such a way as to frustrate the Kremlin design and hasten the decay of the Soviet system.

. . . It is quite clear from Soviet theory and practice that the Kremlin seeks to bring the free world under its dominion by the methods of the cold war. . . .

Four possible courses of action by the United States in the present situation can be distinguished. They are:

a. Continuation of current policies . . . ;

b. Isolation;

c. War; and

d. A more rapid building up of the political, economic, and military strength of the free world than provided under *a*, with the purpose of reaching, if possible, a tolerable state of order among nations without war and of preparing to defend ourselves in the event that the free world is attacked.

. . . [Choice D] is the only course which is consistent with progress toward achieving our fundamental purpose. . . . It is necessary to have the military power to deter, if possible, Soviet expansion, and to defeat, if necessary, aggressive Soviet or Soviet-directed actions of a limited or total character. . . .

A program for rapidly building up strength and improving political and economic conditions will place heavy demands on our courage and intelligence; it will be costly; it will be dangerous. But half-measures will be more costly and more dangerous, for they will be inadequate to prevent and may actually invite war. Budgetary considerations will need to be subordinated to the stark fact that our very independence as a nation may be at stake.

A comprehensive and decisive program . . . would probably involve:

(1) *The development of an adequate political and economic framework for the achievement of our long-range objectives.*

(2) *A substantial increase in expenditures for military purposes. . . .*

(3) *A substantial increase in military assistance programs, designed to foster cooperative efforts, which will adequately and efficiently meet the requirements of our allies. . . .*

(4) *Some increase in economic assistance programs and recognition of the need to continue these programs until their purposes have been accomplished.*

(5) *A concerted attack on the problem of the United States balance of payments. . . .*

(6) *Development of programs designed to build and maintain confidence among other peoples in our strength and resolution, and to wage overt psychological warfare calculated to encourage mass defections from Soviet allegiance and to frustrate the Kremlin design in other ways.*

(7) *Intensification of affirmative and timely measures and operations by covert means in the fields of economic warfare and political and psychological warfare with a view to fomenting and supporting unrest and revolt in selected strategic satellite countries.*
(8) *Development of internal security and civilian defense programs.*
(9) *Improvement and intensification of intelligence activities.*
(10) *Reduction of Federal expenditures for purposes other than defense and foreign assistance, if necessary by the deferment of certain desirable programs.*
(11) *Increased taxes.*

. . . The Soviet Union is currently devoting about 40 percent of available resources . . . to military expenditures. . . . In an emergency the Soviet Union could increase the allocation of resources to these purposes to about 50 percent, or by one-fourth.

The United States is currently devoting about 22 percent of its gross national product . . . to military expenditures. . . . In an emergency the United States could devote upward of 50 percent of its gross national product to these purposes (as it did during the last war), an increase of several times present expenditures for direct and indirect military purposes and foreign assistance. . . .

The threat to the free world involved in the development of the Soviet Union's atomic and other capabilities will rise steadily and rather rapidly. For the time being, the United States possesses a marked atomic superiority over the Soviet Union which . . . inhibits aggressive Soviet action. This provides an opportunity for the United States, in cooperation with other free countries, to launch a build-up of strength which will support a firm policy directed to the frustration of the Kremlin design. . . .

The whole success of the proposed program hangs ultimately on recognition by this Government, the American people, and all free peoples, that the cold war is in fact a real war in which the survival of the free world is at stake. . . . The prosecution of the program will require of us all the ingenuity, sacrifice, and unity demanded by the vital importance of the issue and the tenacity to persevere until our national objectives have been attained.

Questions

1. *What was the fundamental nature of American-Soviet conflict in the late 1940s? How extensively did the worldviews of the two powers differ?*
2. *Was the Truman Doctrine an American effort to preserve the independence of Greece and Turkey, or an American quest to gain dominance over both countries?*
3. *Were the policy prescriptions in NSC-68 valid, in your judgment, on the basis of circumstances facing the United States in 1950?*
4. *On the basis of these documents, which power do you think was most accountable for the Cold War?*

FURTHER READING

Traditional histories of the early Cold War include Herbert Feis, From Trust to Terror: The Onset of the Cold War, 1945–1950 *(New York, 1970); Hugh Thomas,* Armed Truce: The Beginnings of the Cold War, 1945–1946 *(New York, 1987); and Randall B. Woods and Howard Jones,* Dawning of the Cold War: The United States, Quest for Order *(Athens, Georgia, 1991). For revisionist accounts, see Gar Alperovitz,* Atomic Diplomacy: Hiroshima and Potsdam *(New York, 1965); Lloyd C. Gardner,* Architects of Illusion: Men and Ideas in American Foreign Policy, 1941–1949 *(Chicago, 1970); Thomas G. Paterson,* Soviet-American Confrontation: Postwar Reconstruction and the Origins of the Cold War *(Baltimore, 1973); and Joyce and Gabriel Kolko,* The Limits of Power: The World and United States Foreign Policy, 1945–1954 *(New York, 1972). Post-revisionist and synthetic works are Melvyn P. Leffler,* A Preponderance of Power: National Security, the Truman Administration, and the Cold War *(Stanford, 1992); James Gormly,* The Collapse of the Grand Alliance, 1945–1948 *(Baton Rouge, 1987); and John Lewis Gaddis,* The United States and the Origins of the Cold War, 1941–1947 *(New York, 1972). On specific aspects of U.S. policy, see Bruce Cumings,* The Origins of the Korean War, *vol.* 2: The Roaring of the Cataract, 1947–1950 *(Princeton, 1990); Michael J. Hogan,* The Marshall Plan: America, Britain, and the Reconstruction of Western Europe, 1947–1952 *(New York, 1987); and Lawrence Kaplan,* The United States and NATO: The Formative Years *(Lexington, Kentucky, 1984).*

Nonviolence and the Civil Rights Movement

Penny A. Russell

INTRODUCTION

Some histories of the civil rights movement begin in 1954 with the Brown v. Board of Education *decision that struck down separate but equal in public education. Other writers insist that the movement began in August 1955 with the decision of an all-white Mississippi jury to set free the two white men who brutally tortured and murdered fourteen-year-old Chicago native Emmett Till for allegedly whistling at a white woman. Many scholars begin their analysis with Rosa Parks, Martin Luther King, Jr., and the Montgomery Bus Boycott that started in December 1955. Recently, a few scholars have searched for the origins of the movement in the decades before the 1950s.*

Historians also disagree on how to characterize the ideology, politics, strategies, and tactics of the movement. A few have insisted that the commonly used term "the civil rights movement" is inadequate because this social movement was concerned with more than securing citizenship rights for Blacks. Some people saw the movement as a search for community, others spoke of it as a religious crusade, and still others believed it was a battle for the soul of America. To understand how and why African-American activism and politics came to be one of the dominant forces in American life from the mid-1950s to the mid-1960s, you must understand the origins and the foundation of the civil rights movement.

African Americans attempted to mobilize mass movements before the 1950s. The first call for a march on Washington came in May 1941, twenty-two years before Martin Luther King, Jr., told the nation about his dream of equality for all people. In May 1941,

A. Philip Randolph urged African Americans to demonstrate in Washington for an end to discrimination in defense industries and in the military. The march was canceled only after President Franklin D. Roosevelt issued Executive Order 8802, which outlawed discrimination in employment in defense industries that held government contracts and created a Fair Employment Practices Committee (FEPC) to investigate companies that violated the order.

The mass movement that Randolph had wanted to create became a reality fourteen years later. On 1 December 1955, Rosa Parks left her seamstress job in a tailor shop, boarded a city bus for home, and was arrested for refusing to give up her seat to a white passenger, a violation of Alabama's segregation laws. In response, the Women's Political Council, a black women's organization that had been petitioning Montgomery's mayor about discrimination and segregation on the city buses, called for a boycott of the buses on 5 December when Parks's case went to trial. E. D. Nixon and other black men in Montgomery met to discuss the situation and they endorsed the idea of a boycott and called for a mass meeting on the night of 5 December as well.

The city buses were virtually empty of black riders on the morning of the boycott. That same afternoon, Nixon and other male leaders created the Montgomery Improvement Association and elected a young minister, Martin Luther King, Jr., as head of the organization. African Americans in Montgomery walked for a year, enduring intimidation, loss of employment, violence, and bombings until the U.S. Supreme Court declared Montgomery's bus segregation laws unconstitutional.

African-American college students became the leaders and innovators during the next phase of the movement. On 1 February 1960, Franklin McCain, David Richmond, Joseph McNeil, and Izell Blair, Jr., four black college students attending North Carolina Agricultural and Technical College in Greensboro, asked to be served at a Woolworth's lunch counter and refused to leave their seats when they were denied service. Their actions sparked sit-ins by black college students, who were sometimes joined by a few white students, all across the South. In mid-April 1960 local student sit-in leaders met at Shaw University in Raleigh, North Carolina, and, with the assistance of Ella Baker of the Southern Christian Leadership Conference (SCLC), created the Student Nonviolent Coordinating Committee (SNCC) to organize their struggles against segregation.

SNCC's first efforts to register African-American voters were in McComb, Mississippi, under the direction of Robert Moses, a Harlem school teacher who had attended graduate school at Harvard and who had worked with Ella Baker in the past. Despite intimidation, humiliation, violence, and arrests, SNCC members worked with local activists to establish voting rights projects in other communities in Mississippi where they supported the efforts of African Americans to register to vote. SNCC workers were often arrested for their actions and chose to serve their sentences instead of accepting bail. This was a dangerous choice, for African Americans were routinely beaten and mistreated in southern jails.

In April 1963, Martin Luther King, Jr., was arrested in Birmingham, Alabama. While he was incarcerated, in response to a letter from white clergymen, he composed the most famous statement on the philosophy of nonviolent direct action. They had accused King and the SCLC of promoting violence and argued that civil rights activists were outsiders who should not have come to the city. In his letter from jail, King explained the use of nonviolence and assured the clergymen that they would join African Americans in their protests if they knew how the police had tortured Blacks both in the streets and the jails of Birmingham.

Most African-American organizations involved in the struggle for social and political change from the mid-1950s to the mid-1960s adopted the philosophy of nonviolence and the tactics of nonviolent direct action. The definition of nonviolence and how it should be used differed from individual to individual and from group to group, but most civil rights activists agreed on the goals of their movement. They wanted to destroy segregation and transform the nation. They embraced the spirit of urgency that Martin Luther King, Jr., spoke about at the August 1963 March on Washington: "Now is the time to make real the promises of democracy; now is the time to rise from the dark and desolate valley of segregation to the sunlit path of racial justice; now is the time to lift our nation from the quicksands of racial justice to the solid rock of brotherhood; now is the time to make justice a reality for all God's children."

The Strategies of Nonviolence and the Dangers of Activism

These documents offer different views of nonviolence, activism, and resistance by African Americans. Some of these people, such as Rosa Parks, Malcolm X, and King, are familiar while others, such as Ella Baker, James Forman, or A. Philip Randolph, are not. These selections are a small example of the creativity and innovation that activists employed in their efforts to transform the United States into a nation where all citizens could enjoy justice, equality, and freedom.

A. Philip Randolph Calls for a March on Washington, 1941

A. Philip Randolph was the head of the Brotherhood of Sleeping Car Porters, a predominantly African-American labor union, an early civil rights activist, and publisher of The Black Worker, *a labor magazine. In this excerpt from his May 1941 call for a march on Washington, Randolph wanted "mass action that is orderly and lawful, but aggressive and militant, for justice, equality and freedom."*

Taken from "To March On Washington for Jobs and Equal Participation in National Defense," The Black Worker, *May 1941, p. 4.*

Greetings:

We call upon you to fight for jobs in National Defense.

We call upon you to struggle for the integration of Negroes in the armed forces, such as the Air Corps, Navy, Army and Marine Corps of the Nation.

We call upon you to demonstrate for the abolition of Jim-Crowism in all Government departments and defense employment.

This is an hour of crisis. It is a crisis of democracy. It is a crisis of minority groups. It is a crisis of Negro Americans.

What is this crisis?

To American Negroes, it is the denial of jobs in Government defense projects. It is racial discrimination in Government departments. It is widespread Jim-Crowism in the armed forces of the nation. . . .

What shall we do? . . .

With faith and confidence of the Negro people in their own power for self-liberation, Negroes can break down the barriers of discrimination against employment in National Defense. . . .

Most important and vital to all, Negroes, by the mobilization and coordination of their mass power, can cause PRESIDENT ROOSEVELT TO ISSUE AN EXECUTIVE ORDER ABOLISHING DISCRIMINATIONS IN ALL GOVERNMENT DEPARTMENTS, ARMY, NAVY, AIR CORPS AND NATIONAL DEFENSE JOBS. . . .

In this period of power politics, nothing counts but pressure, more pressure, and still more pressure, through the tactic and strategy of broad, organized, aggressive mass action behind the vital and important issues of the Negro. To this end, we propose that ten thousand Negroes MARCH ON WASHINGTON FOR JOBS IN NATIONAL DEFENSE AND EQUAL INTEGRATION IN THE FIGHTING FORCES OF THE UNITED STATES.

An "all-out" thundering march on Washington, ending in a monster and huge demonstration at Lincoln's Monument will shake up white America.

It will shake up official Washington.

It will give encouragement to our white friends to fight all the harder by our side, with us, for our righteous cause.

It will gain respect for the Negro people.

It will create a new sense of self-respect among Negroes. . . .

We summon you to mass action that is orderly and lawful, but aggressive and militant, for justice, equality and freedom.

From "To March on Washington for Jobs and Equal Participation in National Defense" by A. Philip Randolph as it appeared in *The Black Worker*, p. 4, May 1941.

Rosa L. Parks is Arrested in Montgomery, Alabama on 1 December 1955

In a 1977 interview Rosa Parks remembers that she told the city bus driver to "go on and have me arrested" for not giving up her seat to a white man who boarded the bus after her. In this selection, she discusses the events that ignited a community-wide protest.

Taken from Howell Raines, My Soul Is Rested: Movement Days in the Deep South Remembered *(New York, 1977), 40-42.*

As I got up on the bus and walked to the seat I saw there was only one vacancy that was just back of where it was considered the white section. So this was the seat I that I took, next to the aisle, and a man was sitting next to me. . . . The third stop is when all the front seats were taken, and this one man was standing and when the driver looked around and saw he was standing, he asked the four of us, the man in the seat with me and the two women across the aisle, to let him have those front seats.

At his first request, didn't any of us move. Then he spoke again and said, "You'd better make it light on yourselves and let me have those seats." At this point, of course, the passenger who would have taken the seat hadn't said anything. In fact, he never did speak to my knowledge. When the three people, the man who was in the seat with me and the two women, stood up and moved into the aisle, I remained where I was. When the driver saw that I was still sitting there, he asked if I was going to stand up. I told him no, I wasn't. He said, "Well, if you don't stand up, I'm going to have you arrested." I told him to go on and have me arrested.

He got off the bus and came back shortly. A few minutes later, two policemen got on the bus, and they approached me and asked if the driver had asked me to stand up, and I said yes, and they wanted to know why I didn't. I told them I didn't think I should have to stand up. After I had paid my fare and occupied a seat, I didn't think I should have to give it up. They placed me under arrest then and had me to get in the police car, and I was taken to jail and booked on suspicion, I believe. The questions were asked,

Rosa Parks' courageous challenge to segregated busing in Montgomery ignited a community-wide protest and proved to be one of the first major successes of the civil rights movement. (Courtesy of Bettmann/Corbis.)

the usual questions they ask a prisoner or somebody that's under arrest. They had to determine whether or not the driver wanted to press charges or swear out a warrant, which he did. Then they took me to jail and I was placed in a cell. In a little while I was taken from the cell, and my picture was made and fingerprints taken. I went back to the cell then, and a few minutes later I was called back again, and when this happened I found out that Mr. E.D. Nixon and Attorney and Mrs. Clifford Durr had come to make bond for me.

In the meantime before this, of course . . . I was given permission to make a telephone call after my picture was taken and fingerprints taken. I called my home and spoke to my mother on the telephone and told her what had happened, that I was in jail. She was quite upset and asked me had the police beaten me. I told her, no, I hadn't been physically injured, but I was being held in jail, and I wanted my husband to come and get me out. . . . He didn't have a car at that time, so he had to get someone to bring him down. At the time when he got down, Mr. Nixon and the Durrs had just made bond for me, so we all met at the jail and we went home.

Student Nonviolent Coordinating Committee Statement of Purpose

The Reverend James Lawson was a divinity student who was expelled from Vanderbilt University after sit-ins in the spring of 1960. Later that year he would be influential in the founding of the Student Nonviolent Coordinating Committee. In May 1960, he drafted the statement of purpose for the new organization that appeared in the first issue of the newspaper the students created, The Student Voice *1 (June 1960): 1.*

Statement of Purpose

"Carrying out the mandate of the Raleigh Conference to write a statement of purpose for the movement, the Temporary Student Nonviolent Coordinating Committee submits for careful consideration the following draft. We urge all local state or regional groups to examine it closely. Each member of our movement must work diligently to understand the depths of nonviolence.

We affirm the philosophical or religious ideal of nonviolence as the foundation of our purpose, the pre-supposition of our faith, and the manner of our action. Nonviolence as it grows from Judaic-Christian tradition seeks a social order of justice permeated by love. Integration of human endeavor represents the crucial first step towards such a society.

Through nonviolence, courage displaces fear; love transforms hate. Acceptance dissipates prejudice; hope ends despair. Peace dominates war; faith reconciles doubt. Mutual regards cancel enmity. Justice for all overthrows injustice. The redemptive community supercedes [supersedes] systems of gross social immorality.

Love is the central motif of nonviolence. Love is the force by which God binds man to himself and man to man. Such love goes to the extreme; it remains loving and forgiving even in the midst of hostility. It matches the capacity of evil to inflict suffering with an even more enduring capacity to absorb evil, all the while persisting in love.

By appealing to conscience and standing on the moral nature of human existence, nonviolence nurtures the atmosphere in which reconciliation and justice become actual possibilities."

Prepared by-Rev. J.M. Lawson, Jr. Saturday, May 14, 1960

Bigger Than A Hamburger

Ella Baker, executive director of the Southern Christian Leadership Conference, organized the student conference in Raleigh, North Carolina, from which SNCC emerged. She encouraged the student leaders attending the Raleigh conference to create their own organization where they would be free to work "to rid America of the scourge of racial segregation and discrimination—not only at lunch counters, but in every aspect of life."

Baker's ideas about leadership and community organizing were adopted by SNCC and they are presented in Ella J. Baker, "Bigger Than A Hamburger," Southern Patriot *(June 1960): 1.*

Raleigh, N.C.—The Student Leadership Conference made it crystal clear that current sit-ins and other demonstrations are concerned with something bigger than a hamburger or even a giant-sized Coke.

Whatever may be the difference in approach to their goal, the Negro and white students, North and South, are seeking to rid America of the scourge of racial segregation and discrimination—not only at lunch counters, but in every aspect of life.

In reports, casual conversations, discussion groups, and speeches, the sense and spirit of the following statement that appeared in the initial newsletter of the students at Barer-Scotia College, concord, N.C., were re-echoed time and again:

We want the world to know that we no longer accept the inferior position of second-class citizenship. We are willing to go to jail, be ridiculed, spat upon and even suffer physical violence to obtain First Class Citizenship.

By and large, this feeling that they have a destined date with

From "Bigger Than A Hamburger" by Ella J. Baker as it appeared in *The Southern Patriot*, June 1960.

freedom, was not limited to a drive for personal freedom for the Negro in the South. Repeatedly it was emphasized that the movement was concerned with the moral implications of racial discrimination for the "whole world" and the "Human Race."

"This universality of approach was linked with a perceptive recognition that "it is important to keep the movement democratic and to avoid struggles for personal leadership."

It was further evident that desire for supportive cooperation from adult leaders and the adult community was also tempered by apprehension that adults might try to "capture" the student movement. The students showed willingness to be met on the basis of equality, but were intolerant of anything that smacked of manipulation or domination.

This inclination toward group-centered leadership, rather than toward a leader-centered group pattern of organization, was refreshing indeed to those of the older group who bear the scars of the battle, the frustrations and the disillusionment that come when the prophetic leader turns out to have heavy feet of clay.

However hopeful might be the signs in the direction of group-centeredness, the fact that many schools and communities, especially in the South, have not provided adequate experience for young Negroes to assume the initiative and think and act independently accentuated the need for guarding the student movement against well-meaning, but nevertheless unhealthy, overprotectiveness.

Here is an opportunity for adult and youth to work together and provide genuine leadership—the development of the individual to his highest potential for the benefit of the group. . . .

In Jail in Greenwood, Mississippi

James Forman provides the following glimpse of life for SNCC activists in the Greenwood, Mississippi jail in his book The Making of Black Revolutionaries: A Personal Account *(New York, 1972), 299-301.*

April 2, 1963: We have been in jail one week today. Our morale is good, although there are serious undertones of a desire to be free among some members of the group. . . .

The cell in which we are being held is not so bad so far as American prisons go. (The entire penal system needs reforming.) We are eight in a cell with six bunks. We have two mattresses on the floor. There is an open shower, a sink, a stool. It took us two days to get a broom and five days to get some salt for our food. The inner cell in which we are "contained" is approximately 15' x 12'. Not much room is there? . . .

We are also improving our minds. We have been allowed to keep our books and we have sufficient cigarettes. I even have my pipe and some tobacco. Personally, I have tried to organize our lives. Do you expect anything else of me? We have occasional classes. Moses gave us an excellent math lecture the other day. I gave one lesson in writing and English. Guyot has delivered several in biology. We are always having discussions. Sometimes one of us will read a passage from a book and then we will discuss the meaning of it. We have had several stimulating conversations on Thoreau's essay on Civil Disobedience and Nkrumah's thoughts on Positive Action. . . .

My personal opinion as to the significance of our staying in jail follows: I am convinced that all the people connected with SNCC are busily engaged in protesting our unjust imprisonment. This is as it should be. I am also convinced that others sympathetic to the cause of Freedom are also alarmed at this travesty of justice. Only our bodies are confined to this cell. Our minds are free to think what we wish and we know our stay here will also pass away. Our imprisonment serves to dramatize to the nation and to the world that the black man does not even have the right to *try* to be an American citizen in some parts of our so-called democracy. Our jail-without-bail may also serve to remind others in the movement of the need for some of us to stay in jail to dramatize the situation.

On a local and state level it is important that we stay in jail, for people are remembered more by what they do than by what they say. We have been telling Mississippians that we must prepare to die. We have encouraged them to accept our beliefs. Thus it follows that we must lead by example rather than by words.

Letter from the Birmingham City Jail

King presents his ideas on the use of nonviolence and reminds the white clergymen that he is in Birmingham because "injustice anywhere is a threat to justice everywhere." This version of his famous letter is in Martin Luther King, Jr., "Letter from Birmingham Jail," in Why We Can't Wait *(New York, 1963), 77-83, 98-100.*

April 16, 1963

MY DEAR FELLOW CLERGYMEN:

While confined here in the Birmingham city jail, I came across your recent statement calling my present activities "unwise and untimely." Seldom do I pause to answer criticism of my work and ideas. If I sought to answer all the criticisms that cross my desk, my secretaries would have little time for anything other than such correspondence in the course of the day, and I would have no time for constructive work. But since I feel that you are men of genuine good will and that your criticisms are sincerely set forth, I want to try to answer your statement in what I hope will be patient and reasonable terms.

I think I should indicate why I am here in Birmingham, since you have been influenced by the view which argues against "outsiders coming in." . . . Several months ago the [local SCLC] affiliate here in Birmingham asked us to be on call to engage in a nonviolent direct-action program if such were deemed necessary. We readily consented, and when the hour came we lived up to our promise. So I, along with several members of my staff, am here because I was invited here. I am here because I have organizational ties here.

But more basically, I am in Birmingham because injustice is here. . . .

Moreover, I am cognizant of the interrelatedness of all communities and states. I cannot sit idly by in Atlanta and not be concerned about what happens in Birmingham. Injustice anywhere is a threat to justice everywhere. We are caught in an inescapable network of mutuality, tied in a single garment of destiny. Whatever affects one directly, affects all indirectly. Never again can we afford to live with the narrow, provincial "outside agitator" idea. Anyone who lives inside the United States can never be considered an outsider anywhere within its bounds.

You deplore the demonstrations taking place in Birmingham. But your statement, I am sorry to say, fails to express a similar concern for the conditions that brought about the demonstrations. . . .

In any nonviolent campaign there are four basic steps: collection of the facts to determine whether injustices exist; negotiation; self-purification; and direct action. We have gone through all these steps in Birmingham. There can be no gainsaying the fact that racial injustice engulfs this community. Birmingham is probably the most thoroughly segregated city in the United States. Its ugly record of brutality is widely known. Negroes have experienced grossly unjust treatment in the courts. There have been more unsolved bombings of Negro homes and churches in Birmingham than in any other city in the nation. These are the hard, brutal facts of the case. On the basis of these conditions, Negro leaders sought to negotiate with the city fathers. But the latter consistently refused to engage in good-faith negotiation. . . .

You may well ask: "Why direct action? Why sit-ins, marches and so forth? Isn't negotiation a better path?" You are quite right in calling for negotiation. Indeed, this is the very purpose of direct action. Nonviolent direct action seeks to create such a crisis and foster such a tension that a community which has constantly refused to negotiate is forced to confront the issue. It seeks so to dramatize the issue that it can no longer be ignored. . . .

. . . My friends, I must say to you that we have not made a single gain in civil rights without determined legal and nonviolent pressure. Lamentably, it is an historical fact that privileged groups seldom give up their privileges voluntarily. . . .

We know through painful experience that freedom is never voluntarily given by the oppressor; it must be demanded by the oppressed. Frankly, I have yet to engage in a direct-action campaign that was "well timed" in the view of those who have not suffered unduly from the disease of segregation. For years now I have heard the word "Wait!" It rings in the ear of every Negro with piercing familiarity. This "Wait" has almost always meant "Never." We must come to see, with one of our distinguished jurists, that "justice too long delayed is justice denied." . . .

Before closing, I feel impelled to mention one other point in your statement that has troubled me profoundly. You warmly commended the Birmingham police force for keeping "order" and "preventing violence." I doubt that you would have so warmly commended the police force if you had seen its dogs sinking their teeth into unarmed, nonviolent Negroes. I doubt that you would so quickly commend the policemen if you were to observe their ugly and inhumane treatment of Negroes here in the city jail; if you were to watch them push and curse old Negro women and young Negro girls; if you were to see them slap and kick old Negro men and young boys; if you were to observe them, as they did on two occasions, refuse to give us food because we wanted to sing our grace together. I cannot join you in your praise of the Birmingham police department. . . .

I wish you had commended the Negro sit-inners and demonstrators of Birmingham for their sublime courage, their willingness to suffer and their amazing discipline in the midst of great provocation. One day the South will recognize its real heroes. They will be the James Merediths, with the noble sense of purpose that enables them to face jeering and hostile mobs, and with the agonizing loneliness that characterizes the life of the pioneer. They will be old, oppressed, battered Negro women, symbolized in a seventy-two-year-old woman in Montgomery, Alabama, who rose up with a sense of dignity and with her people decided not to ride segregated buses, and who responded with ungrammatical profundity to one who inquired about her weariness: "My feets is tired, but my soul is at rest." They will be the young high school and college students, the young ministers of the gospel and a host of their elders, courageously and nonviolently sitting in at lunch counters and willingly going to jail for conscience' sake. One day the South will know that when these disinherited children of God sat down at lunch counters, they were in reality standing up for what is best in the American dream and for the most sacred values in our Judaeo-Christian heritage, thereby bringing our nation back to those great wells of democracy which were dug deep by the founding fathers in their formulation of the Constitution and the Declaration of Independence. . . .

. . . Let us all hope that the dark clouds of racial prejudice will soon pass away and the deep fog of misunderstanding will be lifted from our fear-drenched communities, and in some not too distant tomorrow the radiant stars of love and brotherhood will shine over our great nation with all their scintillating beauty.

Yours for the cause of Peace and Brotherhood,
MARTIN LUTHER KING, JR.

To Mississippi Youth from Malcolm X

Malcolm X, originally Malcolm Little, took the surname X to represent the lost identity of African slaves. Malcolm became the main spokesman for the Nation of Islam during the 1950s. While in the Nation of Islam, he emphasized racial separatism and black self-reliance and was described by some as militant and extremist. He became disillusioned with and left the Nation of Islam in March 1964 and subsequently founded the Organization of Afro-American Unity (OAAU). From his break with the Nation of Islam in 1964 until his assassination in February 1965, he distanced himself from racial separatism and sought solidarity with the civil rights movement. In this excerpt from a speech on 31 December 1964, Malcolm presents his views on nonviolence and the movement in Mississippi.

Excerpted from Malcolm X, "To Mississippi Youth," in George Breitman, ed., Malcolm X Speaks: Selected Speeches and Statements *(New York, 1965), 138, 142-44.*

My experience has been that in many instances where you find Negroes talking about nonviolence, they are not nonviolent with each other, and they're not loving with each other, or forgiving with each other. Usually when they say they're nonviolent, they mean they're nonviolent with somebody else. I think you understand what I mean. They are nonviolent with the enemy. A person can come to your home, and if he's white and wants to heap some kind of brutality on you, you're nonviolent. . . . But if another Negro just stomps his foot, you'll rumble with him in a minute. Which shows you that there's an inconsistency there.

Condemned by many as a racist and extremist, Malcolm X, provided an important alternative to Martin Luther King's nonviolent tactics. (Courtesy of Bettmann/Corbis.)

I myself would go for nonviolence if it was consistent, if everybody was going to be nonviolent all the time. I'd say, okay, let's get with it, we'll all be nonviolent. But I don't go along with any kind of nonviolence unless everybody's going to be nonviolent. If they make the Ku Klux Klan nonviolent, I'll be nonviolent. If they make the White Citizens Council nonviolent, I'll be nonviolent. But as long as you've got somebody else not being nonviolent, I don't want anybody coming to me talking any nonviolent talk. . . .

In studying the process of this so-called [racial] progress during the past twenty years, we of the Organization of Afro-American Unity realized that the only time the black man in this country is given any kind of recognition, or even listened to, is when America is afraid of outside pressure, or when she's afraid of her image abroad. . . .

And today you'll find in the United Nations, and it's not an accident, that every time the Congo question or anything on the African continent is being debated, they couple it with what is going on, or what is happening to you and me, in Mississippi and Alabama and these other places. In my opinion, the greatest accomplishment that was made in the struggle of the black man in America in 1964 toward some kind of real progress was the successful linking together of our problem with the African problem, or making our problem a world problem. . . .

So we here in the Organization of Afro-American Unity are with the struggle in Mississippi one thousand per cent. We're with the efforts to register our people in Mississippi to vote one thousand per cent. But we do not go along with anybody telling us to help nonviolently. We think that if the government says that Negroes have a right to vote, and then some Negroes come out to vote, and some kind of Ku Klux Klan is going to put them in the river, and the government doesn't do anything about it, it's time for us to organize and band together and equip ourselves and qualify ourselves to protect ourselves. And once you can protect yourself, you don't have to worry about being hurt. . . .

If you don't have enough people down there to do it, we'll come down there and help you do it. Because we're tired of this old runaround that our people have been given in this country. For a long time they accused me of not getting involved in politics. They should've been glad I didn't get involved in politics, because anything I get in, I'm in it all the way. If they say we don't take part in the Mississippi struggle, we will organize brothers here in New York who know how to handle these kind of affairs, and they'll slip into Mississippi like Jesus slipped into Jerusalem.

Questions

1. *How did these people and organizations use nonviolent direct action? Do they have similar ideas about nonviolence?*
2. *What are some of the dangers that activists in the movement faced?*
3. *Did King and his allies, members of SNCC, and Malcolm X understand each others' views on nonviolence and activism? Was there any common ground between them?*
4. *Do these documents suggest that some people were more idealistic in the 1950s and 1960s? Why or why not?*
5. *Do you think that you could have been an activist like any of these people? What factors would encourage or inhibit you?*

FURTHER READING

Race & Democracy: The Civil Rights Struggle in Louisiana, 1915-1972 by Adam Fairclough (Athens, 1995) demonstrates that civil rights struggles began with the twentieth century. Two studies that analyze the indigenous roots of the movement and emphasize the roles of local leaders are Charles M. Payne, *I've Got the Light of Freedom: The Organizing Tradition and the Mississippi Freedom Struggle* (Berkeley, 1995); and John Dittmer, *Local People: The Struggle for Civil Rights in Mississippi* (Urbana, 1994). The best history of SNCC is still Clayborne Carson, *In Struggle: SNCC and the Black Awakening of the 1960s* (Cambridge, 1995); and there is a collection of fascinating interviews with organizers in *A Circle of Trust: Remembering SNCC*, ed. Cheryl Lynn Greenberg (New Brunswick, 1998). *But for Birmingham: The Local and National Movements in the Civil Rights Struggle* by Glenn T. Eskew (Chapel Hill, 1997) examines one of the most important civil rights campaigns of the 1960s. Belinda Robnett's *How Long? How Long? African-American Women in the Struggle for Civil Rights* (New York, 1997) is a long-awaited study of women's activism that provides a theoretical framework for exploring their unique roles in the movement. Biographies have provided some of the best scholarship on the movement, and the second volume of Taylor Branch's biography of King, *Pillar of Fire: America in the King Years, 1963-65* (New York, 1998), is now available. The life of a significant, but overlooked, woman who was responsible for running SNCC is eloquently presented in Cynthia Griggs Fleming, *Soon We Will Not Cry: The Liberation of Ruby Doris Smith Robinson* (Lanham, Maryland, 1998). A thoughtful comparison of the ideas of King and Malcolm X can be found in James H. Cone, *Martin & Malcolm & America: A Dream or a Nightmare* (Maryknoll, New York, 1992).

Why Did the United States Lose the Vietnam War?

Mark Grimsley

INTRODUCTION

Ordered to return to Southeast Asia at the beginning of Rambo: First Blood Part II *(1985), the title character caustically inquires, "Do we get to win this time?" The premise of the film, and a raft of others like it, was that the United States betrayed the soldiers it sent to fight in Vietnam—in part because the U.S. government allegedly abandoned POWs and MIAs it knew were being held after the war's end (Rambo's mission is to retrieve them), but more fundamentally because the American military could have won the war if only the American government and people had let them. The fictional Rambo's bitterness reflects a very real bitterness among certain segments of American society. Equally bitter are those who believe that the United States could not possibly have won the war at reasonable cost, and therefore should not have intervened in the first place. Thus, the question, "Why did the United States lose the Vietnam War?" is possibly the most divisive issue in recent American history.*

The United States plainly lost the war in the sense that it committed its armed might and prestige to a venture that ultimately failed. But in an important sense—as people on both sides of the issue acknowledge—the United States could not have "won" the Vietnam War. Only the South Vietnamese government could do that. From the first, American policy in Vietnam was designed to assist the South Vietnamese toward that end. The difficulty lies in assessing the extent to which that policy succeeded—or might *have succeeded—in helping the South Vietnamese regime prevail against its Communist rivals, the North Vietnamese and the Viet Cong.*

Both North and South Vietnam were barely a decade old when the first American combat troops splashed ashore in 1965. Before 1954, Vietnam had been part of French Indochina, a colony that also included present-day Laos and Cambodia. France's defeat by the Germans in 1940 had allowed the Japanese to occupy Indochina during World War II. After Japan's defeat in 1945, the French had returned to find that Vietnamese nationalists, led by Ho Chi Minh, now sought complete independence from any foreign power. A long, bitter guerrilla war began soon thereafter. Because Ho Chi Minh and his followers were avowed Communists, the United States supported the French with money and equipment. After a stunning defeat in 1954 led the French to abandon Indochina, the United States was party to an agreement whereby Vietnam was divided at the 17th parallel into two parts—North Vietnam, controlled by the Communists, and South Vietnam, controlled by Ngo Dinh Diem, a ruler friendly to the United States but only weakly supported by the South Vietnamese people.

In 1961, the Communist North Vietnamese organized the National Liberation Front, composed of South Vietnamese who wished to defeat the Diem regime and unite with North Vietnam. Dubbed the "Viet Cong"—short for Vietnamese Communists—the National Liberation Front soon began a guerrilla war against the Diem regime, supported directly by North Vietnam and indirectly by the Soviet Union and Communist China. The John F. Kennedy administration regarded South Vietnam as a bulwark against communism in Southeast Asia and supported the South Vietnamese government with money, equipment, and military advisers. By 1963, however, it was clear that the Diem regime was too inept to defeat the Viet Cong. Hoping that new leadership might improve the situation, the U.S. government approved a military coup in which Diem was killed. When the situation in South Vietnam continued to decline, Kennedy's successor, Lyndon B. Johnson, began bombing attacks against North Vietnam in August 1964, followed by the commitment of ground troops in early 1965.

By deploying American armed forces directly, the Johnson administration believed it could force the North Vietnamese and

Viet Cong to desist from further aggression against South Vietnam. But the Johnson administration deliberately chose to conduct the war in a limited fashion, fearing that unrestricted bombing or an invasion of North Vietnam risked intervention by the Communist Chinese (as had occurred during the Korean War). The Johnson administration also feared that a full military mobilization would undercut its ambitious domestic spending program, the Great Society. But surely, it was thought, complete military mobilization was unnecessary to defeat a small Third World nation. A Marine lieutenant sent to Vietnam spoke for many Americans when he remarked, "[W]e carried, along with our packs and rifles, the implicit conviction that the Viet Cong would be quickly beaten."

Eight years later, in 1973, after losing more than fifty-eight thousand American lives, the United States withdrew from South Vietnam. The South Vietnamese regime fell to a final North Vietnamese invasion in 1975. What happened?

The Turning Point: Tet 1968

Until early 1968, Americans were told—and most believed—that the United States was winning the war in Vietnam. Although this reflected the sincere opinions of many U.S. policymakers, it also was due to a deliberately orchestrated public relations campaign of "accentuating the positive." In their public pronouncements, American officials emphasized U.S. and South Vietnamese successes, while carefully downplaying elements that suggested a bleaker picture.

Then, on 31 January 1968, the North Vietnamese and Viet Cong launched surprise attacks all over South Vietnam, striking at over a hundred cities and towns, including the capital city of Saigon itself. Timed to take advantage of a temporary truce in observance of the Lunar New Year—"Tet"—this massive wave of attacks at once became known as the Tet Offensive. Historians agree that it was a major turning point in America's involvement in Vietnam.

It would be wrong to say that, prior to Tet, most Americans were enthusiastic about the war. A poll taken in November 1967 revealed that 44 percent of Americans favored a gradual or total withdrawal from Vietnam, while another 55 percent believed the United States should pursue a more vigorous policy. But the Tet Offensive greatly intensified doubts that the United States could defeat the Communists within an acceptable time frame and at an acceptable cost. This was not because the Tet Offensive was a victory for North Vietnamese and Viet Cong forces. On the contrary, in purely military terms it was a Communist disaster. Gen. William C. Westmoreland, the commander of U.S. forces in Vietnam, estimated that as many as fifty thousand North Vietnamese and Viet Cong soldiers were killed. Yet two thousand Americans (and four thousand South Vietnamese soldiers, as well as over twelve thousand South Vietnamese civilians) also perished—a staggering casualty list that made a hollow boast of predictions that the war could be won within a year or two. Respected and influential television journalist Walter Cronkite captured the mood of many Americans in the wake of Tet: "To say that we are mired in stalemate seems the only reasonable, yet unsatisfactory conclusion."

The following excerpts portray the shock of the Tet Offensive, its impact on American public opinion and policymakers, and the shift in U.S. policy it generated.

The Attack on the U.S. Embassy

The initial phase of the Tet Offensive included a strike against the U.S. Embassy in Saigon. Militarily it was—as one American officer said dismissively—"a piddling platoon action," but politically it was stunning. If the huge American military presence in South Vietnam could not prevent Viet Cong commandos from storming the U.S. Embassy, the feeling went, how could it possibly be achieving the success that American generals and officials were promising?

American journalist Don Oberdorfer drew on dozens of personal interviews as well as official sources for his account of the Tet Offensive, published in 1971. Here he describes the embassy attack. Excerpted from Don Oberdorfer, Tet! *(1971; reprint ed., New York, 1984), 6–8, 28.*

On a Saigon street corner just before midnight, a wiry, muscular man named Nguyen Van Sau kept a rendezvous with an officer of the Viet Cong C-10 Battalion. Sau was a squad leader normally stationed at battalion base headquarters, which was near the Michelin Rubber Plantation only thirty miles north of the capital. He came to the site of the battle the day before not as a soldier in formation, but as an ordinary civilian on the back of a commercial truck on a main highway—just one more traveling celebrant of the national festival of Tet.

Like many soldiers of the revolution, Sau had been an illiterate farmer when he was recruited for the cause. Born in a village on the outskirts of Saigon, he attended only one year of school before going to work in the rice fields. He joined the Liberation

Army [the Viet Cong] in 1964. . . . When the C-10 battalion was established for sapper [a term, normally used to describe a combat engineer, but used by the Viet Cong to mean a commando-raider] and sabotage activities in the Saigon area in late 1965, Sau was assigned to the unit. In 1966 he was promoted to squad leader and in March of 1967 he was permitted to join the People's Revolutionary Party, the Communist Party of South Vietnam.

In November of 1967—three months prior to Tet—Sau's section of the C-10 Battalion began to ship ammunition and explosives to Saigon from a supply cache at headquarters. The first shipment of ammunition and TNT [explosive] moved in a rented truck piled high with firewood. Three other shipments were concealed in large baskets of tomatoes which came into the city down Route 1.

Two days before Tet, big and unusually heavy baskets of "tomatoes" and large bamboo containers of "rice" were moved to a house adjoining the small automobile repair shop at 59 Phan Thanh Gian Street. The house and garage were owned by Mrs. Nguyen Thi Phe, who had been working for the Viet Cong in Saigon for thirteen years and had been arrested several times for subversive activities.

Shortly after midnight on Tet night, sapper Sau and the other members of the team assembled at the garage. The shipments of weapons were broken out and distributed, and the soldiers briefed for the first time on their combat mission. It is probable that most of them, including Sau, had barely heard of the United States Embassy and had little understanding of the significance of their mission that night. Sau did not learn what he was supposed to do after penetrating the exterior wall of the Embassy compound. Nothing was said about replacements or an escape route, but there is no indication the soldiers were told this was a suicide raid.

At 2:45 A.M. they were rolling through the streets toward the Embassy in a small Peugeot truck and a taxicab. . . . The truck and taxi turned the corner onto Thong Nhut (Reunification) Boulevard, a broad, tree-lined avenue dominated on one side by the eight-foot outer wall of the American Embassy compound. As the taxicab rounded the corner, its passengers opened fire with automatic weapons at the two MPs [military policemen] standing just outside the night gate of the Embassy on the side street. The small truck stopped on the boulevard side of the high compound wall.

American soldiers guard the U.S. embassy building in Saigon after its attack by Viet Cong snappers during the Tet Offensive. News of the attack shocked the American home front, exploding the myth that the United States was on the brink of victory in Vietnam. (Courtesy of Dick Swanson/ Life Magazine © Time, Inc.)

The men, wearing neckerchiefs and arm bands for identification, climbed out and quickly began unloading rockets and explosive charges.

Specialist Fourth Class Charles L. Daniel, twenty-three, of Durham, North Carolina, and Private First Class William E. Sebast, twenty, of Albany, New York, fired back at the taxicab, then moved inside. They slammed the steel gate and locked it with a heavy padlock and chain. At 2:47 A.M. they radioed "Signal 300"—MP brevity code for enemy attack.

A moment later an explosion rocked the compound. With a flash and a blast, a fifteen-pound explosive charge blew a three-foot hole in the high wall of the compound near the corner where the truck had stopped.

Daniel and Sebast wheeled around and began firing at the invaders scrambling through the hole. Daniel shouted into the MP radio: "They're coming in! They're coming in! Help me! Help me!" Then the radio went dead. Daniel's body was found later with bullet wounds in the head; Sebast had been shot through the chest. From the positions of their bodies and the bullet holes in the wall behind them, it appeared they were facing the invaders when they died. It is likely that their first shots killed the two Viet Cong leaders, the first men through the hole in the wall.

A Military Police jeep patrol cruising several blocks away heard the call for help and responded immediately. Sergeant Jonnie B. Thomas, twenty-four, of Detroit, and Specialist Fourth Class Owen E. Mebust, twenty, of Lynwood, California, sped down the boulevard toward the Embassy. They were met by a hail of automatic weapons fire. Thomas and Mebust were the third and fourth Americans to be killed at the Embassy in the first five minutes.

U.S. Public Learns of Attack

The first news reports of the attack on the Embassy flashed worldwide barely fifteen minutes after it began. An Associated Press correspondent wired a steady stream of updates by teletype. His reports reached New York just as the major television networks were about to air their evening news programs. Here is the lead story that night as broadcast by NBC anchorman Chet Huntley:

> The Vietcong seized part of the U.S. Embassy in Saigon early Wednesday, Vietnam time. Snipers are in the buildings and on roof tops near the Embassy and are firing on American personnel inside the compound.
>
> Twenty suicide commandos are reported to be holding the first floor of the Embassy.
>
> The attack on the Embassy and other key installations in Saigon, at Tan Son Nhut Air Base and Bien Hoa north of Saigon came as the climax of the enemy's biggest and most highly coordinated offensive of the war. There was no report on Allied casualties in Saigon, but they're believed to be high.

In the Vietnam War, stunning images like this one frequently undercut a more nuanced view of the conflict. Here South Vietnam's National Police Chief summarily executes a Viet Cong officer in the early days of the Tet Offensive. This image horrified the American public; few learned the officer had been captured after murdering several civilian hostages, including a mother and her children. (Photograph by Eddie Adams. Courtesy of AP/Wide World Photos.)

The attacks came as thousands of civilians were celebrating the Lunar New Year, and at times it was almost impossible to distinguish the explosion of mortar shells and small arms fire from those of the firecrackers the celebrants were setting off.

General Westmoreland Reacts

Although surprised by the scope and ferocity of the Tet Offensive, Gen. Westmoreland, the commander of MACV (Military Assistance Command, Vietnam), regarded it with some reason as a major Communist miscalculation and a potential U.S. opportunity. As for the attack on the embassy, to him it was tactically insignificant, virtually a blip on the screen. He was therefore somewhat surprised that the White House seemed inordinately concerned about it, and even more so when he arrived at the embassy shortly after its recapture by U.S. troops—an event that occurred barely six hours after Sau and his comrades first entered the compound. Taken from William C. Westmoreland, A Soldier Reports, *(Garden City, New York, 1976), 324–25.*

With the coming of daylight a platoon of U.S. airborne troops landed on the helicopter pad on the roof of the Chancery [the main embassy building], but by that time the fight was over. All fifteen VC sappers were dead, along with the five Americans and four Vietnamese employees of the Embassy, one of whom may have been a VC collaborator.

As soon as I learned that the airborne troops had landed, I drove by car to the Embassy. It was about 8:30 A.M. Like any battlefield, the compound was in disarray, bodies of Americans and Vietnamese still lying about. Yet unlike most battlefields, American reporters and television cameramen were seemingly everywhere. Their faces mirrored dismay and incredulity, as if the end of the world was at hand.

... [I was asked] to hold a press conference on the scene. I took the opportunity to try to put the Embassy raid and the countryside attacks into perspective.

Contrary to rumor, I said, none of the Viet Cong had gotten inside the Chancery. Damage to the building was superficial. As for the big offensive throughout the country, the enemy, by coming into the open, was exposing himself to tremendous casualties. Fully conscious of American and South Vietnamese strength and ability, I had no hesitation in saying that the enemy was inviting defeat.

My efforts at perspective went for nought. The attack on the Embassy, [journalist] Don Oberdorfer wrote later, "seemed to give the lie to the rosy projections and victory claims that Westmoreland and others had been dishing out." Oberdorfer said that the reporters could hardly believe their ears. "Westmoreland was standing in the ruins and saying everything was great."

That attitude on the part of the American reporters undoubtedly contributed to the psychological victory the enemy achieved in the United States. What would they have had me say, that the walls were tumbling down when I knew they were not? That the enemy was winning when I knew he was on the verge of a disastrous military defeat? . . .

In the race to drain every possible sensation from the Embassy story, reporters made little apparent effort to check facts. . . . Chet Huntley on the NBC Evening News had the VC inside the Chancery, the defenders in the compound outside. There was no report on Allied casualties in Saigon, said Huntley, "but they're believed to be high." Was that kind of gratuitous speculation justified? Was the long, costly American effort in Vietnam to be sacrificed to the idols of sensation and competition?

A Reporter's View

Peter Braestrup was the Saigon bureau chief for the Washington Post at the time of the Tet Offensive. In later years he wrote a study of news coverage during the offensive that echoed the criticisms made by Westmoreland. "[M]any of these reporters," Braestrup acknowledged, "were inexperienced in military operations or in the tactics of the Communists. Particularly the television people had no real grip on the football game. They could go out and take pictures of the players and the drama. But they were like sportswriters who had no concept of the game they were covering." Even so, Braestrup rejected the view that the media was the primary culprit in shaping the myth that Tet was a military disaster for the Americans and South Vietnamese. Abridged from Al Santoli, To Bear Any Burden: The Vietnam War and Its Aftermath in the Words of Americans and Southeast Asians, *(New York, 1985), 180–81.*

The press, in terms of themes they convey, are a reflective institution. They have cultural biases and there are trends and fashions. But on the big issues, the president of the United States dominates when he wants to. Why did the media press the panic button at Tet? President Lyndon Johnson seemed to have been struck by a kind of immobility. . . .

Johnson knew that something big was coming because General Westmoreland had told him. He had sent reinforcements ahead of time—the 11th Infantry Brigade from Hawaii and two brigades of the 101st Airborne.

But Johnson never mentioned this in his State of the Union Address [just prior to the Tet Offensive]. He was doing everything possible to downplay the idea of war—and, with an election year in progress, upgrade the idea of peace negotiations. So he failed to prepare the public or the press.

From the start, the President had failed to define a clear strategy for winning the war. He failed to mobilize the country or decide how we were going to end the war. He was grasping for straws and buying time, hoping something would turn up. Public opinion—the man on the street—doesn't quite know what's going on, but he's not satisfied with this. So Lyndon brought home the famous "progress campaign" of 1967. Everybody was brought in from Vietnam, including General Westmoreland, to say, "We're making progress." That was short-term relief in the Gallup polls for Lyndon. Then comes Tet.

All of a sudden, everybody is saying, "We can't go on like this." The hawks are saying it behind closed doors, the doves are saying it out loud. And Johnson isn't saying anything. For two months he doesn't say anything and takes no decisive action. He did not do what Richard Nixon did in the 1972 election year—send in the B-52s and mine Haiphong Harbor—take a forceful retaliatory posture against the North Vietnamese. Nixon's popularity went up. And though he wasn't popular with the press, his policy was coherent. They understood that he had a scenario. He did not leave a vacuum. He was a decisive, forceful president in a time of crisis. That is what the public looks to. And that is what the press looks to also.

At Tet, Lyndon Johnson in effect got into his bunker. He left the political debate and furor in the hands of his critics and to the press. Johnson was in a crisis of his own making. The press will aggravate any president's problems. If the President is nervous or indecisive, the press will make it worse. And more of his critics will come out of the woodwork.

The press, in effect, becomes a prism. Concentrating the heat on the White House. But the President starts the demoralization himself. He's like the platoon leader. If they run into an ambush, all the troops look to the platoon leader to take charge. If he's lying on the ground for ten, twenty, a hundred seconds, the troops get demoralized himself. That's what happened at Tet. One trooper, like Walter Cronkite, who's a little shook, will say, "Let's get the hell out of here." Panic will start. And the press will overreact to everything. That's the way they are.

Questions in the Wake of Tet

In fact, President Lyndon B. Johnson briefly wanted to redouble the American military effort after Tet, as Gen. Westmoreland advised. But many of his advisers had doubts, among them, newly-appointed Secretary of Defense Clark Clifford. Clifford replaced Robert S. McNamara, who had quietly resigned the office because of misgivings about American policy in Vietnam (policy he had done as much as anyone to create). Clifford soon had misgivings of his own. Taken from Clark M. Clifford, "A Viet Nam Reappraisal: The Personal History of One Man's View and How It Evolved," Foreign Affairs *47 (July 1969): 609–13.*

I took office on March 1, 1968. The enemy's Tet offensive of late January and early February had been beaten back at great cost. The confidence of the American people had been badly shaken. The ability of the South Vietnamese Government to restore order and morale in the populace, and discipline and esprit in the armed forces, was being questioned. At the President's direction, General Earle G. Wheeler, Chairman of the Joint Chiefs of Staff, had flown to Viet Nam in late February for an on-the-spot conference with General Westmoreland. He had just returned and presented the military's request that over 200,000 troops be prepared for deployment to Viet Nam. These troops would be in addition to the 525,000 previously authorized. I was directed, as my first assignment, to chair a task force named by the President to determine how this new requirement could be met. We were not instructed to assess the need for substantial increases in men and matériel; we were to devise the means by which they could be provided.... Try though we would to stay with the assignment of devising means to meet the military's requests, fundamental questions began to recur over and over.

... [H]ere are some of the principal issues raised and some of the answers as I understood them:

"Will 200,000 more men do the job?" I found no assurance that they would.

"If not, how many more might be needed—and when?" There was no way of knowing.

"What would be involved in committing 200,000 more men to Viet Nam?" A reserve call-up of approximately 280,000, an increased draft call and an extension of tours of duty of most men then in service.

"Can the enemy respond with a build-up of his own?" He could and he probably would.

"What are the estimated costs of the latest requests?" First calculations were on the order of $2 billion for the remaining four months of that fiscal year, and an increase of $10 to $12 billion for the year beginning July 1, 1968.

"What will be the impact on the economy?" So great that we would face the possibility of credit restrictions, a tax increase and even wage and price controls. The balance of payments would be worsened by at least half a billion dollars a year.

"Can bombing stop the war?" Never by itself. It was inflicting heavy personnel and matériel losses, but bombing by itself would not stop the war.

"Will stepping up the bombing decrease American casualties?" Very little, if at all. Our casualties were due to the intensity of the ground fighting in the South. We had already dropped a heavier tonnage of bombs than in all the theaters of World War II. During 1967, an estimated 90,000 North Vietnamese had infiltrated into South Viet Nam. In the opening weeks of 1968, infiltrators were coming in at three to four times the rate of a year earlier, despite the ferocity and intensity of our campaign of aerial interdiction.

In the wake of the Tet Offensive, Lyndon Johnson wearily reviews the text of a major televised address on Vietnam. The address, given on March 31, 1968, ended with his announcement that he would not seek a second full term as president—a surprise decision for which the Tet Offensive was largely responsible. (Courtesy of Corbis-Bettmann.)

"How long must we keep on sending our men and carrying the main burden of combat?" The South Vietnamese were doing better, but they were not ready yet to replace our troops and we did not know when they would be.

When I asked for a presentation of the military plan for attaining victory in Viet Nam, I was told that there was no plan for victory in the historic American sense. Why not? Because our forces were operating under three major political restrictions: The President had forbidden the invasion of North Viet Nam because this could trigger the mutual assistance pact between North Viet Nam and China; the President had forbidden the mining of the harbor at Haiphong, the principal port through which the North received military supplies, because a Soviet vessel might be sunk; the President had forbidden our forces to pursue the enemy into Laos and Cambodia, for to do so would spread the war, politically and geographically, with no discernible advantage. These and other restrictions which precluded an all-out, no-holds-barred military effort were wisely designed to prevent our being drawn into a larger war. We had no inclination to recommend to the President their cancellation.

"Given these circumstances, how can we win?" We would, I was told, continue to evidence our superiority over the enemy; we would continue to attack in the belief that he would reach the stage where he would find it inadvisable to go on with the war. He could not afford the attrition we were inflicting on him. And we were improving our posture all the time.

I then asked, "What is the best estimate as to how long this course of action will take? Six months? One year? Two years?" There was no agreement on an answer. Not only was there no agreement, I could find no one willing to express any confidence in his guesses. Certainly, none of us was willing to assert that he could see "light at the end of the tunnel" or that American troops would be coming home by the end of the year.

After days of this type of analysis, my concern had greatly deepened. I could not find out when the war was going to end; I could not find out the manner in which it was going to end; I could not find out whether the new requests for men and equipment were going to be enough, or whether it would take more and, if more, when and how much; I could not find out how soon the South Vietnamese forces would be ready to take over. All I had was the statement, given with too little self-assurance to be comforting, that if we persisted for an indeterminate length of time, the enemy would choose not to go on.

And so I asked, "Does anyone see any diminution in the will of the enemy after four years of our having been there, after enormous casualties and after massive destruction from our bombing?"

The answer was that there appeared to be no diminution in the will of the enemy. . . .

And so, after these exhausting days, I was convinced that the military course we were pursuing was not only endless, but hopeless. A further substantial increase in American forces could only increase the devastation and the Americanization of the war, and thus leave us even further from our goal of a peace that would permit the people of South Viet Nam to fashion their own political and economic institutions. Henceforth, I was also convinced, our primary goal should be to level off our involvement, and to work toward gradual disengagement.

Partly as a result of these meetings, Johnson soon decided against a major increase in the military effort in Vietnam. Instead he suspended the bombing of North Vietnam and began to pursue peace negotiations with the North Vietnamese and Viet Cong. (These dragged on for several years, with little result until the 1973 Paris Peace Accords.) With his popularity at an all-time low, Johnson also declared that he would not run for a second term as president. From then on, he and his successor, Richard Nixon, worked toward disengaging the United States from the "quagmire" in Vietnam.

Questions

1. *Compare the views of Gen. Westmoreland and Peter Braestrup on the American press corps during the Tet Offensive. Whose perspective do you find more persuasive and why?*
2. *The German military philosopher Carl von Clausewitz maintained that in war the ultimate objective is to break the enemy's will to continue the struggle. Evaluate the Tet Offensive in this light. Did it break the American will to continue the struggle?*
3. *Did Secretary of Defense Clark Clifford ask the right questions in his reevaluation of America's involvement in Vietnam? Are there other questions you believe he ought to have asked as well?*
4. *Did American policymakers make the right decision in choosing to disengage gradually from Vietnam after Tet? What other courses were available to them? What would you have done?*

Further Reading

The best survey of America's involvement in Vietnam is George C. Herring, America's Longest War: The United States and Vietnam, 1950–1975 *(New York, 1986). Stanley Karnow,* Vietnam: A History *(New York, 1983) is a sound, readable treatment of the entire thirty-year conflict, prepared as a companion to the PBS television series of the same name. (The PBS series, available on video, is well worth watching.) Don Oberdorfer,* Tet! *(Garden City, New York, 1971) remains the best account of the pivotal Communist offensive.* After Tet: The Bloodiest Year in Vietnam *(New York, 1993), by Ronald H. Spector, cogently weaves together political and military developments to create an effective snapshot of the American war effort at its height. As secretary of defense under both Kennedy and Johnson, Robert S. McNamara contributed heavily to the flawed American policy in Vietnam. His memoir,* In Retrospect: The Tragedy and Lessons of Vietnam *(New York, 1995) describes, in heavily self-critical tones, how that policy evolved.* On Strategy: A Critical Analysis of the Vietnam War *(Novato, California, 1982), by Harry G. Summers, Jr., makes the case that the United States could have prevailed in Vietnam had it adopted a better strategy. Although marred by bias and a turgid style, Gabriel Kolko,* Anatomy of a War: Vietnam, the United States, and the Modern Historical Experience *(New York, 1985), best illuminates the Vietnamese Communist revolutionary movement; it is unyielding in its insistence that the United States could not possibly have won.*

The Vietnam Era Antiwar Movement

David H. Steigerwald

Introduction

The vast expansion of American military intervention in Vietnam kicked off the most divisive episode in twentieth-century national life. Culminating almost two decades of growing involvement, the Johnson administration initiated a systematic bombing campaign and introduced ground troops in 1965 while avoiding sustained public debate. President Johnson wanted to leave the impression that no new policy was being set, and he believed that Congress had given him the necessary approval when it allowed him "to take all necessary measures to repel any armed attacks" against U.S. forces in Southeast Asia in the Gulf of Tonkin resolution (August 1964). Beneath this reasoning, however, lay the knowledge that the majority of Americans showed no fervor for a war in Vietnam. The successful prosecution of American military policy, the administration came to believe, required not a cultivation of public support but a campaign that made as little public noise as possible, as National Security Advisor McGeorge Bundy once advised. Johnson and his advisors faced an even deeper problem in regard to public opinion: they had launched a war that was, at best, extremely difficult to justify. Because it was difficult to defend an intervention on behalf of an incompetent and disorganized regime in South Vietnam, the administration traded debate for accusation and charged its opponents with everything from naiveté to treason. In so doing, the administration itself helped fuel a substantial antiwar movement.

It is little wonder that many Americans spoke out against both the expansion of the war and the disingenuous politics of the administration. The earliest opponents of the war included the nation's foremost foreign policy authorities, George Kennan,

Walter Lippmann, Hans Morgenthau, and J. William Fulbright, each of whom voiced serious misgivings about American involvement in Vietnam even before 1965. Military expansion, meanwhile, reignited a latent peace movement by galvanizing old organizations, such as the pacifist Fellowship of Reconciliation (FOR), with newer antinuclear groups, such as Women Strike for Peace (WSP) and Citizens for a Sane Nuclear Policy (SANE). Many of these groups represented mainstream political progressives, but the movement accumulated a large left wing with the emergence of Students for a Democratic Society (SDS), the main organization of radical students. Unlike the mainstream groups, SDS had a "non-exclusion" policy of cooperation with the Communist Progressive Labor Party (PL), which insinuated itself into the movement through SDS. Yet another type of activist, the hippie, entered the movement by 1967, less through any organization than simply by virtue of the increasingly influential counterculture. The movement ultimately included teachers and students, young and old, pacifist nuns and Maoists preaching armed revolution.

These many voices generated varied arguments against the war. The establishment critics attacked the American anti-Soviet and anti-Communist policy of "containment" and the domino theory, which held that if any one country would fall to communism, others were sure to follow. These detractors believed that American foreign policy in practice imprudently extended American resources and expanded American interests to where they neither belonged nor could be sufficiently protected. As the administration spurned them, antiwar activists began to argue that the war revealed much deeper problems in American life. That the liberal Johnson administration could initiate great reform at home while waging war against an impoverished people fighting for independence from Western imperialism indicated, so activists argued, that the American system, for all its wealth and technology—indeed, because of these very things—was out of control. More radical activists, largely emerging out of SDS, insisted that the war grew out of the will to dominate inherent in Western capitalism. This same system concentrated wealth in a few hands, suppressed racial minorities at home, and could be brought to an end, therefore, only through wholesale revolution. These were not readily compatible positions and they reveal the deep differences within the antiwar movement that discourage decisive assessments of the movement's importance.

VOICES OF DISSENT

Though the internal politics of the antiwar movement were often divisive and its public protests messy and chaotic, the path of antiwar argument ran along a fairly coherent path: fairly narrow criticisms of U.S. foreign policy turned, in the face of official lying, harassment, and ongoing war, increasingly strident and radical. Even the most conservative dissenters gradually concluded that the war revealed deep flaws in the very nature of America. J. William Fulbright, for example, chair of the Senate Foreign Relations Committee, came to see the war as a regrettable result of an "arrogance of power," while younger activists argued that only a dehumanized, bureaucratized society could unleash such senseless destruction. The radical turn was mirrored by the media-assisted rise of SDS and also of more confrontational forms of protest. In the midst of intellectual, organizational, and strategic radicalization, many movement leaders embraced an increasingly dogmatic preoccupation with anti-capitalist and anti-imperialist theory, a dogmatism much at odds with the variety and openness of the movement itself.

LBJ Launches the Quiet War

Lyndon Johnson attempted to militarize American policy in Vietnam with little public notice, a sure sign that neither public support nor pressing national interests lay behind that policy. As the antiwar journalist I. F. Stone points out in the following piece, the public relations hush was completely out of character with Johnson's method of centralized, high-profile decision making. Stone implies that the administration proceeded in this fashion because the policy itself was indefensible. The following piece is one of the many broadsides that the independent Stone launched at Johnson through the years.

Excerpted from I. F. Stone, In a Time of Torment, 1961-1967 *(Boston, 1967), 58-61.*

There seems to be a peculiar division of labor here in Washington. The President makes peace speeches and the Pentagon makes foreign policy but the unpleasant task of declaring war is left to the poor State Department. The news that U.S. troops in Vietnam have been authorized to engage in full combat is the news that we are embarking on a new war. Article I, Section 8, of the Constitution, that half-forgotten document, put the power to declare war in the hands of Congress. Its members might insist at least that they have the right to hear declarations of war from some official higher up than the press officer of the State Department. It is hard to find any Constitutional or administrative reason to explain why Robert J. McCloskey, the press officer, should have been pushed suddenly into the pages of history by being assigned the task of announcing at his daily, usually routine and almost always boring, noon press briefing that we were no longer advising or patrolling or defensively shooting back in Vietnam but going full-scale into war. As a major decision, it should have been announced at the White House. As a change in military orders, it might have been made public at the Pentagon. As a hot potato, both seem to have passed it on to the State Department. There in turn it was passed on down from the Secretary through the many Assistant Secretaries to the lowest echelon available. Maybe the higher-ups are hoping it will be called not Johnson's or [Secretary of Defense Robert] McNamara's but Bob McCloskey's war.

Nothing better attests [to] the slim popular support for the war than the care thus exercised by Lyndon Johnson not to be photographed marching at the head of the troops straight into it. The White House acted as if it couldn't be bothered by such trivial matters. . . . This genius at obfuscation was evident in the very form of the announcement given McCloskey to read: the U.S. commander in Saigon had been authorized to commit U.S. troops to "combat support" of South Vietnam units *if* asked to do so by the South Vietnamese government. This would seem to put the

The march on the Pentagon, October 1967. (Courtesy of Corbis Images.)

power to declare America at war in the hands of whoever happened to be on top in Saigon's Ferris wheel changes of government and military command. This is quite a departure from the tight centralization of powers characteristic of the Johnson Administration. Here in Washington minor officials can hardly announce a new post office for Chilicothe, Ohio, without clearing it with the White House. But whether or not our troops move into full combat will be decided by someone 9000 miles away whose name the papers can't even spell properly. Delegation of powers has never been so distant. It looks as if while the rest of us may be plunged into war, Lyndon Johnson wants to keep as far away from it as possible. . . .

The truth is that the South Vietnamese army is out of reserves. . . . The political situation is as precarious as the military. . . . The shaky government and its shakier military needed the shot in the arm of a public announcement that they were being given a blank check to draw as they pleased on American manpower. But worse is in the offing. Military planners here must be prepared to deal with the possibility that the Viet Cong may soon inflict so heavy a blow as to demoralize the South Vietnamese forces and make impossible the maintenance of any governmental façade in beleaguered Saigon. Very shortly the problem may be more serious than providing mobile reserves to rescue South Vietnamese forces from unexpected attacks. The problem soon may be that if resistance is to go on, the U.S. will have to take over the government and the war altogether.

So we will do what we swore after the Korean war we would never do again—commit American troops to an Asian land war. Militarily and politically, McCloskey's war is folly. It will tie down a major portion of U.S. military power in a minor theatre of conflict, and create an image made to order for hostile propaganda. White men will be fighting colored men in an effort to put down a rebellion so deeply rooted that it has gone on for two decades, and extended its power steadily during the four years in which we trained, directed and supplied a satellite native army. . . .

If our troops meet serious reverses in the South, it will be hard to resist the clamor for a tougher bombing policy in the North. If Hanoi and Haiphong are bombed, the North will have nothing to lose and will escalate the war by moving its army south. Those elements in our military itching for a preventive war against China will press for bombing the roads and railroads which connect it with Vietnam. Whether and how China will react, what Russia will do, are unknowns. . . . To go to war is to leave oneself at the mercy of the unexpected. How far it will spread and how many lives it will cost depends on the capricious roulette of war. One thing alone is certain. The further we get in, the harder it will be to get out.

The Establishment Critics' Dissent

In the following excerpt, Hans Morgenthau, perhaps the most influential international relations scholar of the 1950s and 1960s, lays out the critique of American policy typical of the early establishment critics: that our involvement in Vietnam was unrealistic and moralistic; that Viet-

Excerpted from *Vietnam and the United States* by Hans Morgenthau. Copyright © 1965 by Public Affairs Press.

nam was irrelevant to the nation's vital interests; and that policymakers had stretched national commitments well beyond the limits of even America's power. Much as Melvin Small argues, in making such a case, these staid critics both legitimized dissent and articulated objections to U.S. policy that many of their less well placed citizens intuitively sensed. Morgenthau personally experienced the chilling of reasoned debate when he participated in a nationally televised "teach-in" with National Security Advisor McGeorge Bundy, who ignored Morgenthau's criticisms of policy and instead attacked his scholarship. The Morgenthau-Bundy debate marked the end of the "teach-in movement," the grass-roots effort to initiate public debate over Vietnam.

Taken from Hans J. Morgenthau, Vietnam and the United States *(Washington, D.C., 1965), 81-82, 87-91.*

American foreign policy has tended in this century to move back and forth between the extremes of an indiscriminate isolationism and an equally indiscriminate internationalism or globalism. While these two positions are obviously identified with utterly different foreign policies—indiscriminate involvement here, indiscriminate abstention there—it is important to note that they share the same assumptions about the nature of the political world and the same negative attitude toward foreign policy correctly understood. They are equally hostile to that middle ground of subtle distinctions, complex choices, and precarious manipulations, which is the proper sphere of foreign policy.

Both deny the existence of priorities in foreign policy which are derived from a hierarchy of interests and the availability of power to support them. For both extremes, it is either all or nothing. . . . Both refuse to concern themselves with the concrete issues of foreign policy on their own merits, that is, in terms of the interests involved and the power available. . . . Both assume the self-sufficiency of American power to protect and promote the American national interest either in indiscriminate abstention or indiscriminate involvement. . . .

Both attitudes, in different ways oblivious of political reality, substitute for the complex and discriminating mode of political thought a simple approach, which in its simplicity is commensurate with the simplicity of their picture of the political world: the moral crusade. The isolationist's moralism is naturally negative . . . ; it seeks to protect the virtue of the United States from contamination by the power politics of evil nations. . . . Contemporary globalism tries to protect the virtue of the "free world" from contamination by Communism and to create a world order in which that virtue [American democracy] has a chance to flourish. The anti-Communist crusade has become both the moral principle of contemporary globalism and the rationale of our global foreign policy. . . .

A foreign policy which takes for its standard the active hostility to a world-wide political movement . . . confuses the sphere of philosophic or moral judgment with the realm of political action and for this reason it is bound to fail. For there are narrow limits, defined by the interest at stake and the power available, within which a foreign policy has a chance to be successful, and a foreign policy which would oppose Communist revolution and subversion throughout the world oversteps those limits. It does so in three different aspects.

First, the resources of even the most powerful nation are limited. They may suffice for intervening in two or three small countries simultaneously. But if one considers . . . [the] suggestion that the United States might have to send a million men to Vietnam, one realizes the extent to which available resources fall short of the unlimited commitment.

Second, the task such a foreign policy sets itself is unending. You suppress Communism in South Vietnam and it raises its head, say, in Thailand; you suppress it in the Dominican Republic and it raises its head, say, in Colombia. The successful suppression of revolution in one spot does not discourage revolution elsewhere, provided the objective conditions are favorable. . . .

Third, the attack upon a particular revolution as part of a world-wide, anti-revolutionary campaign is bound to have world-wide repercussions. Local successes against a particular revolution may have to be paid for by loss of support elsewhere and even by the strengthening of revolutionary forces throughout the world.

The only standard by which a sound foreign policy must be informed is not moral and philosophic opposition to Communism as such, but the bearing which a particular Communism in a particular country has upon the interests of the United States. . . .

. . . [W]e can oppose all revolutionary movements around the world. But in consequence of such opposition and in spite of our reformist intentions, we shall then transform ourselves into the anti-revolutionary power *per se* . . ., and we will find ourselves defending a *status quo* which we know to be unjust and in the long run indefensible. For we know of course that the rational choice open to us is not between the *status quo* and revolution, but between non-Communist and different types of Communist revolutions. But it is our fear of Communism that forces us into an anti-revolutionary stance. . . .

This policy is bound to be ineffective in the long run against the local revolution to which it is applied. It is also ineffective in its own terms of the anti-Communist crusade. For the very logic which makes us appear as the anti-revolutionary power *per se* surrenders to Communism the sponsorship of revolution everywhere. Thus the anti-Communist crusade achieves what it aims to prevent: the exploitation of the revolutions of the age by the Soviet Union and China.

Finally, our reliance upon a simple anti-Communist stance and its corollary, military intervention, is bound to corrupt our judgment about the nature and the limits of our power. We flatter ourselves to defend right against wrong, to discharge the self-imposed duty to establish a new order throughout the world, and to do so effectively within the limits of military logistics. Thus we may well come to think that all the problems of the political world will yield to moral conviction and military efficiency, and that whatever we want to do we shall be able to do because we possess those two assets in abundance.

Name the System!

Surely one of the great contradictions of national life in the sixties was how the same administration that had launched an unprecedented effort in domestic reform like the Great Society could embrace a disastrous foreign policy that made war against an impoverished, non-white people, in an abstract sense the same sort of people whose counterparts in the United States had become the object of great national concern. American policymakers, "the best and the brightest," were enlightened, liberal men paradoxically engaged in a brutish war. At the first notable protest march, SDS president Paul Potter on Easter of 1965 influenced antiwar thinking by portraying American society as a dehumanizing social system running out of control.

Taken from Massimo Teodori, ed., The New Left: A Documentary History *(Indianapolis, 1969), 246-48.*

The incredible war in Vietnam has provided the razor, the terrifying sharp cutting edge that has finally severed the last vestiges of illusion that morality and democracy are the guiding principles of American foreign policy. The saccharine, self-righteous moralism that promises the Vietnamese a billion dollars of economic aid at the very moment we are delivering billions for economic and social destruction and political repression is rapidly losing what power it might ever have had to reassure us about the decency of our foreign policy. The further we explore the reality of what this country is doing and planning in Vietnam the more we are driven toward the conclusion of Senator Morse that the U.S. may well be the greatest threat to peace in the world today. . . .

The President mocks freedom if he insists that the war in Vietnam is a defense of American freedom. Perhaps the only freedom that this war protects is the freedom of the warhawks in the Pentagon and the State Department to "experiment" with "counter-insurgency" and guerrilla warfare in Vietnam. . . .

Thus far the war in Vietnam has only dramatized the demand of ordinary people to have some opportunity to make their own lives, and of their unwillingness, even under incredible odds, to give up the struggle against external domination. We are told however that that struggle can be legitimately suppressed since it might lead to the development of a Communist system—and before that menace, all criticism is supposed to melt. . . .

But the war goes on; the freedom to conduct that war depends on the dehumanization not only of Vietnamese people but of Americans as well; it depends on the construction of a system of premises and thinking that insulates the President and his advisers thoroughly and completely from the human consequences of the decisions they make. I do not believe that the President or [Secretary of State] Mr. Rusk or [Secretary of Defense] Mr. McNamara or even McGeorge Bundy are particularly evil men. If asked to throw napalm on the back of a 10-year-old child they would shrink in horror—but their decisions have led to mutilation and death of thousands and thousands of people.

What kind of system is it that allows "good" men to make those kinds of decisions? What kind of system is it that justifies the U.S. or any country seizing the destinies of the Vietnamese people and using them callously for our own purpose? What kind of system is it that disenfranchises people in the [American] South, leaves millions upon millions of people throughout the country impoverished and excluded from the mainstream and promise of American society, that creates faceless and terrible bureaucracies and makes those the place where people spend their lives and do their work, that consistently puts material values before human values—and still persists in calling itself free and still persists in finding itself fit to police the world? . . .

We must name that system. We must name it, describe it, analyze it, understand it and change it. For it is only when that system is changed and brought under control that there can be any hope for stopping the forces that create a war in Vietnam today or a murder in the [American] South tomorrow.

From Protest to Resistance

The rising conviction that the war was merely one result of corporate capitalism—a conviction induced by military escalation—had a number of momentous consequences for the movement. First, it linked antiwar activism with other insurgencies such as black nationalism, anti-colonialism, and student rebellion. If the war grew from a rotten system instead of misguided policy, then nothing short of overthrowing "the system" would end it. Revolution just as obviously recommended increasingly confrontational tactics. In place of prayer vigils and speeches came the "guerrilla warfare" of the 1967 Oakland protest and the chaos of the Pentagon march; dramatic, individual acts of "resistance" such as draft-card burning became expected. As the movement radicalized, so its rhetoric became increasingly shrill. The radical turn is illustrated in the

From "Talking With the Troops" by George Dennison as it appeared in *Liberation,* November 1967.

following selections.

The first excerpt is from an eyewitness account of the famous Siege of the Pentagon, 21 October 1967, during which a large and boisterous crowd of antiwar protesters clashed with regular troops pressed into crowd control and federal marshals, who by all accounts attacked the protesters with relish. Note how the author, George Dennison, distinguishes between the protesters and the forces with whom they clashed, a distinction that to Dennison rested on nothing less than a gulf between a decaying civilization and a new one in the process of being born.

From George Dennison, "Talking With the Troops," Liberation 12 *(Nov. 1967): 12-14.*

It is hard to make these feelings clear. Guns and acts of violence do, after all, enforce powerful simplifications. Here on one side were the animated faces and the lively voices of the young, there on the other the grim monotony of military force. We might have been a delegation from the modern world saying only, "Let Us Live." We said much more than that, and said it clearly, but our sense of one deep issue—the plight of individual life brimming against repressive force—was so acute that we felt the deepest emotion over incidents which, except symbolically, were hardly of great consequence.

As we poured into the blacktop parking ramp—designed for the cars of VIP's—a torrent of helmets gushed from the building and came bubbling down the steps. Three youths made a dash for the door and were clubbed with rifles. We other hundreds sat down immediately, in close order, and linked arms, expecting an assault. But the troops, some leveling their rifles at our heads, lined up in front of us. . . . We could see masses of troops, all helmets and guns, streaming along the side of the building so as to close the rampway we had entered. . . .

While daylight lasted, I looked as closely as I could at the soldiers in front of us. Many were Negro; almost all were young. These were not violent faces, but those of boys from small towns and city slums, many with an unfinished, hangdog look of profound uncertainty in the conduct of life. Their cheeks and jaws were wooden with embarrassment. Their eyes flitted here and there, some with hungry surprise, others with a kind of wide-eyed fearfulness, drinking in the age-mate faces of those who sat before them. . . .

Whereas the soldiers, taken in the mass, were much as I have described them. . . , their sergeants and officers tended to have closed faces and guarded eyes. We became acutely aware that night of the meaning of faces. The marshals' were the worst, and it was only they, as a group, who kept up a tactic of violence and provocation. Most of their arrests, especially after nightfall, were made brutally. . . .

It would be interesting to draw out the political meaning of faces and bodies. When lives are coerced and thought is rendered valueless, these facts show in the face. Self-conflict is a political-moral fact. Self-contempt is ugly. Chronic anger is ugly. Stupidity shows in the face as a form of fear; it is ugly. Envy, resentment, complacency—all these feelings, under certain conditions, become chronic; they are fixed in the face as if by molds. . . . Social criticism, in one of its deepest aspects, is nothing but the criticism of the ugliness of Americans.

I say all this because in order to make clear why I was so deeply moved by the beauty of the young faces all around me. They were, of course, vivified by the integrative and liberating action at hand. But more than this, they were simply beautiful. It was the ordinary beauty of man—so rare: the beauty of intelligence, of natural pride. . . .

But let me put it in terms of youth's own rebellion against the prevailing norms of individual life, for the long hair and the beards of many collegians are first a refusal to be the shorn and colorless Duplicate of Man of the business world, who attests in every gesture and by dress that no imperative—be it moral, religious, intellectual or sexual—will interfere with his employer's demands. The beard is a tribute to vanished patriarchs and it means, "You must take my manhood into account," just as the long hair, in the mechanical landscapes of our cities, announces, in the form of loyalty, the animality of the human animal. No one who has heard the angry complaints of parents and authorities doubts for a moment their jealousy and shame. Nor is their own suffering a small matter, for they have already paid the price these young have refused. . . .

It is an extraordinary thing that in the midst of this rot our present generation of radical young should have emerged. They are their own men. They have not knuckled under, nor will they. Their self-respect, their love for and admiration of each other, their moral courage and independent thought, their sense of a world to be gained—all this is like a burst of sunlight after the longest, longest fog. . . .

It is not easy to imagine sweeping changes based only on resentment, or on the insights of sociology, however true. But to see young men who are patently free men demanding a world for their manhood—this is truly a different matter. At the Pentagon they were faced by the very image of man at his worst, all thought and feeling submerged in the uniform and reduced to robot response. Yet the long hours of the confrontation salvaged the soldiers' faces. The demonstrators spoke to them as men, and were acutely aware of the individual's plight. "We're not against the *soldiers*! We're against the *war*!" This was the first of many chants intended to clarify the confrontation.

Staughton Lynd

In this second selection, radical historian Staughton Lynd clarifies what the shift to resistance meant for the movement. Excerpted from "Resistance: From Mood to Strategy," Liberation *(November 1967): 40-41.*

Since roughly January 1967, the Movement has turned toward what it terms resistance. The new slogans are "from protest to resistance". . . , "from dissent to resistance" . . . or just "resist." . . . Resistance is thus far a mood rather than a strategy. Often when a movement is groping toward a new strategy there must be an initial period when individuals take a new kind of action without fully understanding what strategy the action implies. . . .

The activity of draft resistance may express either a mood or a strategy. When young men say "hell no, we won't go," what is uppermost in their minds may be either a personal, conscientious refusal to fight or the hope of producing consequences that will help to stop the war. Naturally, any given man, any particular action, is likely to reflect both of these attitudes in some measure, but as draft resistance moves from a mood toward a strategy the concern to produce consequences will be increasingly important.

This means that the traditional pacifist scenario which leads from dramatic individual witness to the martyrdom of jail will be questioned in terms of its effects. Thus Carl Davidson of S.D.S. inquired last spring whether the onlooker, watching the pacifist dragged off to jail, may find his own will to resistance weakened

---

One of four students killed by the Ohio National Guard during a 1970 antiwar protest at Kent State University. (Courtesy of Getty Images.)

rather than made stronger. Thus, too, the question has been raised as to whether ways cannot be found such that the draft resister publicly says "No". . . yet does not permit himself to be jailed and thereby lost to the Movement for the period of his imprisonment. Finally, conceptualization of draft resistance from the standpoint of strategy will mean understanding this act of refusal as a transition to long-term radical activity. In the Movement, saying "No" to the draft at the inception of one's adulthood will become a characteristic rite of initiation—a commencement exercise, so to speak—for the man brave or foolish enough to drop out of preparation for a conventional career. . . . And the draft-resistance organizer will seek to create conditions such that as many persons as possible from the groups most exposed to the draft undergo this radicalization in the shortest possible time.

Clearly, draft resistance—thus far the characteristic expression of the new resistance mood—is linked to another widespread concern of the past year: the tendency to visualize radicalism as the work of a lifetime rather than a two-year or three-year "experience," with the attendant need to ask how one can be a radical if he is married and has children, or is involved with a professional career. . . .

. . . [T]he problem to be solved is seen more seriously and somberly than was the case only a few years ago. A liberal ideology was implicit in the pattern of dropping out for a few years and then returning to graduate school, catching up and proceeding to a conventional career. America, basically a good society, was understood to have a problem: "the Negro problem." Just as the problem was small compared to the goodness of the society as a whole, so one devoted only a fraction of a lifetime to its solution. Two or three years was felt to be equivalent to the magnitude of the difficulty.

Now there is a different vision. The civil-rights movement has become a black-liberation movement. The movement against the war in Vietnam has been understood to be necessarily a movement against all the similar wars which will follow the termination of this one. The Movement as a whole—even though operating in separate white and black parts—has redefined itself as a movement against racist capitalist imperialism at home and abroad. The question is no longer that American society *has* a problem. What we think now is that American society *is* a problem. . . . [W]e are now clear that nothing less than all our lives will be enough.

Questions

1. *What are the differences between the critiques of the war found in Morgenthau and Stone, on the one hand, and Potter and Lynd, on the other? What are the underlying political or moral concerns of each? What are some of the factors that might explain the different perspectives found among the dissenters? Could class background, age, or occupation explain the differences?*
2. *To what extent could the breadth and variety of conviction in the different emphases of Morgenthau, Potter, and Lynd be a source of strength in a political movement, rather than an indication of division and weakness? Are there times and places where such divisions are productive and desirable?*
3. *Potter and Lynd clearly share the radical conviction that the war revealed a corrupt system. Note, however, the subtle differences in tone between the two. What are the political and organizational implications that might grow from Potter's open-ended allusion to "the system" as compared to Lynd's condemnation of America's "racist capitalist imperialism"?*
4. *Staughton Lynd calls activists to a lifetime of radical politics in his consideration of resistance. How might the kind of violence set loose on demonstrators at the Pentagon encourage or discourage that sort of sustained commitment?*

FURTHER READING

Thomas Powers, The War at Home: Vietnam and the American People, 1964-1968 *(New York, 1973), remains generally valuable because the author links the shift to confrontational politics with the obduracy of the administration. Nancy Zaroulis and Gerald Sullivan,* Who Spoke Up?: American Protest Against the War In Vietnam, 1963-1975 *(Garden City, New York, 1984) is thorough but uncritical and has been superseded by Tom Wells,* The War Within: America's Battle Over Vietnam *(Berkeley, 1994). Charles DeBenedetti, with Charles Chatfield,* An American Ordeal: The Antiwar Movement of the Vietnam Era *(Syracuse, 1990) includes the best account of mainstream groups in the movement. The self-analytical age of the sixties has produced many autobiographical accounts of the movement. David Harris,* Dreams Die Hard *(New York, 1982); Tom Hayden,* Reunion: A Memoir *(New York, 1988); Todd Gitlin,* The Sixties: Years of Hope, Days of Rage *(New York, 1987); and David Dellinger,* From Yale to Jail: The Life Story of a Moral Dissenter *(New York, 1993) are variously informative.*

Dissent in the 1960s: Definitions and Context

Steven Conn

Introduction

Sex, drugs, and rock 'n roll.

For many people this has become the easiest way to summarize the tumultuous decade of the 1960s. Perhaps the most enduring images of those times remain hippies, flower children, rock music festivals, and be-ins. Needless to say this assessment of the decade as one dominated by dope-smoking hippies vastly oversimplifies. It obscures much about the nature of the dissent that took place during the 1960s. The easiest way to understand the nature of that dissent, and its role in shaping the 1960s, is to recognize and delineate three broad streams of youth and student activity that converged during the decade.

The first of these streams found its source in the American South and in the struggle for civil rights. Initially this movement based itself in black churches and other community institutions. Throughout the 1950s, the Southern Christian Leadership Conference (SCLC) had been the organizational heart of the civil rights movement. By the early 1960s, however, younger activists were challenging their elders for leadership of the movement. In February 1960, black college students led dramatic sit-ins at the segregated Woolworth's lunch counter in Greensboro, North Carolina. Later that year, the formation of the Student Non-Violent Coordinating Committee (SNCC) boldly announced the arrival of a new generation of civil rights activists.

By the second half of the decade, that younger generation had grown impatient with the slow progress of the civil rights move-

ment and angry with the violent white backlash. A militant wing of the black youth movement split from the older generation, following the banner of "Black Power." Under that banner, younger black activists experimented with increasingly militant and separatist politics, embodied most famously in the Black Panther Party, and with a variety of cultural expressions exploring ideas of black pride.

The second stream originated in Port Huron, Michigan. There, roughly fifty college students from Ivy League and Big Ten universities gathered to form Students for a Democratic Society (SDS) in 1962. Their founding document, the Port Huron Statement, *offered an impassioned critique of an American society grown comfortably complacent. For these students, the nation they now inherited gorged itself on consumerism, and while it starved spiritually, it remained politically indifferent despite the ever-present threat of nuclear annihilation, and it trumpeted pompous patriotism even while black Americans fought their second-class status. SDS called on students to lead a reinvigoration of American politics through the mechanism of "participatory democracy." Hundreds of SDS chapters organized on campuses from coast to coast and these formed the backbone of what became known as the "New Left."*

The third stream formed in this context. The counter culture made its unofficial national debut in the summer of 1967 in San Francisco. In that summer, thousands of young people flocked to the Bay area to participate in the "Summer of Love." The summer began with the Monterey Pop Festival in June, which proved to be the first large-scale counter-cultural musical event. Throughout the late 1960s, large music festivals became unofficial conventions for counter-cultural rebels. The musical event that seemed to demonstrate most dramatically the promise of the counter culture took place near Woodstock, New York, in August 1969. For the most enthusiastic participants in the counter culture, Woodstock stood as a gentle alternative to the rest of American society. Some participants called themselves "Woodstock Nation."

The legacy of the counter culture is complicated and is still unfolding. For many involved, the counter culture really meant nothing more than sex, drugs, and rock. At the same time, such glib dismissals do not do justice to the sincerity and creativity with which some experimented with different ways of living and the depth to which they explored the connection between the personal and the political. The varieties of personal expression that college students today take for granted have their origins in the explorations of the counter culture. The counter culture did, for better or worse, alter the American social landscape.

To separate dissent in the 1960s into these three categories reflects, at some level, a convenience for historians. Surely these three broad groups involved different people, dealt with different issues, and employed different methods to achieve their goals. But it is also important to recognize that they overlapped in significant ways as well. There were certainly black hippies and those who believed in communal living and political engagement. The job for the historian is to analyze both the differences and the similarities.

VOICES FROM THE 1960s

The young people who joined the various dissent movements of the 1960s made self-conscious efforts to define who they were and what they saw wrong with American society. Through poems, manifestos, books, and interviews they worked to explain their beliefs and to critique the social and political status quo. In the following selections, the leaders of the three main streams of dissent describe their goals and methods.

The Black Panther movement defined itself against the nonviolent tradition of the earlier civil rights movement. Stokely Carmichael and others rejected the methods of peaceful collaboration with white allies in favor of radical action. They linked racism, poverty, and America's foreign policy in Vietnam with the domestic repression of African Americans and called for armed struggle to replace the exploitative system.

Tom Hayden and other "New Left" activists believed in the possibility of constructive engagement in the political system as a means to create a more just society. Disillusioned with the perceived gap between American ideals and reality, these activists advocated wider political participation by the young in order to achieve social justice. Concentrating on the university as the focal point of activism, they hoped to bring these young people to the forefront of political mobilization.

Others rejected the possibility of constructive change in the status quo that the first two groups implicitly believed. Adherents of the "counter culture" movement called for either a complete disruption of "an insane society" or the rejection of society and a retreat to a separate and simple lifestyle.

FIRST STREAM: SNCC, BLACK PANTHERS, BLACK CULTURE

"Black Power!"

During a march from Tennessee to Mississippi led by Martin Luther King, Jr., a small knot of young marchers refused to sing the civil rights movement's anthem "We Shall Overcome." Frustrated by the slow pace of civil rights progress, they decided to introduce a new slogan to the vocabulary of protest: "Black Power!" The young black activist Stokely Carmichael led this symbolic break with the older civil rights movement.

A member of the Student Non-Violent Coordinating Committee (SNCC) and eventually its head, Carmichael had soured on the possibilities of Gandhian non-violence to achieve racial equality and on the utility of working with white allies. In the selection below, Carmichael explains the philosophy of black power and its origins. Excerpted from Stokely Carmichael, "What We Want," New York Review of Books *7 (September 22, 1966): 5-7.*

One of the tragedies of the struggle against racism is that up to now there has been no national organization which could speak to the growing militancy of young black people in the urban ghetto. There has been only a civil rights movement, whose tone of voice was adapted to an audience of liberal whites. It served as a sort of buffer zone between them and angry young blacks. None of its so-called leaders could go into a rioting community and be listened to. In a sense, I blame ourselves—together with the mass media—for what has happened in Watts, Harlem, Chicago, Cleveland, Omaha. Each time the people in those cities saw Martin Luther King get slapped, they became angry; when they saw four little black girls bombed to death, they were angrier; and when nothing happened, they were steaming. We had nothing to offer that they could see, except to go out and be beaten again. We helped to build their frustration.

For too many years, black Americans marched and had their heads broken and got shot. . . . After years of this, we are at almost the same point—because we demonstrated from a position of weakness. We cannot be expected any longer to march and have our heads broken in order to say to whites: come on, you're nice guys. For you are not nice guys. We have found you out. . . .

Capturing a central paradox for African Americans in the 1960s, this demonstrator wonders why blacks should fight for a country which continued to deny them basic civil and political rights. In this way, the civil rights movement and the anti-war movement became two sides of the same coin. (Courtesy of Media Image Resource Alliance.)

An organization which claims to be working for the needs of a community—as SNCC does—must work to provide that community with a position of strength from which to make its voice heard. This is the significance of black power beyond the slogan.

Black power can be clearly defined for those who do not attach the fears of white America to their questions about it. We should begin with the basic fact that black Americans have two problems: they are poor and they are black. All other problems arise from this two-sided reality: lack of education, the so-called apathy of black men. Any program to end racism must address itself to that double reality.

. . . Thus we determined to win political power, with the idea of moving on from there into activity that would have economic effects. With power, the masses could *make or participate in making* the decisions which govern their destinies, and thus create basic change in their day-to-day lives. . . .

. . . We have no infallible master plan and we make no claim to exclusive knowledge of how to end racism; different groups will work in their own different ways. SNCC cannot spell out the full logistics of self-determination but it can address itself to the problem by helping black communities define their needs, realize their strength, and go into action along a variety of lines which they must choose for themselves. Without knowing all the answers, it can address itself to the basic problem of poverty; to the fact that in . . . [one southern county] 86 white families own 90 per cent of the land. What are black people in that county going to do for jobs, where are they going to get money? There must be reallocation of land, of money.

Ultimately, the economic foundations of this country must be shaken if black people are to control their lives. The colonies of the United States—and this includes the black ghettoes within its borders, north and south—must be liberated. . . . For racism to die, a totally different America must be born.

This is what the white society does not wish to face; this is why that society prefers to talk about integration. But integration speaks not at all to the problem of poverty, only to the problem of blackness. Integration today means the man who "makes it," leaving his black brothers behind in the ghetto as fast as his new sports car will take him. It has no relevance to the Harlem wino or to the cotton-picker making three dollars a day. . . .

Integration, moreover, speaks to the problem of blackness in a despicable way. As a goal, it has been based on complete acceptance of the fact that *in order to have* a decent house or education, blacks must move into a white neighborhood or send their children to a white school. This reinforces, among both black and white, the idea that "white" is automatically better and "black" is by definition inferior. This is why integration is a subterfuge for the maintenance of white supremacy. It allows the nation to focus on a handful of Southern children who get into white schools, at great price, and to ignore the 94 per cent who are left behind in unimproved all-black schools. Such situations will not change until black people have power—to control their own school boards, in this case. Then Negroes become equal in a way that means something, and integration ceases to be a one-way street.

Then integration doesn't mean draining skills and energies from the ghetto into white neighborhoods; then it can mean white people moving from Beverly Hills into Watts. . . .

Whites will not see that I, for example, as a person oppressed because of my blackness, have common cause with other blacks who are oppressed because of blackness. . . .

The need for psychological equality is the reason why SNCC today believes that blacks must organize in the black community. Only black people can convey the revolutionary idea that black people are able to do things themselves. Only they can help create in the community an aroused and continuing black consciousness that will provide the basis for political strength. In the past, white allies have furthered white supremacy without the whites involved realizing it—or wanting it, I think. Black people must do things for themselves; they must get poverty money they will control and spend themselves, they must conduct tutorial programs themselves so that black children can identify with black people. This is one reason Africa has such importance: The reality of black men ruling their own natives gives blacks elsewhere a sense of possibility, of power, which they do not now have. . . .

Black people do not want to "take over" this country. They don't want to "get whitey"; they just want to get him off their backs, as the saying goes. . . .

But our vision is not merely of a society in which all black men have enough to buy the good things of life. When we urge that black money go into black pockets, we mean the communal pocket. We want to see money go back into the community and used to benefit it. . . . The society we seek to build among black people, then, is not a capitalist one. It is a society in which the spirit of community and humanistic love prevail. . . . We can build a community of love only where we have the ability and power to do so: among blacks.

As for white America, perhaps it can stop crying out against "black supremacy," "black nationalism," "racism in reverse," and begin facing reality. The reality is that this nation, from top to bottom, is racist; that racism is not primarily a problem of "human relations" but of an exploitation maintained—either actively or through silence—by the society as a whole.

The Black Panther Party

One of the most spectacular and controversial outgrowths of the Black Power movement was the Black Panther Party. Founded in 1966 by Huey Newton and Bobby Seale in Oakland, the party attracted a great deal of media attention for its commitment to armed self-defense. The image of the Panther dressed in military fatigues and armed became for many white Americans their worst nightmare of Black Power.

The party did not only attract media attention. The Panthers were hounded by the police and the FBI almost everywhere they established chapters. These encounters often led to violent, tragic encounters, many provoked by the police. Panthers were routinely harassed, arrested, and on several occasions, killed.

The media focus on the party's militancy also obscured the positive work many members did in inner-city communities, especially in Chicago where the party ran a successful school breakfast program for needy children.

In this excerpt from a 1973 interview, founder Huey Newton describes the Panther ethos of using armed violence to achieve political goals. His discussion of the "doomed" revolutionary now seems poignantly ironic—Newton died in a drug-related shoot-out in 1989. Taken from "Playboy Interview: Huey Newton," 20 Playboy *(May 1973): 76, 78, 90.*

PLAYBOY: Do you think the *only* way to achieve your revolutionary goals is through armed violence?
NEWTON: Yes, and I think that ultimately it will be through armed violence, because the American ruling circle will not give up without a bitter struggle. But America will not be changed until the world is changed. To say that change will come here just through the ballot box would be a fantasy. We're running for city-council offices today. But if you ask if we would be prepared to fight with armed force when the time is right, I would say yes, when the occasion presents itself—and I think it will come, at some point in the future. . . .

From "Playboy Interview: Huey Newton" *Playboy*, Vol. 20 (May 1973).

PLAYBOY: So you would feel no hesitation about using violence as a tool, even to the point of killing people, provided it advanced your movement or your principles?
NEWTON: That's right.
PLAYBOY: And you say that without reservation?
NEWTON: The death of any man diminishes me, but sometimes we may have to be diminished before we can reconstruct.
PLAYBOY: That raises our last question: If you're ready to kill for the cause, you must also be ready to die for it. Are you?
NEWTON: I will fight until I die, however that may come. But whether I'm around or not to see it happen, I know we will eventually succeed, not just in America but all over the world, in our struggle for the liberation of all oppressed peoples. The revolution will win. But [Russian revolutionary anarchist Mikhail] Bakunin wrote that the first lesson the revolutionary *himself* must learn is that he's a doomed man. If that sounds defeatist, you don't understand the nature of revolution: that it's an ongoing process and that we don't get out of life alive, anyway. All we can do as individuals is try to make things better now, for eventually we all die. I think Mao's statement sums it up best: "Death comes to everyone, but it varies in its significance. To die for the reactionary is as light as a feather. But to die for the revolution is heavier than Mount Tai."

The Black Panthers achieved the highest profile of any of the militant black power organizations. As a consequence, they often found themselves in conflict with the police. Here volunteers raise money to support Panther members about to go on trial. (Courtesy of Leonard Freed/Magnum Photos, Inc.)

Black Power and Black Culture

Black Power and black pride served as the wellspring for extraordinary cultural, as well as political, achievements. A new-found desire to celebrate black heritage, black history, and black culture helped heal some of the psychological damage inflicted on American blacks by generations of denying or denigrating their traditions. No one articulated this sensibility better than James Brown when he sang: "Say it strong, say it loud / I'm black and I'm proud."

Nikki Giovanni is one of a host of black writers who found their voice in the Black Power struggles of the 1960s. In this poem, written in 1968, she describes how the accumulated effects of violence against leaders for peace and justice transformed her personally. Taken from Nikki Giovanni, Black Feeling, Black Talk, Black Judgement *(New York, 1979), 68-70.*

Adulthood
(For Claudia)

i usta wonder who i'd be
when i was a little girl in indianapolis
sitting on doctors porches with post-dawn pre-debs
(wondering would my aunt drag me to church sunday)
i was meaningless
and i wondered if life
would give me a chance to mean

i found a new life in the withdrawal from all things
not like my image

when i was a teen-ager i usta sit
on front steps conversing
the gym teacher's son with embryonic eyes

about the essential essence of the universe
(and other bullshit stuff)
recognizing the basic powerlessness of me

but then i went to college where i learned
that just because everything i was was unreal
i could be real and not just real through withdrawal
into emotional crosshairs or colored bourgeois
intellectual pretensions
but from involvement with things approaching reality
i could possibly have a life

so catatonic emotions and time wasting sex games
were replaced with functioning commitments to logic
and
necessity and the gray area was slowly darkened into
a Black thing

for a while progress was being made along with a certain
degree
of happiness cause i wrote a book and found a love
and organized a theatre and even gave some lectures on
Black history
and began to believe all good people could get
together and win without bloodshed
then
hammarskjöld was killed
and lumumba was killed
and diem was killed
and kennedy was killed
and malcolm was killed
and evers was killed
and schwerner, chaney and goodman were killed
and liuzzo was killed
and stokely fled the country
and le roi was arrested
and rap was arrested
and pollard, thompson and cooper were killed
and king was killed
and kennedy was killed
and i sometimes wonder why i didn't become a

debutante
sitting on porches, going to church all the time,
wondering
is my eye make-up on straight
or a withdrawn discoursing on the stars and moon
instead of a for real Black person who must now feel
and inflict
pain

[Note: Dag Hammarskjöld, United Nations Secretary General, 1961; Patrice Lumumba, Prime Minister of Congo, 1961; Ngo Dinh Diem, President of South Vietnam, 1963; President John F. Kennedy, 1963; Malcolm X, black nationalist leader, 1965; Medgar Evers, NAACP official, 1963; Michael Schwerner, James Chaney, Andrew Goodman, volunteers in Mississippi "Freedom Summer," a black voter registration project, 1964; Viola Liuzzo, white civil rights worker in Alabama, 1965; Stokely Carmichael, SNCC; Leroi Jones, black activist and playwright; H. Rap Brown, SNCC; Martin Luther King, Jr., civil rights leader, 1968; Robert F. Kennedy, Democratic presidential candidate, 1968.]

SECOND STREAM: STUDENTS AND THE "NEW LEFT"

The Port Huron Statement

The Port Huron Statement was the result of a conference held in Port Huron, Michigan, in 1962. Written largely by Tom Hayden, the statement offers a critique of American society and a call to action for America's students. The statement became the founding document for the Students for a Democratic Society, and it announced the arrival of the "New Left" in this country. Excerpted from "An Official Statement of Students for a Democratic Society," in How Democratic Is America? Responses to the New Left Challenge, *ed. Robert A. Goldwin (Chicago, 1969), 1-3, 5-15.*

Introduction: Agenda for a Generation

We are people of this generation, bred in at least modest comfort, housed now in universities, looking uncomfortably to the world we inherit.

When we were kids, the United States was the wealthiest and strongest country in the world: the only one with the atom bomb, the least scarred by modern war, an initiator of the United Nations that we thought would distribute Western influence throughout the world. Freedom and equality for each individual, government of, by, and for the people—these American values we found good, principles by which we could live as men. Many of us began maturing in complacency.

As we grew, however, our comfort was penetrated by events too troubling to dismiss. First, the permeating and victimizing fact of human degradation, symbolized by the Southern struggle against racial bigotry, compelled most of us from silence to activism. Second, the enclosing fact of the Cold War, symbolized by the presence of the Bomb, brought awareness that we ourselves, and our friends, and millions of abstract "others" we knew more directly because of our common peril, might die at any time. We might deliberately ignore, or avoid, or fail to feel all other human problems, but not these two, for these were too immediate and crushing in their impact, too challenging in the demand that we as individuals take the responsibility for encounter and resolution.

While these and other problems either directly oppressed us or rankled our consciences and became our own subjective concerns, we began to see complicated and disturbing paradoxes in our surrounding America. The declaration "all men are created equal . . ." rang hollow before the facts of Negro life in the South and the big cities of the North. The proclaimed peaceful intentions of the United States contradicted its economic and military investments in the Cold War status quo.

We witnessed, and continue to witness, other paradoxes. With nuclear energy whole cities can easily be powered, yet the dominant nation-states seem more likely to unleash destruction greater than that incurred in all wars of human history. Although

---

our own technology is destroying old and creating new forms of social organization, men still tolerate meaningless work and idleness. While two-thirds of mankind suffers undernourishment, our own upper classes revel amidst superfluous abundance. Although world population is expected to double in forty years, the nations still tolerate anarchy as a major principle of international conduct and uncontrolled exploitation governs the sapping of the earth's physical resources. Although mankind desperately needs revolutionary leadership, America rests in national stalemate, its goals ambiguous and tradition-bound instead of informed and clear, its democratic system apathetic and manipulated rather than "of, by, and for the people." . . .

Some would have us believe that Americans feel contentment amidst prosperity—but might it not better be called a glaze above deeply felt anxieties about their role in the new world? And if these anxieties produce a developed indifference to human affairs, do they not as well produce a yearning to believe there *is* an alternative to the present, that something *can* be done to change circumstances in the school, the workplaces, the bureaucracies, the government? It is to this latter yearning, at once the spark and engine of change, that we direct our present appeal. The search for truly democratic alternatives to the present, and a commitment to social experimentation with them, is a worthy and fulfilling human enterprise, one which moves us and, we hope, others today. . . .

We regard *men* as infinitely precious and possessed of unfulfilled capacities for reason, freedom, and love. In affirming these principles we are aware of countering perhaps the dominant conceptions of man in the twentieth century: that he is a thing to be manipulated, and that he is inherently incapable of directing his own affairs. We oppose the depersonalization that reduces human beings to the status of things—if anything, the brutalities of the twentieth century teach that means and ends are intimately related, that vague appeals to "posterity" cannot justify the mutilations of the present. We oppose, too, the doctrine of human incompetence because it rests essentially on the modern fact that men have been "competently" manipulated into incompetence—we see little reason why men cannot meet with increasing skill the complexities and responsibilities of their situation, if society is organized not for minority, but for majority, participation in decision-making.

Men have unrealized potential for self-cultivation, self-direction, self-understanding, and creativity. It is this potential that we regard as crucial and to which we appeal, not to the human potentiality for violence, unreason, and submission to authority. The goal of man and society should be human independence: a concern not with the image of popularity but with finding a meaning in life that is personally authentic; a quality of mind not compulsively driven by a sense of powerlessness, nor one which unthinkingly adopts status values, nor one which represses all threats to its habits, but one which has full, spontaneous access to present and past experiences, one which easily unites the fragmented parts of personal history, one which openly faces problems which are troubling and unresolved; one with an intuitive awareness of possibilities, an active sense of curiosity, an ability and willingness to learn. . . .

We would replace power rooted in possession, privilege, or circumstance by power and uniqueness rooted in love, reflectiveness, reason, and creativity. As a *social system* we seek the establishment of a democracy of individual participation, governed by two central aims: that the individual share in those social decisions determining the quality and direction of his life; that society be organized to encourage independence in men and provide the media for their common participation.

In a participatory democracy, the political life would be based in several root principles:

that decision-making of basic social consequence be carried on by public groupings;

that politics be seen positively, as the art of collectively creating an acceptable pattern of social relations;

that politics has the function of bringing people out of isolation and into community, thus being a necessary, though not sufficient, means of finding meaning in personal life;

that the political order should serve to clarify problems in a way instrumental to their solution; it should provide outlets for the expression of personal grievance and aspiration; opposing views should be organized so as to illuminate choices and facilitate the attainment of goals; channels should be commonly available to relate men to knowledge and to power so that private problems—from bad recreation facilities to personal alienation—are formulated as general issues.

The economic sphere would have as its basis the principles:

> that work should involve incentives worthier than money or survival. It should be educative, not stultifying; creative, not mechanical; self-directed, not manipulated, encouraging independence, a respect for others, a sense of dignity and a willingness to accept social responsibility, since it is this experience that has crucial influence on habits, perceptions, and individual ethics;
>
> that the economic experience is so personally decisive that the individual must share in its full determination;
>
> that the economy itself is of such social importance that its major resources and means of production should be open to democratic participation and subject to democratic social regulation. . . .

In social change or interchange, we find violence to be abhorrent because it requires generally the transformation of the target, be it a human being or a community of people, into a depersonalized object of hate. It is imperative that the means of violence be abolished and the institutions—local, national, international—that encourage nonviolence as a condition of conflict be developed. . . .

Almost no students value activity as citizens. Passive in public, they are hardly more idealistic in arranging their private lives. . . . "Students don't even give a damn about apathy," one has said. Apathy toward apathy begets a privately constructed universe, a place of systematic study schedules, two nights each week for beer, a girl or two, and early marriage; a framework infused with personality, warmth, and under control, no matter how unsatisfying otherwise. . . .

But apathy is not simply an attitude; it is a product of social institutions, and of the structure and organization of higher education itself. . . . Tragically, the university could serve as a significant source of social criticism and an initiator of new modes and molders of attitudes. But the actual intellectual effect of the college experience is hardly distinguishable from that of any other communications channel—say, a television set—passing on the stock truths of the day. Students leave college somewhat more "tolerant" than when they arrived, but basically unchallenged in their values and political orientations. With administrators ordering the institution, and faculty the curriculum, the student learns by his isolation to accept elite rule within the university, which prepares him to accept later forms of minority control. The real function of the educational system—as opposed to its more rhetorical function of "searching for truth"—is to impart the key information and styles that will help the student get by, modestly but comfortably, in the big society beyond. . . .

The very isolation of the individual—from power and community and ability to aspire—means the rise of a democracy without publics. With the great mass of people structurally remote and psychologically hesitant with respect to democratic institutions, those institutions themselves attenuate and become, in the fashion of the vicious circle, progressively less accessible to those few who aspire to serious participation in social affairs. The vital democratic connection between community and leadership, between the mass and the several elites, has been so wrenched and perverted that disastrous policies go unchallenged time and again. . . .

TOWARDS AMERICAN DEMOCRACY

Every effort to end the Cold War and expand the process of world industrialization is an effort hostile to people and institutions whose interests lie in perpetuation of the East-West military threat and the postponement of change in the "have not" nations of the world. Every such effort, too, is bound to establish greater democracy in America. The major goals of a domestic effort would be:

1. America must abolish its political party stalemate. . . .
2. Mechanisms of voluntary association must be created through which political information can be imparted and political participation encouraged. . . .
3. Institutions and practices which stifle dissent should be abolished, and the promotion of peaceful dissent should be actively promoted. . . .
4. Corporations must be made publicly responsible. . . .
5. The allocation of resources must be based on social needs. A truly "public sector" must be

> established, and its nature debated and planned. . . .
> 6. America should concentrate on its genuine social priorities: abolish squalor, terminate neglect, and establish an environment for people to live in with dignity and creativeness. . . .

THE UNIVERSITY AND SOCIAL CHANGE

. . . The civil rights, peace, and student movements are too poor and socially slighted, and the labor movement too quiescent, to be counted with enthusiasm. From where else can power and vision be summoned? We believe that the universities are an overlooked seat of influence.

. . . Social relevance, the accessibility to knowledge, and internal openness—these together make the university a potential base and agency in the movement of social change.

1. Any new left in America must be, in large measure, a left with real intellectual skills, committed to deliberativeness, honesty, and reflection as working tools. The university permits the political life to be an adjunct to the academic one, and action to be informed by reason.
2. A new left must be distributed in significant social roles throughout the country. The universities are distributed in such a manner.
3. A new left must consist of younger people who matured in the postwar world, and must be directed to the recruitment of younger people. The university is an obvious beginning point.
4. A new left must include liberals and socialists, the former for their relevance, the latter for their sense of thoroughgoing reforms in the system. The university is a more sensible place than a political party for these two traditions to begin to discuss their differences and look for political synthesis.
5. A new left must start controversy across the land, if national policies and national apathy are to be reversed. The ideal university is a community of controversy, within itself and in its effects on communities beyond.
6. A new left must transform modern complexity into issues that can be understood and felt close-up by every human

> being. It must give form to the feelings of helplessness and indifference, so that people may see the political, social, and economic sources of their private troubles and organize to change society. In a time of supposed prosperity, moral complacency, and political manipulation, a new left cannot rely on only aching stomachs to be the engine force of social reform. The case for change, for alternatives that will involve uncomfortable personal efforts, must be argued as never before. The university is a relevant place for all of these activities. . . .

The bridge to political power, though, will be built through genuine cooperation, locally, nationally, and internationally, between a new left of young people, and an awakening community of allies. In each community we must look within the university and act with confidence that we can be powerful, but we must look outwards to the less exotic but more lasting struggles for justice.

Third Stream: Yippies!, Communes, Counter Culture

The Yippies! in Chicago, 1968

The demonstrations in Chicago during the 1968 Democratic Convention were initially conceived by the Yippies! who sought to turn politics into a theater of the absurd and in doing so attract media attention. Abbie Hoffman, Jerry Rubin, and Paul Krassner founded the Yippies!, and Krassner is credited with coining the name. In his essay "The Birth of the Yippie! Conspiracy," Krassner succinctly described the purpose of the Yippies!: "No more marches. No more rallies. No more speeches. The dialogue is over baby. . . . The goal now is to disrupt an insane society."

In the following selection, Abbie Hoffman describes the goals of the Yippies! and the plans for the demonstrations in Chicago. Taken from Abbie Hoffman, Revolution for the Hell of It *(New York, 1968), 102-3, 106-8.*

Last December [1967] a group of us in New York conceived the Yippie! idea. We had four main objectives:

1. The blending of pot and politics into a potlitical grass leaves movement—a cross-fertilization of the hippie and New Left philosophies.
2. A connecting link that would tie together as much of the underground as was willing into some gigantic national get-together.
3. The development of a model for an alternative society.
4. The need to make some statement, especially in revolutionary action-theater terms, about LBJ, the Democratic Party, electoral politics, and the state of the nation.

To accomplish these tasks required the construction of a vast myth, for through the notion of myth large numbers of people could get turned on and, in that process of getting turned on, begin to participate in Yippie! and start to focus on Chicago. *Precision was sacrificed for a greater degree of suggestion.* People took off in all directions in the most sensational manner possible:

"We will burn Chicago to the ground!"

"We will fuck on the beaches!"

"We demand the Politics of Ecstasy!"

"Acid for all!"

"Abandon the Creeping Meatball!"

And all the time: "Yippie! Chicago — August 25-30."

Reporters would play their preconceived roles: "What is the difference between a hippie and a Yippie?" A hundred different answers would fly out, forcing the reporter to make up his own answers; to distort. And distortion became the life-blood of the Yippies.

Yippie! was in the eye of the beholder. . . .

From *Revolution for the Hell of It* by Abbie Hoffman. The Dial Press, Inc., 1968.

A Constitutional Convention is being planned. A convention of visionary mind-benders who will for five long days and nights address themselves to the task of formulating the goals and means of the New Society.

It will be a blend of technologists and poets, of artists and community organizers, of anyone who has a vision. We will try to develop a Community of Consciousness.

There will be a huge rock-folk festival for free. Contrary to rumor, no groups originally committed to Chicago have dropped out. In fact, additional ones have agreed to participate. In all about thirty groups and performers will be there.

Theater groups from all over the country are pledged to come. They are an integral part of the activities, and a large amount of funds raised from here on in will go for the transportation of street theater groups.

Workshops in a variety of subjects such as draft resistance, drugs, commune development, guerrilla theater and underground media will be set up. The workshops will be oriented around problem-solving while the Constitutional Convention works to developing the overall philosophical framework.

There will probably be a huge march across town to haunt the Democrats.

People coming to Chicago should begin preparations for five days of energy-exchange. Do not come prepared to sit and watch and be fed and cared for. It just won't happen that way. It is time to become a life-actor. The days of the audience died with the old America. If you don't have a thing to do, stay home, you'll only get in the way. . . .

We are negotiating, with the Chicago city government, a six-day treaty. . . . We have had several meetings, principally with David Stahl, Deputy Mayor of Chicago, and there remains but to iron out the terms of the treaty—suspension of curfew laws, regulations pertaining to sleeping on the beach, etc.—for us to have a bona fide permit in our hands.

The possibility of violence will be greatly reduced. There is no guarantee that it will be entirely eliminated.

This is the United States, 1968, remember. If you are afraid of violence you shouldn't have crossed the border.

This matter of a permit is a cat-and-mouse game. The Chicago authorities do not wish to grant it too early, knowing this would increase the number of people that descend on the city. They can ill afford to wait too late, for that will inhibit planning on our part and create more chaos.

It is not our wish to take on superior armed troops who outnumber us on unfamiliar enemy territory. It is not their wish to have a Democrat nominated amidst a major bloodbath. The treaty will work for both sides. . . .

Prepare a street theater skit or bring something to distribute, such as food, poems or music. Get sleeping bags and other camping equipment. . . .

The point is, you can use Chicago as a means of pulling your local community together. It can serve to open up a dialogue between political radicals and those who might be considered hippies. The radical will say to the hippie: "Get together and fight, you are getting the shit kicked out of you." The hippie will say to the radical: "Your protest is so narrow, your rhetoric so boring, your ideological power plays so old-fashioned."

Each can help the other, and Chicago . . . might well offer the medium to put forth that message.

Counter Culture

Some of those who participated in the New Left and the "counter culture" did so as an expression of their thorough disgust with American society. They became increasingly infatuated with Third World liberation struggles and made heroes of revolutionaries like Che Guevara and Mao Zedong. Many, however, had a much more ambivalent relationship to American culture. Indeed, at some level the "counter culture" can be seen as part of a deep strain in American culture that has always valued personal expression over conformity.

This short poem by Jerry Rubin captures this ambivalence. Rubin, a cofounder of the Yippies!, was certainly seen by the public as one of those who disliked what America stood for and advocated its destruction, yet his writing reveals him to be very much in love with American culture despite the alienation he feels because of its corruption. Excerpted from Jerry Rubin, Do It! Scenarios of the Revolution *(New York, 1970), 12-13.*

Child of Amerika

I am a child of Amerika.

If I'm ever sent to Death Row for my revolutionary "crimes," I'll order as my last meal: a hamburger, french fries and a Coke.

I dig big cities.

I love to read the sports pages and gossip columns, listen to the radio and watch color TV.

I dig department stores, huge supermarkets and airports. I feel secure (though not necessarily hungry) when I see Howard Johnson's on the expressway.

I groove on Hollywood movies—even bad ones.

I speak only one language—English.

I love rock 'n' roll.

San Francisco's Haight-Ashbury became one center of America's counter culture. Some came looking for an alternative to a sterile, consumer-based society, others merely looked for sex, drugs and rock and roll. (Courtesy of AP/Wide World Photos.)

I collected baseball players' cards when I was a kid and wanted to play second base for the Cincinnati Reds, my home team.

I got a car when I was sixteen after flunking my first driver's test and crying for a week waiting to take it a second time.

I went to the kind of high school where you had to pass a test to get *in*.

I graduated in the bottom half of the class.

My classmates voted me the "busiest" senior in the school.
I had short, short, short hair.
I dug *Catcher in the Rye.*
I didn't have pimples.

I became an ace young reporter for the Cincinnati *Post and Times-Star*. "*Son*," the managing editor said to me, "*someday you're going to be a helluva reporter, maybe the greatest reporter this city's ever seen.*"

I loved Adlai Stevenson.

My father drove a truck delivering bread and later became an organizer in the Bakery Drivers' Union. He dug Jimmy Hoffa (so do I). He died of heart failure at fifty-two.

My mother had a college degree and played the piano. She died of cancer at the age of fifty-one.

I took care of my brother, Gil, from the time he was thirteen.

I dodged the draft.

I went to Oberlin College for a year, graduated from the University of Cincinnati, spent 1 1/2 years in Israel and started graduate school at Berkeley.

I dropped out.

I dropped out of the White Race and the Amerikan nation.
I dig being free.
I like getting high.
I don't own a suit or tie.
I live for the revolution.
I'm a yippie!
I am an orphan of Amerika.

Communes and Alternative Living

The "counter culture" also found some of its members among those for whom New Left politics and the civil rights and anti-war movements had become equally corrupt power struggles. Raymond Mungo was such a wounded veteran of the movement. As the Yippies! prepared to go to Chicago in 1968, Mungo embarked on a personal odyssey that landed him at Total Loss Farm, a commune in Vermont.

Mungo, and others like him, retreated from the chaotic, and ultimately futile, world of opposition politics to experiment with alternative ways of living. Often these experiments embraced a "back to the land" philosophy that manifested itself in the creation of primitive rural communities. Mungo turned his back on American society, but he did so in a thoroughly American way. His experiences, and the book from which this selection is taken, were clearly inspired by the journeys of Beat generation author Jack Kerouac and the descent of Henry David Thoreau. Taken from Raymond Mungo, Total Loss Farm: A Year in the Life *(New York, 1970), 16-17, 133, 157-59.*

When we lived in Boston, Chicago, San Francisco, Washington (you name it, we lived there; some of us still live there), we dreamed of a New Age born of violent insurrection. We danced on the graves of war dead in Vietnam, every corpse was ammunition for Our Side; we set up a countergovernment down there in Washington, had marches, rallies and meetings; tried to fight fire with fire. Then Johnson resigned, yes, and the universities began to fall, the best and the oldest ones first, and by God every 13-year-old in the suburbs was smoking dope and our numbers multiplying into the millions. But I woke up in the spring of 1968 and said, "This is not what I had in mind," because the movement had become my enemy; the movement was not flowers and doves and spontaneity, but another vicious system, the seed of a heartless bureaucracy, a minority Party vying for power rather than peace. It was then that we put away the schedule for the revolution, gathered together our dear ones and all our resources, and set off to Vermont in search of the New Age.

The New Age we were looking for proved to be very old indeed, and I've often wondered aloud at my luck for being 23 years old in a time and place in which only the past offers hope and inspiration; the future offers only artifice and blight. I travel now in a society of friends who heat their houses with hand-cut wood and eliminate in outhouses, who cut pine shingles with draw-knives and haul maple sugar sap on sleds, who weed potatoes with their university-trained hands, pushing long hair out of their way and thus marking their foreheads with beautiful penitent dust. We till the soil to atone for our fathers' destruction of it.

We smell. We live far from the marketplaces in America by our own volition, and the powerful men left behind are happy to have us out of their way. They do not yet realize that their heirs will refuse to inhabit their hollow cities, will find them poisonous and lethal, will run back to the Stone Age if necessary for survival and peace. . . .

Over the crest of the hill, for the first time the road descends—walking downhill for a stretch we can catch our breath. That's why we built the road so, that horses pulling loads up the farm could recuperate from the uphill struggle and, freshened, go on. The road dips down to a wooden bridge crossing a stream of many colors in which pickerel, trout, salmon, tuna, and whales have been spotted by the sharpest of eyes. Most folks see only an occasional small trout or sunfish in this Noname Brook, which leads nowhere, but that is because they are all nearsighted. They wear glasses in the faith that the real, or actual, universe is not the one their own eyes can see, but a standard, universal universe dictated by prescription, or politics. You'd certainly be welcome to hang on to your specs here, but this is a place where you *could* take them off without fear of ridicule or violence to your body. Without my glasses, the brook becomes a dazzling pulsating streak of sunlight across the earth, ill-defined and like the great Source difficult to watch for long. They say it can blind you, but how to know which things you might better be blind to? Our great adventure after all is in searching for something not only better but new, nothing less than the next step in the evolution of the race, which may be somewhere we've been before. It goes in spells. And in racing toward the New Age, we can't be expected to carry all the dead weight of the past—all the schools, factories, newspapers, jobs, religions, and movements—which would drag us under. Just do whatever comes to mind, do something you hadn't thought of before, it's bound to get you *somewhere.* And you'll then decide whether you like it and where to move on to. We might stay at the brook all day and be perfectly happy, even dangle our toes in the chilly clear water, but me I'm now anxious to get on up to the farm. Coming? . . .

We *are* saving the world, of course, as the world for us extends to the boundaries of Total Loss Farm and the limits of our own experience; and Total Loss Farm is everywhere now, perhaps under your own rhubarb patch if you looked at it a little closer, and our experience all that anyone could hope to know of life. We were born and raised by parents who loved us at least until they lost us to a certain high-pitched whistle in the wind which they had gotten too old to hear; we work at maintaining ourselves, though our shared labor is seldom very taxing, for it takes little enough work to make plants grow, most of it is out of our hands, and our relationship to the work one of direct gratification and reward, as children insist on; we have children of our own, though they are fully peers by the time they've learned to eat and eliminate without physical help, and soon become more our masters than our students; and we die, sometimes in sulphurous flames, dramatic and shocking, other times silent and mysterious like the gone children wandering Europe with scenes of the parents engulfed in atrocity scrawled across their minds, but never to be spoken: "I come from Auschwitz, or Hué, or Boston, my father was shot for believing in God and hangs limp forever in front of our home as a reminder to the others; my mother was sold to the grim green soldiers for their sport, my brother to be used as a woman; I escaped the country of the somnambulent and blind on the back of a wolf who prowled the ruins and took pity on me; I have come here to begin again."

Our parents must wonder where we are, this story is, as much as anything else, an attempt to fill them in, but it grows harder and harder to speak. Fortunately, it grows simultaneously less necessary. I have clothes on my back, though they are old, and a roof over my head and food for my belly. In this, I am luckier than many. I am surrounded by people who would give their own lives in defense of mine, for they know we will make it together or not at all. I wish to be reconciled with all of my enemies, and to live on the planet and glory in peaches to a ripe old age. I am willing to help you as much as I'm able, as a single person can help another, not as a movement or government can help a mass. I may ask for some help from you as well. If you come to my house with love in your heart and there's room for one more—for there isn't always—you may know I will feed you and house you for the night, if you need it. You may see me walking from town to town with my thumb outstretched to the highway, seeking a lift: don't pass me by.

You have seen me everywhere. I am not asking for the vote. I do not seek to be represented. I do not seek to tear down your buildings or march on your castle or sit at your desk. I am interested neither in destroying what you have put up nor in gaining control of your empire. I demand nothing, and nothing is my inheritance. I live in the world, in the woods, with my friends, where not many people come by and the planet is entire and friendly; we like to be left alone except by those who can help. You can help by giving the planet, and peace, a chance. I ask only that you treat yourself right, give yourself the best of everything; and in so doing, you will be acting for me as well. If you can't stop, at least wave as you go by. Slow down, perhaps stop working: you'll find the time for everything you really want to do.

The "Silent Majority" Responds

In the autumn of 1969 President Richard Nixon, in a nationally televised address, contrasted what he believed to be a minority of Americans engaging in disruptive protest, with what he called "the silent majority"— suburban, law-abiding, conservative, middle-class citizens. It was this majority whose opinion Nixon courted in dealing with protesters and the "counter culture."

Promising to bring the nation together, and heal its wounds, Nixon often tried to play the elder statesman when he publicly discussed demonstrators, leaving it to his vice president, Spiro Agnew, to set a more strident and bellicose tone against protesters. Agnew was surely given this assignment by Nixon, who we now know was enraged at student demonstrators who challenged his policies. Asked by a reporter whether his aggressive posturing differed from the president's attitude, Vice President Agnew responded: "When the president said 'bring us together' he meant the functioning, contributing portions of the American citizenry."

In the speech excerpted below, Agnew calls for a "positive polarization" of the American public. It is an extraordinary gesture for a vice president to announce division as official government policy, but such was the nature of the Nixon administration. Nearly three decades later Agnew's demands for "law and order" strike us as richly ironic. Spiro Agnew was forced to resign for taking bribes, and Nixon, the great champion of law and order, came to think of impeachment before resigning in disgrace because of the Watergate scandal. Taken from Spiro T. Agnew, Frankly Speaking: A Collection of Extraordinary Speeches *(Washington, 1970), 44-49, 51.*

What I said before, I will say again. It is time for the preponderant majority, the responsible citizens of this country, to assert *their* rights. It is time to stop dignifying the immature actions of arrogant, reckless, inexperienced elements within our society. The reason is compelling. It is simply that their tantrums are insidiously destroying the fabric of American democracy. . . .

Last week I was lambasted for my lack of "mental and moral sensitivity." I say that any leader who does not perceive where persistent street struggles are going to lead this nation lacks mental acuity. And any leader who does not caution this nation on the danger of this direction lacks moral strength.

I believe in Constitutional dissent. I believe in the people registering their views with their elected representatives, and I commend those people who care enough about their country to involve themselves in its great issues. I believe in legal protest within the Constitutional limits of free speech, including peaceful assembly and the right of petition. But I do not believe that demonstrations, lawful or unlawful, merit my approval or even my silence where the purpose is fundamentally unsound. In the case of the Vietnam Moratorium [15 October 1969, a day of demonstrations, actions, vigils, and petition drives across the nation], the objective announced by the leaders—immediate unilateral withdrawal of all our forces from Vietnam—was not only unsound but idiotic. The tragedy was that thousands who participated wanted only to show a fervent desire for peace, but were used by the political hustlers who ran the event. . . .

Think about it. Small bands of students are allowed to shut down great universities. Small groups of dissidents are allowed to shout down political candidates. Small cadres of professional protestors are allowed to jeopardize the peace efforts of the President of the United States.

It is time to question the credentials of their leaders. And, if in questioning we disturb a few people, I say it is time for them to be disturbed. If, in challenging, we polarize the American people, I say it is time for a positive polarization.

It is time for a healthy in-depth examination of policies and a constructive realignment in this country. It is time to rip away the rhetoric and to divide on authentic lines. It is time to discard the fiction that in a country of 200 million people, everyone is qualified to quarterback the government. . . .

Now, we have among us a glib, activist element who would tell us our values are lies, and I call them impudent. Because anyone who impugns a legacy of liberty and dignity that reaches back to Moses, is impudent.

I call them snobs for most of them disdain to mingle with the masses who work for a living. They mock the common man's pride in his work, his family and his country. It has also been said that I called them intellectuals. I did not. I said that they characterized themselves as intellectuals. No true intellectual, no truly knowledgeable person, would so despise democratic institutions.

America cannot afford to write off a whole generation for the decadent thinking of a few. America cannot afford to divide over their demagoguery, to be deceived by their duplicity, or to let their license destroy liberty. We can, however, afford to separate them from our society—with no more regret than we should feel over discarding rotten apples from a barrel. . . .

. . . [I]t is time to stop demonstrating in the streets and start doing something constructive about our institutions. America must recognize the dangers of constant carnival. Americans must reckon with irresponsible leadership and reckless words. The mature and sensitive people of this country must realize that their freedom of protest is being exploited by avowed anarchists and communists who detest everything about this country and want to destroy it. . . .

Will we defend fifty centuries of accumulated wisdom? For that is our heritage. Will we make the effort to preserve America's bold, successful experiment in truly representative government? Or do we care so little that we will cast it all aside?

Questions

1. *Compare and contrast the"three streams" of dissent.*
2. *To what extent did "culture" play a role in these movements? Can cultural rebellion be the same thing as political rebellion? Why or why not?*
3. *What is the role of violence, or the threat of violence, for each of these groups?*
4. *What is the legacy of each "stream" today?*

FURTHER READING

For the most complete accounts of SDS and related movements, see Todd Gitlin, The Sixties: Years of Hope, Days of Rage *(New York, 1987) and James Miller,* "Democracy is in the Streets": From Port Huron to The Siege of Chicago *(New York, 1987). Stewart Burns's* Social Movements of the 1960s: Searching for Democracy *(Boston, 1990) provides a largely sympathetic survey of these movements. One of the best studies of SNCC remains Carson Clayborne,* In Struggle: SNCC and the Black Awakening of the 1960s *(Cambridge, Massachusetts, 1981). Perhaps the most insightful, best-written analysis of the relationship between protest movements and the Nixon administration is Jonathan Schell's* The Time of Illusion *(New York, 1975). For the best contextualization of the drama of the 1960s see Godfrey Hodgson's* America in Our Time *(New York, 1976).*